CRITICAL THINKING AND THE PROCESS

OF EVIDENCE-BASED PRACTICE

Critical Thinking and the Process of Evidence-Based Practice

Eileen Gambrill

OXFORD
UNIVERSITY PRESS

OXFORD
UNIVERSITY PRESS

Oxford University Press is a department of the University of Oxford. It furthers
the University's objective of excellence in research, scholarship, and education
by publishing worldwide. Oxford is a registered trade mark of Oxford University
Press in the UK and certain other countries.

Published in the United States of America by Oxford University Press
198 Madison Avenue, New York, NY 10016, United States of America.

© Oxford University Press 2019

Library of Congress Cataloging-in-Publication Data
Names: Gambrill, Eileen D., 1934– author.
Title: Critical thinking and the process of evidence-based practice / Eileen Gambrill.
Description: New York, NY : Oxford University Press, [2019] |
Includes bibliographical references and index.
Identifiers: LCCN 2018015258 (print) | LCCN 2018016003 (ebook) |
ISBN 9780190463366 (updf) | ISBN 9780190463373 (epub) |
ISBN 9780190463359 (pbk. : alk. paper)
Subjects: LCSH: Evidence-based social work. | Evidence-based medicine. |
Critical thinking. | Decision making.
Classification: LCC HV10.5 (ebook) | LCC HV10.5 .G36 2019 (print) | DDC 361.3/2—dc23
LC record available at https://lccn.loc.gov/2018015258

Contents

1. *Thinking about Decisions* 1

2. *Origins, Characteristics, and Controversies Regarding the Process of Evidence-Based Practice* 22

3. *Evidence: Sources, Uses, and Controversies* 48

4. *Steps in the Process of Evidence-Based Practice* 85

5. *Critically Appraising Research* 120

6. *Cultivating Expertise in Decision-Making* 157

7. *Argumentation: Its Central Role in Deliberative Decision-Making* 186

8. *Avoiding Fallacies* 212

9. *The Influence of Language and Social-Psychological Persuasion Strategies* 228

10. *Communication Skills (Continued)* 242

11. *Challenges and Obstacles to Evidence-Informed Decision-Making* 270

12. *Being and Becoming an Ethical Professional* 284

REFERENCES 299
INDEX 327

CRITICAL THINKING AND THE PROCESS

OF EVIDENCE-BASED PRACTICE

1

Thinking about Decisions

DECISION-MAKING IS CENTRAL in the helping professions. Related literature lies in many different interrelated areas including judgment and decision-making (reasoning), the study of expertise, and critical thinking. Decisions are made about what outcomes to focus on, how to frame concerns, what theories and methods to use, what interventions to recommend (including watchful waiting), how (or if) to evaluate outcome, and whether to involve clients/patients as informed participants. Here are a few examples of decisions.

- Ms. Richards, a child welfare worker, has to make a decision about what parent training program to refer a client to.
- Ms. Reed, a psychologist, has to determine whether Ms. X who started to say to staff "You are a devil," just as she was about to be released from a mental hospital, is still "mentally ill."
- Dr. B, an oncologist, must decide whether a pathology report regarding possible cancer is accurate.
- Ms. Garcia must decide whether her dentist's recommendation that she must get a "deep cleaning of her teeth" (which is quite intrusive) is really needed.

Decisions in the helping professions are characterized by ill-defined goals, ambiguity, missing data, and shifting and competing goals and values. They are influenced by agency policies and practices. They often involve high stakes and multiple players and are made under time pressures. We may feel pressure to "go-along" with our peers with a decision that may harm others or neglect standards we value (Baron, 1987).

Decisions have life-affecting consequences as in deciding how to discourage another suicide attempt, whether a biopsy shows malignancy, and whether social anxiety should be treated with medication. Questions include, What information do I need to make a sound decision? Do I have this information? If not, is it available and how can I obtain it? What should I do if I cannot get it? Decisions made involve moral and ethical issues in a number of ways including problems/behaviors selected for attention and how they are defined (e.g., as legal, ethical, medical, or moral). Uncertainty is a constant companion highlighting ethical questions about how this is handled. Rarely is all relevant information available. Baron (2008) emphasizes three types of questions as integral to decision-making:

1. "The *normative* question: How should we evaluate thinking, judgment and decision-making? By what standards?" (p. 3; emphasis in original). Do we behave in such a manner that our goals are met? Do our judgments correspond with the world? (Baron, 2012).
2. "The *descriptive* question: How do we think? What prevents us from doing better than we do according to normative standards?"
3. "The *prescriptive* question: What can we do to improve our thinking, judgment and decision-making, both as individuals and society?" (p. 3; emphasis in original).

BARON'S SEARCH-INFERENCE FRAMEWORK

Forming and evaluating beliefs, selecting goals, and making decisions all involve thinking. Baron (2008) suggests, "We think when we are in doubt about how to act, what to believe or what to desire . . . thinking helps us to resolve our doubts: It is purposive" (p. 6). A decision involves a choice regarding what to do or what to believe. We think about options. Baron (1985, 2008) suggests that in making decisions we search for "possibilities, evidence and goals and [make] inferences from these" (Baron, 2008, p. 7); "the whole point of good thinking is to increase the probability of good outcomes (and true conclusions)" (p. 64). A good outcome is one that decision makers value; it results in valued goals. Good decision makers "do the best they can with what is knowable" (p. 64). Decisions are made to achieve goals and they are based on beliefs about what actions [possibilities] will achieve the goals" (p. 6). Thinking can be defined as "a method of finding and choosing among potential possibilities, that is, possible actions, beliefs, or personal goals" (p. 8). Thus, "thinking is, in a way, like exploration" (p. 7).

Possibilities are possible answers that may remove doubt. "Goals are the criteria by which [we] evaluate possibilities—for ending the thinking process (criteria or standards of evaluation) and evidence consists of any belief that is valuable in determining 'the extent to which a possibility achieves some goal'" (Baron, 2008, p. 8). It changes "the strengths assigned to possibilities, i.e., the thinker's tendency to adapt them" (Baron, 1985, p. 87). It may be sought or not. "One possibility can serve as evidence against another" (p. 87). Goals determine the way evidence is used and what evidence is sought (p. 87). They may change based on evidence.

> We look for other possibilities to make sure that the current favorite is really the best, or to look for ways to modify it to make it better, by taking pieces of other possibilities. The reason we look for counter-evidence is, again, to prevent error and to suggest ways to modify a possibility. More generally, the reason for all of these elements is to increase our [warranted] confidence in whatever possibility we choose in the end. (Baron, 2017, p. 6)

Consider the decision confronting Mrs. Garcia. Her goals include keeping her teeth and avoiding over- or undertreatment. She can take her dentist's advice and make an appointment with someone to do a "deep cleaning." She could seek another dentist's advice first. Or, she could do nothing. If a specialist tells her deep cleaning is not only not necessary but will do more harm than good, this offers evidence against the possibility (option) of getting deep cleaning. Consider Dr. B's situation. He could accept the lab report that the biopsy shows cancer. He could send the specimen to another laboratory for a check. Dr. B's goal (as well as the client's goal) is to obtain the most accurate answer to the question "Is this cancer or not?" If the second report from a pathologist with greater experience with this particular cancer states that the biopsy is not cancer, this is evidence against the possibility of immediately starting very invasive treatment.

Inference is used to evaluate the relevance of the evidence to goals drawing on certain rules (see Chapter 7).

> Thinking can be described in terms of search and inference. The objects searched for consist of possibilities, evidence (in the form of beliefs) and goals (criteria, values, desires). In decision making, the possibilities are options, and inference is the evaluation of options in the light of evidence and goals. We can also think about beliefs themselves, by evaluating them in

terms of other beliefs. . . . And, similarly, we can evaluate goals in terms of other goals. (Baron, 2017, p. 4)

Thus, Baron (2008) defines thinking as "*a method of finding and choosing among potential possibilities (possible actions, beliefs and personal goals)*" (p. 8; emphasis in original). "Fairness to possibilities" (Baron, 1985, p. 107) is a key characteristic: "Aside from optimal search, good thinking involves being fair to all possibilities . . . when searching for evidence and using evidence" (p. 107). This requires looking for reasons why you may be wrong. Returning to our examples, maybe an error was made in the second lab. Maybe the expert periodontist Mrs. Richards consulted was wrong. The term *judgment* refers to "evaluation of one or more possibilities with respect to a specific set of evidence and goals" (Baron, 2008, p. 8). Within Baron's search-inference framework "our goal is to bring our beliefs into line with the evidence" (p. 12). As Baron notes, our goals may prevail, for example maintaining a belief despite a lack of evidence. And, goals may change in addressing a problem.

Search may be characterized by its objects (evidence, possibilities, or goals), its duration or extent (time, or number of objects sought), and, importantly, its direction. Direction is defined in terms of whether search is directed at whatever favors currently strong possibilities (usually just one) or opposes them. Inferences may also be characterized by direction. For example, evidence may be weighted more heavily as a function of whether it favors or opposes strong possibilities (Baron, 2017, p. 4).

Baron (2008) defines a bias as "a departure from the normative model in a particular direction" (p. 41). Biases result in ignoring counter-evidence related to preferred beliefs encouraged by insufficient search for possibilities and goals and "under-weighing evidence against favored possibilities when it is available" (Baron, 2017, p. 2). Insufficient search for information regarding a decision is common as is confirmation bias (i.e., looking only for data that supports a position) and belief perseverance (i.e., ignoring data against favored views). Richard Paul and his colleagues emphasize the role of both *egocentric* and *sociocentric* biases (Paul, 1993; Paul & Elder, 2014) in compromising decisions. The former refers to biases that result from focusing on our own interests. The second refers to biases that result from the particular society in which we live. People differ in their tendency to reflect biases in their thinking (e.g., Stanovich & West, 2008). Epistemic rationality refers to "how well our beliefs map on to the actual structure of the world" (p. 6). Instrumental rationality refers to how well our beliefs allow us to accomplish our goals.

ACTIVE OPEN-MINDED THINKING: INTEGRAL TO CRITICAL THINKING

Discussions about what makes a good thinker are as old as philosophy itself. "Thinking is in its most general sense, a method of choosing among potential possibilities, that is possible beliefs or actions" (Baron, 1985, p. 90). Thouless (1974) suggests that the essence of crooked thinking is not acting when you must act. The term *reflection* is popular. But, as Brookfield (1995) notes, "Reflection is not by definition critical" (p. 8). Nor is thinking necessarily informed. For example, an expert in an area can draw on a vast knowledge base; a novice cannot (see Chapter 6). Exhibit 1.1 describes examples of critical thinking skills, knowledge, attitudes, and ways of behavior. Active open-minded thinking (AOT) is useful in selecting and achieving goals and providing a guide about what sources to trust. AOT is integral to critical thinking, for example searching for reasons why we may be wrong. Baron (2017) defines AOT as "the disposition to be fair to different conclusions even if they go against one's initially favored or pet conclusion" (p. 1). These characteristics illustrate the close relationship between AOT and the process of evidence-based practice (see Chapters 2 and 4).

AOT involves the careful examination and evaluation of beliefs and actions to arrive at well-reasoned decisions regarding actions, beliefs, and goals. Here are sample items on the scale of AOT (agreement is indicated on a scale of 1 to 7). (See Baron, Scott, Fincher, & Metz, 2015; Haran, Ritov, & Mellers, 2013). The last four items are coded in reverse.

1. Allowing oneself to be convinced by an opposing argument is a sign of good character.
2. People should take into consideration evidence that goes against their beliefs.
3. People should revise their beliefs in response to new information or evidence.
4. Changing your mind is a sign of weakness.
5. Intuition is the best guide in making decisions.
6. It is important to persevere in your beliefs even when evidence is brought to bear against them.
7. One should disregard evidence that conflicts with one's established beliefs.

EXHIBIT 1.1
EXAMPLES OF THINKING SKILLS, KNOWLEDGE, ATTITUDES AND WAYS
OF BEHAVING RELATED TO ACTIVE OPEN-MINDED THINKING

- Demonstrates fairness to possibilities: Searches for counter-evidence
  to preferred views; accurately weighs evidence for both preferred and
  non-preferred views.
- Reviews goals in relation to possibilities/evidence.
- Questions one's own views and attempts to understand related assumptions
  and implications.
- Searches for goals and possibilities not obvious.
- Raises vital questions and problems.
- Gathers, assesses, and accurately describes the evidentiary status of relevant
  information.
- Uses evidence skillfully and impartially.
- Recognizes the fallibility of one's opinions and the probability of bias in them
  and the danger of differentially weighing evidence according to personal
  preferences.
- Listens carefully to other people's ideas.
- Recognizes that most real-world problems have more than one possible so-
  lution and that solutions may differ and be difficult to compare in terms of a
  single criterion of merit.
- Describes differing views without distortion, exaggeration, or
  caricaturization.
- Demonstrates understanding of the differences among conclusions,
  assumptions, and hypotheses.
- Is sensitive to the difference between the validity of a belief and the intensity
  with which it is held.
- Understands the difference between reasoning and rationalizing.
- Has a sense of the value and cost of information and knows how to seek
  needed information.
- Looks for unusual approaches to complex problems.
- Tries to anticipate consequences of alternative possibilities before
  choosing one.
- Makes valuable generalizations of problem-solving techniques to different areas.
- Can learn independently and has an interest in doing so.
- Understands the difference between winning an argument and being right.
- Is aware that understanding is always limited.
- Distinguishes between logically valid and invalid inferences.
- Can structure informally presented problems so that formal techniques
  (e.g., mathematics) can be used to solve them.

Source: J. Baron, 2008, *Thinking and Deciding* (4th ed.), New York, NY: Columbia University Press; Baron, 2008; Nickerson, 1986, pp. 29–30; and R. Paul, 1993, *Critical Thinking: What Every Person Needs to Survive in a Rapidly Changing World* (3rd ed. rev.). Santa Rosa, CA: Foundation for Critical Thinking. www.criticalthinking.org

"The main conceptual contribution of AOT is its concern with direction, as well as extent. This is because AOT is intended as the antidote to myside bias" (Baron, 2017, p. 5). Although one could search too much as well as too little, departures from what is needed to avoid myside bias are more common. Thus, "we call it a virtue when people resist myside bias by looking for reasons why their pet belief or favored option might be wrong" (p. 5). Haran, Ritov, and Mellers (2013) found that AOT has positive associations "with greater persistence in searching for information, higher accuracy of estimates and lower overconfidence" (p. 197).

Paul and Elder (2014) suggest that "critical thinking begins when we think about our thinking with a view to improving it" (p. 366), drawing on relevant knowledge and skills, including metacognitive skills such as questioning favored assumptions. Here is a description of critical thinking by Scriven and Paul (2005) written for the National Council for Excellence in Critical Thinking:

> Critical thinking is the intellectually disciplined process of actively and skillfully conceptualizing, applying, analyzing, synthesizing, and/or evaluating information gathered from, or generated by, observation, experience, reflection, reasoning, or communication, as a guide to belief and action. In its exemplary form, it is based on universal intellectual values that transcend subject matter divisions: clarity, accuracy, precision, consistency, relevance, sound evidence, good reasons, depth, breadth, and fairness. It entails proficiency in the examination of those structures or elements of thought implicit in all reasoning: purpose, problem or question-at-issue, assumptions, concepts, empirical grounding, reasoning leading to conclusions, implications and consequences, objections from alternative viewpoints, and frame of reference. Critical thinking—in being responsive to variable subject matter, issues, and purposes—is incorporated in a family of interwoven modes of thinking, among them: scientific thinking, mathematical thinking, historical thinking, anthropological thinking, economic thinking, moral thinking, and philosophical thinking.

Critical thinking involves clearly describing and carefully evaluating claims and arguments, no matter how cherished, and considering alternative views. This means paying attention to the *process* of reasoning (how we think), not just the product. Critical thinking and intelligence are only modestly associated (Stanovich, 2008; 2010). In weak sense critical thinking, we focus on supporting our own views as in egocentric bias (Paul, 1993); "much of our thinking, left to itself, is biased, distorted, partial, uninformed, or downright prejudiced" (Brookfield, 1995, p. 8). Indeed, Feynman (1974) suggests, "The first principle is that you must not fool yourself and you are the easiest person to fool" (p. 12). Increasing attention has been focused on our vulnerability to misinformation (Carey, 2017; Lewandowsky, Ecker, Seifert, Schwarz, & Book, 2012) and the play of cognitive biases such as cherry-picking (reporting only data that support a preferred view).

 Socratic questioning is integral to critical thinking (AOT), evidence-based practice and science. (See Exhibit 1.2). Critical thinking values, skills, and knowledge can protect us from being bamboozled and misled by deceptive claims. Consider the examples that follow. Each makes a claim concerning the effectiveness of a practice method. Are they true? What questions would you ask to evaluate the accuracy of these claims? How would you search for related research findings?

- Eye movement desensitization is effective in decreasing anxiety.
- "Four hours a month can keep a kid off drugs forever. Be a mentor" ("Four Hours a Month," 2002; Partnership for a Drug-Free America [www.drugfreeamerica.org]).
- Anatomically detailed dolls can be used to accurately identify children who have been sexually abused.
- Stents improve longevity.

Paul and his colleagues at the Center for Critical Thinking in Sonoma (Paul, 1993; Paul & Elder, 2014) include four domains in their conceptualization of critical thinking, highlighting the role of Socratic questioning in arriving at well-reasoned decisions. (See Exhibit 1.2). These domains are elements of thought, abilities, affective dimensions (dispositions), and intellectual standards. Related Socratic questions include:

1. What is my purpose or goal? (This may be unrealistic or conflict with other goals.)
2. What is the question I am trying to answer? Is it clear? Is it important?
3. What information do I need to answer my question?
4. What is the most basic concept in the question?
5. What assumptions am I using?
6. What is the point of view with respect to the issue? This may be too narrow, contain contradictions, or be based on false data.
7. What are my fundamental inferences or conclusions?
8. What are the implications of my reasoning (if I am correct)?

EXHIBIT 1.2

A TAXONOMY OF SOCRATIC QUESTIONS

Questions about the Question

What question am I trying to answer?
What kind of question is this?
Why is this question important?

To answer this question, what questions would we have to answer first?
What does this question assume?
Is this the same issue as_____?

Questions of Clarification

What do you mean by _____?
What is your main point?
How does ____ relate to _____?
Could you put that another way?
Let me see if I understand: do you
    mean ____ or _____?

• Could you give me an example?
• Would this be an example: _____
    _____?
• Could you explain that further?
• Does ___ work for all problems?

Questions That Probe Assumptions

What are you assuming?
What could we assume instead?

You seem to be assuming _____?
Do I understand you correctly?

Questions that Probe Reasons and Evidence

What information is needed to answer
    the question?
How can we gather this?
How can we determine if it is accurate?
Why do you think that is true?
Is there any evidence for that?

Do we need other information?
Is there reason to doubt that evidence?
Who is in a position to know if that is so?
Are these reasons adequate?
How does that apply to this example?
What would change your mind?

Questions about Viewpoints/Perspectives

What might someone who
    believed ____ think?
Can/did anyone view this in
    another way?

What would someone who disagrees say?
What is an alternative?

Questions That Probe Implications and
    Consequences

What are you implying by that?
What effect would that have?

Should we consider other implications?
What is an alternative?

Source: Adapted from *Critical Thinking: What Every Person Needs to Survive in a Rapidly Changing World*, by R. Paul, 1993 (3rd ed. rev.), Santa Rosa, CA: Foundation for Critical Thinking. www.criticalthinking.org

Proposed stages in development of critical thinking suggested by Paul, 1993 include:

Stage One: The Unreflective Thinker (we are unaware of significant problems in our thinking).

Stage Two: The Challenged Thinker (we become aware of problems in our thinking).

Stage Three: The Beginning Thinker (we try to improve but without regular practice).

Stage Four: The Practicing Thinker (we recognize the necessity of regular practice).

Stage Five: The Advanced Thinker (we advance in accordance with our practice).

Stage Six: The Master Thinker (skilled and insightful thinking become second nature to us). (www.criticalthinking.org) Downloaded 11/15/17.

Paul (1993) and Paul and Elder (2014) view critical thinking as a unique kind of purposeful thinking in which we use intellectual standards such as clarity and fairness. It is:

- Clear versus unclear.
- Precise versus imprecise.
- Specific versus vague.
- Accurate versus inaccurate.
- Relevant versus irrelevant.
- Consistent versus inconsistent.
- Logical versus illogical.
- Deep versus shallow.
- Complete versus incomplete.
- Significant versus trivial.
- Adequate (for purpose) versus inadequate
- Fair versus biased or one-sided.

RELATED SKILLS AND KNOWLEDGE

Decisions are made to solve problems. Related skills include searching for information relevant to a decision, accurately weighing the quality of evidence, reviewing resources, and avoiding biases (see Exhibit 1.1; also see discussion of

Baron's search-inference framework and AOT). Other skills include identifying assumptions and their implications (consequences), suspending judgment in the absence of sufficient evidence to support a claim/decision, understanding the difference between reasoning and rationalizing, and stripping an argument of irrelevancies and phrasing it in terms of its essentials (see Chapter 7). Seeking counter-evidence to preferred views and understanding the difference between the accuracy of a belief and the intensity with which it is held is vital. *Critical thinking skills are not a substitute for problem-related knowledge.* As Baron (2008) emphasizes, "without *knowledge* or beliefs that correspond to reality, thinking is an empty shell" (p. 15). However, as he notes, thinking about a problem can contribute to expertise. Specialized knowledge may be needed to evaluate the plausibility of premises related to an argument. Consider the following example:

- Depression always has a psychological cause.
- Mr. Draper is depressed.
- Therefore, the cause of Mr. Draper's depression is psychological in origin.

Even though the logic of this argument is sound, the conclusion may be false; the cause of Mr. Draper's depression could be physiological. The greater the content knowledge that is available and needed about a problem to solve it, the more important it is to be familiar with this knowledge (see Chapter 6). Taking advantage of practice-related theory and research is a hallmark of the process of evidence-based practice as described in Chapter 2.

In addition to content knowledge, related performance skills are needed. For example, being aware of common errors in reasoning will not be useful without skills to avoid them and values that encourage their use such as fair-mindedness. Critical thinking encourages us to identify and question assumptions and to consider the possible consequences of different beliefs or actions. It requires clarity rather than vagueness; "one cannot tell truth from falsity, one cannot tell an adequate answer to a problem from an irrelevant one, one cannot tell good ideas from trite ones—unless they are presented with sufficient clarity" (Popper, 1994, p. 71). The term *meta-cognitive* refers to being aware of and influencing our reasoning process by asking questions such as:

- "Do I understand this point?"
- "What mistakes may I be making?"
- "Is this claim true?"
- "How good is the evidence?"
- "Who presented it as accurate?" "How reliable are these sources?"

- "Are conflicts of interest involved?"
- "Are the facts presented correct?"
- "Have any facts been omitted?"
- "Can an intervention tested and found to be successful in one setting be used with success in other settings?"

RELATED VALUES, ATTITUDES, AND STYLES: AFFECTIVE DIMENSIONS

Predispositions and attitudes include recognizing the fallibility of beliefs and the probability of bias in them, valuing the discovery of ignorance as well as knowledge, active open-mindedness (e.g., seeking counter-evidence to preferred views), a desire to be well informed, a tendency to think before acting, and curiosity (Baron, 2000; Ennis, 1987; Paul, & Elder, 2014). AOT "is the disposition to be fair toward different conclusions even if they go against one's initially favored or pet conclusion" (Baron, 2017, p. 1). (See earlier description of items on the AOT scale.) Related moral values suggested by Paul (1993) include humility (awareness of the limits of knowledge including our own; lack of arrogance), integrity (honoring the same standards of evidence to which we hold others), and persistence (willingness to struggle with confusion and unsettled questions; see Exhibit 1.3).These attitudes highlight the role of affective components, such as empathy for others and a tolerance for ambiguity and differences of opinion. They emphasize the importance of critical doubt (examining beliefs) and open-mindedness (understanding and considering opposing views before judging them; Walton, 1999, p. 71).

> To think critically about issues we must be able to consider the strengths and weaknesses of opposing points of view. Since critical thinkers value fairmindedness, they feel that it is especially important that they entertain positions with which they disagree. They realize that it is unfair either to judge the ideas of another until they fully understand them, or act on their own beliefs without giving due consideration to relevant criticisms. The process of considering an opposing point of view aids critical thinkers in recognizing the logical components of their beliefs (e.g., key concepts, assumptions, implications, etc.) and puts them in a better position to amend those beliefs. (Paul, Binker, & Charbonneau, 1986, p. 7)

Critical thinkers are skeptics rather than believers. That is, they are neither gullible (believing anything) or cynical (believing nothing). Cynics have a

EXHIBIT 1.3
VALUES AND TRAITS INTEGRAL TO CRITICAL THINKING

- *Fair-mindedness*: Adhering to intellectual standards without reference to our own advantage or the advantage of our group.
- *Intellectual humility:* Recognizing the limits of our own knowledge, including circumstances in which we are likely to deceive ourselves; maintaining a sensitivity to bias, prejudice, and limitations of our viewpoint. Recognizing that we should never claim more knowledge/expertise than we have. Questions include: How much do I really understand/know about _____? Am I competent to help this client?
- *Intellectual courage*: Facing and fairly addressing ideas, beliefs, or viewpoints toward which we have strong negative emotions and to which we have not given a serious hearing. This courage is connected with the recognition that ideas considered dangerous or absurd may be reasonable. To determine for ourselves what is accurate, we must not accept what we have "learned" passively and uncritically. Intellectual courage comes into play here, because we will come to see some truth in some ideas strongly held by others. The penalties for nonconformity can be severe.
- *Intellectual empathy*: Putting ourselves in the place of others to understand them, accurately describing the viewpoints and reasoning of others. It includes remembering occasions when we were wrong despite a conviction that we were right.
- *Intellectual integrity*: Honoring the same rigorous standards of evidence to which we hold others; practicing what we advocate and admitting discrepancies and inconsistencies in our own thoughts and actions.
- *Intellectual perseverance*: Pursuing accuracy despite obstacles and relying on rational principles despite the irrational opposition of others; recognizing the need to struggle with confusion and unsettled questions to achieve deeper understanding.
- *Confidence in reason*: Confidence that, in the long run, our higher interests and those of humankind will be best served by giving the freest play to reason by encouraging others to develop their rational faculties; faith that, with proper encouragement and education, people can learn to think for themselves, form rational views, draw reasonable conclusions, think coherently and logically, persuade each other by reason, and become reasonable persons, despite obstacles to doing so.
- *Intellectual autonomy*: Being motivated to think for ourselves.
- *Intellectual curiosity*: An interest in deeply understanding things and learning.
- *Intellectual discipline*: Thinking guided by intellectual standards such as clarity and relevance.

Source: Adapted from *Critical Thinking: What Every Person Needs to Survive in a Rapidly Changing World* (3rd ed. rev.), by R. Paul, 1993, Santa Rosa, CA: Foundation for Critical Thinking, pp. 467–472. www.criticalthinking.org

contemptuous distrust of all knowledge. Skeptics (critical thinkers) value truth and seek approximations to it through critical discussion and the testing of theories. Critical thinkers question what others view as self-evident. They ask: Is this claim accurate? Have critical tests been performed? If so, were they relatively free of bias? Have the results been replicated? How representative were the samples used? Are there alternative well-argued points of view? Criticism of all views, including our own, is viewed as essential to forward understanding. Critical thinking discourages arrogance, the assumption that our beliefs should not be subject to critical evaluation. Popper (1992) emphasized, "In our infinite ignorance we are all equal" (p. 50). It prompts questions such as "Could I be wrong?" "Have I considered alternative views?" "Do I have sound reasons to believe that this plan will help this client?"

Critical thinking encourages us to think *contextually*, to consider the big picture, and to connect personal troubles to social issues. It requires accurate description of alternative views and a candid discussion of controversies and problems with preferred views, including empirical data that contradict them. Both critical thinking and evidence-based practice value transparency (honesty) concerning what is done to what effect, including candid description of lack of knowledge. Stanovich, West, and Toplak (2016) developed CART (Comprehensive Assessment of Rational Thinking) to evaluate rational thinking and characteristics that compromise this. Concepts include:

- Avoiding miserly information processing (override intuition; see Chapter 2).
- Avoiding irrelevant context effects such as framing and anchoring.
- Avoiding myside bias.
- Avoiding overconfidence.
- Avoiding superstitious thinking.
- Avoiding antiscience attitude.
- Being actively open-minded.
- Using deliberative thinking style.
- Considering future consequences.

THE IMPORTANCE OF THINKING CRITICALLY ABOUT DECISIONS

The history of the helping professions reflects great achievements as well as missed opportunities and avoidable harming in the name of helping. Related literature shows that avoidable errors are common (James, 2013). Avoidable errors may result in (a) failing to offer help that could be provided and is desired by clients, (b) forcing clients to accept practices they do not want, (c) offering help that is not needed, or (d) using procedures that aggravate rather than alleviate client concerns. Errors may occur during assessment by overlooking important data, using invalid measures, or attending to irrelevant data; during intervention by using ineffective methods; and during evaluation by using inaccurate indicators of progress. Reliance on irrelevant or inaccurate sources of data during assessment may result in incorrect and irrelevant accounts of client concerns and recommendation of ineffective or harmful methods. Important factors may not be noticed. For example, a clinician may overlook the role of physiological factors in depression. Failure to consider physical causes may result in inappropriate decisions.

Failure to seek information about the evidentiary status of claims may result in use of ineffective methods. Errors may result from reliance on questionable criteria such as anecdotal experience to evaluate the accuracy of claims (see related discussion in Chapter 2). Critical thinking knowledge, skills, and values contribute to minimizing mistakes such as not recognizing a problem, confusing the consequences of a problem for the problem, ignoring promising alternatives, harmful delay in decision-making, and lack of follow-up (Caruth & Handlogten, 2000). Professionals do not necessarily acquire critical thinking skills in their professional education (Heidari & Ebrahimi, 2016). Critical thinking skills, values, and knowledge are integral to the process of evidence-based practice.

Practices and policies include those based on sound evidence in which clients are involved as informed participants, as well as continued use and dissemination of services that have been carefully evaluated and found to be harmful (Hochman, 2014). False beliefs and misinformation are common, encouraged by our tendency to look for support for our beliefs and ignore contradictory information (DiResta, 2017; Gambrill, 2012a; Lewandowsky, Ecker, Seifert, Schwartz, & Cook, 2012). Cognitive errors in decision-making in medicine such as failure to search for contradictory information are common (Croskerry, 2003). Problems may remain unsolved because of reliance on questionable criteria to evaluate claims about what is accurate, such as tradition, popularity, or authority; we may fail to distinguish between evidence and pseudoevidence (see Chapter 2). Consider a claim that recovered memory therapy works. Too often, the questions that should be asked to reveal the evidentiary status of a claim are not asked, such as "The method works for what?" "What kind of research was conducted to test this claim? "Could such research rigorously test the claim?" "Has anyone been harmed by this method?"

Clients may be harmed rather than helped if we do not use AOT in which we search for counter-evidence and arguments against preferred views when considering possibilities, goals, and evidence regarding decisions. Are they well-reasoned?

Are they informed by related research? Have we avoided being bamboozled either by ourselves and/or others into accepting bogus claims about the effectiveness of a method (Gambrill, 2012a)? Have we avoided common errors in reasoning such as premature closure? As Karl Popper (1994) suggests, "there are always many different opinions and conventions concerning any one problem or subject matter. . . . This shows that they are not all true. For if they conflict, then at best only one of them can be true?" (p. 39). Gaps between knowledge available and what was used were a key reason for the development of evidence-based practice and policy (Gray, 2001a). The following findings suggest that clinical decisions can be improved:

- There are wide variations in practices (Wennberg & Thomson, 2011).
- Most services provided are of unknown effectiveness (Frakt, 2013).
- Medical reversals are common (Prasad, 2016; Prasad, Vandross, Toomey, Cheung, Rho, Quinn, Chako . . . Cifu, 2013).
- Clients are often harmed in the name of helping (Scull, 2005; 2015).
- Intervention methods found to be harmful continue to be used (Petrosino, Turpin-Petrosino, & Buehler, 2013).
- Assessment methods shown to be harmful continue to be used (e.g., Lilienfeld, Lynn, & Lohr, 2015; Thyer & Pignotti, 2015).
- Overdiagnosis and overtreatment is common (Hafner & Palmer, 2017; Pathirana, 2017; Welch, Schwartz, & Woloshin, 2011).
- Methods found to be effective are often not offered to clients (e.g., Jacobson, Foxx, & Mulick, 2005).
- There are large gaps between claims of effectiveness and evidence for such claims in the peer-reviewed literature (Ioannidis, 2005, 2016).
- Avoidable errors are common (James, 2013).
- Clients are typically not involved as informed participants regarding the evidentiary status of recommended services and alternatives.

There has been continuing parade of revelations of problems in the peer-reviewed literature including hiding of negative trials and adverse effects of medications, creating bogus categories of illness, overmedicating young children and the elderly with antipsychotics, and related conflicts of interest (Gambrill, 2012a). Consider these quotes from current and former editors-in-chief of major medical journals:

It is simply no longer possible to believe much of the clinical research that is published, or to rely on the judgment of trusted physicians or authoritative medical guidelines. I take no pleasure in this conclusion, which I reached slowly and reluctantly over my two decades as an editor of the *New England Journal of Medicine*. (Angell, 2009, p. 11).

The case against science is straightforward much of the scientific literature, perhaps half, may simply be untrue. Afflicted by studies with small sample sizes, tiny effects, invalid exploratory analyses, and flagrant conflicts of interest, together with an obsession for pursuing fashionable trends of dubious importance, science has taken a turn towards darkness, . . . scientists too often sculpt data to fit their preferred theory of the world. Or they retrofit hypotheses to fit their data—acquiescence to the impact factor fuels an unhealthy competition to win a place in a select few journals. Our love of "significance" pollutes the literature with many a statistical fairytale— Universities are in a perpetual struggle for money and talent, end points that foster reductive metrics, such as high-impact publication. National assessment procedures, such as the Research Excellence Framework, incentivize bad practices. (Horton, 2015, p. 1380)

Ioannidis (2005, 2016) argues that most research findings reported in the biomedical literature are false and that most systematic reviews are misleading, redundant, and conflicted. Hiding well-argued alternative views is common, such as failure to describe anxiety in social situations as a learned reaction created by a unique learning history (Gambrill & Reiman, 2011). Much of the material in peer-reviewed sources has more of the quality of advertisements (e.g., inflated claims based on misleading appeals to statistical significance, hiding negative information) than scholarly discourse (Gambrill, 2012a). Billions of dollars in settlements have been made based on whistle-blowing suits filed under the False Claim Act against drug and device makers (Silverman, 2010). Good intentions do not prevent harming in the name of helping. Consider the blinding of 10,000 children by routine use of oxygen at birth (Silverman, 1980). Scull (2015) illustrates the "orgy of experimentation with somatic treatments for mental disorder" in the 1930s including "surgical evisceration in pursuit of hypothesised septic causes of mental illness: fever therapy . . . barbiturates, injections of insulin, convulsive therapies, lobotomies" (p. 401). Gøtzsche (2015) argues that prescribed psychotropic medication taken by people 65 and over kills more than 500,000 people per year and disables tens of thousands more.

ATTENDING TO CONTEXT

Decisions are made in an environment that may be known only in part and the part that is knowable may be deliberately obscured or neglected (Oreskes &

Conway, 2010). They are made in real-life circumstances characterized by incomplete knowledge, ill-structured problems, involvement of many players, changing environments, time pressures, and conflicting goals such as offering effective services versus saving money. Problems that confront clients, such as lack of housing or health care, may be "wicked" problems with no clear formulation (Rittel & Webber, 1973). Practice is carried out in the context of policies and related legislation that certain patterns of behavior are problems and certain remedies are appropriate. Problems are defined in different ways at different times. Many players influence what is viewed as a problem and promoted as a remedy including politicians, the media, advocacy groups, clients, marketers of products (e.g., drugs), researchers, governmental agencies, patients, insurance companies, and regulatory agencies.

Changing ideas about what is and what is not mental illness illustrate the consensual nature of psychiatric diagnoses. Homosexuality was defined as a mental illness until 1974, when the American Psychiatric Association, under pressure from gay and lesbian advocacy groups and bitter infighting, decided that it was not. One of the ongoing debates concerns whether to locate the source of problems in individuals and to focus on changing them and/or to examine related environmental causes and pursue environmental change. The widespread use of medical language—healthy/unhealthy, wellness/sickness, health/disease—directs attention toward medical remedies. The word *health* has been applied to an ever-widening range of behaviors, feelings, and thoughts.

Related industries such as the pharmaceutical industry influence what problems are focused on and how they are framed (Moynihan & Cassels, 2005). Commercial interests in making money at the expense of harming clients are daily revealed (e.g., in successful lawsuits brought under the False Claims Act) as are conflicts of interest of individual practitioners with ties to corporations (e.g., Angel, 2009; Gambrill, 2012a). Political and economic influences and related efforts to hide important information highlight the need for critical appraisal of claims. Those who have products to sell, including residential centers, pharmaceutical companies, and professional organizations, use a variety of strategies to encourage purchase of their products including giving gifts to physicians (Wood et al., 2017). These range from the obvious, such as advertisements, to the hidden, such as offering workshops and sponsoring conferences without identifying funding sources. It is estimated that pharmaceutical companies spend $61,000 per medical student per year to market their products to these individuals (Gagnon, 2010). A review of advertising on marketing brochures distributed by drug companies to physicians in Germany revealed that 94% of the content in these had no basis in scientific evidence (reported in Tuffs, 2004). In advertising we are usually aware of the purpose of the advertiser—to sell a service or product. In other venues such as conferences, we may not be aware of sponsorship by a source that may encourage deceptive presentations. As we become immersed in the everyday world of practice, it is easy to forget about the economic, political, and social context in which problems are defined and reacted to. We may forget that problems are defined in accord with popular grand narratives of the times; we may forget to ask: "Who benefits and who loses form a particular view?"

Governmental agencies may be complicit in hiding adverse effects of policies and practices (e.g., Hatcher, 2014; Lenzer, 2005). The Internet as well as newspapers and journals are a source of false as well as accurate claims and allow repetition of misinformation that may bias us unknowingly. The marketing function of sites such as Facebook has received increased attention including their role in spreading mis-information. Our biases, including our world views contribute to the influence of mis-information (Carey, 2017; Nyhan & Reifler, 2010). They contribute to stereotypes and prejudice in making decisions (FitzGerald & Hurst, 2017).

UNCERTAINTY AS A CONSTANT COMPANION

The very nature of clinical practice leaves room for many sources of error. Decisions must be made in a context of uncertainty; the criteria on which decisions should be made are in dispute, and empirical data about the effectiveness of different intervention options are often lacking. Uncertainty may concern the nature of the problem, what is needed to attain valued outcomes, the likelihood of attaining them, and the measures that will best reflect degree of success. Information about options may be missing or unreliable, and accurate estimates of the probability that different alternatives will result in desired outcomes may be unknown. Let's return to the decision that must be made by Mrs. Richards regarding choice of parent training programs. Uncertainties here include: Is the program selected most likely to help her client? Is she informed about the competence of the individual who will provide it? With what percentage of clients like her client is success found? Consider also the patient in the mental hospital who starts to call the staff a devil just as she was about to be discharged. Does this indicate that treatment has been a failure? Should we inquire about the "function" of this behavior (e.g., that she is about to be discharged to an abusive situation; Layng, 2009)? Even when empirical information is available, this knowledge is usually in the form of general principles that do not allow specific predictions about individuals (Dawes, 1994). Problems may have a variety of causes and potential solutions. Most interventions are of unknown effectiveness. It is estimated that in medicine, 11% of treatments are clearly beneficial, 24% are likely to be beneficial, in 7% there is a tradeoff of harm and benefit, 3% are likely to be harmful or ineffective, and 50% of are unknown effectiveness (Frakt, 2013).

More often than not, it is not clear what intervention will be most effective, highlighting the importance of attending to ignorance (both avoidable and unavoidable) as well as knowledge in addition to client preferences and involving clients as informed participants. Interventions long promoted as effective may be found to be unneeded, such as use of stents (Kolata, 2017a). Clients seek relief from suffering, and professionals hope to offer it; there is a pressure from both sides to view proposed options in a rosy light. In the classic description of sources of uncertainty in making medical decisions, Fox (1957) suggests three that remain pertinent in the helping professions.

The first results from incomplete or imperfect mastery of available knowledge. No one can have at his command all skills and all knowledge of the lore of medicine. The second depends upon limitations in current medial knowledge. There are innumerable questions to which no physician, however well trained, can as yet provide answers. A third source of uncertainty derives from the first two. This consists of difficulty in distinguishing between personal ignorance or ineptitude and the limitations of present medical knowledge. (pp. 208–209).

Increased attention to the poor quality of much research and problems of generalizing findings from one individual and/or setting to another has increased uncertainty in many areas as has rigorous research that shows that previous views were incorrect (Kolata, 2017). Promising developments include AllTrials (www.alltrials.net, which is dedicated to registering and reporting all clinical trials; the RAIT (Restoring Invisible and Abandoned Trials) initiative; open science METRICS (Meta-Research Innovation Center) at Stanford, established to decrease the enormous waste in conducting research that cannot answer the questions addressed; and the Science Exchange Reproducibility Initiative.

SUMMARY

Decision-making is at the heart of clinical practice. Unless we critically reflect on the reasoning process used to make decisions, clients may be harmed rather than helped; we may be bamboozled by slick advertising and deceptive research reports. The helping professions are huge industries comprised of many stakeholders competing for resources. As a result, misleading claims may be forwarded that harm clients. This highlights the importance of AOT in making decisions in which we search for and critically appraise possibilities, goals, and evidence. Problems often remain unsolved not because we lack intelligence but because we fail to use AOT as well as content knowledge needed to make informed decisions; we fail to search for and critically appraise possibilities, goals, and evidence. Informed decision-making requires questioning beliefs and actions drawing on critical thinking, knowledge, skills, and values as well as content knowledge and related skills regarding problems addressed.

2

Origins, Characteristics, and Controversies Regarding the Process

of Evidence-Based Practice

A KEY CHOICE is how to view evidence-based practice (EBP; Gambrill, 2006). One view, which is the subject of this book, is what Eddy (2005) refers to as "evidence-based individual decision making" (p. 14)—the process of evidence-based practice. Other approaches include the EBPs (evidence-based practices) and EBIs (evidence-based interventions) approach and related guidelines. A third choice is the propaganda approach—redubbing interventions of unknown or weak evidentiary status as "evidence-based". The term *evidence-based medicine* entered the professional literature in 1991 in an article by Guyatt. The original vision of EBP is an alternative to authority-based decision-making in which appeals are made to personal anecdotes, clinical experience, reports of committees, tradition, and unsystematic observation. As suggested by Isaacs and Fitzgerald (1999), EBP is an alternative to eminence-based, eloquence-based, and vehemence-based decision-making (among others). Eddy (2005) notes that the term *evidence-based* spread to other areas including "evidence-based coverage, evidence-based performance measures, quality improvement, and policy." Other areas include evidence-based purchasing, evidence-based policy, and evidence-based organizations (Gray, 2001a). Evidence-based practice describes a philosophy as well as a process designed to forward effective use of professional judgment in integrating information about each client's unique circumstances and characteristics including their preferences and values with external research findings. "It is a guide for thinking about how decisions should be made" (Haynes et al., 2002).

Sackett et al. (1997) note that the philosophical origins of evidence-based medicine "extend back to mid-19th century Paris and earlier." Although its philosophical roots are old, the blooming of EBP as a process highlighting evidentiary, ethical, and application issues in all professional venues (education, practice/policy, and research) is fairly recent, facilitated by the Internet revolution. Professionals and clients often need information to make decisions, for example, about what services are most likely to be of value in attaining hoped-for outcomes. The term *evidence-based practice* calls attention to the extent to which decisions are informed by "evidence." And, what *is* evidence? Most people assumed that decisions were based on "evidence"; the use of this term seemed to imply that decisions were not necessarily informed by related research regarding the evidentiary status of interventions used including diagnostic tests. And, indeed, this was the case (Hochman, 2014). That is, in many cases, clients were not offered (or informed about), interventions most likely to help them, and some were receiving interventions with harmful effects (see later discussion of the origins of EBP).

Ethical obligations require practitioners to involve clients as informed participants concerning potential harms and benefits of recommended services and well-argued alternatives. In their discussion of EBP, Guyatt and Rennie (2002) include obligations of professionals to advocate for changes in environmental conditions that contribute to problems. Sackett and his co-authors published a book describing the process of evidence-based practice in 1997. Policy and requirements for evidence-based organizations suggested by Gray in 1997 and 2001a are still relevant today. Some prefer the term *evidence-informed practice* (Chalmers, 2003). I use both terms interchangeably in this book as well as the term *evidence-informed decision-making*.

The process of EBP as described by its originators involves "the conscientious, explicit and judicious use of current best evidence in making decisions about the care of individual [clients]" (Sackett, Richardson, Rosenberg, & Haynes, 1997, p. 2). Being explicit calls for clarity regarding what is done, why it is done, and with what outcomes. Judiciousness calls for thinking critically about life-affecting decisions and drawing on available research as well as other vital information. Conscientiousness implies being motivated to do the right thing and engage in the effort required to maximize the likelihood of a positive outcome. What is the best answer to vital questions? Increased recognition of harming in the name of helping as well as variations in practices used for the same concern, together with technological advances such as the Internet, contributed to the development of EBP (see later discussion in this chapter).

The process of EBP is a way for individual practitioners and clients to handle the inevitable uncertainty in making decisions in an informed, ethical manner, attending to ignorance as well as knowledge. It is designed to decrease the gaps between research and practice to maximize opportunities to help clients attain outcomes they value and avoid harm (Gray, 2001a, 2001b; Straus, Glasziou, Richardson, & Haynes, 2011). It is hoped that professionals who consider relevant research findings together with other vital information including client characteristics and circumstances will provide more effective, ethical services than those who rely on anecdotal experience, tradition, or popularity. Critical appraisal often shows that current practices result in more harm than good (Hochman, 2014). Examples include lobotomy, routine mammography for women in their forties, and Vioxx among many others (Prasad & Cifu, 2015). When ineffective methods fail, clients may feel more hopeless about achieving hoped-for outcomes.

The process of EBP requires "the integration of the best research evidence with our clinical expertise and our [client's] unique values and circumstances" (Straus et al., 2011). There may be no related research and well-argued theory must be drawn on as a guide. Clinical expertise refers to use of practice skills, including effective decision-making and relationship skills, and past experience to rapidly identify each client's unique circumstances and characteristics including their preferences and expectations and "their individual risks and benefits of potential interventions. . . ." (Straus et al., 2011, p. 1). It includes knowledge of relevant theory. Clinical expertise is drawn on to integrate information from varied sources (Haynes, Devereaux, & Guyatt, 2002) including information about resources (Health Sciences Library hsl.mcmaster.libguides.com downloaded 7/3/15).

> Without clinical expertise, practice risks becoming tyrannized by external evidence, for even excellent external evidence may be inapplicable to or inappropriate for an individual [client]. Without current best external evidence, practice risks becoming rapidly out of date, to the detriment of [clients]. (Sackett, et al., 1997, p. 2)

Client values refer to "the unique preferences, concerns and expectations each [client] brings to a clinical encounter and which must be integrated into clinical decisions if they are to serve the [client]" (Straus et al., 2011, p. 1; see Exhibit 2.1). Political economic, and social contingencies and organizational characteristics, including inter-agency relationship, influence application of the process as described in Chapter 11.

Evidence-based practice requires drawing on research findings related to important questions and sharing what is found (including nothing) within a supportive relationship with clients (Elwyn, Edwards, & Thompson, 2016). It involves a search not only for knowledge but also for ignorance. Such a search is required to involve clients as informed participants (e.g., to identity uncertainties related

EXHIBIT 2.1

KEY COMPONENTS OF THE PROCESS OF EVIDENCE-BASED PRACTICE

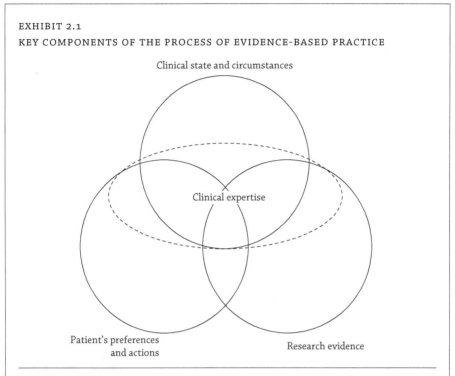

Clinical state and circumstances

Clinical expertise

Patient's preferences
and actions

Research evidence

Source: Clinical Expertise in the Era of Evidence-Based Medicine and Patient Choice by R. B. Haynes, P. J. Devereaux, and G. H. Guyatt, 2002, ACP Journal Club, 136, pp. A11-14. Reprinted with permission.

to decisions). When little or no research is available regarding a concern, well-argued theory is drawn on; this should be informed by empirical research, for example, about behavior and/or physiology. Client values and expectations are vital to consider (see later description of Step 4 in the process of EBP). The process of EBP highlights the uncertainties involved in making decisions and offers tools to handle these constructively and ethically, for example, by locating and critically appraising research related to decisions, taking advantage of technologies such as systematic reviews. Uncertainties include the relevance of research to individual clients, client characteristics and circumstances that may influence outcome, and resources available. Steps in EBP include:

Step 1: convert information needs related to decisions into well-structured questions.

Step 2: track down the best evidence with which to answer them.

Step 3: critically appraise that evidence for its validity (closeness to the truth), impact (size of the effect), and applicability (usefulness in our clinical practice).

Step 4: integrate the critical appraisal with our clinical expertise and with our [clients'] unique characteristics including their values and circumstances (e.g., Is a client similar to those studied? Is there access to services needed?).

Step 5: evaluate our effectiveness and efficiency in executing steps 1 to 4 and seek ways to improve them both for next time. (Straus, Glasziou, Richardson, & Haynes, 2011, pp. 3–4).

Not keeping up with new research findings related to important decisions renders knowledge increasingly out of date. As a result, helpers cannot honor informed consent obligations and decisions may harm rather than help clients (e.g., Jacobson, Foxx, & Mulick, 2005; Lilienfeld, Lynn, & Lohr, 2015; Thyer & Pignotti, 2015).

EXAMPLES

1. Dr. Price works in a mental health crisis center. The administrator of this agency sent a memo to staff that he had heard that brief psychological debriefing was effective in decreasing post-traumatic stress disorder following a crisis and suggested that his staff use this method. His question was: In clients experiencing a potentially traumatic event, is brief, one-hour psychological debriefing, compared to no service, more effective in preventing post-traumatic stress disorder? This is an effectiveness question. He found a systematic review prepared by Rose, Bisson, Churchill, and Wessely (2009). This review concluded that not only was single session individual debriefing not effective, there was increased risk of PTSD for those receiving debriefing. Based on this review, he sent an e-mail to his colleagues questioning the use of this method for clients.

2. Jake complained of pain in his knee and consulted a surgeon. The surgeon recommended repair of his meniscus tear. Jake googled knee pain and meniscus repair and discovered a study comparing sham surgery with arthroscopic surgery that reported similar outcomes (Sihvonen et al., 2013). He decided not to have the surgery.

3. Diane works in a child protection agency that uses a consensus-based risk assessment to estimate the likely recurrence of child abuse among parents alleged to have abused their children. This is based on the opinions of a group of experts on what they consider risk factors. Her question was: Among parents alleged to have abused their children,

are actuarial compared to consensus-based measures most accurate in predicting the likelihood of future abuse? This is a question about risk. Diane found that actuarial measures based on empirical relationships between certain factors and the likelihood of an outcome, such as child abuse, outperformed consensus-based measures (Cuccaro-Alamin, Foust, Vaithianathan, & Putnam-Hornstein, 2017). She brought this research to the attention of other staff and suggested preparation of a CAT (critically appraised topic) for the next journal club meeting (see ACP Journal Club, http://annals.org).

THREE PHILOSOPHIES OF EVIDENCE-BASED PRACTICE

Evidence-based practice and policy involve a philosophy of ethics of professional practice, a philosophy of science (epistemology—views about what knowledge is and how it can be gained), and a philosophy of technology. Ethics involves decisions regarding how and when to act; it involves standards of conduct. For example, is it ethical to refer clients to agencies that do not provide effective services or to refer clients to agencies when you are unfamiliar with the quality of services they provide? Is it ethical to rely on the opinion of "experts" and lists of "evidence-based practices" to select services? Is it ethical to expect staff to provide services but not give them the needed training and resources required to do so? Is it ethical to ignore fraud and corruption that compromises services clients receive? Is it ethical to involve clients as uninformed participants? Is it ethical for policy makers to require or encourage implementation of a program without carefully reviewing whether it is likely to be effective with given individuals and/or communities? Epistemology involves views about knowledge and how to get it or if we can (see Chapter 3). The philosophy of technology concerns questions such as: What criteria should we rely on in deciding what technology to develop and how or if it can be successfully applied? What criteria should we use to examine the consequences of a given technology? Evidence-informed practice emphasizes the importance of critically appraising research and developing a technology to help clinicians to do so.

The process of EBP offers practitioners a philosophy that is compatible with obligations described in professional codes of ethics and accreditation policies and standards (e.g., for informed consent and to draw on practice- and policy-related research findings) as well as an evolving technology for integrating evidentiary, ethical, and practical issues. Related literature highlights the interconnections among these three concerns and suggests specific steps (a technology) to decrease gaps among them in all professional venues, including practice and policy (e.g., drawing on related research), research (e.g., preparing systematic reviews and clearly describing limitations of studies), and professional education (e.g., exploring the value of problem-based learning in developing life-long learners). The uncertainty associated with decisions is acknowledged, not hidden. EBP requires considering research findings related to important practice/policy decisions and sharing what is found (including nothing) with clients (see Chapter 4). Transparency and honesty regarding the evidentiary status of services is a hallmark of this philosophy.

AN ALTERNATIVE TO AUTHORITY-BASED PRACTICE

Evidence-based decision-making arose as an alternative to authority-based decision-making in which criteria such as consensus, anecdotal experience,

---

EXHIBIT 2.2
DIFFERENCES BETWEEN AUTHORITY-BASED AND EVIDENCE-BASED
PRACTITIONERS

Authority-Based	Evidence-Informed
• Clients are not informed or are misinformed.	• Clients are involved as informed participants regarding ignorance of and knowledge.
• Ignores client preferences ("We know best").	• Seeks and considers client values and preferences.
• Does not identify information needs, pose specific related questions, search for and critically appraise what is found, and share with clients.	• Identifies information needs, poses clear related questions, seeks related research findings, critically appraises them, and shares what is found with clients and significant others (including nothing).
• Ignores errors and mistakes, avoids criticism.	• Seeks out errors and mistakes; values criticism as vital for learning.
• Accepts claims based on misleading criteria such as tradition and expert consensus.	• Relies on rigorous criteria to appraise claims and select practices and policies (e.g., those that control for biases).
• Relies on self-report of clients or anecdotal observations to evaluate progress.	• Seeks both subjective (self-report) and objective (e.g., observation) data to evaluate progress.

status, or tradition are relied on (see Exhibit 2.2.) This is reflected in a handout distributed to new residents in the Department of Obstetrics, Gynecology, and Reproductive Sciences at San Francisco General Hospital: "Everyone's clinical opinion counts equally regardless of rank or experience. We value opinions only to the extent that they are supported by scientific evidence and not according to the perceived prestige of the proponent" (Grimes, 1995). Evidence-based is designed to break down the division between research, practice, and policy—highlighting the importance of honoring ethical obligations. Although misleading in the incorrect assumption that EBP means that decisions are based only on evidence of the effectiveness of different services, use of the term does call attention to the fact that available evidence may not be used or the current state of ignorance shared with clients. It is hoped that professionals who consider related research findings regarding life-affecting decisions and inform clients about them will provide more effective and ethical care than those relying on criteria such as anecdotal experience, available resources, or popularity. The following examples illustrate reliance on authority-based criteria for selection of service methods.

> Ms. Riverton has just been to a workshop on eye movement desensitization therapy. The workshop leader told the participants that this method "works and can be used for a broad range of problems." Ms. Riverton suggests to her supervisor at the mental health clinic where she works that agency staff should use this method. When asked why, she said because the workshop leader is a respected authority in the field.
>
> Mr. Davis read an editorial that describes the DARE programs as very effective in decreasing drug use. No related empirical literature was referred to. He suggested to his agency that they use this effective method.

In the first example, the authority of a workshop leader is appealed to. In the second, the authority of an author of an editorial is appealed to. Evidence-based decision-making involves use of quite different criteria; a key one is information about the accuracy of claims. Is eye movement desensitization effective for certain kinds of problems? Are DARE programs effective? (See Gorman & Huber, 2009). EBP draws on the results of systematic, rigorous, critical appraisals of research related to questions, such as "Is this assessment measure valid?" "Does this intervention do more good than harm?" For example, review groups in the Cochrane and Campbell Collaborations prepare reviews of all research related to a question.

THE EVIDENCE-BASED PRACTICES AND GUIDELINES APPROACH

One popular view is the EBPs approach in which some source recommends or mandates use of certain programs and related guidelines and/or manuals (also known as the EBIs approach—evidence-based interventions). Websites such as the National Institute for Health and Care Excellence (NICE), the California Evidence-Based Clearinghouse for Child Welfare (www.cebc4cw.org), and the Social Care Institute for Excellence (SCIE; (www.scie.org.uk) include lists of what are described as "evidence-based practices." Programs are rated in terms of their assumed effectiveness. Many sources promote "evidence-informed policies" (e.g., Alliance for Useful Evidence; www.alliance4usefulevidence.org) and describe practice guidelines. Criteria for labeling a method/program as "evidence-based" vary in rigor so buyer-beware applies. And, to what degree can programs tested in one setting be successfully applied in others? Many people confuse the process of EBP as described in original sources with the EBPs approach. Thus, if someone uses the term *evidence-based practice or policy*, find out how she is using this term.

The *process* of evidence-informed decision-making on the part of individual clients and practitioners differs in important ways from the promotion of EBPs and EBIs. The process requires deliberative reasoning for considering the applicability an EBP/EBI guideline. It requires integrating multiple kinds of information in making decisions regarding individuals.

THE PROPAGANDA APPROACH

Choices regarding new ideas and related technology include (1) ignoring it, (2) claiming there is nothing new, (3) saying "We've been doing it," (4) relabeling the old as new because it sounds good and is in "fashion," (5) misrepresenting it and then attacking the distortion (e.g., picking off fragments and asserting that the fragment selected is the idea), or (6) accurately describing it and considering what it has to offer. Many uses of the term *EBP* reflect avoidable distortions and dubbing dubious programs as "evidence-based" (Gambrill, 2010a, 2010b, 2016). Material referred to as "evidence-based" reflects critical thinking values, knowledge, and skills to different degrees, ranging from a close relationship to little overlap, as illustrated by use of the term *evidence-based* without the substance; excessive claims are made regarding possible generalization of practices and/or policies. The old is relabeled as the new (as an "evidence-based" practice or policy); the term is used without the substance (e.g., Gorman & Huber, 2009). Claims to be "scientific" have long been used to forward quackery and fraud as discussed in Chapter 3.

ORIGINS OF THE PROCESS OF EVIDENCE-BASED PRACTICE

The origins of the process of EBP reflect ongoing ethical and evidentiary concerns, including the uncertainties concerning decisions made. Sackett, Straus, Richardson, Rosenberg, and Haynes (2000) suggest four realizations made possible by five recent developments for the rapid spread of EBP. Realizations include: (1) practitioner need for valid information about decisions; (2) the inadequacy of traditional sources for acquiring this information, for example because they are out-of-date, frequently wrong, overwhelming in volume, and variable in their validity; (3) the gap between assessment skills and clinical judgment "which increase with experience and our up-to-date knowledge and clinical performance which decline" (p. 2); and (4) lack of time to locate, appraise, and integrate this evidence (p. 2). There were increasing gaps between information available on the Internet that could be of value to clients and clinicians in making decisions and what was drawn on. Developments that Sackett et al. suggest that have allowed improvement in this state of affairs included (1) the creation of strategies for efficiently tracking down and appraising evidence (for its validity and relevance); (2) the invention of the systematic review and concise summaries of the effects of healthcare (epitomized by the Cochrane Collaboration); (3) the creation of evidence-based journals of secondary publications; (4) the creation of information systems for bringing the foregoing to us in seconds; and (5) the creation and use of effective strategies for lifelong learning and for improving the soundness of decisions (p. 3).

Variations in Services Offered

There was increased attention to variations in services offered for similar problems across regions and their outcomes (Wennberg, 2002). As Gray (2001a) notes, variations occurred between countries, between services in a country, between services in an area, and between staff in an agency. Questions arise such as: "Are they of equal cost and effectiveness?" "Do some harm?" Wide variations in practices continue including rates of caesarean births and hysterectomies (e.g., Brownlee et al., 2011; McPhearson, Gon, & Scott, 2013; Wennberg & Thomson, 2011). Children are prescribed medication for (mis)behavior at far higher rates in the United States compared to France (Cohen, 2013). Children in foster care in the United States are prescribed much higher rates of psychotropic medication compared to other children (U.S. Government Accountability Office, 2014) as are children of low socioeconomic status (Bonnot et al., 2017). The Wennberg International Collaborative (www.wennberg.collaborative) tracks variations in medical practices. We should have similar sites in other professions.

Gaps among Ethical, Evidentiary, and Application Concerns

A key reason for the creation of the process of EBP was the discovery of gaps showing that professionals were not acting systematically or promptly on re-search findings. There was a failure to start services that work and to stop services that did not work or harmed clients. Gray (2001b) suggests that current service patterns have the following characteristics:

- overenthusiastic adoption of interventions of [unknown] efficacy or even [demonstrated] ineffectiveness;
- failure to adopt interventions that do more good than harm at a reasonable cost;
- continuing to offer interventions demonstrated to be ineffective;
- adoption of interventions without adequate preparation (such that the benefits demonstrated in a research setting cannot be reproduced in the ordinary service setting);
- wide variations in the rates at which interventions are adopted or discarded. (p. 366)

Although linked in professional codes of ethics and accreditation standards, eth-ical and evidentiary issues are often far apart in practice. Gaps between obligations described in professional codes of ethics to help and avoid harm, to involve clients as informed participants and everyday practices and policies continue. Accurate claims based on sound investigations compete with bogus claims about what works as illus-trated by the history of fraud and quackery (Lilienfeld, Lohr, & Lohr, 2015; Thyer & Pignotti, 2015; Young, 1992). Unnecessary medical care is common (e.g., Gawande, 2015). Underuse of effective practices is common (Glasziou et al., 2017) as is overuse (Brownlee et al., 2017). Prasad and his colleagues (2013) describe reversals of 146 contradicted medical practices. If professionals are uninformed about the evidentiary status of practices and policies, they cannot honor informed consent obligations.

Economic Considerations

Economic concerns were another factor (e.g., wasting money on ineffective and/ or harmful services). No matter what system of care exists, resources are lim-ited. Wasting money on harmful or ineffective services leaves less for effective programs. A concern in evidence-based policy to consider both individuals and populations (do all residents with a particular need have access to similar quality care?), encourages evidence-informed decisions (e.g., Gray, 2001).

Increased Attention to Harming in the Name of Helping

Common practices thought to help people may be ineffective or harmful. Related reports increased awareness that services designed to help clients including assessment methods may have negative effects. Makary and Daniel (2016) argue that medical errors, many avoidable, are the third leading cause of death in the United States. Diagnostic errors are common (Singh, Meyers, & Thomas, 2014). We do not know how many standards of medical care are wrong (Prasad, Cifu, & Ioannidis, 2012). We can ask the same question regarding other helping professions.

Limitations of Traditional Methods of Knowledge Dissemination

Increased recognition of the flawed nature of traditional means of knowledge dissemination such as texts, editorials, and peer review was another factor. Reviews of texts showed that many were out of date. There were gaps between responsibilities of researchers and scholars to be honest brokers of knowledge and ignorance and what was found in related venues, including the peer-reviewed literature such as inflated claims of "what works" and hiding limitations of research. Revelations of the flawed nature of the peer-reviewed literature continue (Ioannidis, 2005, 2016). There were (and are) troubling gaps between obligations of researchers to report limitations of research, prepare rigorous reviews, and accurately describe well-argued alternative views and what we find in published literature. We find:

- Inflated claims.
- Biased estimates of the prevalence of concerns, advocacy in place of careful weighing of evidence.
- Hiding limitations of research.
- Haphazard reviews.
- Ignoring counterevidence to preferred views.
- Ignoring or distorting well-argued alternative perspectives and related evidence.
- Pseudoinquiry; little match between questions and methods used to address them.
- Ad hominem rather than ad rem arguments (see Chapter 8).
- Ignoring knowledge of clients and service providers in making decisions about the appropriateness of guidelines.

In 2005 Ioannidis argued that most published research findings are false (see also Ioannidis, 2016). Statistical analyses are often flawed (Nuijten, Hartgerink, van Assen, Epskamp, & Wicherts, 2016; Nuzzo, 2014). A variety of strategies are used to give the illusion of successful outcomes including focusing on surrogates (reducing plaque in the arteries rather than mortality), data dredging (searching for significant findings unguided by specific hypotheses), describing only outcomes found to be positive and not reporting negative ones, and folding outcome measures not found to be significant into a composite score and claiming that this composite reflects effectiveness. Such ploys are common in the peer-reviewed literature (e.g., Gorman & Huber, 2009). Many studies cannot be replicated (Baker, 2015). Examples of flaws and fallacies in the medical literature include Significance Turkey (lauds significant results even if they are not clinically significant) and Diagnostic Zealot (overzealous peddler of the latest diagnostic test; Michael, Boyce, & Wilcox, 1984). As Rosenthal (1994) suggests in his description of hyperclaiming (telling others that proposed research is likely to achieve goals that it will not) and causism (implying a causal relationship when none has been established), "Bad science makes for bad ethics" (p. 128).

Reasons for lack of transparency regarding limitations of research include special interests of those who fund research such as pharmaceutical companies that censor negative findings (e.g., Angell, 2009) and conflicts of interest between academics/researchers and Big Pharma (Lo & Field, 2009). Fake peer reviews are common (authors create fake email accounts and review their own manuscripts). Retractionwatch.com has flagged thousands of retractions. Initiatives designed to increase transparency include open access and open science (www.alltrials. net). The Meta-Research Innovation Center (METRICS) has been established at Stanford University to plan how to decrease the enormous waste in conducting research that cannot answer questions addressed (see also Ioannidis, 2012; Prasad & Ioannidis, 2014).

Invention of the Systematic Review

Recognition of limitations in traditional research reviews such as lack of rigorous appraisal of research encouraged the development of the systematic review for synthesizing research findings. The Cochrane Collaboration was created in 1992 to prepare, maintain, and disseminate high-quality research reviews related to a specific practice/policy question. The Campbell Collaboration was established in 1999. Systematic reviews focus on a clear question, use explicit rigorous criteria for inclusion and exclusion of studies, clearly describe these criteria, search widely for related research including in the "gray literature" (unpublished sources), and use clear methods for combining data. The Cochrane and Campbell Databases provide systematic reviews regarding thousands of questions. Examples include antidepressants for treatment of depression in people with cancer, social skills programs for people diagnosed as schizophrenic, and exercise programs for people with dementia. Here, too, skepticism is required because reviews differ in rigor (Gambrill, 2015; Ioannidis, 2016).

The Internet Revolution

Inventions in technology were key in the origins of EBP such as the Web revolution that allows quick access to databases and preparation of meta-analyses and systematic reviews (research syntheses), which, if well done, make it easier to discover the evidentiary status of interventions and claims about causes. The Internet allows speedy searches and routine updating of reviews.

The Appeal of EBP to Professionals and Clients

Gray (2001b) attributes the rapid spread of EBP in part to its appeal to clinicians and to clients. He notes that clients initially experience surprise to the concept of EBP because they thought doctors were basing their decisions on best current evidence.

> It also came as a shock that even the knowledge, where it was available, was often deficient (or commonly not even utilized by doctors who had been left behind the knowledge frontier). They therefore welcomed EBM enthusiastically and it is remarkable how quickly that access to information has turned the table on professional expertise and power. It is no longer feasible to feign knowledge: patients are just as likely to have searched for the evidence before they consult a clinician (p. 27).

HALLMARKS AND IMPLICATIONS OF THE PHILOSOPHY OF EBP

The philosophy and related technology of the process of EBP has implications for all individuals and institutions involved with helping clients, including educators, researchers, practitioners/policy makers, and those who provide funding (see Exhibit 2.3). Hallmarks such as considering the values and expectations of clients, involving clients as informed participants and making what professionals do to what effect transparent, should help to counter influences that contribute to ignoring outcomes of interest to clients, using ineffective or harmful services and

EXHIBIT 2.3
INTERRELATED HALLMARKS AND CONTRIBUTIONS OF THE
PROCESS OF EBP

1. *Move away from authority-based practices and policies*
   - Encourage critical appraisal of claims; decrease reliance on questionable criteria for making decisions such as popularity.
   - Avoid pseudo-inquiry (research that cannot critically test questions raised).
   - Minimize influence by and promotion of human service propaganda (Gambrill, 2012a).

2. *Honor ethical obligations*
   - Focus on client concerns and hoped-for outcomes.
   - Attend to individual and cultural differences in client circumstances and characteristics including client values and preferences.
   - Clearly describe gaps between evidentiary and ethical concerns.
   - Involve clients as informed participants. Be honest brokers of knowledge and ignorance; clearly describe the evidentiary status of recommended services and alternatives.
   - Minimize harming in the name of helping.
   - Be competent to offer services.
   - Make judicious use of scarce resources.
   - Blow the whistle on fraud and corruption that harms clients.

3. *Promote transparency and accountability regarding what is done to what effect*
   - Describe variations in services and their outcomes.
   - Acknowledge ignorance and uncertainties associated with decisions.
   - Critically appraise claims of knowledge and ignorance.
   - Describe gaps between research findings and services and policies.
   - Blow the whistle on pseudoscience, propaganda, quackery, and fraud.
   - Clearly describe services offered and outcomes attained on agency websites.

4. *Encourage a systemic approach to implementation challenges*
   - Identify and minimize implementation challenges including dysfunctional organizational practices and policies.
   - Educate professionals who are lifelong learners.
   - Promote accurate reporting of research findings.

5. *Maximize knowledge flow* (see also number 3)
   - Decrease gaps between available knowledge and what is used (e.g., draw on high-quality systematic reviews regarding important questions).
   - Welcome critical appraisal of beliefs and actions.
   - Minimize biases and fallacies that contribute to flawed decisions.
   - Help all involved parties to rapidly locate and critically appraise research regarding life-affecting decisions.

- Encourage lifelong learning.
- Create transparent, accountable agency complaint and compliment systems.
- Design and implement effective programs for identifying and minimizing errors.

Source: E. Gambrill, May 2000, *Evidence-Based Practice: Implications for Knowledge Development and Use in Social Work*, Paper presented at the Conference on Developing Practice Guidelines for Social Work Interventions. George Warren Brown School of Social Work, Washington University. Shortened version in A. Rosen, & E. K. Proctor (Eds.), 2003, *Developing Practice Guidelines for Social Work Intervention: Issues, Methods and Research Agenda*, New York: Columbia University Press, pp. 37–58.

failure to involve clients as informed participants. Research, practice, and educational issues are intertwined. For example, uncritical reviews of research may result in misleading "practice guidelines" (Gorman, 2017). Promotion of transparency contributes to knowledge flow.

Move Away from Authority-Based Practices and Policies

The key contribution of the process of EBP is moving from authority-based professions to those in which ethical obligations to clients are honored—for example, to draw on and critique related research findings and involve clients as informed participants. Honest brokering of knowledge and ignorance is valued. There is an openness to and welcoming of criticism (McIntyre & Popper, 1983). Indicators of authority-based decision-making include relying on criteria such as opinion and tradition, failing to involve clients as informed participants, and promoting inflated claims of effectiveness regarding practices and/or policies (Cartwright & Hardie, 2012). Although professional codes of ethics call on practitioners to inform clients regarding the risks and benefits of recommended services and alternatives, this is typically not done. Transparency regarding the evidentiary status of interventions is emphasized. Interventions include assessment frameworks and measures. There is candidness and clarity in place of secrecy, obscurity, and paternalism. These characteristics are at odds with authority-based practice (e.g., Chalmers, 1983; Gambrill, 1999).

Honor Ethical Obligations

Evidence-informed practice has ethical implications for clients, practitioners, policymakers, researchers, and educators. Hallmarks include focusing on client concerns and hoped-for outcomes, attending to individual differences in client circumstances and characteristics including client values and expectations, and involving clients as informed participants in decision-making. EBP involves sharing responsibility with clients for decision-making in a context of recognized uncertainty. A striking characteristic of EBP and related developments is the extent to which clients are involved in many different ways. One is reflected in the attention given to individual differences in client characteristics, circumstances, actions, values, and preferences in making decisions, including recognizing their unique knowledge in relation to application concerns. A second is helping clients to develop critical appraisal skills. A third is encouraging client involvement in the design and critique of research (e.g., Hanley, Truesdale, King, Elbourne, & Chalmers, 2001). A fourth is attending to outcomes clients value, and a fifth is involving clients as informed (rather than as uninformed or misinformed) participants.

The client-focused nature of evidence-informed decision-making requires helpers to attend to client interests: What are *their* desired outcomes, what are *their* preferences regarding practices and policies, and what are *their* questions (information needs)? Sharpe and Faden (1998) describe the struggle in medicine to focus on client outcomes and highlight how recent this focus is and what a contentious issue it has been and continues to be. A concern for involving clients as informed participants in making decisions has encouraged the development of client decision aids (e.g., Elwyn, Edwards & Thompson, 2016).

Reduce Harm by Learning from Errors

EBP encourages programmatic research regarding error, both avoidable and not, its causes and consequences for clients and other involved parties, and exploring how to minimize errors, including comprehensive (systemic) risk management programs (e.g., Gambrill & Shlonsky, 2001; Jenicek, 2011; Vincent, 2010). If we understand the circumstances that contribute to errors, we are in a better position to minimize avoidable ones. Research regarding errors highlights systemic causes, including quality of feedback concerning outcomes of decisions, staff training, and organizational culture.

Increase Transparency

Evidence-based practice encourages transparency concerning what is done to what effect including criteria used to make decisions in all venues of interest, including practice and policy, research, and professional education. Some programs do more good than harm, some more harm than good, and most have not been critically tested. EBP emphasizes the importance of accurately describing the evidentiary status of claims about assessment, intervention, and evaluation methods. It calls for candid descriptions of the limitations of research studies. A key contribution is discouraging inflated claims of knowledge that mislead involved parties and hinder the development of knowledge. Consider terms such as *well established* and *validated* that convey a certainty that is not possible (see Chapter 3). Ignorance and uncertainty are recognized rather than hidden. Involving clients as informed participants increases transparency of what is done to what effect. Transparency will reveal services that are ineffective, allowing a more judicious distribution of scarce resources (Eddy, 1994a, 1994b; Prasad & Ioannidis, 2014). It will reveal gaps between causes of client problems and interventions used and promoted. Transparency will reveal the extent to which ethical obligations are met including involving clients as participants who are accurately informed about the evidentiary status of recommended services and alternatives. And, it will suggest impossible tasks. Consider the requirement to "ensure" that children in protective care will not be harmed. This cannot be done.

Encourage a Systemic Approach to Pursuit of Quality of Care

The process of EBP encourages a systemic approach to improving quality of services: (1) educating professionals who are life-long learners, (2) involving clients as informed participants, (3) attending to organizational practices and policies that influence service, (4) considering the implications of scarce resources, and (5) attending to implementation challenges such as the provision of tools that facilitate tracking down and appraising relevant research findings (for their validity and relevance; Gray, 2001b). Related literature describes a wide variety of efforts to address application concerns (see Chapter 11), some of which may be so severe that Sackett et al. (2000) refer to them as "Killer Bs" (e.g., organizational barriers and reliance on tradition or authority when making decisions; p. 181). Differences in settings and individuals may prohibit successful use of a practice or policy that has been found to be of value in one setting. User-friendly websites have been created to enhance critical appraisal skills as described in Chapter 5. Quality of services is unlikely to improve in a fragmented approach, that is, without attending to all links in the system of service provision (e.g., England, Butler, & Gonzales, 2015; Fixen, Blasé, Naoom, & Wallace, 2009). Decisions concerning the distribution of scarce resources are a key ethical concern in the helping professions. This requires consideration of populations as well as individuals.

Maximize Knowledge Flow Including Knowledge about Ignorance

Evidence-informed practice and policy are designed to maximize knowledge flow among all involved parties. In a culture in which knowledge flow is free, criticism is welcomed, and ignorance is acknowledged. Counterevidence regarding popular views is sought. Gray (2001b) suggests that evidence-based organizations should include systems that are capable of providing evidence and promoting the use of evidence, including both explicit (created by researchers) and tacit (created by clinicians, clients, and managers). Evidence-informed agencies encourage knowledge flow by using services that maximize the likelihood of attaining hoped-for outcomes. Clinicians and clients are involved as informed participants—there is no privileged knowledge in the sense of not sharing information about the evidentiary status of services. Benefits of a democratic knowledge market include:

1. Critical appraisal of claims.
2. Increased staff morale because decisions will be informed (e.g., regarding important uncertainties) and staff are rewarded for sharing knowledge and are free to raise questions and learn from colleagues and others throughout the world.
3. Increase in informed decisions.
4. Recognition of uncertainty and ignorance. This is often swept under the rug; staff would no longer be blamed for not considering knowledge that, in fact, does not (or did not) exist.

Critical appraisal may reveal that programs being widely disseminated are not effective or have harmful effects. Accountable complaint and compliment systems are another way to increase knowledge flow.

MISREPRESENTATIONS OF AND OBJECTIONS TO EVIDENCE-BASED PRACTICE

Inaccurate descriptions of the process and philosophy of EBP (Gambrill, 2010a, 2010b) emphasize the importance of reading original sources. Criticism of ideas is vital but should be based on accurate understanding and descriptions (Popper, 1994). And, what is proclaimed as new may not be. Given the clash with authority-based practice (making decisions based on criteria such as tradition and popularity) often influenced by commercial interests, it is not surprising that the original vision of evidence-informed decision-making, which highlights ignorance and uncertainty is often ignored or misrepresented. Misrepresenting new ideas saves time in accurately understanding and describing them and allows current practices and policies to continue and now to be dubbed as "evidence-based." Both censorship and distortion of new ideas is common in the history of the helping professions and in science (e.g., Campanario, 2009).

One objection is that EBP started in medicine and thus is not relevant to other helping professions. Similarities among helping professions include the need to make complex decisions in uncertain environments, a reluctance to face uncertainty, the vital role of communication skills, the play of political and economic influences, and ethical obligations. The typical physician works in an atmosphere of uncertainty. (Medicine has the advantage that there are *signs* as well as *symptoms*. That is, if we feel warm [a symptom], we can take our temperature [a sign] to check on this.) All helping professionals must struggle with deciding how (or if) research findings apply to a particular client.

Objections due to misunderstandings and misrepresentations of the process of EBP include:

- It ignores clinical expertise (e.g., relationship skills).
- It ignores clients' values and preferences.
- It promotes a cookbook approach (e.g., ignores individual differences in clients' circumstances and characteristics).
- It is simply a cost-cutting tool.
- It is limited to clinical research.
- It is an ivory-tower concept (it cannot be done).
- Only randomized controlled trials are considered.
- It leads to therapeutic nihilism in the absence of evidence.
- It ignores organizational obstacles.
- We are already doing it; there is nothing new (see Exhibit 2.4).

Reading original sources shows the incorrectness of all these objections. (See Gibbs and Gambrill, 2002, for replies to objections based on distortions of EBP.) Attention to the unique characteristics and circumstances of clients including cultural differences prohibit a "cookbook" approach as does attention to unique settings. Organizational obstacles are of key concern (Gray, 1997, 2001) as are uncertainties. Review of research related to a question may show that effective programs will cost more, not less. Many (most?) practitioners do not search for external research findings related to important decisions. Many (most?) do not clearly describe to clients the criteria they use to select interventions or describe the risks and benefits of recommended services and alternatives.

EXHIBIT 2.4
MISREPRESENTATIONS OF THE PROCESS OF EVIDENCE-BASED PRACTICE

Distortion	Reply
1. EBP stems from behaviorism and positivism.	1. It does not stem from either. (See original sources as well as discussion in this chapter.)
2. EBP ignores client values.	2. Attending to client values and preferences is a hallmark of the process of EBP.
3. EBP ignores clinical expertise.	3. Clinical expertise is drawn on in all steps in the process of EBP. It includes tacit knowledge and effective communication skills (see Chapter 5).
4. EBP simply substitutes another form of authority.	4. In propagandistic uses of the term "evidence-based" this is true.
5. EBP is a cookbook approach.	5. EBP involves the use of clinical expertise to consider unique client characteristics and circumstances and available resources and related factors.
6. EBP is simply a cost-cutting tool.	6. A review of possible options related to a concern may result in more money being spent.
7. Only randomized controlled trials are drawn on.	7. A wide variety of research is drawn on to match the question raised as described in original sources.
8. Research shows it cannot be done.	8. Research suggests there are many obstacles but that it can be done and valuable aids continue to be developed (Elwyn, Wiersinga, & Greenhalgh, 2016).
9. EBP results in therapeutic nihilism.	9. If no evidence is found, this is shared with clients, clinical expertise and client values and interests are drawn on to guide decisions.
10. There is nothing new about EBP; we are already doing it.	10. New developments in technology have occurred and most practitioners do not use the process.

Distortion	Reply
11. No evidence is available that can guide practice.	11. Relevant evidence is available regarding many questions and EBP requires a search for ignorance as well as knowledge.
12. It ignores organizational and other contextual factors.	12. Contextual factors have always been (and are) a concern. (See Gray, 1997, 2001, as well as more recent sources.)
13. EBP assumes that professionals are rational agents.	13. One reason EBP originated was because clinicians often do not draw on related research.
14. It only applies if evidence is found.	14. See no. 11.
15. Effectiveness is a matter of personal opinion.	16. EBP emphasizes the importance of critical appraisal.
16. You can always find evidence for a point of view.	17. But is it compelling (see Chapters 3 and 5)?
17. All methods are of equal value in evaluating claims.	17. This is not so (see Chapters 3 and 5).

Source: Based in part on "Evidence-Based Practice: Counterarguments to Objections," by L. Gibbs and E. Gambrill, 2002, *Research on Social Work Practice*, 14, 452–476, and "Evidence-Based Medicine: A Commentary on Common Criticisms," by S. E. Straus and D. C. McAlister, 2000, *Canadian Medical Journal*, *163*, 837–841.

Professional codes of ethics require characteristics of EBP including informed consent and drawing on practice-related literature. EBP calls on professionals to identify important information needs, to search for related research findings, and to share what is found, including nothing, with clients. If no related research findings are located, clients are so informed and client preferences and well-argued theory are drawn on. EBP describes a process for integrating research and practice facilitated by innovations such as the Internet; such advances have been applied to practice primarily during the past two decades. They are new. It is true that there is a search for relevant well-argued theory and research concerning life-affecting decisions and critical appraisal of what is found. For example, randomized controlled trials (RCTs) are important in evaluating many questions including those concerning effectiveness and prevention. RCTs have saved thousands of lives, for example, by showing that current methods harm clients (e.g., Hochman, 2014). However critical appraisal of RCTs is vital; like any other research method, RCTs may be poorly constructed and, even if well constructed and carried out, often have limitations due to concerns regarding both internal and external validity (e.g. generalizing results to other locals and/or individuals; Deaton & Cartwright, 2016). Other research methods are needed to critically appraise other kinds of questions as described in Chapter 5. Some claim that if you look diligently enough, you can always find a study that supports your conclusion and find fault with a study that does not. An ethical search requires seeking all published research that meets standards for inclusion regardless of whether it supports or refutes a favored assumption.

OBSTACLES

There are many obstacles to making informed decisions (see Exhibit 2.5.) As Straus and McAlister (2000) suggest, some limitations of EBP are universal, such as lack of scientific evidence related to decisions and challenges in applying evidence to individuals. Obstacles include lack of relevant information; authoritarian organizational cultures; lack of critical thinking values, skills, and knowledge; and limited resources including access to needed databases. Both professionals and clients may lack health and statistical literacy (Gigerenzer, 2014a). Problems that confront clients (e.g., lack of housing or day care) are often difficult ones that challenge the most skilled of helpers. Rarely is all relevant information available, and it is difficult to integrate different kinds of data. Professionals usually work in a state of uncertainty. They can only estimate the probability that a client has a certain illness. Challenges include disagreements about criteria to use to assess the accuracy of decisions, cultural difference in views of personal troubles and social problems, and gaps in knowledge about how to achieve given outcomes.

There are pressures on clinicians to act more certain than they are, including the rhetoric of professional organizations that oversell the success of clinicians and clients who seek more certainty than is possible. Clinicians may not be aware of the influence of the biomedical-industrial complex in framing and creating problems and promoting methods that do more harm than good (Angell, 2009; Gotzsche, 2013; Lexchin, 2012). Organizations differ in how conducive they are to learning and critical thinking as described in Chapter 11. Raising questions about accepted practice may result in negative reactions from colleagues. Thinking critically about practices and policies and related factors increases personal responsibility because more accurate distinctions are possible between artificial and real constraints on helping clients. Critically evaluating the accuracy of practice- and policy-related claims requires time, effort, and skills.

EXHIBIT 2.5
BARRIERS TO PROBLEM-SOLVING

1. *Limited Knowledge Is Available About*
   - The prevalence, variability, and natural history of behaviors/conditions of concern
   - The causes of problems
   - Methods that are most effective in attaining hoped-for outcomes
   - How to arrange generalization over time and settings

2. *Task Environment*
   Social, Political, and Economic
   - Prevalence of propaganda (e.g., misinformation, pseudoscience, and quackery)
   - Competing contingencies (to make money, protect turf)
   - Anti-intellectualism
   - Taboo topics such as questioning claims of effectiveness
   - Misunderstandings of science
   - Lack of cues and positive feedback for desired behaviors
   - Lack of corrective feedback regarding decisions
   Agency
   - Failures of communication among parties (e.g., clients, staff)
   - Authoritarian administrators
   - Time pressures
   - Lack of resources
   - Lack of corrective feedback and deliberate practice of skills
   - Dysfunctional recording systems
   - Lack of service coordination

3. *Information Processing Barriers*
   - Memory is often inaccurate
   - Our emotions influence our thinking
   - Failure to over-ride intuitive beliefs with analytic thinking
   - We may rely on "rules" that lead us astray
   - We jump to conclusions
   - Plethora of misinformation

4. *Personal*
   Motivational
   - Conflicts of interest
   - Lack of curiosity
   - Lack of caring
   - Unrealistic expectations
   - Lack of courage and intellectual empathy

- Lack of interest in discovering what is accurate
- Lack of integrity

Emotional
- Fear of making mistakes
- Fatigue, anger, anxiety
- Low tolerance for ambiguity; inability to "incubate"
- Appeal of vivid material

Perceptual/Intellectual
- Define problems too narrowly (e.g., overlook environmental causes)
- Overlook alternative views
- Stereotyping (we see what we expect to see)
- Judging rather than generating ideas
- Avoidable discrepancies between personal and objective ignorance
- Inflexible use of problem-solving strategies
- Limited use of varied problem-solving languages—words, figures
- Rely on questionable criteria to evaluate claims; fail to evaluate beliefs
- Cynicism

Expressive
- Inadequate skills in writing and speaking clearly
- Lack of skills in communicating empathy and caring

The good news is that tools for discovering and sharing ignorance and knowledge regarding life-affecting decisions continue to be developed as described in the chapters that follow. Debiasing strategies can be acquired. We can learn how to allocate scarce resources, such as time more wisely. We can enhance critical thinking values, knowledge, and skills that contribute to informed decision-making. We can learn how our emotions affect our decisions and take steps to counter this by using active open-minded thinking. The costs of forgoing critical thinking in clinical practice are substantial. "In exchange for the time saved, clinicians must preserve and encourage unwarranted complacency, unverified dogma, and self-perpetuating error" (Feinstein, 1967, p. 310).

SUMMARY

The process of evidence-based practice is designed to facilitate the integration of ethical, evidentiary, and application concerns in making decisions. Uncertainties are recognized, and efforts made to reveal and decrease them. Interrelated implications include moving away from authority-based practices and policies in which professionals depend on criteria such as opinion, popularity, and tradition. The process of evidence-informed practice provides a way to honor ethical obligations to help and avoid harm and to involve clients as informed participants by honest brokering of knowledge and ignorance, for example, clearly describing criteria used to make decisions. The EBPs approach in which some authority designates what is effective and should be used is quite different from the process and philosophy of EBP as described by its originators, as is the "business-as-usual" approach in which interventions of weak or of unknown effects are redubbed as "evidence-based." It is important to distinguish between objections based on misunderstandings of the process of EBP and those based on an accurate understanding. Otherwise, this approach that is so compatible with ethical obligations of professionals may be prematurely discarded and opportunities lost to help clients and to continue to learn.

Critical thinking, the process of EBP, and scientific reasoning are closely related. All use reasoning for a purpose (i.e., to solve problems), relying on standards such as clarity, relevance, and accuracy. All encourage active open-mindedness in which we ask questions designed to make the invisible visible (search for possibilities, evidence, and goals). All contribute to minimizing common fallacies and biases accuracy. All regard criticism as essential to forward understanding by challenging assumptions, considering opposing views, and checking reasoning for errors, such as overlooked possibilities. All are anti-authoritarian. All value transparency (honesty) concerning what is done to what effect including candid description of uncertainty and ignorance.

3

Evidence

SOURCES, USES, AND CONTROVERSIES

⌒⟋——————————————————————————————————————

THE PHRASE *EVIDENCE-BASED practice* (EBP) draws attention to the kind of evidence needed (and used) to make decisions and how to obtain it. We draw on certain evidence to evaluate knowledge claims—to explore the extent to which different possibilities may contribute to achieving certain goals (Baron, 2008, p. 8). Concerns about inflated claims of knowledge and failure to use knowledge available to help clients attain valued goals were key reasons for the origin of EBP as described in Chapter 2. There are few more loaded words than "evidence." Differences of opinion abound regarding evidence. When do we have enough evidence to recommend a practice or policy and of what should this consist? Related arguments should be clearly described (see Chapter 7). Consider these examples.

Dr. A has to make a decision about how to assess a client's depression. Should she draw on cognitive-behavioral assessment methods and related theory? What sources of assessment information should she use, and what criteria should she use to evaluate their accuracy? Should she ask her client to complete the Beck Depression Inventory and/or talk to family members and take a careful history? Should she prescribe an antidepressant? Should she use a practice guideline recommended by her agency? Has the methodological quality of this guideline been assessed (see Chapter 5 for more detail)?

Ms. Ross has to make a decision about how to help foster parents encourage positive behaviors and enhance the development of a five-year-old boy who has been removed from his biological parents because of persistent neglect. How can she locate accurate guidelines regarding the most effective methods? Do recommendations pertain to her client? What criteria should she use to review the claim: "Attention deficit hyperactive disorder (ADHD) is due to a biochemical disorder"?

How much evidence and what kind is needed to recommend a particular intervention? Is one study enough (Gorman, 2017)? Must we understand all parameters that influence outcome to intervene effectively? What evidence is needed to avoid harmful errors? Criteria used to evaluate the evidentiary status of claims that affect personal well-being may differ from those used to evaluate claims that affect clients (Gambrill & Gibbs, 2002). Beliefs and related decisions are based on varied criteria including folklore, tradition, practice wisdom, common sense, and research findings (see Exhibit 3.1). Davies (2004) suggests that a broad view of evidence is needed to review policy choices including (1) experience and expertise, (2) judgment, (3) resources, (4) values, (5) habits and traditions, (6) lobbyists and pressure groups, and (7) pragmatics and contingencies.

EXHIBIT 3.1
EXAMPLES OF DIFFERENT KINDS AND SOURCES "EVIDENCE"

- habits/tradition
- emotions
- common sense
- scientific (empirical/theoretical)
- arguments (e.g., convincing, misleading)
- intuition
- superstition
- cultural/ folklore/tradition
- legal/forensic
- ethical guidelines/values
- observation, eyewitness/examples
- imagined
- views of famous people/experts
- consensus/popularity/"prevailing understanding"
- testimonials/case examples
- "moral-political denunciations" (Webster, 1997, p. 194)
- circumstantial
- hearsay
- expert witness
- reluctant (provided under duress)
- pseudoevidence
- genuine evidence
- doubtful evidence

Let's say you attend a conference to learn about a new method for helping clients, and the presenter encourages the audience to adopt the method because it is new. Would that be sufficient grounds to use the method? What if the presenter describes a few clients who he claims have been helped by the method? Would you use the method? Or, let's say that staff who manage a refuge for battered women tested residents' self-esteem before and after residents participated in a support group and found that the women scored higher after taking part in the group. Can we assume that participation in the group caused an increase in residents' self-esteem? Lastly, let's say the leader of an interdisciplinary team encourages the group to arrive at a unanimous decision about whether a child requires special education services. Can we assume that because no one raised objections that important evidence and relevant arguments have been heard? In the first situation, the presenter encourages acceptance of a method because it is new (appeal to newness). Everything was new at one time. In the second example, acceptance is encouraged by describing a few selected instances (reliance on case examples). In the third, staff assume that because improvement followed intervention, the intervention caused improvement (the post-hoc-ergo-proc fallacy). In the final example, dissenting opinions may not be shared because of fear of negative reactions (groupthink). Should we rely on a theory of "how things work"? Problems with mechanistic reasoning include conflating plausibility with accuracy and oversimplifications (Howick, Glasziou, & Aronson, 2010). Placing babies on their stomachs to sleep is an example of harm due to reliance on low-quality mechanistic reasoning (Howick, 2011).

To make informed decisions, we need skill in spotting claims, identifying what kind they are (e.g., about facts, values, policies), and what kind of evidence is needed to evaluate their accuracy in comparison with what is offered. Questions are vital to discovery—to the discovery that accepted views are false, in some cases resulting in considerable harm. Socrates emphasized the value of questions in exploring the soundness of beliefs. His fate attests to the unhappy fate that often awaits those who question accepted views and/or the views of the powerful. Scientific discoveries often clash with religious views as shown by the reaction to Copernicus and Galileo who questioned whether the sun revolved around the earth. This illustrates that questions are not benign; they probe the soundness of claims and related arguments. They question authority—believing something simply because of who said it or how many said it (see Exhibit 3.2).

Baron (2008) views evidence as any belief that helps "users to determine the extent to which a possibility achieves some goal" (p. 8). Baron's search-inference framework of thinking suggests that all goal-directed thinking and decision-making can be described in terms of inferences made from possibilities, evidence,

EXHIBIT 3.2

KINDS OF CLAIMS AND RELATED QUESTIONS

1. *About "problems"/outcomes*
   - What problems (outcomes) are selected for attention? Who selects these and on what basis?
   - What problems are ignored? Who stands to gain by _____ decisions?
   - Exactly how is it defined? What are specific examples?
   - What kind of problem is it claimed to be? What are underlying assumptions?
   - What is the prevalence?
   - What controversies exist regarding this "problem"?
   - Is there a remedy?
   - Should action be taken? What should be done?
   - What evidence is there regarding these questions? Are claims true?

2. *About assessment, diagnosis, risk, and prediction*
   - Is a measure reliable? Were important kinds of reliability checked?
   - Is a measure valid? Does it measure what it is designed to measure? What kinds of validity were investigated?
   - What risks are focused on and who promotes this focus?
   - What is the false positive rate?
   - What is the false negative rate?
   - What is the absolute risk reduction
   - Are key valued "end states" accurately predicted (rather than surrogates)?
   - What percentage of predictions are accurate?
   - How good is the evidence for all of these issues? Are claims accurate?

3. *About causes*
   - Is correlation confused with causation?
   - How strong are associations?
   - Could associations found be coincidental?
   - Could a third factor be responsible?
   - Are root causes distinguished from secondary causes?
   - Are boundaries or necessary conditions clearly described (circumstances where relationships do not hold; Haynes, 1992)?
   - Are well-argued alternative views accurately presented?
   - Are interventions based on presumed causes effective?
   - Are vague multifactorial claims made that do not permit critical tests?
   - How good is the evidence for all of these issues? Are claims true?

4. *About effectiveness/prevention*
   - Are claims true? Were critical tests carried out? What were the results?

- What is the number needed to treat (NNT) What is the number needed to harm (NNH)?
- Was the possibility of harmful effects investigated? What is the number needed to harm?
- How rigorous were the tests?
- Were outcomes of key value to clients focused on?
- Are reviews of related research of high quality (e.g., rigorous, comprehensive in search and transparent in description of methods and findings)?
- How long do effects persist? What was the duration of follow up

and goals that are discovered through searching (p. xiii). Possibilities are possible answers to a question or resolutions of the original doubt. "Goals are the criteria by which you evaluate the possibilities" (p. 7). Goals influence evidence sought and how it is used. We make inferences about the importance of evidence regarding different possibilities in view of our goals. "Evidence is defined by its function in changing the strengths assigned to possibilities, i.e., the thinker's tendency to adopt them. . . . One possibility can serve as evidence against another as when we challenge a scientific hypothesis by giving an alternative and incompatible explanation of the data" (Baron, 1985, p. 87). Baron's comparison of how we should evaluate thinking (the normative question), how we do think and what prevents us from doing better (the descriptive question), and what we can do to enhance our thinking, judgment, and decision-making (the prescriptive question) highlights the importance of active-open mindedness in which we seek evidence *against* our favored views. It emphasizes the vital role of sensitivity to evidence.

The question "What is knowledge?" has been of concern to philosophers throughout the ages. Controversies abound. People differ in their beliefs about knowledge and how it can be gained (epistemology). Knowledge differs in many ways (e.g., deep vs. superficial, procedural compared to content, fluid vs. labored, tacit vs. explicit; Jong & Ferguson-Hessler, 1996). Views of knowledge and how to attain it differ in the extent to which they highlight uncertainty and enable discovery of ignorance, both personal and objective, and the weeding out of false knowledge. The dissemination of information may result in hazards (Bostrom, 2011).

Epistemological beliefs affect learning and how information is processed (Bromme, Kienhuses, & Stahl, 2008; Kuhn, 1993; Kuhn & Udell, 2003). Examples of kinds of knowledge related to the helping professions is shown in Exhibit 3.3. In Walton's theory of argumentation

EXHIBIT 3.3
DIFFERENT KINDS OF KNOWLEDGE IN THE HELPING PROFESSIONS

Content Knowledge
- ethical obligations
- cause–effect relationships
- assessment methods
- developmental norms
- research findings regarding behavior and how it is influenced
- intervention options
- evaluation methods
- service systems and related public policies and related legislation
- common biases and fallacies in decision-making
- criteria of value in critically appraising different kinds of research

Procedural Knowledge
- how to use different kinds of assessment methods
- how to carry out different kinds of intervention
- how to critically appraise different kinds of claims and related research reports
- how to search effectively and efficiently for research related to life-affecting decisions
- how to integrate different sources of information in a way that contributes to sound decisions
- how to accurately evaluate programs
- how to store and retrieve information

Inert Knowledge
- content knowledge unaccompanied by procedural knowledge
- failure to use content or procedural knowledge
- censored knowledge

Self-Knowledge
- about personal biases
- about gaps between personal knowledge and skills and what is available (e.g., regarding causes, risks, accuracy of assessment methods, effectiveness of intervention methods)
- about vulnerability to burnout
- about the quality of learning skills
- about skill in avoiding biases and fallacies

False Knowledge
- Beliefs that are not true and are not questioned

Knowledge of Ignorance
- Match between personal and objective knowledge

> Knowledge is based on three factors (1) the evidence collected at a given point in the investigation, (2) the kinds of arguments that can properly be used to justify a claim in that type of investigation, and (3) the standard of proof set for knowledge in this particular type of investigation. (Walton, 2013, p. 185)

Nickerson (1986) defines knowledge as information that decreases uncertainty about how to achieve a certain outcome. (I would add—or reveals uncertainty.) We can ask: "What knowledge will help us to solve problems clients confront (e.g., elder abuse)?" Is it helpful to use terms such as *well established,* which imply a certainty that cannot be had or *probably effective,* which is quite vague? Do two well-designed independent RCTs warrant a description of "well-established"?

Nickerson (1986) suggests that three kinds of knowledge are important in critical thinking: critical thinking itself, domain-specific knowledge, and self-knowledge. Domain-specific knowledge, including both content (knowing what) and procedural knowledge (knowing how to apply content knowledge), may be needed. Self-knowledge includes familiarity with the strengths and limitations of thinking in general as well as knowledge of your personal strengths and limitations that influence how you approach learning, problem-solving and decision-making. Three of the basic building blocks of reasoning are suggested by Paul—ideas and concepts drawn on, what is taken for granted, and point of view used influence how we approach problems. Paul (1993) uses the term *sociocentric biases* to refer to societal influences on our beliefs (see also Paul & Elder, 2014).

Popper (1992) defines knowledge as problematic and tentative guesses about what may be true. It results from selective pressures from the real world in which our guesses come into contact with the environment through a process of trial and error (Munz, 1985).

> In Panrationalism, nothing is exempt from criticism and *all* criticism is legitimate. It is just as legitimate to criticize by saying, "I have a gut feeling that . . ." as by saying, "It is self-evident that . . ." as by saying, "Observation shows that . . .". . . . Somebody may criticize by appealing to authority; somebody else, by appealing to tradition or to consensus. It is then open to the opponent to rebut and an appeal to, say, authority is only reprehensible if it implies a denial of Panrationalism—that is, if it implies an invitation that the authority appealed to must not be criticized. No criticism can be ruled out in advance. One has to allow any criticism and see what happens. (Munz, 1985, p. 50).

THE POLITICS OF EVIDENCE

Different views and assertions about how much "we know" (or "don't know") reflect use of different criteria for evaluating the soundness of claims that are influenced by different agendas including pursuit of money, status, or preference for the latest fashion (Sperber, 1990). Political, economic, and social factors influence what evidence is drawn on to support claims, the soundness of the evidence, and what evidence is hidden as do egocentric biases in which we search only for data that support our views. For example, advocates of a view may engage in "moral-political denunciation of ideas rather than assessment of their logical structure" (Webster, 1997, p. 198). Misinformation abounds including misleading claims of "what we know" or what we "do not know" in the peer-reviewed literature as well as in the media and is often difficult to counter (Lewadowsky et al., 2012). Consider controversies regarding the effects of smoking on health, climate change, use of psychotropic medication for the elderly, and the wisdom of getting mammograms. Each of these examples illustrates the play of special interests and contested claims regarding "evidence." Millions, even billions, of dollars are at stake in many areas. Claims made on websites funded by drug companies may present misleading views (Gambrill, 2012a).

Deceptive strategies used to shape views of "evidence" include the misleading creation of doubt, hiding negative findings including harmful effects of medication and distorting views, and then attacking the distorted view. These ploys represent age-old propaganda methods of censorship, distortion, fabrication, and the creation of confusion (Gambrill, 2012a). As Rank (1984) suggests in *The Pitch*, propagandists hide negative evidence about their view and promote positive evidence and hide positive evidence regarding disliked views and promote negative evidence. Rigorous scientific investigation and publication of relevant findings may threaten profits gained via deceptive claims. It may threaten world views such as religious beliefs (e.g., evolutionary theory). Those who make claims may not care about the truth or falsity of a claim, just whether the claim is acted on (see discussion of palaver and bullshit in Chapter 9).

Bauer (2004) argues that there are knowledge monopolies/cartels that impede attention to well-argued alternative views and counterevidence to views promoted, for example, regarding global warming. A variety of individuals and institutions may be involved in forwarding a particular view and excluding contradictory evidence including expert committees, universities, research centers, the professional literature, and drug and device manufacturers. "The blurring of the scientific and the nonscientific aspects of problems and their solutions is a tactic used in persuasion oration (Bromme & Goldman, 2014, p. 65). Ploys that contribute to inflated claims of knowledge include hiding of flaws in research, misusing statistics, ignoring alternative well-argued views, and changing outcome measures. This illustrates the social uses of science for example to bolster reputations of individuals and institutions and to gain money and status as well as the "statistical-ritual hypothesis" (Gigerenzer, 2018). Hundreds of predatory journals exist that publish manuscripts without peer review for money encouraged by the need for publications on the part of academics for promotion and gaining research funds. Failure of replication is common (Pashler & Wagenmakers, 2012).

The status of science is used to forward misinformation (as in scientism). Related misuses highlight the importance of understanding what science is and what it is not so we are less susceptible to misinformation. It highlights the rhetorical nature of scientific publications—their use for persuasion (Hilgartner, 2000; Latour, 1988). Misrepresenting the evidentiary status of clams often results in lawsuits based on the False Claims Act (e.g., see list of largest pharmaceutical settlements in Wikipedia). Many are for billions of dollars. If we understand what science is and what it is not, we are more likely to avoid the influence of lookalikes for science—for example, claims based on studies without blind testing, without a control group, and with small samples. This highlights the importance of critical thinking values, skills, and knowledge—of skeptical appraisal of preferred as well as disliked views to avoid the effects of motivated skepticism (looking only for data that confirm preferred views).

Munz (1985) argues that "any culture interferes with the process of critical selection of theories because it consists in an important sense, of the nurture of a body of knowledge which enables people to gauge in advance what they set out to discover" (p. 55). This prevents "radical and relentless criticism" (p. 51). "Knowledge is placed in bondage to society" (p. 301)—it is protected from critical appraisal-encounters with the outside world, which provide corrective feedback (p. 163). Munz (1985) suggests that the function of *false knowledge* (beliefs that are not true and that are not questioned) is to maintain social bonds among people by protecting shared beliefs from criticism (the growth of knowledge). This may be necessary to encourage cooperation in a group. He argues that the adaptive value of ritualistic practices in the history of humankind has been enormous (p. 83). Cultures often thrive because of false knowledge. Such cultures "are doubly effective in promoting social behavior because, not being exposed to rational criticism, they enshrine emotionally comforting and solidarity-producing attitudes" (pp. 283–284). This view suggests that the growth of knowledge can only take place in certain circumstances (i.e., cultures)—those in which alternative views are entertained and all views are subject to criticism. Only in this way do beliefs confront the environment. Certain "ways of knowing" compared to others are designed to critically test guesses (e.g., about effectiveness). (See later discussion of science.)

THE ETHICS OF EVIDENCE

When should we seek information needed to solve a problem? When is it unethical not to do so? How can we recognize our ignorance? How can we recognize important uncertainties? Practitioners make decisions about what information they need to help clients attain hoped-for outcomes, whether and how to pursue it, and what to share with clients. They make decisions about how informed to be about the evidentiary status of assessment, intervention, and evaluation methods used; has the accuracy of a related claim been critically tested (see Chapter 5)? Pellegrino (1999) suggests, "Because evidence has the power to convince others, it has an inescapable moral dimension. It can lead or mislead, enhance or diminish the lives of individuals and communities. . . . When we use evidence to convince or persuade, we become de facto accomplices in what results from our efforts" (p. 34). There is thus an ethics of evidence as highlighted in professional codes of ethics (to help, to avoid harm, and to involve clients as informed participants). Is there evidence for these claims:

- Scared Straight programs decrease delinquency.
- Brief psychological debriefing programs prevent post-traumatic stress disorder.
- Eyewitness testimony can be trusted.
- Screening for depression on the part of general practitioners always does more good than harm.

Research shows that these claims are false. If you act on misleading accounts, you may focus on irrelevant factors and recommend ineffective or harmful methods. Given that decisions affect clients' quality of life, there is an ethical obligation to be informed about important uncertainties and research that may decrease or reveal them. Pellegrino (1999) argues: "There is a clear duty to provide assessment and explanation with appropriate reservations about the preliminary state of evidence and the fact that it may change with more data" (p. 37). There is an ethical duty to be skeptical—to recognize flaws in research, for example. There is an ethical obligation to be honest brokers of knowledge and ignorance to enable clients to make rational (informed) decisions. Related rules include use of the best possible evidence and recognizing inevitable uncertainties (Mike, 1999).

Practitioners make decisions about what problems to focus on and how to frame them, for example, as psychological, medical, moral, or political concerns and how critically to appraise decisions. Focusing on individuals as the cause of their problems ignores related environmental circumstances (e.g., Conrad, 2007; Speed, Moncrieff, & Rapley, 2014; Ryan, 1976; Szasz, 2007). Attention to environmental circumstances, such as lack of employment opportunities that pay a living wage, encourages empathic understanding of clients; "there too may go I." It is in this sense that Gøtzsche (2008) considers humanistic thinking as two of the four components that form the basis of clinical decisions: ethical norms (e.g., to help and to avoid harm) and "understanding the client as a fellow human being" (p. 150). Given the history of the helping professions (e.g., bogus claims of effectiveness and harming in the name of helping), the ethical road is to make accurate claims. Reliance on false claims or theories may result in clients being harmed rather than helped. False hopes may be created and opportunities to use effective methods forgone. Consider the many claims of effectiveness based on anecdotal case reports that were later shown to be false in controlled research. (See, for example, the description of facilitated communication, a method alleged to help nonverbal people talk; Jacobson, Foxx, & Mulick, 2005.) Many methods have been found to be harmful (e.g., Lilienfeld, Lynn, & Lohr, 2015). Thus, the quality of decision-making and related arguments is an ethical matter as highlighted in codes of ethics calling on professionals to help and not harm clients and to involve clients as informed participants.

IGNORANCE: AVOIDABLE OR NOT

The process of EBP, as described by its originators, is a way to handle the inevitable uncertainty in making decisions in an informed, ethical manner, attending to ignorance as well as knowledge (see Chapter 2). Critical tests may show that an intervention works, but we may not understand how it works. This may be revealed in later research. Theories put forward may be more of a metaphor than a grand generalization (Lewontin, 1994). Uncertainties may be created by ambiguity of research related to a decision, unknown probabilities regarding natural causes of behavior, and complexities in care programs and structures as well as existential characteristics of clients (Han, Klein, & Arora, 2011). There may be no related research concerning decisions; this is an important finding. Error is a constant companion. As Walton (2015) suggests, "one of the most important characteristic of rationality is the awareness of the likelihood of error, the recognition of the constant need to search for errors, and a willingness to correct them. Mistakes are inevitable. Reasoning requires a vigilance to try to avoid mistakes" (p. 26). Popper (1992) argues that we are all equal "in our infinite ignorance" (p. 50). There has been increased attention to the importance of attending to ignorance as well as knowledge and the many factors that contribute to avoidable ignorance including biases such as overconfidence. "We need to think about the conscious, unconscious, and structural production of ignorance, its diverse causes and conformations, whether brought about by neglect, forgetfulness, myopia, extinction, secrecy or suppression" (Proctor & Schliebinger, 2008, p. 3). As these authors point out, the distribution of ignorance is unequal; who knows what, and why not? (p. 6). Inquiry is always selective.

Proctor and Schliebinger (2008) argue that the study of ignorance is just as important as the study of knowledge. The study of ignorance is propelled in part by increased recognition of the deliberate creation of ignorance for strategic purposes such as evading revelations that certain programs and products are worthless or harmful. Roberts and Armitage (2008) use the term *ignorance economy* to refer to such activity and its consequences. There are many things people do not want you to know, such as the results of negative trials in drug studies and hidden changes in end points—the moving goal post (e.g., Gotzsche, 2013, 2015a; Whitaker & Cosgrove, 2015). Collective avoiding (denial) of information is common (Norgaard, 2006, 2011). Some topics may be taboo. Gaudet (2013) argues that researchers value, actively produce, and thereby mobilize ignorance. Ignorance is a resource (Gross & McGoey, 2015; McGoey, 2012). Strategies to evade sharing of evidence needed to appraise claims is key in propaganda (censorship, fabrication, confusion, and diversion). Over the past years, there has been a tsunami of publications revealing the hiding of adverse side effects of prescribed psychotropic medication (Gotzsche, 2013), failure to publish all clinical trials (Glasziou & Chalmers, 2017), harmful promotion of off-label uses of prescribed medication, lying on the part of pharmaceutical companies, and related conflicts of interest between academic researchers and the pharmaceutical industry (e.g., Cosgrove, Bursztajn, Krimsky, Anaya, & Walker, 2009).

Ignorance and related uncertainties may be avoidable or unavoidable; they may matter or not matter. We can explore the extent to which ignorance and related uncertainties as well as knowledge is attended to concerning a topic, claim, or decision and identify interested parties as well as strategies used to "tip the scales" (such as the creation of doubt; Oreskes & Conway, 2010). Some have more power (resources) than do others to create and maintain ignorance. "Secrecy and non-knowledge are indispensable to the operation of power. Not only because power imposes secrecy on those whom it dominates, but because it is perhaps just as indispensable to the latter" (Taussig, 1999, p. 57; cited in McGooey, 2010, p. 68).

HELPFUL DISTINCTIONS

A number of distinctions are of value in making decisions about possibilities, goals, and evidence.

Genuine and Pseudoevidence

Kuhn (1992) distinguishes between *genuine evidence* (evidence external to the asserted cause such as disconfirming alternatives) and *pseudoevidence* (a simple restatement of the phenomenon using a specific instance, so losing opportunities to critique a theory (p. 170; see Chapter 7).

Widely Accepted/True

What is widely accepted may not be true. Many people believe in the influence of astrological signs (their causal role is widely accepted). However, to date, there is no evidence that they have a causal role in influencing behavior; that is, risky predictions based on related beliefs have not survived critical tests.

Good Intentions and Good Outcomes

Good intentions do not ensure good results. Many publications document the harmful effects of efforts intended to help clients (e.g., Gotzsche, 2013, 2015a, 2015b; Jacobson, Foxx, & Mulick, 2015; Scull, 2015; Welch et al., 2011). Moncrieff and Cohen (2006) argue that medication prescribed to alter abnormal brain states assumed to be related to "mental illness" may create such states. Intensive social casework offered to a sample of frail elderly individuals in the Cleveland area increased mortality (Blenkner, Bloom, & Nielsen, 1971).

A Feeling That Something Is True Versus Whether It Is True

Hastie and Dawes (2011) suggest that failing to distinguish between a feeling that something is true and whether it is true helps to account for the widespread belief in many questionable causes of behavior such as astrological influences, crystals, and spirit guides. A feeling that something is true may or may not be supported by a sound argument. As Baron (1985) notes, "only certain sentiments, namely those that encourage an unwillingness to think, to consider alternatives, to evaluate evidence correctly, and so on" are the enemy of reason (p. 278). Basing actions and beliefs on feelings discourages an examination of their soundness, and, in professional contexts, this may result in decisions that do not benefit clients.

Truth and Credibility

Popper (1994) defines truthful statements as those that correspond with the facts (p. 174). Credible statements are those that are possible to believe. Phillips (1992) suggests that just about anything may be credible. Simply because it is possible to believe something does not mean that it is true. Although scientists seek true answers (statements that correspond to the facts), this does not mean that there is certain knowledge. Rather, certain beliefs (theories) have (so far) survived critical tests or have not yet been exposed to them. An error "consists essentially of our regarding as true a theory that is not true" (Popper, 1992, p. 4).

Personal and Objective Knowledge

Personal knowledge refers to what you as an individual believe you "know." Objective knowledge refers to assumptions that have survived critical tests or evaluation. It is public; it is criticizable by others. Personal and objective knowledge may overlap to different degrees. Knowledge of our own ignorance is a vital kind of personal knowledge that may be compromised by self-censorship(e.g., discounting evidence against preferred views). We tend to overestimate what "we know"—that is, our self-assessments of our "knowledge" and skills are inflated (Dunning, Heath, & Suls 2004).

Reasoning Compared to Rationalizing

Reasoning involves the review of evidence against as well as evidence in favor of a position. Rationality requires an openness to criticism: "A limitless invitation to criticism is the essence of rationality" (Munz, 1985, p. 50). It requires active open-minded thinking. Related items in the Comprehensive Assessment of Rational Thinking (CART) include avoiding myside bias by being actively open-minded (Stanovich, West, & Toplak, 2016). *Rationalizing* entails a selective search for evidence in support a belief or action encouraged by both *egocentric* (searching for data that supports our views) and *sociocentric* biases (influence by the culture in which we live). When we rationalize, we are interested in building a case rather than weighing evidence for and against an argument; we engage in defensive thinking. We ignore counterevidence. Reasoning also differs from political thinking that "is motivated by a need to be accepted, or to get ahead. To think politically is to forget about what you think is true and to voice opinions that you think are likely to win approval from your friend. . . ." (Notturno 2000, p. 13).

Propaganda, Bias, and Point of View

Propaganda is primarily interested in shaping beliefs and actions with little thought (Ellul, 1965). Much propaganda is "a set of methods employed by an organized group that wants to bring about the active or passive participation in its actions of a mass of individuals, psychologically unified through psychological manipulations and incorporated in an organization" (Ellul, 1965, p. 61). Ellul (1965) argues that we live in a technological society in which propaganda is essential. The media, advertising, public relations, and bureaucracies are techniques. Case records and surveillance systems are technologies as are human relations and psychotherapy. The Internet provides vast opportunities to spread misinformation and efforts to correct this often fails (Nyhan & Reifer, 2010; 2015). Technology presses for ever greater efficiency and standardization. Stivers (2001) describes misuses of technology in management, such as assuming that implementation of a new system is in itself proof of success.

   A major function of propaganda is to squelch and censor dissenting points of view. Propagandists take advantage of our biases and prejudices. Common propaganda methods include creation of confusion, diversion, distortion, and censorship of alternative views and contradictory evidence (Gambrill, 2012a). The inflation of knowledge claims (puffery) is a key propaganda strategy (Rank, 1984). Those who market ideas attempt to forward a view, not through a balanced and accurate presentation of related evidence and alternative views, but through reliance on strategies such as distorted presentations of disliked positions, presentation only of data that support a favored position, and question begging (asserting what must be argued; see www.pharmedout.org). Inflating risk and encouraging fear is a key ploy (Altheide, 2002; see Exhibit 3.4). There is a partiality in the use of evidence, such as hiding adverse effects of a drug and selective publication of drug trials (e.g., Turner Mathew, Linardaros, Tell, & Rosenthal, 2008).

   In propaganda, realities are constructed that are partial-tilted toward those that forward beliefs and actions favored by the claims maker. Consider the assertion that smoking marijuana is gateway drug to use of heroin. This

---

EXHIBIT 3.4
EXAMPLES OF PROPAGANDA IN THE HELPING PROFESSIONS

Censorship
- Hide lack of evidence for claims.
- Hide well-argued alternative views.

Distortion
- Present inaccurate negative versions of competing views.
- Prepare inaccurate positive account of preferred view.

Diversion
- Create fears based on inaccurate accounts.
- Encourage ridicule.
- Appeal to vague ideologies that obscure consequences.

Fabrication
- Make up data (see retractionwatch.com).

(false) claim has been used to rationalize the criminalization of marijuana resulting in imprisoning tens of thousands of (mostly African American) men (Alexander, 2010). Propagandists may present only one side of an argument, hide counterarguments to preferred views, and attack the motives of critics to deflect criticism. For example, they may say that anyone who doubts the effectiveness of services for battered women must be trying to undermine efforts to help women. Messages are posed in a way to encourage uncritical acceptance. There may be an *illusion of argument*—pieces are missing; hoped-for actions ("Fight terror"), effects ("Be safe"), and efforts to understand a problem ("He is paranoid") are vague, and critical appraisal is discouraged. Belief may be encouraged by visual images such as pictures of brains (McCabe & Castel, 2008). Our fears and hopes may cloud our judgment and propagandists take advantage of this. Unless we are familiar with an area, we may not detect what is missing such as accurate description of well-argued alternative views (Gambrill & Reiman, 2011). Here, as with fraud, websites, and organizations have been developed to counter propaganda such as the National Coalition Against Censorship.

The term *bias* refers to "a partiality that prevents objective consideration of an issue or situation" (www.wordreference.com, accessed 12/22/06). (See Chapters 5 and 6.) Biases result from preference for particular values and/or theories coupled by an absence of active open-mindedness in critically appraising views.

In statistics, the term refers to "a tendency of an estimate to deviate in one direction from a true value" (Webster's *Third New International Dictionary*, 1987). The term *point of view* refers to the frame of reference we bring to a question such as a theory (Paul, 1993). This view may be too broad or too narrow.

Reasoning and Truth

Reasoning does not necessarily yield the truth. However, effective reasoning is more likely to reveal the evidentiary status of claims. The accuracy of a conclusion does not necessarily indicate that the reasoning used to reach it was sound. And, lack of evidence for a claim does not mean that it is incorrect. Similarly, surviving critical tests does not mean that a claim is true; further tests may show that it is false.

Knowing and the Illusion of Knowing

There is a difference between accurately understanding content and the *illusion of knowing*. The illusion of knowing is encouraged by thinking in terms of absolutes (e.g., "proven," "well established") rather than thinking conditionally (e.g. "This may be . . ." "This could be . . ."; Zechmeister & Johnson, 1992). Claims regarding causality and effectiveness are often overstated (Cartwright & Hardie, 2012). The promise of technology in solving problems may be oversold (Stivers, 2001). Familiarity with a claim or concept creates an (often incorrect) impression of knowledge as in the validity effect (Renner, 2004). This effect is a hindrance to acquiring knowledge because we believe we already have it. The illusion of knowing is encouraged by lack of active open-minded thinking, for example, not monitoring understanding by asking questions such as "Do I understand this?" "Could I be wrong?" "What is this person claiming?" and "What are his reasons?" There is a failure to take remedial action such as rereading and a failure to detect contradictions and unsupported claims. Redundant information may be focused on, creating a false sense of accuracy.

What to Think and How to Think

Thinking critically about any subject requires us to examine our reasoning process including the accuracy of our beliefs. This is quite different than being required to memorize a list of alleged facts. Examining the accuracy of assertions requires us to think critically about them.

Consistency and Critical Testing

Assigning appropriate weight to evidence for or against a claim is a key part of what it means to be reasonable. Two or more assertions thus may be consistent with each other but yield little or no insight into the soundness of an argument. A psychiatrist may search for consistent evidence when exploring a depressed client's history of depression. An assertion should be consistent with other beliefs held; that is, self-contradictory views should not knowingly be accepted. However, two or more assertions may be consistent with each other but yield little or no insight into the soundness of an argument. Saying that A (a history of "mental illness") is consistent with B (alleged current "mental illness") is to say only that it is possible to believe B given A.

Facts, Beliefs, and Preferences

A belief can be defined as "confidence that a particular thing is true, as evidenced by a willingness to act as though it were" (Nickerson, 1986, p. 2). *Beliefs* are assumptions about what is true or false. They may be testable (e.g., support groups help the bereaved) or untestable (God exists). They may be held as convictions (un-questioned assumptions) or as guesses about what is true or false, which we seek to critically test. Beliefs involve claims that vary in their accuracy. Popper (1972) suggests that *facts* refer to well-tested data, intersubjectively evaluated. These can be contrasted with "factoids"—claims with no related evidence, which, because they are repeated so often, may be believed—the "Woozle Effect." In a scientific approach, it is assumed that the accuracy of an assertion is related to the unique-ness and accuracy of related critical appraisals. Facts are capable of verification; beliefs may not be. Preferences reflect values; someone may say: "I prefer insight-oriented treatment." Beliefs are statements that in principle, can be shown to be true or false. An example is "Play therapy helps children to overcome anxiety." Here, evidence can be gathered to determine whether this is the case.

Logic and Reasoning

Logic is concerned with the form or validity of deductive arguments. "It provides methods and rules for restating information so as to make what is implicit ex-plicit. It has little to do with the determination of truth or falsity" (Nickerson, 1986, p. 7). Deliberative reasoning requires much more than logic. It requires skill in developing arguments and hypotheses, establishing the relevance of informa-tion to an argument, and evaluating the plausibility of assertions (see Chapter 7).

It requires a willingness to change beliefs on the basis of evidence gathered. Knowledge is required to evaluate the plausibility of premises related to an argument as in this example: (1) Depression always has a psychological cause; (2) Mr. Draper is depressed; (3) therefore, Mr. Draper's depression is psychological in origin. The logic of this argument is sound, but the conclusion may be false because the first premise is false. The cause of Mr. Draper's depression could be physiological. "Like most everyday problems that call for reasoning, the explicit premises [may] leave most of the relevant information unstated. Indeed, the real business of reasoning in these cases is to determine the relevant factors and possibilities, and it therefore depends on a knowledge of the specific domain" (Johnson-Laird, 1985, p. 45).

Intuitive and Analytic Thinking

Another common distinction is between mindful action in which an effort is made to understand something and automatic associative functioning in which we carry out tasks with little thought (the dual process theory). The effectiveness of a style depends on knowledge and skills reflected in intuition and what is needed to solve a problem. (See later discussion of intuition in this chapter and critique of the dual process model of decision-making in Chapter 6.)

COMMON APPEALS

Criteria such as popularity, testimonials, newness, emotions, and tradition are often used to support claims, for example, of effectiveness. These criteria do not provide sound grounds on which to accept claims. If claims appear in peer-reviewed journals, does that mean that these are true? If a claim is accompanied by a reference, is this a good reason to assume it is accurate? We may accept claims of effectiveness because we believe that those who make them have good intentions; they want to help clients. But, as illustrated in Chapter 1, good intentions and good outcomes do not necessarily go together. The confident manner in which a claim is presented may encourage acceptance. Being swayed by the style of presentation underlies persuasion by entertainment. How interesting is a view? Does it sound profound? Does it claim to "empower" clients? Testing (systematic exploration) as well as guessing is needed to explore the accuracy of claims.

Conclusions about many clients may be made based on a few unrepresentative case examples. Case examples are easy to remember; they have a story-like quality. So too do testimonials—reports by people who have used a product or service and claim that it is beneficial. Someone who has attended Alcoholics Anonymous may say, "I tried it and it works." The testimonial is a variant of the case example and is subject to the limitations of case examples; neither case examples nor testimonials provide comparative information needed to evaluate whether an assumption is true or false. Testimonials are widely used in advertising. The problem is not that the report about an individual's experience with a method is not accurate, but the further step of making a claim that this experience means that the method works. Certain claims may "make sense." `You may read that expressing anger in frustrating situations is helpful in decreasing anger. This may make sense to you. But is it true?

Experience

Appeals to experience range from those of a naive realist to those of a highly experienced professional who has a vast memory of related knowledge about how to solve certain kinds of problems. In naive realism, we believe that our senses (what we see, hear, and feel) reflect what is true; we fail to question this source. Professionals may appeal to anecdotal experience to support claims of effectiveness as in case examples. A psychologist may state, "I know cognitive behavioral methods are effective with depressed clients because they are effective with my clients." Experience in everyday practice and knowledge and beliefs based on this is a key source of what is known as practice wisdom and clinical expertise (see Chapter 6). The value of experience depends in part on feedback gained and acted on. Anecdotal reports can be valuable in suggesting promising hypotheses, for example, regarding adverse events and possible causes, and provide telling counterexamples to a claim (Aronson, 2003). They may be used to demonstrate diagnostic methods and how to handle challenging clinical situations.

A key problem with relying on anecdotal experience as a guide to the effectiveness of an intervention is lack of comparison (Dawes, 1988). An interest in comparison is a hallmark of scientific thinking; our experience may be restricted and/or biased. For example, when relying on experience, we may fail to recognize that conditions have changed—that what worked in the past no longer works in the present. We tend to recall our successes and forget our failures; that is, we tend to selectively focus on our "hits." "Myside" bias may occur—evaluating, generating, and testing assumptions in a way that is biased toward one's views (Paul, 1993; Stanovich, West, & Toplak, 2013). Unless we have kept track of both our hits and our misses (unless we gain corrective feedback), we may arrive at incorrect conclusions.

Reliance on personal stories in making decisions may lead us astray if they do not accurately represent important characteristics that should be considered. Overconfidence in a belief may create an *illusion of control* in which we overestimate how much control we really have. We do not know what might have happened if another sequence of events had occurred. Overlooking this, we may unfairly praise or blame ourselves (or someone else). And, we tend to create our own experience. If we are friendly, others are likely to be friendly in return. If we are hostile, others are likely to be hostile. Another problem with relying on experience concerns changes in memory; we may alter views about the past to conform to current moods or views. We tend to remember what is vivid, which may result in biased samples (see discussion of cognitive biases in Chapter 6).

Our tendency to look for causes may encourage premature closure on a cause, for example, on a pattern that is not really there. We may assume that "mental illness" results in homelessness because many homeless people are diagnosed as "mentally ill." Being homeless may create survival behaviors (mis)labeled as indicators of "mental illness." A child welfare worker may assume that few child abusers stop abusing their children because she sees those who continue to abuse their children more often than those who do not. Her experience with this biased sample may result in incorrect inferences about the recurrence of child abuse (i.e., an overestimate). Relying on a carefully documented track record of success is quite different; this offers a systematic record. Experience may encourage a reluctance to consider new ideas. Indeed, one advantage of being a novice may be a greater willingness to question beliefs. King (1981) suggests that "For Flexner (1915), as for us today, severely critically handling of experience was an important part of scientific method, applicable to clinical practice as well as to research investigation" (pp. 303–304).

Hogarth (2001) suggests that a key step in becoming aware of the limitations of experiential learning is creating an awareness of its potential deficiencies, and, that as part of this, we should be aware of the different conditions under which we learn which range from kind to wicked. In wicked environments we receive irrelevant or no feedback. Professionals who receive no feedback concerning the outcomes of their decisions work in "wicked" environments (see also discussion of expertise in Chapter 6).

Intuition

Intuition (our "gut reaction") involves a quick, often emotion-laden judgment (Kahneman, 2011). It may be informed (based on extensive content knowledge and multiple experiences in applying this in which we gain corrective feedback) or uninformed (Hogarth, 2001; see discussion of the dual process model in Chapter 6).

When our "gut reaction" is based on correct cues, it serves us well. When it is not (when in Hogarth's term, it is not an "informed intuition" based on relevant content knowledge and multiple opportunities for corrective feedback), it may lead us astray. The view that intuition involves a responsiveness to information that, although not consciously represented, yields productive insights is compatible with research regarding expertise (Klein, 1998, 2011). Dreyfus and Dreyfus (1986) found that experts rely on "internalized" rules that they no longer may be able to describe. No longer remembering where or when something was learned encourages attributing effective problem-solving to "intuition." When an expert is asked: "What made you think that a particular method would be effective?" her answer may be, "My intuition." When asked to elaborate, she may offer sound reasons reflecting multiple experiences providing corrective feedback. That is, her "hunch" was an informed one.

Intuitive judgments may be based on heuristics (simple rules of thumb) such as asking "Could I be wrong?" Heuristics (strategies for making decisions) may be used with or without awareness. Gigerenzer (2005) refers to intuition as the "unconscious use of a heuristic"—you can sense what to do without being able to explain why (Gigerenzer & Gaissmaier, 2011). "Imitate the successful" is one heuristic suggested by Gigerenzer and Brighton (2011)—"Look for the most successful person and imitate his or her behavior" (p. 24). We make what Gigerenzer calls, a "fast and frugal decision." It is rapid (fast) and relies on key environmental cues (it is frugal). We ignore irrelevant data; we do not calculate pros and cons. Thus, a heuristic "is a strategy that *effectively* matches the structure of information in the environment. . . . Heuristic strategies in fact ignore some of the complexity of the environment . . . in order to reduce both the estimation error and effort. . . . Less effort can lead to more accurate judgments" (Mousavi & Gigerenzer, 2014, p. 1673). Gigerenzer (2008) suggests that we select a heuristic based on reinforcement learning. He argues that it is correspondence with a certain environment that matters (Gigerenzer & Brighton, 2011, p. 2).

Intuition is not a sound guide for making decisions when misleading cues are focused on. This highlights the importance of relevant knowledge and memory of it in making decisions as discussed in Chapter 6. Research comparing clinical judgments to those based on empirical relationships between variables and an outcome, such as future child abuse, shows the superior accuracy of the latter (Cuccaro-Alimin, Foust, Vaithianathan, & Putnam-Hornstein, 2017; Grove & Meehl, 1996). Clinicians' judgments of outcomes in psychotherapy are inflated (Boswell, Kraus, Miller, & Lambert, 2015; Walfish, McAlister, O'Donnell, & Lambert, 2012). Intuition cannot show which method is most effective in helping clients; a different kind of evidence is required for this. Relying on intuition or what "feels right" is ethically questionable when other grounds, including a critical examination of beliefs, results in better reasoned decisions. Attributing judgments to "intuition" decreases opportunities to teach others; one has "it" but does not know how or why "it" works. If you ask your supervisor, "How did you know to do that at that time?" and she says, "My intuition," this will not help you learn what to do.

SCIENCE AND SCIENTIFIC CRITERIA

A concern for helping and not harming clients obliges us to critically evaluate assumptions about what is true and what is false as well as their consequences. Relying on scientific criteria offers a way to do so. It is important to understand what science is so we can avoid influence by look-a-likes (e.g., pseudoscience) that may lure us into embarking on courses of action that do more harm than good and that obscure promising options. With this understanding, we are less likely to be a patsy for bogus claims. It can help us to avoid *scientism*—misleading adherence to the methods of science when they are not appropriate (Phillips, 1987, p. 206). It will help us to recognize advocacy in the guise of science (e.g., distortion or hiding information to attain a goal).

Propagandists use the discourse of science (e.g., jargon) to promote an illusion of objectivity and scientific rigor. The corruption of science by special interests highlights the importance of understanding what science is and what it is not (Gambrill, 2012a). (See earlier discussion of the politics of evidence.) The study of the social dimensions of scientific knowledge includes "the effects of scientific research on human life and social relations, the effects of social relations and values on scientific research, and the social aspects of inquiry itself" (Longino, 2002). If we do not understand science and its social as well as knowledge functions and history, we are likely to make the following errors:

1. Assume science can discover final answers and so make and act on inflated claims of knowledge that may harm clients.
2. Assume that there is no way to discover what may be true and what may be false because scientists make errors and have biases.
3. Prematurely assume that those who question popular views, for example, about mental illness, prescribed medication or screening are crackpots.
4. Throw out the baby (science) with the bath water (pseudoscience and scientism).

WHAT IS SCIENCE?

The essence of science is creative, bold guessing, and rigorous testing in a way that offers accurate information about whether a guess (conjecture or theory) is accurate (Asimov, 1989; e.g., "Evidence becomes capable of disconfirming the theory"; Kuhn 1993, p 100). It is a way of "learning how not to fool ourselves" (Feynman, 1974, p. 4). Science is a process for solving problems in which we learn from our mistakes. It is evolutionary in the sense that, theories/beliefs encounter corrective feedback from the environment (Munz, 1985), unless artificially protected from criticism. Science rejects a reliance on authority, for example, pronouncements by officials or professors, as a route to knowledge. Authority and science are clashing views of how knowledge can be gained. The history of science and medicine shows that new ideas and the results of critically testing these often frees us from false beliefs and results in discoveries (e.g., Hochman, 2014).For example, the cause of ulcers was found to be Helicobacter pylori, not stress or spicy foods (Marshall & Warren, 1984; Van der Weyden, Armstrong, & Gregory, 2005).

There are many ways to do science and many philosophies of science. The terms *science* and *scientific* are sometimes used to refer to any systematic effort— including case studies, correlational studies, and naturalistic studies—to acquire information about a subject. All methods are vulnerable to error, which must be considered when evaluating the data they generate. Nonexperimental approaches to understanding include natural observation, as in ethology (the study of animal behavior in real-life settings), and correlational methods that use statistical analysis to investigate the degree to which events are associated. These methods are of value in suggesting promising experiments, as well as when events of interest cannot be experimentally altered or if doing so would destroy what is under investigation. We are subject to a variety of superstitions; the occult and mysterious forces have an allure of special powers encouraged by wishful thinking.

Criticism: Critical to the Growth of Knowledge

The scientific tradition is the tradition of criticism (Popper, 1994, p. 42). Popper (1994) argues that "the growth of knowledge, and especially of scientific knowledge, consists of learning from our mistakes" (p. 93). Scientific statements are those that can be tested (they can be refuted). If an agency for the homeless claims that it succeeds in finding homes for applicants within 10 days, you could accept this claim at face value or systematically gather data to see whether this claim is true. A claim may be testable or not, and, if testable, tested or not and found to be true, false, or uncertain (Bunge, 1984). The view of science presented here, critical rationalism, is one in which the theory-laden nature of observation is assumed (i.e., our assumptions influence what we observe) and rational criticism is viewed as the essence of science (Miller, 1994; Phillips, 1987, 1990a, 1990b; Popper, 1972). Concepts are assumed to have meaning and value even though they are unobservable.

Popper's (1994) view of science can be summed up in four steps: (1) we start with some problem; (2) we propose a tentative theory (solution); (3) we critically discuss and test our theory, (4) which always reveals new problems (P1 →TT →CD →P2) (p. 140). Thus, in Popper's view, knowledge starts with problems. "The tension between our knowledge and ignorance is decisive for the growth of knowledge . . . The word 'problem' is only another name for this tension" (p. 100). We use severe criticism to test our guesses about how to solve problems. This view of science emphasizes the elimination of errors by means of criticism. The growth of knowledge is not in accuracy of depiction or certainty but in an increase in universality and abstraction (Munz, 1985). That is, a better theory can account for a wider range of events. Corrective feedback from the physical world allows us to test our guesses. We learn which of our guesses are false. Popper (1994) suggests that "the more our knowledge grows, the more we realize how little we know . . . to become educated is to get an inkling of the immensity of our ignorance" (Popper, 1994, 141–142). Evolutionary epistemologists highlight two different histories of science: the creation of theories (e.g., through random variation) and their selection (by testing; Munz, 1985). Without criticism, common fallacies and biases are more likely to hinder problem-solving; we are less likely to recognize our ignorance regarding important questions that affect clients' lives.

Active open-minded thinking is integral to science. Critical thinking requires asking questions we (as well as others) may prefer to ignore such as: "Do our services do more good than harm?" It may require blowing the whistle on harmful practices and policies. "The ability to recognize the possible falsehood of a theory and the identification of evidence capable of disconfirming it are foundational obligations that lie at the heart of both informal and scientific reasoning" (Kuhn, 1993, p. 100). History as well as current day events show that many do not welcome probing questions such as "What evidence do you have for your position?" and "Are there well-argued alternative views?" Thus, in addition to people simply not understanding what science is and what it is not, criticism is a threat to current views. That is why there is so often lots of talk about critical thinking, but little actual critical inquiry and why caring and honoring ethical obligations to clients are so important in providing the courage to raise questions that may have life-affecting consequences.

Munz (1985) argues that "when one is rational, one is open to criticism and an absolutely limitless invitation to criticism is the essence of rationality. . . . "Nothing is exempt from criticism and *all* criticism is legitimate" (p. 50). "We say a person is rational when he is prepared to offer his non-rational thoughts or behavior to criticism" (p. 53). Skeptics may or may not be rational; they may dogmatically reject ideas out of hand (see discussion of critical/rational thinking in Chapter 1). A lack of skepticism is illustrated by promoting claims based on biased samples, confusing correlation and causation, and ignoring conflicts of interest that may color claims.

Scientific Statements Are Refutable/Testable

Science is concerned with knowledge that can be pursued through the consideration of alternatives. It is assumed that we can test our guesses about what is true or false by means of rational argument and critical tests of our theories and that the soundness of an assertion is related to the uniqueness and rigor of relevant critical tests. A theory should describe what cannot occur as well as what can occur. If you can make contradictory predictions based on a theory, it cannot be tested. If you cannot discover a way to test a theory, it is not falsifiable. Theories can be falsified only if specific predictions are made about what can happen and also about what cannot happen.

In a justification approach to knowledge we focus on gathering support for (justifying, confirming) our beliefs. Let's say that you see 3,000 swans, all of which are white. Does this mean that all swans are white? Can we generalize from the particular (seeing 3,000 swans, all of which are white) to the general, that all swans are white? Karl Popper (and others) contend that we cannot discover what is true by means of induction (making generalizations based on particular instances) because we may later discover exceptions (swans that are not white). In fact, black swans are found in New Zealand. He maintains that falsification (attempts to falsify, to discover the errors in our beliefs) by means of critical discussion and testing is the only sound way to develop knowledge (Popper, 1992, 1994). Confirmations of a theory can readily be found if one looks for them. (For critiques of Popper's view of knowledge, see, for example, Schilipp, 1974.)

Popper uses the criterion of falsifiability to demark what is or could be scientific knowledge from what is not or could not be. For example, there is no way to refute the claim that "there is a God," but there is a way to refute the claim that "assertive community services for the severely and chronically mentally ill reduces substance abuse." We could, for example, randomly distribute clients to a group providing such services and compare those outcomes with those of clients receiving no services or other services. Although we can argue for the selection of a theory by its having survived more risky tests concerning a wider variety of hypotheses (not been falsified), compared with other theories that have not been tested or that have been falsified, we can never accurately claim that this theory is "the truth." We can only eliminate false beliefs.

Some Tests Are More Rigorous Than Others

Some tests are more rigorous than others in controlling sources or bias and so offer more information about what may be true or false. Compared with anecdotal reports, experimental tests are designed to rule out alternative hypotheses and so provide more opportunities to discover that a theory is not correct. Still, they may be quite flawed (see Chapter 5). Theories differ in the extent to which they have been tested and in the rigor of the tests used. Every research method is limited in the kinds of questions it can rigorously explore (see www.testingtreatments.org). For example, if our purpose is to discover the emotional complexity of a certain experience such as parental responses to the death of an infant, then qualitative methods are needed, for example detailed case examples, thematic analyses of journal entries, and/or open-ended interviews over different times.

A Search for Patterns and Regularities

It is assumed that the universe has some degree of order and consistency. This does not mean that unexplained phenomena or chance variations do not occur or are not considered. For example, chance variations contribute to evolutionary changes. Uncertainty is assumed. Since a future test may show an assumption to be incorrect, even one that is strongly corroborated (has survived many critical tests), no assertion can ever be "proved." This does not mean that all beliefs are equally sound; some have survived more rigorous tests than have others (Asimov, 1989).

Parsimony

An explanation is parsimonious if all or most of its components are necessary to explain most of its related phenomena. Unnecessarily complex explanations may get in the way of detecting relationships, for example, between behaviors and related events.

Scientists Strive for Objectivity

Popper (1994) argues, "What we call *scientific objectivity* is nothing else than the fact that no scientific theory is accepted as dogma, and that all theories are tentative and are open all the time to severe criticism—to a rational, critical discussion aiming at the elimination of errors" (p. 160). Basic to objectivity is openness regarding what is done and the critical discussion of theories (eliminating errors through criticism). This requires fair-mindedness to possibilities such as the possibility of being wrong. Honesty is a key requirement for fairmindedness. The theory-laden nature of observation is assumed. Observation is always selective (influenced by our theories, concepts). Scientists are often wrong and find out that they are wrong by testing their predictions. In this way, better theories (those that can account for more findings) replace earlier ones. Thus, we have an obligation to recognize and learn from our mistakes:

1. To recognize that mistakes will be made; "it is impossible to avoid making mistakes" (p. 64).
2. To recognize that it is our duty to minimize avoidable mistakes.
3. To learn how to do better from recognizing our mistakes.
4. To "be on the lookout" for mistakes (p. 64).
5. To embrace a self-critical attitude.
6. To welcome others pointing out our mistakes; we need others to discover and point out our mistakes; criticism by others is a necessity.
7. Objective criticism "would always be specific" "would give specific reasons why specific statements or specific hypotheses appear to be false or specific arguments invalid. It must be guided by the idea of getting nearer to objective truth. In this sense it must be impersonal, but also sympathetic (Popper, 1998, addendum 2, pp. 62–65).

Science is conservative in its insisting that a new theory account for previous findings. (For critiques of the view that advancing knowledge means abandoning prior knowledge, see Phillips, 1987.) Science is revolutionary in calling for the overthrow of previous theories shown to be false, but this does not mean that the new theory has been "established" as true. Although the purpose of science is to seek true answers to problems (statements that correspond to facts), this does not mean that we can have certain knowledge. Rather, we may say that certain beliefs (theories) have (so far) survived critical tests or have not yet been exposed to them. Certain theories have been shown to have more universal application than others. Some theories have been found to be false. An error "consists essentially of our regarding as true a theory that is not true" (Popper, 1992, p. 4). We can avoid error or discover it by doing all that we can to discover and eliminate falsehoods (p. 4). The study of errors when making decisions has received increased attention (Jenicek, 2011; Makary & Daniel, 2016).

Other Characteristics

Science deals with specific problems that may be solvable. For example, is intensive in-home care for parents of abused children more effective than the usual social work services? Is the use of medication to decrease depression in elderly people more (or less) effective than cognitive-behavioral methods? Asking "Is there a God?" is an example of an unsolvable question. Saying that science deals with problems that can be solved does not mean, however, that other questions are unimportant or that a problem will remain unsolvable. New methods may be developed that enable exploration of questions previously unapproachable in a systematic way. Scientific knowledge is publicly reviewed by a community. Science is collective. Scientists communicate with one another, and the results of one study inform the efforts of other scientists. Scientists critique each other. Baron (2017) argues that it is active open-minded thinking that "distinguishes true science from pseudo-science" (p. 6).

THE ETHICS OF CRITICAL RATIONALISM

Popper's critical rationalism entails moral obligations regarding pursuit of accurate answers (Koertge, 2007); his philosophy of science entails a moral philosophy. "For critical reason is the only alternative to violence so far discovered" (Popper, 1994, p. 69). Personal freedom is Popper's (1994) fundamental value—self-emancipation through knowledge. "The search for truth and the idea of approximations to the truth are also ethical principles; as are the ideas of intellectual integrity and of fallibility which lead us to a self-critical attitude and to toleration" (Popper, 1992, p. 199). He argued that "scientists have a special responsibility to seek the truth" and emphasized the obligations of social scientists to draw our attention to less visible developments that may endanger freedom directly, such as tools for mass-manipulation (Koertge, 2007, p. 10). Thus, there a moral obligation to seek information when this affects client outcome including information about avoidable errors and their causes. Minimizing avoidable suffering is another core value

Popper promotes. "Thus the imperative of avoiding cruelty, both physical and mental" (Koertge, 2009, p. 5).

"Because of the central position of epistemology in Popper's moral philosophy, behaviors that interfere with or enhance a community's ability to engage in efficient problem-solving take on moral significance" (Koertge, 2009, p. 5). Popper rejected the view that participants in a discussion must share basic assumptions (Popper, 1994). Indeed, as Koertge (2009) notes, he rejected this as dangerous because it may encourage people to believe that if they do not agree on basic premises, the only resort is to drop the goal of objective truth, and that can encourage propaganda, inciting men to hatred. "Toleration is the necessary consequence of realizing our human fallibility: to err is human, and we do it all the time. *So let us pardon each other's follies*" (Popper, 1992, p. 190). We are obligated to avoid unnecessary mistakes and acknowledge mistakes when they occur. This close connection between ethics and epistemology calls for intellectual honesty and accountability and open dialogue and an obligation to critically appraise ideas and data (e.g., do they contribute to decreasing avoidable miseries?). Popper emphasized our obligation to write clearly and to learn from mistakes.

> From the single goal of self-emancipation through knowledge, much follows: a dedication to communal problem solving, honesty, openness to criticism, tolerance for other views and society that supports freedom of expression. When we add the imperatives to relieve suffering and avoid cruelty, we have the building blocks for a pretty adequate moral philosophy. (Koertge, 2007, p. 10)

Criticizing someone's theory/data contributes to problem-solving.

SCIENCE AND NORMAL SCIENCE

Kuhn (1970) argued that most investigators work within accepted (and often wrong) paradigms. They do "normal science."

> . . . the "normal" scientist, as Kuhn describes him, is a person one ought to be sorry for. . . . The "normal" scientist, in my view, has been taught badly. I believe, and so do many others, that all teaching on the University level (and if possible below) should be training and encouragement in critical thinking.

The "normal" scientist, as described by Kuhn, has been badly taught. He has been taught in a dogmatic spirit: he is a victim of indoctrination. He has learned a technique which can be applied without asking for the reason why. . . . As a consequence, he has become what may be called an applied scientist, in contradistinction to what I should call a pure scientist. He is, as Kuhn puts it, content to solve "puzzles." (quoted in Notturno, 2000, p. 237; Popper, 1970, pp. 52–53).

Research regarding new ideas often show that currently accepted theories are not correct, however as Kuhn (1970) argued, old paradigms may continue to be uncritically accepted until sufficient contradictions (anomalies) force recognition of the new theory. Spirited disagreements about evolution continue (see publications of the National Science Education Center). The history of science shows that new ideas are often censored and that those proposing them may have difficulty getting a hearing in scientific journals and the media. Prestigious journals typically rejected the work of scientists who made major discoveries and overturned prevailing beliefs (Campanario, 2009; Campanario & Acedo, 2007). Entrenched views may result in an inability to even conceive of radical new discoveries such as the existence of germs. (See for example Nuland's (2003) description of the life of Ignas Semmelweiss).

Commenting on Kuhn's notion of "normal science," that is, its concrete institutional embodiment, Popper (1970) wrote:

"Normal" science, in Kuhn's sense, exists. It is the activity of the non-revolutionary, or more precisely, the not-too-critical professional: of the science student who accepts the ruling dogma of the day; who does not wish to challenge it; and who accepts a new revolutionary theory only if almost everybody else is ready to accept it—if it becomes fashionable by a kind of bandwagon effect. To resist a new fashion needs perhaps as much courage as was needed to bring it about. . . . (p. 52)

MISUNDERSTANDINGS AND MISREPRESENTATIONS OF SCIENCE

Surveys show that most people do not understand science (National Science Foundation, 2006). Here are some common misconceptions (undsci@berkeley.edu):

- There is a search for final answers.
- Creative thinking has no role.

- It is assumed that science knows, or will soon know, all the answers.
- Objectivity is assumed.
- Chance occurrences are not considered.
- Scientific knowledge is equivalent to scientific thinking.
- The accumulation of facts is the primary goal.
- Linear thinking is required.
- Passion and caring have no role.
- There is one kind of scientific method all scientists follow.
- Unobservable events are not considered.

Bromme and Goldman (2014) argue that the public has a "bounded understanding" of science; that is, they make decisions based on an incomplete understanding of science and the specific topic addressed. Challenges to understanding science include determining the relevance of information, the tentativeness of scientific truth, distinguishing between scientific and nonscientific issues and determining what is true and what is false (p. 59). Textbooks often omit controversy and personality, giving "an incorrect illusion of a logical progression of uncomplex discovery when indeed the history is quite different: "serendipitous, personality-filled, conjectural, and controversial" (Bell & Linn, 2002, p. 324). Journal articles may omit controversy about causes and evidence (Gambrill & Reiman, 2011). Misunderstandings about science may result in ignoring this problem-solving method and the knowledge it has generated (e.g., Hochman, 2014). Misunderstandings and misrepresentations of science are so common that D. C. Phillips entitled one of his books *The Social Scientist's Bestiary: A Guide to Fabled Threats to and Defenses of Naturalistic Social Science* (1992). Even some academics confuse logical positivism (discarded by scientists long ago) and science as we know it today. Logical positivism emphasizes direct observation by the senses. It is assumed that observation can be theory free. It is justification focused, assuming that greater verification yields closer approximations to the truth. This approach to knowledge was discarded decades ago because of the induction problem (see earlier discussion of justification/falsification), the theory-laden nature of observation, and the utility of unobservable constructs.

Science is often misrepresented as a collection of facts or as referring only to controlled experimental studies. Many people confuse science with pseudoscience and scientism. Some people protest that science is misused. Anything can be misused. Some believe that critical reflection is incompatible with passionate caring. Reading the writings of any number of scientists, including Loren Eiseley, Carl Sagan, Karl Popper, and Albert Einstein, should quickly put this false belief to rest. Far from reinforcing myths about reality, science is likely to question them. All sorts of questions that people may not want raised may be raised, such as: "Does this residential center really help residents?" "Would another method be more effective?" "Does what I'm doing really help clients?" and "How accurate is my belief about _____?" Many scientific discoveries, such as Charles Darwin's theory of evolution, clashed with (and still does) some religious views of the world. Consider the Church's reactions to the discovery that the earth was not the center of the universe. Only after 350 years did the Catholic Church agree that Galileo was correct in stating that the earth revolves around the sun. An accurate understanding of science will help you to distinguish among accurate, trivializing, and bogus uses.

PSEUDOSCIENCE

The term *pseudoscience* refers to material that makes science-like claims but provides no evidence for them (Bunge, 1984). Pseudoscience is characterized by a casual approach to evidence (weak evidence is accepted as readily as strong evidence). Indicators include irrefutable hypotheses, a reluctance to revise beliefs when confronted with a relevant criticism, equation of an open-mind with an uncritical one, inflated claims of knowledge and ignorance (what is true and what is false), use of scientific sounding words, reliance on anecdotal examples, failure to draw on related research, and failure to test claims (see www.quackwatch.org). There is a search only for confirming evidence for a claim. Results of a study may be referred to in many sources until they achieve the status of a law without any additional data being gathered (the "Woozle Effect"—evidence by citation).

Examples of pseudoscience in professional journals include carrying decimal points to two or three places for data that does not warrant this degree of exactitude offering an illusion of rigor and focusing on the significance of correlations that could have occurred by chance. Pseudoscience is a multibillion-dollar industry. Products include self-help books, "subliminal" tapes, and call-in advice from "authentic psychics" who have no evidence that they accomplish what they promise. It can be found in all fields (Lilienfeld, Lynn, & Lohr, 2015; Thyer & Pignotti, 2015). The terms *science* and *scientific* are often used to increase the credibility of a view or approach, even though no evidence is provided to support it; they are applied to activities that in reality have nothing to do with science. This can be seen in bogus uses of the term *evidence-based* (e.g., Gambrill, 2010a, 2010b). The misuse of appeals to science to sell products or encourage certain beliefs is a form of propaganda (encouraging beliefs and actions with the least thought possible; Ellul, 1965).

ANTISCIENCE

Antiscience refers to rejection of scientific methods as valid. Some people believe that there is no such thing as privileged knowledge—that some is sounder than others. Typically, such views are not problem focused, allowing a critical appraisal of competing views. Antiscience is common in academic settings (Gross & Levitt, 1994; Patai & Koertege, 2003), as well as in popular culture (e.g., Burnham, 1987). Many people confuse science, scientism, and pseudoscience, resulting in an antiscience stance.

RELATIVISM

Relativists argue that all methods are equally valid in testing claims (e.g., anecdotal reports and experimental studies). It is assumed that knowledge and morality are inherently bounded by or rooted in culture (Gellner, 1992, p. 68). "Knowledge or morality outside of culture is, it claims, a chimera. Meanings are incommensurate, meanings are culturally constructed, and so all cultures are equal" (p. 73). Postmodernism is a form of relativism (all grounds for knowledge claims are considered equally questionable). Gellner (1992) argues that in the void created, some voices predominate; throwing us back on authority, not a criterion that will protect clients' rights and allow those in the helping professions to be faithful to their code of ethics. If there is no means by which to tell what is accurate and what is not, if all methods are equally effective, the vacuum is filled by an "elite" who are powerful enough to say what is and what is not (Gellner, 1992). Gellner argues that the sole focus on cognitive meaning in postmodernism ignores political and economic influences. He argues that postmodernism "denies or obscures tremendous differences in cognition and technical power" (p. 71). He points out that there are real constraints in society that are obscured by this recent form of relativism (postmodernism) and suggests that such cognitive nihilism constitutes a "travesty of the real role of serious knowledge in our lives" (p. 95). Gellner argues that this view undervalues coercive and economic constraints in society and overvalues conceptual ones. "If we live in a world of meanings, and meanings exhaust the world, where is there any room for coercion through the whip, gun, or hunger?" (p. 63).

Gellner (1992) argues that postmodernism is an affectation: "Those who propound it, or defend it against its critics, continue, whenever facing any serious issue in which their real interests are engaged, to act on the non-relativistic assumption that one particular vision is cognitively much more effective than others" (p. 70). Consider the different criteria social work students want their physicians to rely on when confronted with a serious medical problem compared to criteria they say they rely on to select a service method offered to clients. They reported that they rely on criteria such as intuition, testimonials, and experience with a few cases when making decisions about clients but want their physicians to rely on the results of controlled experimental studies and demonstrated track record of success based on data collected systematically and regularly when making decisions about a serious medical problem of their own (Gambrill & Gibbs, 2002). Descriptions of "critical postmodernism" include questions key in science such as "What constitute acceptable knowledge" (Fawcett, 2011, p. 232). Munz (1992) argues that postmodernism is "pre- rather than postmodern" in reviving "old and decidedly premodern positions (p. 347).

QUACKERY

Quackery refers to the promotion and marketing, for a profit, of untested, often worthless and sometimes dangerous health products and procedures, by either professionals or others (Jarvis, 1990; Young, 1992).

> People generally like to feel that they are in control of their life. Quacks take advantage of this fact by giving their clients things to do—such as taking vitamin pills, preparing special foods, meditating, and the like. The activity may provide a temporary psychological lift, but believing in false things can have serious consequences. The loss may be financial, psychological (when disillusionment sets in), physical (when the method is harmful or the person abandons effective care), or social (diversion from more constructive activities). (Barrett, Jarvis, Kroger, & London, 2002, p. 7)

Barrett and his colleagues (2002) suggest that victims of quackery usually have one or more of the following vulnerabilities: (1) lack of suspicion; (2) desperation; (3) alienation (e.g., from the medical profession); (4) belief in magic; or (5) overconfidence in discerning whether a method works. Advertisers, both past and present, use the trappings of science (without the substance) to encourage consumers to buy products. Indicators of quackery include the promise of quick cures, the use of anecdotes and testimonials to support claims, privileged power (only the great Dr. _____ knows how to _____), and secrecy (claims are not open to objective scrutiny). Reasons suggested by William Jarvis (1990) for why some professionals become quacks include the profit motive (making money) and the prophet motive (enjoying adulation and discipleship resulting from a pretense of superiority). Quackery and pseudoscience make use of propaganda strategies.

FRAUD AND CORRUPTION

Fraud is the intentional misrepresentation of the effect of certain actions, such as taking a prescribed drug to decrease depression, to persuade people to part with something of value (e.g., money; Levy & Luo, 2005). It does this by means of deception and misrepresentation, drawing on a variety of propaganda ploys, such as the omission of information concerning harmful side effects. Drug makers now top the fraud pay-out list (Tanne, 2010). Legal aspects of fraud include (1) misrepresentation of a material fact; (2) knowledge of the falsity of the misrepresentation or ignorance of the truth; (3) intent; (4) acting on the misrepresentation; and (5) damage to the victim (*The Free Dictionary*; see also False Claims Act, 1863 (31 USC 3729).

Corruption includes deceitful practices, such as dumping unsafe drugs in developing countries and misrepresenting evidence (e.g., Gotzsche, 2013; Union of Concerned Scientists, 2012). It includes bribery of officials and kickbacks for referrals. Classification systems may give an illusion of validity. Seeking status and profit have corrupted even the peer-review literature (e.g., Angell, 2009; retractionwatch.org). Corruption in the health area is vast. Examples include selling or prescribing pills with no active ingredients or containing harmful substances. Institutional corruption occurs "when there is a systemic and strategic influence which is legal, or even currently ethical, that undermines the institution's effectiveness by diverting it from its purpose or weakening its ability to achieve its purpose, including . . . weakening either the public's trust in that institution or the institution's inherent trustworthiness" (Lessig, 2015). Corruption, fraud, quackery, and the propaganda ploys used in their service compromise informed consent. Valuable websites include Bad Science, Bad Science Watch, Center for Open Science, Center for Science in the Public Interest, Berkeley Initiative for Transparency in the Social Sciences, Healthy Skepticism, METRICS, Project for Scholarly Integrity, Center for Scientific Integrity, and Sense About Science.

SUMMARY

People differ in what evidence is drawn on to make and/or to explore the accuracy of claims and soundness of decisions. There are many views of knowledge, what it is, and how to get it. Some, compared to others, are more likely to enable evidence-informed decisions. Our concern for helping and not harming clients obliges us to critically appraise evidence in relation to possibilities and goals, attending to ignorance as well as knowledge. Professional codes of ethics call on professionals to draw on practice- and policy-related research in making decisions and to involve clients as informed participants. Sound criteria for evaluating claims and making decisions include well-reasoned arguments and critical tests that suggest that one option is more likely than another to result in valued outcomes. "Nowhere is the obligation to be well-informed, up-to-date, objective, and forthcoming about uncertainties more pressing than in clinical decisions" (Pellagrino, 1999, p. 4). The history of science shows that our beliefs are often wrong. This highlights the importance of active open-minded thinking and understanding science.

4

Steps in the Process of Evidence-Based Practice

EVIDENCE-BASED PRACTICE (EBP) is a process for handling the uncertainty surrounding decisions regarding individual clients or patients in an ethical, informed manner—informed about ignorance as well as knowledge. It requires a willingness to recognize uncertainty, for example, in choosing among alternative interventions. Sources of uncertainty include limitations in knowledge, lack of familiarity with knowledge that is available, and difficulties distinguishing between personal ignorance and lack of competence and actual limitations of knowledge (Fox & Swazy, 1974; Han, Klein, & Arora, 2011). Bogus claims in the media as well as in the peer-reviewed literature highlight the need for critical appraisal of claims. Uncertainties may be related to lack of information about important individual differences in client circumstances and characteristics including cultural differences and quality of resources. A willingness to say "I don't know" and to ask questions others may find disturbing combined with taking steps to see if needed information is available increases the likelihood of identifying important uncertainties and involving clients as informed participants (Chalmers, 2003).

Skills in searching, appraising, and storing information and the motivation to use them are needed. Gray (2001b) suggests that performance (*P*) is a function of level of motivation (*M*) and competence (*C*) and the barriers (*B*) we confront (p. 13):

$$P = \frac{M \times C}{B}$$

Challenges include gaining timely access to research findings and critically appraising this knowledge (Galbraith, Ward, & Heneghan, 2017). Highlighting application problems has been a key contribution of evidence-informed practice (e.g., Gray, 1997; 2001a; Montori & Guyatt, 2007).

POSING WELL-FORMED QUESTIONS REGARDING INFORMATION NEEDS

What information do you need to attain a hoped-for outcome? Can you get it? If not, why not? It is important to recognize gaps between your personal knowledge and what is available (objective knowledge) and to acknowledge uncertainties. Some may be resolvable; many may not be. Translating information needs, for example, about causes related to a problem, into questions that facilitate a search for related research is a key step in the process of EBP(Sackett et al., 1997; Straus, Glasziou, Richardson, & Haynes., 2011). Reasons include:

- Vague questions lead to vague answers; specific questions are needed to gain specific answers to guide decisions.
- If we do not pose clear questions, we are less likely to discover helpful research findings and change what we do; we may harm clients or offer clients ineffective methods.
- It is a countermeasure to arrogance that interferes with learning and the integration of practice and research; we will discover important uncertainties.
- It can save time. The better formed the question, the more quickly may related literature (or the lack of it) be revealed.
- It is necessary for self-directed, lifelong learning (See Gibbs, 2003).

Different questions may arise during assessment, intervention and evaluation. Both background and foreground questions may arise. The former refers to information about a problem or situation including possible remedies. Question include who, what where, when, how, and why and concern a particular problem, test, intervention or other aspect of care (Straus, Glasziou, Richardson, & Hayners, 2011, p. 16). Experts are more likely to raise vital questions compared to novices (see Chapter 6). Foreground questions refer to "specific knowledge to inform specific clinical decisions or actions" related to a client (p. 16) and include four parts (see Exhibit 4.1). Straus, Glaszious, Richardson, & Haynes, (2011) suggest that as you have experience with a concern, knowledge need for foreground information increases and need for background information decreases.

EXHIBIT 4.1
EXAMPLES OF COMPONENTS OF WELL-STRUCTURED QUESTIONS

Question Types	Client Type and Problem	What Might Be Done	Alternative	Outcome	Examples of Quality Filters
Effectiveness	Disoriented elderly residents in a nursing home	Reality orientation therapy	Validation therapy	Better orientation to time, pace, and person	Systematic review Controlled trial Meta-analysis
Prevention	High school students at high risk for pregnancy.	Baby—think it over	Didactic material on the use of birth control	Fewer pregnancies and more knowledge of birth control methods	Systematic review Controlled trial Meta-analysis
Assessment	Elderly nursing home residents who are depressed or have Alzheimer's disease or dementia	Complete a depression screening test	A short mental examination test	Accurately discriminate between depression and dementia	Validity False positive False negative Sensitivity Specificity Inter-related reliability
Description	Children	Raised with depressed mothers	Compared to mothers who are not depressed	Prevalence of developmental delays	Systematic review Representative sample Survey Focus group
Prediction	Preschool children	With antisocial behavior	Children who do not display such behavior	Likelihood of antisocial behavior in adolescence	Predictive validity False positive False negative

(continued)

EXHIBIT 4.1 (*Continued*)

Question Types	Client Type and Problem	What Might Be Done	Alternative	Outcome	Examples of Quality Filters
Risk	Mothers alleged to maltreat their children.	Complete an actuarial risk-assessment measure	Complete consensus-based measure	Best prediction of future abuse	Sensitivity Specificity False positive False negative Systematic review
Harm	In adults	Screen for depression	No screening	Least harm	Systematic review Controlled trial
Cost–benefit	Parenting classes for mothers whose children have been removed from their care	Purchase services from another agency	Offer training in-house	Least costly and most effective	Cost–benefit ratio

Source: Question format is based on *Evidence-Based Medicine: How to Practice and Teach EBM*, by D. L. Sackett, W. S. Richardson, W. Rosenberg, and R. B. Haynes, 1997, New York, NY: Churchill Livingstone, p. 29.

The originators of EBP suggest posing a four-part question that describe the population of clients, the intervention you are interested in, and what it may be compared to (including doing nothing) and hoped-for outcomes (PICO questions). The process of forming a specific question often begins with a vague general question and then proceeds to a well-built one. Synonyms can be used to facilitate a search. For example, if abused children are of concern, other terms for this may be *maltreated children, neglected children,* and *mistreated children.* Background information as well as increased information about a client will help you to focus your question.

Different Kinds of Questions

Different kinds of questions (about effectiveness, prevention, risk, assessment, or description) may require different research methods to critically test them. A variety of information needs, and related questions may arise with a client. Let us say you work in a hospice and counsel grieving parents who have lost a child. *Descriptive* questions include "What are the experiences of parents who lose a young child?" "How long do these last?" "Do they change over time and if so, how?" Both survey data and qualitative research, such as focus groups, in-depth interviews, and participant observation, may be used to explore such questions. Research may be available that describes experiences of grieving parents based on a large randomly drawn sample of such parents. A research report may describe the experiences of clients who seek bereavement counseling using in-depth interviews. Questions concerning *risk* may arise (such as "In parents who have lost a young child, what is the risk of depression?) as well as questions about *effectiveness*: "For parents who have lost a young child, is a support group compared to no service more effective in decreasing depression?" *Prevention* questions may arise. "For parents who have lost a young child, is brief counseling compared to a support group more effective in preventing depression from interfering with care of other children?"

Effectiveness Questions

Many questions concern the effectiveness of services. A question may be: "In people recently exposed to a catastrophic event, would brief psychological debriefing compared to no intervention minimize the likelihood of posttraumatic stress disorder?" Ideally, we would discover a related systematic review or meta-analyses of randomized controlled trials such as Rose, Bisson, Churchill, and Wessely (2009).

Prevention Questions

Prevention questions direct attention to the future. These include questions about the effectiveness of early childhood visitation programs in preventing delinquency at later developmental stages. An example is: "In young children, do early home visitation programs, compared with no service, influence the frequency of delinquency as adolescents?" Here, too, well-designed randomized controlled trials control for more biases than do other kinds of studies.

Prediction (Risk and Prognosis) Questions

Professionals often estimate risk, for example, of future child maltreatment. A key question here is: "Is the risk assessment measure valid?" What is the rate of false positives (clients incorrectly said to have some characteristics such as being suicidal) and false negatives (clients inaccurately said not to have this characteristic, not be suicidal)? A well-built risk question is: "In abused children in foster care, will an actuarial risk assessment measure, compared to a consensus-based measure, provide the most accurate predictions regarding reabuse of children returned to their biological parents?"

Assessment Questions

What is the most evidence informed way to frame a problem? For example, is out-of-control behavior of a child due to "mental illness"? The pharmaceutical industry spends billions of dollars promoting the medicalization of everyday problems to enhance sales of medications (Gambrill, 2012a). This highlights the importance of critically appraising theories promoted, for example, concerning behavior and behavior change. Framing problems is a key part of expertise; experts in an area are more likely to accurately frame problems using valid assessment theories and tools than are novices. Professionals use a variety of assessment methods including self-report measures, interviews, observation, and physiological measures. Assessment methods used reflect underlining theory. Measures differ in their reliability (e.g., consistency of responses in absence of changed circumstances) and validity (do they measure what they purport to measure? See Chapter 5). Inflated claims regarding the accuracy of assessment and diagnostic measures are common. The sample used to gather data and provide "norms" on a measure (scores of a certain group of individuals) may be different than clients with whom you work, and so these norms may not apply. An assessment question may be: "In detecting frail elderly people who are depressed, is the Beck Depression Inventory or the Pleasant Events Schedule more accurate?" Posing and answering relevant descriptive questions contributes to accurate problem framing.

Description Questions

You may need descriptive information, such as the experiences of caregivers of frail elderly relatives. A question here is: "In those who care for dying relatives, what challenges arise and how are they handled?" Some description questions call for qualitative research such as experiences related to living in a nursing home (e.g., in-depth interviews, observation, and focus groups). Some require survey data involving large samples regarding problems and their causes. Survey data may provide information about the percentage of grieving parents who continue to grieve in certain ways with certain consequences over the years. It may provide information about the percentage of divorces and other consequences and describe how parents cope with them. Here, too, we should consider the quality of related research.

Questions about Harm

How many people have to receive some assessment measure or service for one to be harmed? This is known as number needed to harm (NNH). Related questions are: "How many people would we have to screen to identify one person who could benefit from help?" and "How many of these would be harmed by simply taking the test who are not at risk?" Any intervention including assessment may harm as well as help.

Questions about Cost–Benefit

Limited resources highlight the importance of cost–benefit analyses. What is the cost of offering one service compared to another and how many people benefit from each service? Criteria for reviewing cost–benefit studies can be found in Guyatt, Rennie, Meade, and Cook (2015).

Questions About How to Encourage Lifelong Learning

Integrating practice and research requires lifelong learning. An example of a question here is: "In newly graduated social workers, will a journal club, compared to a 'buddy system,' be most effective in maintaining evidence-informed practice skills?"

Common Errors in Posing Questions

Errors that may occur when posing answerable questions include having more than one question in a question and trying to answer the question before stating it clearly (posing vague questions). Gibbs (2003) notes that students often do not distinguish between a practice or policy question useful to guide a search and a research question requiring collection of data using an appropriate research method.

Novices may pose different questions compared to experts in an area who are familiar with research, for example, regarding prevalence of a concern (such as depression) and the complexity of related factors, such as lack of social support, negative thoughts, recent losses, poor nutrition, and so on.

A lack of knowledge may contribute to posing misleading questions that overlook important individual differences in a client's circumstances or characteristics. For example, posing an effectiveness question before discovering factors that contribute to depression (such as "In adults who are depressed, is cognitive-behavioral therapy, compared to medication, most effective in decreasing depression?") may overlook the fact that, for this client, recent losses in social support are uppermost, which suggests a different question, such as "In adults who are depressed because of a recent loss in social support, is a support group or individual counseling most effective in decreasing depression?"

Obstacles to Posing Well-Structured Questions

Obstacles include:

1. Lack of education (e.g., confusing research questions and practice questions, trying to answer a question before clearly posing it, including posing more than one question in a question).
2. Limited background information.
3. Limited foreground information about client characteristics and circumstances.
4. Lack of related tools, such as access to computerized databases.
5. Disinterest in honoring ethical obligations to clients to make informed decisions.
6. Lack of agency support (e.g., threatening nature of posing clear questions to those who favor use of authority-based criteria to select services such as tradition, popularity).
7. Lack of patience in crafting well-structured questions.

Ely et al. (2002) conducted a qualitative study investigating obstacles to answering physicians' questions about patient care with evidence. Participants included 9 academic generalist doctors, 14 family doctors, and 2 medical librarians. They identified 59 obstacles and organized them into the following categories:

- Missing client data requiring unnecessarily broad search. Questions that include demographic or clinical information and information about client preferences may help to focus the search. The kind of information of value will vary depending on the question and may not be clear until the search is under way.

- Inability to answer vague questions such as "What is this rash?" and vague cries for help ("I don't know what to do with this client") with general resources.
- Uncertainty about the scope of the question and unspoken ancillary questions. For example, the original question may have to be expanded to include ancillary questions.
- Obstacles related to modifying the question include unhelpful changes, perhaps due to misunderstandings between helpers and clients, trying to answer too many questions at once, and trying to answer the question while posing it.

Posing clear questions may be viewed a threat. Questions are not benign as illustrated by the fate of Socrates (Plato, 1993). Staff who pose questions may create discomfort among other staff, perhaps because they are doing something unfamiliar or perhaps because others view them as impertinent or disloyal to the agency or profession. Supervisors may not have experience in posing answerable questions and wonder why it is of value. Other obstacles include lack of time, lack of training in how to pose well-structured questions, lack of needed tools to search, lack of motivation to consider criteria on which decisions are made, and fears that there are more questions than answers. Options for addressing challenges include gaining guided experience in posing questions. The more we practice a skill, the more facility we gain with it, if we also gain corrective feedback.

SEARCHING FOR RESEARCH FINDINGS RELATED TO INFORMATION NEEDS

The Internet has revolutionized the search for information, making it speedier and more effective. Google searches can be swift and productive. Let us say you are interested in locating research concerning the effectiveness of brief psychological debriefing to prevent post-traumatic stress. Terms selected for a Google search might be *decreasing stress, psychological debriefing,* and *systematic review.* Always search for a systematic review first (see later discussion). Steps in searching include deciding how to search, conducting a search, evaluating the results, and revising your strategy as needed. Searches can be facilitated by careful selection of search terms including relevant quality filters such as the term *systematic review.*

EXHIBIT 4.2
EXAMPLES OF DATABASES AND HUNTING TOOLS

- ACP Journal Club www.acponline.org.
- Agency for Health Care Research and Quality (AHRQ) www.ahrq.gov, research arm of the U.S. Department of Health and Human Services; see also www.guideline.gov
- Best Practice http://bestpractice-bmj.com
- Campbell Collaboration http://www.campbellcollaboration.org/
- Center for Evidence and Implementation www.ceigloal.org
- Center for Evidence-Based Medicine http://www.cebm.net/. The website includes an EBM Toolbox for practicing and teaching EBM, the CATMaker (a software program allowing the user to create one-page summaries of evidence), a calendar of EBM events, and links to other EBM sites.
- Centre for Reviews and Dissemination (CRD), University of York www.york.ac.uk.crd. This produces reviews of the effectiveness and cost-effectiveness of healthcare interventions and provides access to several databases including a database of abstracts of systematic reviews (DARE).
- CINAHL http://www.cinahl.com, a nursing and allied health database, including health education, occupational therapy, emergency services, and social services in health care (United States).
- ClinicalTrials.gov http://clinicaltrials.gov
- Cochrane Collaboration. http://www.cochrane.org/
- Coalition for Evidence-Based Policy http://www.coalition4evidene.org/
- Database of Abstracts and Reviews of Effects (DARE) www.crd.york.ac.uk
- DUETS http://www.library.nhs.uk/duets, database of uncertainties about the effectiveness of interventions
- DynaMed Plus
- Embase
- EQUATOR. This is an international initiative designed to increase the value of medial research by promoting transparency and accurate reporting of studies.
- Essential Evidence Plus www.essentialevidenceplus.com
- Evidence-Based Mental Health http://ebmh.bmj.com
- Evidence Gap Maps www.3ieimpact.org
- Google Scholar
- HealthEvidence.org
- InfoPOEMS
- James Lind Library http://www.jameslindlibrary.org/
- Joanna Briggs Institute www.joannabrigs.edu.au, provides healthcare research.
- McMaster Optimal Aging Portal, https://www.mcmasteroptimalaging.org/
- McMaster Plus https://plus.mcmaster.ca/mcmasterplusdb/

- MedlinePlus http://medlineplus.gov/
- National Guideline Clearinghouse (www.guideline.gov)
- National Institute for Health and Care Excellence www.nice.org.uk
- National Registry of Evidence-Based Programs and Practices (SAMSA) www.samhsa.gov
- NHS Clinical Knowledge Summaries http://knowledge.nic.nhs.uk
- OVID www.ovid.com
- PROSPERO International Prospectus Register of Systematic Reviews www.crd.york.ac.uk
- PsychInfo www.apa.org
- PubMed: Medline http://www.nlm.nih.gov/pubs/factsheets/pubmed.html
- Scopus www.scopus.com
- OpenGray www.opengrey.eu; see also Sigle (System for Information on gray literature).
- Social Care Institute for Excellence (SCIE) www.scie.org.uk. Provides reports regarding best practices in social care emphasizing value of services to consumers. They produce "knowledge reviews" combining research knowledge with knowledge from practitioners and consumers.
- SumSearchz http://sumsearch.org
- TRIP Database http://www.tripdatabase.com. This database searches over 75 sites of high-quality medical information. It provides direct, hyperlinked access to the largest collection of "evidence-based" material on the web as well as articles from journals such as the *BMJ, JAMA,* and *NEJM.*
- UpToDate www.uptodate.com
- Web of Science www.webofknowledge.comg4

Different kinds of questions require different kinds of research to critically appraise them and related terms are of value in preparing a search. Such terms are referred to as *quality filters* (see Exhibit 4.1). If a question concerns effectiveness, quality filters include terms such as random or controlled trials, meta-analysis, or systematic review. Systematic reviews and meta-analyses include a search for and critical appraisal of related studies (see Chapter 5). Use of Boolean search terms is helpful. Examples include "and," which retrieves only articles with *both* words (child abuse and single parents), and "or," which locates all articles with either word (alcohol abuse or cocaine abuse). The term NOT excludes material containing certain words. Synonyms and key words can be combined by placing parentheses around OR statements such as (parent training OR parent education). Parentheses can be used to group words such as (*frail* and *elderly*). You can limit searches in a variety of ways, for example, by date.

Ease of searching depends in part on access to relevant databases. Sources include those that contain systematic reviews, websites listing interventions in terms of their assumed effectiveness such as the California Evidence-Based Clearinghouse on Child Welfare, sites concerned with harm (www.iatrogenic. org; www,healthyskepticism.org), and those providing practice guidelines such as the National Guideline Clearinghouse (NGC), National Institute for Health and Care 'excellence, and Social Care Institute for Excellence (SCIE; see Exhibit 4.2). Different databases may have different rules about how search terms should be entered for maximum effect. Experience in using relevant databases is an important skill. A clinical question filter can be used in sites such as CINAHL, Medline, EMBASE PsychINFO, and PubMed. POEMS (Patient-Oriented Evidence That Matters) can be obtained from Essential Evidence Plus.

Many sources provide summaries of individual studies such as Evidence-Based Medicine, ACP Journal Club, Evidence-Based Mental Health, and Evidence-Based Health Care and Public Health. Essential Evidence Plus provides a daily POEM, which is a synopsis of new evidence filtered for relevance to client care and evaluated for validity. Examples include "Mixed benefits of palliative care interventions and harms per 100,000 colonoscopies." Sources such as MacPlus, TRIP, and SumSearch search over multiple sites over multiple evidence levels. MacMasters offers special portals for different populations (e.g., elderly, child welfare clients). Evidence Gap Maps are provided by sources such as the world bank group (Openknowledge. worldbank.org and 3ie: International Initiative for Impact Evaluation.

Centers and organizations provide related support and resources including the Health Sciences Library McMaster University (http://hsl.macmaster.ca). The Centre for Evidence-Based Medicine in Oxford was the first of several similar centers in the United Kingdom. See www.cebm.net. Short courses, workshops, and training opportunities are offered by many centers. The *Centre for Evidence-Based Mental Health* offers resources designed to promote and support the teaching and practice of evidence-based mental health care including a list of links to evidence-based mental health and websites and a toolkit of teaching resources including examples of scenarios used in teaching EBP in mental health. See www. cebmh.com. The Centre for Evidence-Based Nursing is designed to help nurses, researchers, nurse educators, and managers to identify EBPs and to encourage use of evidence. Governmental agencies such as the National Health Service provide free statistical information of potential value.

A careful search requires seeking information that challenges (disconfirms) your initial assumptions as well as for information that supports them. A finding that an intervention harms clients or that there is no relevant research provides important information that contributes to an accurate appraisal of the uncertainties surrounding a decision. A finding that an intervention helps but also may have harmful effects requires discussion. (See Step 4.) If you get too many "hits," you could narrow the search by using more specific terms and use more selective quality filters. If you get too few, you could widen the search by using more general terms or select better databases. Search for high-quality reviews. Sources differ in rigor of critical appraisal of research. As always, "buyer beware" applies. And, just because a source has a reputation for providing accurate appraisals, does not guarantee that all material will be accurate. Flaws in peer-reviewed publications such as inflated claims were a key reason for the development of the process and philosophy of EBP. Such flaws continue (e.g., Gorman, 2017).

The Cochrane and Campbell Databases of Systematic Reviews

The Cochrane Collaboration prepares, maintains, and disseminates high-quality reviews of research related to particular questions in the area of health. Cochrane and Campbell reviews are based on a search for all high-quality research, published and unpublished (if possible in all languages), concerning a specific question and critical appraisal of what is found using rigorous criteria. Reviews are prepared and maintained, based on standards described in a Reviewers' Handbook and can be accessed on-line (www.cochrane-handbook.org). Campbell Reviews include those related to education, child welfare, and the criminal justice system. Criteria used to review studies are clearly described and rigorous criteria are used. Abstracts are available without charge and can be searched. Here are some examples:

- Amphetamines for attention deficit hyperactivity disorder (ADHD) in adults
- Day care centers for severe mental illness
- Dietary advice for reducing cardiovascular risk
- Discharge planning from hospital to home
- Parent training support for intellectually disabled parents
- Peer support telephone calls for improving health

As always, skepticism is needed (Ioannidis, 2016).

What about Practice Guidelines?

Helping clients often involves deciding among different alternatives. Practice guidelines have been developed to help practitioners and clients to make informed choices. Clinical practice guidelines are statements that include recommendations intended to optimize patient care that are informed by a systematic review of evidence and an assessment of the benefits and harms of alternative care options (Graham, Mancher, Wolman, Greenfield, & Steinberg, 2011). They are often accompanied by client versions in leaflets and decision aids. Guidelines have been described for preparing (GRADE) and reporting (AGREE) practice guidelines (see Chapter 5). Requirements include a clear question, involvement of a multidisciplinary panel of experts and individuals from affected groups, exhaustive search and rigorous review of related research, and consideration of subgroups of clients and client preferences that may warrant deviations from the recommendations. To be *trustworthy*, guidelines should

> be based on an explicit and transparent process that minimizes distortions, biases, and conflicts of interest; provide a clear explanation of the logical relationships between alternative care options and health outcomes, and provide ratings of both the quality of evidence and the strength of the recommendations; and be reconsidered and revised as appropriate when important new evidence warrants modifications of recommendations. (Graham, Mancher, Miller Welman, Greenfield, & Steinberg, 2011)

Questions here are: "Is the guideline valid?" Were conflicts of interest present such as ties of task force members to pharmaceutical companies (Cosgrove, Bursztajn, Erlich, Wheeler, & Shaughnessy, 2013)? "Has it been rigorously tested regarding effects?" "Has its *effectiveness* been tested, not just its *efficacy*—has it been tested in real-world circumstances in addition to research centers?" (Lenzer, Hoffman, Furberg, & Ioannidis, 2013.) To what percentage of individual clients does it apply (Elwyn et al., 2015). Although the *efficacy* of a method may be tested under ideal conditions, this same program may not achieve the same results when used in real-life settings (when its *effectiveness* is tested). Individual variations may require modification. Application barriers include lack of needed training. Questions include:

1. Were all important decisions, options, and outcomes clearly described? Have well-tested alternatives been described?
2. Was there a rigorous effort to identify and locate all related research? Were rigorous criteria used to appraise studies?
3. Are benefits and risks clearly described as well as costs for each outcome of interest to different stake holders?
4. Does the guideline apply to your clients?

Advantages and disadvantages of reliance on guidelines, both to practitioners and to clients have long been described (e.g., Elwyn, Wieringa, & Greenhalgh, 2016;

Woolf, Grol, Hutchinson, Eccles, & Grimshaw, 1999). Advantages include enhancing informed consent, provision of more effective services, avoidance of harm, and informing research priorities. Potential limitations include making incorrect recommendations and lack of related research. If inaccurate they may harm clients. Guidelines are for populations and care must be exercised in applying them to individuals; what may be effective with one individual or in one setting may not be in another. "The leading figures in EBM (evidence-based medicine) . . . emphasized that clinicians had to use their scientific training and their judgement to interpret (guidelines) and individualize care accordingly" (Gray, 2001b, p. 26). Guidelines may have adverse effects on public policy by requiring ineffective methods. Preparers of guidelines may have conflicts of interest that bias results. Different people may interpret related evidence differently. Guidelines may be out of date.

Outcomes of concern to clients maybe ignored (e.g., Hsu et al., 2011). A recent review of emergency medicine clinical practice guidelines revealed that almost one half were "based on expert opinion and low-level evidence rather than clinical trial evidence" (Venkatesh et al., 2017). Uncertainties may be underplayed including complexities of problems and related factors and resources needed. Wampold and Imel (2015) argue that psychotherapy research shows that "no one treatment is clearly more effective than another" (p. 272). They argue that common factors such as the alliance, warmth and empathy have a greater impact on outcome than specific interventions. If the quality of the helper-client relationship and characteristics of the clinician contribute more to outcome in psychotherapy than specific interventions used (Wampold & Imel, 2015), can a guideline or manualized treatment be "well established" in achieving certain outcomes?

Guidelines are often very long and may not enable choices among alternative options taking into account individual differences, thus the interest in creating more user-friendly but still rigorous reviews of related data. Shaughnessy et al. (2017) developed a "clinician friendly" tool to review guidelines called G-Trust. Items in this list include:

1. The patient populations and conditions are relevant to my clinical setting.
2. The recommendations are clear and actionable.
3. The recommendations focus on improving patient-oriented outcomes, explicitly comparing benefits versus harms to support clinical decision-making.
4. The guidelines are based on a systematic review of the research data.
5. The recommendation statements important to you are based on graded evidence and include a description of the quality (e.g., strong, weak) of the evidence.
6. The guidelines development includes a research analyst, such as a statistician or epidemiologist.

7. The Chair of the guideline development committee and a majority of the rest of the committee are free of declared financial conflicts of interest, and the guideline development group did not receive industry funding for developing the guideline.

8. The guideline development includes members from the most relevant specialties and includes other key stakeholders, such as patients, payer organizations, and public health entities, when applicable. (p. 416).

Elwyn et al. (2016) describe knowledge tools such as the Diabetes Medication Choice Cards and Option Grid decision aids. (See also user-friendly descriptions of how to estimate risk such as use of natural frequencies; Gigerenzer, 2002a & b, 2014; see also Paling, 2006). As Elwyn et al. notes, what is needed is "just-in-time" and "just enough" knowledge tools.

In the common elements approach, components of a complex intervention correlated with outcome are identified and recommended (Chorpita & Daleiden, 2009).

Common Errors in Searching

Errors in this step may be related to the selection of source and precision of terms used in questions posed; they may be too narrow or too broad, resulting in too few or too many reports. You may forget to include the word "systematic"—that is, search first for a good review. Giving up too soon is a common error; it takes practice to select terms most likely to yield valuable information and it often takes persistence. Lack of information about valuable sites may result in overlooking helpful sources. Naiveté regarding accuracy of or relevance of recommended EBPs and guidelines may hinder informed decisions. "In good thinking 1. Search is sufficiently thorough for the question; 2. Search and inference are fair to all possibilities under consideration, and 3. Confidence is appropriate to the amount of search that has been done and the quality of the inferences made" (Baron, 1996, p. 1).

Obstacles and Evolving Remedies

People often depart from good thinking by:

1. Searching too little when the issue is important (or too much when it is unimportant);

2. Searching and making inferences in a way that favors possibilities that are already strong or that the thinker wishes were adopted; [or]

3. Having high confidence when this is not warranted by the search and inference that have been done. (Baron, 1996, p. 1)

You may not be aware of important databases nor have access to skilled librarians. There may be no rigorous research related to a question. Gray (2001a) refers to this as the *relevance gap*. Another is failure to publish research results––the *publication gap*. Clinical guidelines especially those using GRADE research process, may not be available, and, even if available, may not apply to your client. Of the 59 obstacles to EBP identified by Ely et al. (2002), five they considered most important involved search problems:

- Excessive time required to locate information.
- Difficulty selecting an optimal search strategy.
- Failure of a seemingly relevant resource to cover the topic.
- Uncertainty about how to decide when key evidence has been found.
- Inadequate synthesis of multiple sources of evidence into a conclusion that is clinically relevant.

These obstacles continue to be of concern. Time can be saved by taking advantage of the best Internet sources. The importance of ready access to valuable databases is illustrated by the failure to use agency-based libraries even though they are conveniently located. There may be no access to a reference management system. Help of a knowledge manager may be required to gain speedy access to needed information (Gray, 1998). This person's role is to locate and critically appraise research related to specific questions in a timely manner. Searching widely is one way to protect yourself from influence by inaccurate presentations from a single source. For example, content on the website of the American Psychiatric Association may be compared with material on the Critical Psychiatry Network (www.criticalpsychiatry.co.uk).

CRITICALLY APPRAISING RESEARCH LOCATED

Critically appraising the quality and relevance of different kinds of research is a key competency as is knowledge of high quality aids such as guidelines that follow GRADE recommendations. All research has flaws that may compromise its value in answering a question. Possible biases are always of concern (see Chapter 5). The research methods used may be appropriate for the question, and rigorous, but the findings may not apply to your clients or community. Statistical errors are common (Bakker & Wicherts, 2011). Important cultural differences may be neglected (Lynch & Hanson, 2011). Critical appraisal skills will help you to avoid being bamboozled by inflated claims about causes, risks and remedies. (See Critical Appraisal Skills Program [CASP]; testingtreatments.org).

Criteria of value in appraising the accuracy of content include funding source (does it have a reputation for critical appraisal and accurate presentation of well-argued alternative views?), clarity of writing, completeness of description of studies (e.g., sample size, measures used), rigor of description of limitations, and citation of references so you can review original sources for yourself. As emphasized earlier, the kind of research that may provide answers to questions differs depending on the question. Some questions call for qualitative research such as in-depth interviews. Questions pertaining to intervention, prevention, accuracy of diagnostic methods, or harm are most rigorously explored using randomized controlled trials. Often, a mix of both qualitative and quantitative research is best. Take advantage of user-friendly checklists to critically appraise different kinds of research (e.g., CASP [www.casp.org]; testingtreatments.org; Greenhalgh, 2010; Guyatt et al., 2015). Checklists for reviewing research reports differ in degree of detail. The EBM tool kit is a Canadian-based collection of resources to support EPB. It includes appraisal checklists and methodological filters (http//www.med.ualberta.ca/ebm/ ebm.htm). The Cochrane Consumer Network offers a variety of resources for consumers (see consumers.cochrane.org).

Common Errors

Common errors include (1) not critically appraising what you find including programs on lists of EBPs and practice guidelines, (2) becoming disheartened when you find little, and (3) misinterpreting a lack of evidence that a method is effective as evidence that it is not effective. Lack of statistical literacy is a common obstacle among both professionals and clients (e.g., Gigerenzer, 2014a; Paulos, 1988). A method that is untested may be effective or may be harmful. Professionals are obligated to accurately describe to clients the state of knowledge, ignorance, and uncertainty about life-affecting decisions. When little or no research is available regarding important questions, you must draw on practice theory as well as your client's ideas and preferences in a supportive exchange of shared uncertainties.

Obstacles and Evolving Remedies

You can save time by drawing on high-quality reviews of research when these are available such as systematic reviews in the Cochrane and Campbell Databases. Here as always, skepticism is needed (Ioannidis, 2016). Palm pilots are available for evaluating tests as well as for other goals (e.g., clinical decision-making calculators).

INTEGRATING RESEARCH FINDINGS AND RELEVANT THEORY WITH OTHER INFORMATION AND MAKING A DECISION

You and your clients must decide whether material located is relevant. For example, does a recommended EBP or guideline apply to your client? If so, is a guideline based on GRADE criteria? (see Chapter 5). Client preferences should be considered as well as resources available. Understanding a client's unique characteristics including their values and expectations and circumstances (foreground information) may be critical to making decisions that result in valued outcomes. Thus, this step requires drawing on clinical expertise to integrate both background and foreground information. Application barriers reported by my students include:

1. Lack of needed resources (e.g., programs that offer the best likelihood of helping clients achieve a certain outcome are not available).
2. Chaotic working space––shared phone, desk, and computer and no private space for confidential conversations.
3. Disparity between evidentiary standards advocated in school and those used in agencies (e.g., relying on popularity or entertainment value to select service in agencies).
4. Staff work mainly in a crisis mode, which results in lack of time to make informed decisions.
5. Providers feel overwhelmed by the problems/issues clients bring. This may be due to large caseloads and lack of resources.
6. Unsupportive administrative practices such as failure to reinforce staff for raising questions about the effectiveness of services and dysfunctional micro-management.
7. Unclear mission of the organization/agency (confusion of what services to provide).
8. Poor inter-agency communication and collaboration.

Do Research Findings and Guidelines Apply to My Client?

There may be information about certain kinds of clients, but these clients may differ from your client and so findings may not apply. Experts compared to novices in an area have much greater content knowledge that is valuable in making related decisions (see Chapter 6). A great deal of research consists of correlational research (e.g., describing the relationship between characteristics of parents and child abuse) and experimental research describing differences among groups (e.g., experimental and control). In neither case may a finding be generalized to other clients or settings. Individuals in samples used in research studies may differ from your client. Here, too, ethical obligations to inform clients and to consider their preferences provide a guide, for example, to clearly describe limitations of research findings. The unique characteristics and circumstances of a client may suggest that a recommended method should not be used because negative effects are likely or because such characteristics would render a guideline ineffective. Well-constructed guidelines describe important clinical differences that should be considered. Social or cultural factors as well as acceptability of a method to a client may affect the suitability of a method.

Your knowledge of the science of behavior (e.g., how it is influenced by environmental contingencies) may offer helpful guidelines (e.g., Madden, 2013; Staats, 2012). Norms on assessment measures may be available but not for people like your client. (However, norms should not necessarily be used as guidelines for selecting outcomes for individual clients; outcomes they seek may differ from normative criteria and norms may not be optimal such as low rates of positive feedback from teachers to students. See also earlier discussion of EBPs and guidelines.)

Are They Important? The "So-What Question"

If external research findings apply to a client, are they important? Would they make a difference in decisions made? Were all important outcomes considered? Were surrogate outcomes relied on—those that are assumed to (but may not) reflect vital outcomes? For example, does decreasing plaque in arteries decrease mortality? The term POEMS refers to patient-oriented evidence that matters. Grandage, Slawson, and Shaughnessy (2002) suggest the following for judging usefulness:

$$\text{Usefulness} = \frac{\text{validity x relevance}}{\text{work}}$$

How Definitive Are the Research Findings?

There may be strong evidence not to use a method or strong evidence to use a method. Typically, there will be uncertainty. Disagreements among experts are common. Research regarding causes may not allow ruling out rival explanations including placebo effects, the cyclic nature of a concern such as depression, or the influence of other remedies being used.

Can I Use This Method in My Agency?

Can a plan be carried out in a way that maximizes success? Do you have the required skills? How do you know? Can needed resources be created? Lack of needed resources is common. Ethical obligations here include advocacy—involving others in keeping track of needed resources, collating and sharing this information with others, and advocating for provision of these services. Barriers to implementation may be so extensive that Straus, Richardson, Glasziou, and Haynes (2005) refers to them as the "Killer Bs":

1. The "Burden of Illness" (the frequency of a concern may be too low to warrant offering a costly program with high integrity);
2. Beliefs of individual clients and/or communities about the value of services or their outcomes may not be compatible with what is most effective;
3. A Bad Bargain in relation to resources, costs and outcome;
4. Barriers such as geographic, organizational, traditional, authoritarian or behavioral). (Straus et al., 2005, p. 167)

Questions Sackett, Richardson, Rosenberg, and Haynes (1997, p. 182) suggest for deciding whether to implement a guideline include:

1. What barriers exist to its implementation? Can they be overcome?
2. Can you enlist the collaboration of key colleagues?
3. Can you meet the educational, administrative, and economic conditions likely to determine the success or failure of implementing the strategy such as freedom from conflict with economic and administrative incentives and client and community expectations?

Problems may have to be redefined from helping clients attain needed resources to helping them to bear up under the strain of not having them and involving clients with similar concerns in advocacy efforts to acquire better services.

Are Alternative Options Available?

Are other options available—perhaps another agency to which a client could be referred? Perhaps effective self-help programs are available. Here, too, familiarity with practice and policy-related research can facilitate decisions.

Will Potential Benefits Outweigh Harms?

Every intervention, including assessment measures, has potential risks as well as benefits. Diagnostic tests may result in false positives or false negatives. Will the benefits of an intervention outweigh potential risks and costs (Woloshin, Schwartz, & Welch, 2008)? Trade-offs may be necessary in considering potential benefits and harms. Are you and your clients informed about the benefits and risks? This will require statistical literacy (e.g., Gigerenzer, 2014a; Paling, 2006). Sharing information about number needed to treat (NNT; e.g., for one person to benefit, how many must receive a treatment?) and NNH (number of individuals who would have to receive a service to harm one person) will help clients to make informed decisions. Let's say a physician recommends statin treatments for five years for a person with no manifest heart disease to prevent heart disease. One in 104 will be helped (heart attack prevented) and 1 in 10 will be harmed (muscle damage; Bauer, 2015). (See also later section on HELPING CLIENTS MAKE DECISIONS.) GRADE recommendations include a balancing of benefits and harms.

What If the Experts Disagree?

We often appeal to the authority of experts. Recommendations of experts may not match what is suggested by results of carefully controlled research. Checking the evidentiary status of claims by an expert may be fairly easy. At other times it may require considerable time. Indicators of honesty include (1) accurate description of controversies in an area, including methodological and conceptual problems; (2) accurate description of well-argued disliked views; (3) critical appraisal of both preferred and alternative views; and (4) inclusion of references to sources cited, so readers can look these up.

What If Clients Prefer an Untested Method?

Acceptability of an intervention to clients must be considered. Certainly you should not use a method shown to be harmful. What about contradicted, untested, and aspiring methods (Prasad & Ioannidis, 2014)? If there is an effective method, you could describe the costs and benefits of using this compared to an untested method. You could suggest that the client use a relevant decision aid. Untested methods are routinely offered in both health and social care. Review of the evidentiary status of interventions suggests that about 50% are of unknown effect (Frakt, 2013). Whether you should offer them depends on many factors including acceptability to clients and scarcity of resources.

What If I Do Not Find Any Relevant Research or It Is of Poor Quality?

You and your clients will typically have to make decisions in a context of uncertainty. A search may reveal that there is no research that can guide decisions or that it is of poor quality. Uncertainty about the effectiveness of a practice or policy will be more the norm than the exception. The term *best evidence* could refer to programs that differ greatly in their evidentiary status. There may be no high-quality systematic review regarding a question. Instead of well-designed randomized controlled trials you may discover observational reports and pre–post tests. Let us assume that your search has been sound and that no one else could find anything either. This is an important finding. Ethical obligations to clients require sharing what you find (including nothing) and drawing on relevant background and foreground information to guide your work, including valuable theory that offers understanding of client concerns and options for attaining hoped-for outcomes. EBP involves sharing ignorance and uncertainty as well as knowledge in a context of ongoing support.

What If Research Is Available but It Has Not Been Critically Appraised?

One course of action is to critically appraise the literature for yourself. You may not have time to do this. If this concerns a common hoped-for outcome, involve interested others in critically appraising related research.

Balancing Individual and Population Perspectives

One challenging aspect of the process of EBP is considering both individuals and populations in applying research and distributing scarce resources. Decisions made about populations regarding programs offered may limit options of individuals. Both political and ethical issues regarding the distribution of scarce resources are often overlooked as are concerns regarding the evidentiary quality of research.

HELPING CLIENTS TO MAKE INFORMED DECISIONS

Decisions often involve trade-offs between risks and benefits, both short and long term. Available material may be quite deceiving in presenting information (e.g., Gigerenzer, 2014b). Clients differ in how much they want to know regarding problems and potentials for resolution. Shared decision-making between clients and professionals is increasingly emphasized (Elwyn, Edwards, & Thompson, 2016) including creation of user-friendly materials such as option grids to help clients consider potential harms, benefits, and burdens of interventions. Be sure to inform clients about absolute risk as appropriate taking advantage of related tools (e.g., Paling, 2006). Relative risk is very misleading. (See Chapter 5.) Aids are available concerning many kinds of decisions including whether to take a screening test or a prescribed medication (Agoritas et al., 2015; Stacey et al. 2017; see also https:decisionaid.ohri.ca; http://effectivehealthcare.ahrq.gov). Formats include videos, web-based tools, and information leaflets (Elwyn, Wieringa, & Greenhalgh, 2016; see Exhibit 4.3).

Information can be provided concerning available options and related outcomes, including how they may affect the client and the probabilities associated with each outcome. Decision aids can (1) reduce the proportion of clients who are uncertain about what to choose; (2) increase clients' knowledge of problems, options, and outcomes; (3) create realistic expectations of outcomes; (4) improve the agreement between choices and a client's values; (5) reduce decision conflict (feeling uncertain, uninformed, unclear about values, and unsupported in decision-making); and (6) increase participation. Such aids increase client involvement, contribute to informed decisions, and improve communication between helpers and clients (Elwyn, Edwards, & Thompson, 2016). Elwyn et al. (2013) developed a brief client-report measure of shared decision-making. An Evidence-Informed Client Choice Form introduced by Entwistle, Sheldon, Sowden, and Watt (1998) is still highly relevant (see Exhibit 4.4).

We often do not know what we want, our preferences change in accord with a variety of factors, including the visibility of related consequences. Although many people say they want to achieve a certain goal, such as to stop drinking, exercise more, meet more people, or eat a more healthy diet, their actions often do not reflect their preferences. Both *process* resistance (e.g., a reluctance to engage in exposure to feared situations to decrease anxiety) and *outcome* resistance (e.g., costs of giving up a behavior such as drinking) may be an issue (see blog by David Burns; https://feelinggood.com/). A decision aid can help an individual to weigh factors according to his or her unique values while being

EXHIBIT 4.3

INFORMATION NEEDED TO MAKE A DECISION WHETHER TO TAKE A DRUG
BENEFITS AND RISKS

In a study, 13,000 women aged 35 and older who had never had breast cancer but
were considered to be at high risk of getting it were given either Nolvadex or a
placebo each day for five years. Women were considered to be at high risk if their
chance of developing breast cancer over the next five years was estimated at 1.7% or
higher (an estimate arrived at by using a risk calculator available at www.cancer.gov/
bcrisktool). Here's what happened.

What Difference Did Nolvadex Make?	Starting Risk (Placebo Group)	Modified Risk (Nolvadex Group, 20 mg/day)
Did Noladex help?	3.3%	1.7%
Fewer Nolvadex users got invasive breast cancer (1.6% fewer due to drug).	33 in 1,000	17 in 1,000
No difference in death from breast cancer	About 0.09% in both groups	
Did Nolvadex have side effects?		
Life-threatening side effects	0.9 in 1,000	
Blood clots (in legs or lungs)	0.5%	1.0%
(additional 0.5% due to drug)	5 in 1,000	10 in 1,000
Invasive uterine cancer	0.5%	1.1%
(additional 0.6% due to drug)	5 in 1,000	11 in 1,000
Symptom side effects		
Hot flashes	69%	81%
(additional 12% due to drug)	690 in 1,000	810 in 1,000
Vaginal discharge	35%	55%
(additional 20% due to drug)	350 in 1,000	550 in 1,000
Cataracts that needed surgery	1.5%	2.3%
(additional 0.8% due to drug)	15 in 1,000	23 in 1,000
Death from all causes combined	About 1.2% in both groups	
No difference between Nolvadex and placebo	12 in 1,000	

Source: From *Know Your Chances: Understanding Health Statistics,* by S. Woloshin, L. M. Schwartz, and
G. Welch, 2008, Berkeley, CA: University of California Press. p. 78. Reprinted with permission.

accurately informed about possible consequences of different options including uncertainties associated with each one. Woltman, Wilkniss, Teachout, McHugo, and Drake (2011) developed an electronic decision support system to enhance shared decision-making between community mental health clients and their case managers. Occasions when discovering client preferences is especially important include those in which (1) options have major differences in outcomes

---

EXHIBIT 4.4
EVIDENCE-INFORMED CLIENT CHOICE

Agency: _____
_____

Client: _____
_____

Date: _____
_____

Referral agency: _____
_____

Program within agency: _____
_____

Staff member in agency who will offer program: _____
_____

A. *Related External Research*
   1. Research shows that this program will help people like me to attain hoped-for outcomes.
   2. This program has never been rigorously tested in relation to hoped-for outcomes.
   3. Research shows that other programs that help people like me have been critically tested and found to attain hoped-for outcomes.
   4. Research shows that this program is likely to have harmful effects (e.g., decrease hoped-for outcomes).
B. *Agency's Background Regarding Use of This Method*
   1. The agency to which I have been referred has a track record of success in using this program with people like me.
   2. The staff member who will work with me has a track record of success in using this method with people like me.

Source: Adapted from "Evidence-Informed Patience Choice," by V. A. Entwistle, T. A. Sheldon, A. J. Sowden, and I. A. Watt, 1998, *International Journal of Technology Assessment in Health Care, 14,* 212–215.

or complications, (2) decisions require making trade-offs between short-term and long-term outcomes, (3) one choice can result in a small chance of a grave outcome, and (4) there are marginal differences in outcomes between options (Kassirer, 1994). Clients differ in how "risk adverse" they are and in the importance of particular outcomes.

Common Errors in Integrating Information

Lack of valuable content knowledge and related skills contributes to errors in posing relevant questions and integrating information as do biases such as influence by redundant information (see Chapter 6). Lack of content knowledge and related failure to recognize patterns may result in misleading oversimplifications about the causes of client concerns. Or, vague, overly complex accounts may be pursued, none of which provide clear directions. Sources of error that may result in faulty problem structuring can be seen in Exhibit 4.5. Errors can be minimized by skeptically appraising claims, including those in the peer-reviewed literature. Eagerness to help clients may encourage unfounded confidence in a method and premature advice and assurances. Reliance on invalid assessment measures and failure to critically appraise research regarding interventions may result in faulty decisions. Acquiring relevant knowledge and skills requires, in some cases, years of experience and acquiring content knowledge.

Obstacles and Evolving Remedies

Biases may intrude both on the part of researchers, for example, when preparing reviews and at the practitioner level when making decisions. EBP highlights the uncertainty involved in helping clients and options for handling this in an informed manner, for example, increasing critical appraisal skills of both clients and practitioners. Many components of EBP are designed to minimize "jumping to conclusions," for example, by seeking research related to important questions. Basing decisions on a flawed theory as well as lack of knowledge about important cultural differences may hinder sound decisions. Use of clinical pathways and palm pilots with built-in decision aids, such as flow charts, can be helpful, and many are already in use in the health area.

Use of handheld computers to guide decisions may be of value in decreasing errors and biases, for example, by providing reminders to check certain things.

EXHIBIT 4.5
SOURCES OF ERROR THAT MAY RESULT IN INACCURATE OR INCOMPLETE
PROBLEM STRUCTURING

Source	Description
1. Partiality in the use of evidence.	Overlooking, distorting, or discounting contradictory evidence. Giving favored treatment to favored beliefs (e.g., see items 2 to 7).
2. Rationalizing rather than reasoning justifying rather than critiquing; confirmation bias.	Focusing on building a case for a position rather than gathering information impartially. This is an example of item 1.
3. Focusing on irrelevant or incorrect evidence.	Selecting irrelevant or marginally relevant reasons to support beliefs or actions. The conclusion may have nothing to do with the reasons provided.
4. Jumping to conclusions.	Failing to treat a belief or conclusions as a hypothesis requiring scrutiny.
5. Unwarranted persistence	Not changing your mind even when there is compelling evidence to do so.
6. Categorical rather than probabilistic reasoning.	Reducing options to two possibilities (either/or).
7. Confusing naming and explaining (e.g., diagnosing rather than contextually assessing).	Assuming that giving something a name (e.g., bipolar disorder) explains it and offers intervention leverage.
8. Confusing correlation and causation	Assuming that an association between two or more events indicates causation.
9. Confusing shared with distinguishing characteristics	Focusing on characteristics that may not distinguish among different groups or causes.
10. Faulty generalization	Relying on small or biased samples; assuming that what is true of the whole is true of the parts, or vice versa.

Source	Description
11. Stereotyping	Incorrectly estimating the degree of variability in a group.
12. Influence of consistent data	Being influenced by data that do not offer any new information but are merely consistent with data already available.
13. Lack of domain-specific knowledge	Not having information needed to clarify and understand problems (e.g., facts, concepts, theories). This cause of error is related to many others on this list.
14. Confusing form and function.	Mistakenly assuming that similar forms of behavior have similar functions and that different forms of behavior reflect different functions.
15. Oversimplifications	Ignoring important causes or overlooking uncertainties.
16. Vagueness	Vague descriptions of problems, causes, and hoped for outcomes.
17. Uncritical acceptance of theories/ explanations	Accepting explanations without evaluating them and comparing them with well-argued alternative accounts; not checking whether a belief is consistent with known facts; selecting untestable beliefs.
18. Assuming that a weak argument is not true	Assuming that because you cannot offer a convincing argument, a claim is false.
19. Reliance on ad hoc explanations	Making up explanations as you go along, even though they may contradict one or another or be circular (explain nothing).
20. Incorrect weighing of different contributors	Not weighing contributing factors in relation to their importance.
21. Misuse of speculation	Believing that you can find out what is going on just by thinking about it.
22. Overcomplex accounts	Relying on needlessly complicated accounts that obscure causes.

Source	Description
23. Ecological fallacy	Assuming that an association between two variables on a group level is also true on an individual level.
24. Relying on vivid data	Such data may be misleading.
25. Relying on questionable criteria for evaluating the accuracy of claims	Examples include consensus, anecdotal experience, and tradition.
26. Incorrectly applying a general rule to a particular situation	A general rule may not apply to a specific situation/person.
27. Overconfidence	Failure to question views
28. Confusing causes and their effect	Effects may be confused with their causes.
29. Ignoring base rate	Ignoring statistical information regarding a question.
30. Fundamental attribution error	Overlooking environmental influences and focusing on personality characteristics.
31. Failing to question (override) intuitive beliefs	Active open-minded thinking may be needed to make informed decisions.
32. Dead-end and incomplete accounts	Accounts that do not aid in achieving valued outcomes.
33. Underestimating the play of chance	Events may be random.

Computer-based decision aids may be used to prompt valuable behaviors, to critique a decision (e.g., purchasing services from an agency), to match a client's unique circumstances and characteristics with a service program, to suggest options, and to interpret different assessment pictures (Guyatt & Rennie, 2008). And, just as the narratives of clients may help us to understand how we can improve services, so practitioner narratives may help us to identify challenges to and opportunities for enhancing the quality services (e.g., Greenhalgh & Hurwitz, 1998). Learning from experience in ways that improve the accuracy of future decisions is vital (e.g., Chapter 6).

Related Ethical Dilemmas

Ethical issues that arise in integrating data and making decisions illustrate the close connection between ethical and evidentiary issues. These include ethical obligations of practitioners to accurately inform clients regarding the uncertainties involved in making decisions, including the evidentiary status of recommended methods and their risks and benefits together with the risks and benefits of alternative methods. CollaboRATE is a client-report measure of shared decision-making (Elwyn, Barr, Grande, Thompson, Walsh, & Ozanne, 2013). Should clients be informed regarding effective methods which an agency cannot offer? Should practitioners continue to offer methods of unknown effectiveness? Is it ethical to offer an intervention in a diluted from of unknown effectiveness? Should practitioners be well-informed regarding how to accurately present risks and benefits? Although the answers may clearly be yes, descriptions of everyday practice suggests a different picture. Yet another ethical issue concerns controversies regarding the relative contribution of the person of the helper, common factors such as empathy, and the particular intervention used to outcome. If it is true that the former two contribute more than the particular intervention, this should be considered in deciding what to do (Wampold & Imel, 2015).

EVALUATING OUTCOME AND LEARNING
FROM WHAT YOU FIND

Accountability to clients requires transparency of results as well as selection of user-friendly, valid measures to assess progress. On-going monitoring of clear, relevant, accurate progress measures facilitates timely changes in plans and is positively related to outcome (Boswell, Kraus, Miller, & Lambert, 2013; Miller, Hubble, Chow, & Seidel, 2015). There is a rich literature suggesting valid, feasible ways to evaluate outcome, including complex ones such as quality of life attending to reactive effects that may contribute to misleading reports. Single-case (N of 1) studies offer timely feedback (Barlow, Nock, & Hersen, 2009; Bloom & Britner, 2012). Experimental N of 1 trials are ideal in exploring what method works best for a given client when the external research is murky or does not apply well to a client. Following a baseline, services are offered. However, if N of 1 trials are done in a haphazard way, conclusions about effects may be misleading because many concerns are self-limited and improve on their own, extreme levels of a symptom, if untreated and remeasured later, often return to or toward the normal range, the placebo effect can lead to substantial relief of symptoms, and our own and our clients' expectations can bias our conclusions about whether an intervention worked and clients may exaggerate the benefits of treatment (Sackett, Straus, Richardson, Rosenberg, & Haynes, 2000, pp. 150–151).

Objections to obtaining ongoing feedback may be related to misconceptions about careful evaluation, such as the view that this requires selection of trivial outcomes or measures—the belief that rigor requires rigor mortis. Related literature demonstrates that this is not so (e.g., Campbell, 1988). The alternative to careful evaluation is basing decisions on guesstimates (uninformed guesses) that may mislead both you and your clients.

Common Errors

A variety of biases may contribute to incorrect views of progress, including *hindsight bias* and *wishful thinking*. The role of chance variations and contributing causes such as regression effects may be overlooked. One or more of the following reactive effects may contribute to misleading reports:

- *Hello–goodbye effect*: Clients present themselves as worse than they really are when they seek help and as better than they really are when the service has ended. This leads to overestimating progress (Hathaway, 1948).
- *Hawthorne effect*: Improvement may result from being the focus of attention—for example, going to a well-known clinic or being seen by a famous therapist.
- *Rosenthal effect*: We tend to give observers what we think they want—to please people we like or respect.
- *Observer bias*: The observer's expectations may result in biased data.
- *Social desirability effect*: We end to offer accounts viewed as appropriate. For example, clients may underreport drinking.

Selection of vague outcomes and failure to assess degree of progress in an ongoing manner will make it impossible to carefully evaluate outcome and make timely changes in plans. Process measures (how many sessions a client attended) do not reflect changes in hoped-for outcomes unless there is a high positive correlation between services used and hoped-for outcomes.

Surrogate measures (e.g., decrease in cholesterol) may not reflect mortality.

Obstacles and Evolving Remedies

Lack of time and training in selecting relevant, feasible progress indicators will interfere with ongoing monitoring of hoped-for outcomes that guides timely decision-making. Valuable computer programs may not be available (e.g., for handling data regarding progress). Fears about revealing lack of progress or harmful effects may discourage careful evaluation.

ONGOING LEARNING

Keep track of the questions you ask, important research findings you locate, and client progress to learn how to improve future decisions. Self-evaluation questions are shown in Exhibit 4.6. Gray (2001a) emphasizes the importance of information storage and retrieval skills; if you cannot find information when you need it, it is not of value to clients. Lifelong learning is a key part of the process of EBP. You could pursue answers to important questions that arise in your work in a Journal Club. You could scan valuable sources regularly and compare your current knowledge about important questions with information you discover after your search.

EXHIBIT 4.6
SELF-EVALUATION QUESTIONS

Asking Well-Formed Questions
1. Am I asking any practice or policy questions at all?
2. Am I asking well-formed questions?
3. Can I get "unstuck" when asking questions?
4. Do I have a way to save my questions for later answering?
5. Is my success rate of asking clear questions rising?
6. Am I modeling the asking of clear questions for others?

Finding the Best External Evidence
1. Am I searching at all?
2. Do I know the best sources of current evidence for decisions I make?
3. Do I have easy access to tools for searching for the best evidence?
4. Am I finding useful evidence from a wider array of sources?
5. Am I becoming more efficient in searching?

Critically Appraising the Evidence for Its Validity and Usefulness
1. Am I critically appraising external evidence at all?
2. Are critical appraisal guides becoming easier to apply?

3. Am I becoming more accurate and efficient in applying appraisal measures such as pretest probabilities and NNTs?

Drawing on Clinical Experience to Integrate Information Gathered and Applying the Results

1. Am I integrating my critical appraisals in my practice at all?
2. Am I becoming more accurate and efficient in adjusting critical appraisal measures to fit my clients (e.g., NNT)?
3. Can I explain (and resolve) disagreements about decisions in terms of this integration?

Evaluating My Effectiveness

1. Do clients achieve valued outcomes?
2. Have I carried out any audits of my EBP performance?
3. Am I helping others to learn how to use the process of EBP?

Continuing Professional Development

1. Am I a member of an EBP-style journal club?
2. Have I participated in or tutored at a workshop on how to practice EBP?
3. Have I joined an evidence-based e-mail discussion group?
4. Have I established links with other practitioners of EBP?

Source: Adapted from *Evidence-Based Medicine: How to Practice and Teach EBM.* (2nd ed.), by D. L. Sackett, S. E. Straus, W. S. Richardson, W. Rosenberg, and R. B. Haynes, 2000, New York: Churchill Livingstone, pp. 220–228.

SUMMARY

Key steps in EBP include posing well-formed questions related to information needs; seeking efficiently and effectively for related research; critically appraising what is found, for example, drawing on high-quality systematic reviews); using expertise to integrate diverse sources of information including knowledge about the clients' circumstances and characteristics, including their values, expectations, and preferences and available resources; and making a decision together with clients about what to do, trying it out, evaluating what happens, and learning from this experience how to do better next time. These steps increase the likelihood that you and your clients will be informed about the kinds and levels of uncertainties associated with decisions and make well-reasoned decisions and involve clients as informed participants. Although the steps involved in EBP may sound simple and straightforward, there are many challenges including acquiring access to needed resources, such as databases and arranging for ongoing valid feedback about progress. Perhaps the greatest challenge is a willingness to recognize gaps in current knowledge regarding decisions and what is "out there"--a willingness to say "I don't know"—and a commitment to clients to see and share what is out there.

5

Critically Appraising Research

THIS CHAPTER OFFERS a bare-bones guide for critically appraising practice-related research findings related to different kinds of questions that arise in everyday practice. You are urged to consult other sources for additional details such as Testing Treatment Interactive (testingtreatments.org); Greenhalgh (2010), and Guyatt, Rennie, Meade, and Cook (2015). Being informed about different kinds of research and their advantages and disadvantages, including biases that result in misleading results, will help you to draw on practice- and policy-related research in an informed manner. It will help you and your clients to make more informed decisions. Professional codes of ethics obligate us to draw on practice-related research and to involve clients as informed participants. Without this, you will be a pushover for those who try to persuade you to use methods that may not be in the best interests of clients. Drawing on rigorous appraisals of research related to practice and policy decisions and creating tools and training programs designed to facilitate this, are hallmarks of evidence-based practice (EBP).

There are many kinds of research reports including primary studies (such as randomized controlled trials [RCTs] and observational studies such as case reports) and secondary studies (e.g., systematic reviews, practice guidelines, and decision analyses). Research reports differ in their purpose (questions addressed) and the likelihood that the method used can answer the questions. Examples include:

Analytic: Designed to make causal inferences about relationships, for example, between certain risk factors (such as poverty) and an outcome (such as child abuse). Two or more groups are compared.

Descriptive: Designed to provide information about the prevalence or inci-
    dence of a concern, such as "depression," or about the distribution of cer-
    tain characteristics in a group.
Prospective: Subjects are selected and followed up.
Retrospective: Events of interest have already occurred (e.g., children have
    been abused), and data are collected from case records or recall as in case-
    control studies.
Contemporary comparison: Groups that experience a risk factor at the same
    time are compared.

A key question is what works, for what client in what circumstances. Different
kinds of research design control for different kinds of biases. Sackett (1979)
identified thirty-five different kinds of biases in case-control studies.

THE NEED FOR SKEPTICISM

As emphasized in earlier chapters, simply because something appears in print
does not mean that it is accurate including material in the peer-reviewed literature. Continuing revelations of flaws in the peer-reviewed literature, including
systematic reviews (Ioannidis, 2016), require a skeptical view of lists of EBPs and
practice guidelines. Inflated claims of effectiveness or accuracy of diagnostic and
screening tests are common (e.g., Welch, Schwartz, & Woloshin, 2011). Important
differences among subgroups of clients may be ignored. Research flaws are often
hidden as is funding of research by special interests such as pharmaceutical
companies (Lenzer, 2013). And, we should also be skeptical of the skeptics. Just
because someone says a study is flawed does not mean that it is. Learning to critically appraise different kinds of research studies for yourself frees you from misleading influences by others, allowing you to accurately inform your clients about
the potential of given options for attaining hoped-for outcomes. As Chalmers
(2003) notes, "Surveys often reveal wide variations in the type and frequency
of practice and policy interventions, and this evidence of collective uncertainty
should prompt the humility that is a precondition for rigorous evaluation" (p. 22).

MYTHS THAT HINDER CRITICAL APPRAISAL

A variety of myths hinder critical appraisal of research.

It Is Too Difficult for Me to Learn

The ease of identifying important characteristics of rigorous studies is suggested by the fact that six different samples of social workers wanted their physicians to rely on the results of RCTs when making recommendations about treatment methods (Gambrill & Gibbs, 2002). Guidelines have been developed both to report and to critically appraise different kinds of research (e.g., see testingtreatments.org). The Critical Appraisal Skills Program (CASP) in Oxford has been offering workshops on critical appraisal to professionals for years. (See also testingtreatments.org.) Examples of reporting guidelines for different kinds of studies include:

CARE (case studies)
CHERRIES (Internet-based surveys)
CHEERS (economic evaluations)
CONSORT (RCTs; www.consortstatement.org)
COREQ and RATS (qualitative studies)
CReDECI 2 (complex healthcare intervention and evaluation)
PRISMA (research reviews; http://www.prisma-statement.org)
SQUIRE (quality improvement studies)
STaRI (implementation studies)
STROBE (observational studies)
TIDieR (replication of experimental studies)
TREND (nonrandomized studies)
WIDER (implementation of behavior change interventions)

All Research Is Equally Sound

Research designs differ in the questions that can be carefully explored; they differ in the extent to which biases are controlled that may contribute to incorrect conclusions. A variety of errors can be, and are, made in designing and interpreting research. You may conclude that a method was not effective when it is not. A research design may be used that cannot critically test the question raised. Ioannidis (2005, 2016) argues that most research cannot answer questions addressed. Chalmers (2003) defines reliable studies as "those in which the effects of policies and practices are unlikely to be confused with the effects of biases or chance" (p. 28). Less rigorous studies report more positive results than do more rigorous studies.

I Should Trust the Experts

Depending on experts is risky because experts may all be biased in a certain direction (e.g., Rampton & Stauber, 2001). Experts in an area may prepare more biased reviews than those who are well trained in methodological issues but who do not work in that area (Oxman & Guyatt, 1993). Questions to raise about an "expert" are described in Chapter 6. For example, do they use clear language you can understand and describe well-argued alternatives and contradictory evidence to preferred views?

Intuition Is a Better Guide

Myths that hinder critical appraisal include the belief that uninformed intuitive beliefs about what may help people do not result in harmful consequences. But history shows that harm does occur because of reliance on such criteria. Chalmers (2003) points out,

> As Donald Campbell (1969) noted many years ago, selectively designating some interventions as "experiments"—a term loaded with negative associations—ignores the reality that policy makers and practitioners are experimenting on other people most of the time. The problem is that their experiments are usually poorly controlled. Dr. Spock's ill-founded advice [to parents to let babies sleep on their stomachs] would probably not be conceptualized by many people as a poorly controlled experiment, yet that is just what it was. (p. 30)

As a result, many babies died (see also discussion of intuition in Chapters 3).

Only Certain Kinds of Research Must Be Rigorous

Another myth is that only certain kinds of research must be rigorous to avoid biased results. A concern to avoid biases that may result in misleading conclusions is relevant to all research, including qualitative research.

One or Two Studies Can Yield Conclusive Findings

Yet another myth is that one or two well-controlled studies yield the "truth." Such an assumption reflects a justification approach to knowledge in which we assume that certainty is possible.

How the Intervention Works Must Be Known

Ideally, we would understand exactly how an effective intervention works, for example, how it affects physiological reactions. However, often we do not, or we know only in part. Still the intervention may result in valuable outcomes. Fully understanding how it "works" may occur over time. Even very effective interventions do not work for a small percentage of patients or may result in adverse effects.

A Study Must Be Perfect to Be Useful

Another myth is that a study must be perfect to yield valuable findings. All studies are flawed. The question is, are the flaws so great that they preclude any sound conclusions? Examples of valuable experiments that saved many lives can be found in Hochman (2014).

Quantitative Research Is Best/Qualitative Research Is Best

Another myth is that quantitative research is better than qualitative research, or vice versa. It depends on the question. Pursuit of many questions is informed by both kinds of research.

THE QUESTION OF BIAS

Bias is a systematic "leaning to one side" that distorts the accuracy of results. It can be systematic, in which errors are made in a certain direction, or random. Biases hinder fairmindedness to possibilities. Consider Francis Bacon's (1620/1985) four idols of the mind:

> The Idols of the Tribe have their foundation in human nature itself, and in the tribe or race of men. For it is a false assertion that the sense of man is the measure of things . . . and human understanding is like a false mirror, which receiving rays irregularly, distorts and discolors the nature of things by mingling its own nature with it.
> The Idols of the Cave are the idols of the individual man. For everyone (besides the errors common to human nature in general) has a cave or den of his own, which refracts and discolors the light of nature; owing either to his own proper and peculiar nature; or to its education and conversation with others; or to the reading of books, and the authority of those whom he esteems and

admires; or to the differences of impressions, accordingly as they take place in a mind preoccupied and predisposed or in a mind indifferent and settled. . . .

There are also Idols formed by the intercourse and association of men with each other, which I call Idols of the Market-place, on account of the commerce and consort of men there. . . . And therefore the ill and unfit choice of words wonderfully obstructs the understanding. . . . But words plainly force and overrule the understanding, and throw all into confusion, and lead men away into numberless empty controversies and idle fancies.

Lastly, there are Idols, which have immigrated into men's minds from the various dogmas of philosophies and also from wrong laws of demonstration. These I call Idols of the Theater, because in my judgment all the received systems are but so many stage-plays, representing worlds of their own creation after an unreal and scenic fashion. . . .

Biases occur in selection of questions to focus on, the design of research, in how it is interpreted, and in how it is disseminated and used. There are publication biases. For example, studies reporting negative results are less likely to be published than studies reporting positive results. Studies that report a statistically significant effect of intervention are more likely to be published and more likely to be cited by other authors (Sterne, Egger, & Smith, 2001, p. 189). Examples of biases in published research include:

Submission bias (researchers are more strongly motivated to complete, and submit for publication, positive results), publication bias (editors are more likely to publish positive studies), methodological bias (methodological errors such as flawed randomization produce positive biases), abstracting bias (abstracts emphasize positive results), framing bias (relative risk data produce a positive bias). (Gray, 2001b, p. 24; see also Exhibit 5.1)

Allegiance effects (preferences for a certain kind of therapy) contribute to differences in outcome (Dragioti, Dimoliatis, Fountoulakis, & Evangelou, 2015). The steps involved in evidence-based practice are designed to decrease confirmation biases, such as looking only for data that support a preferred theory.

Bias and Validity

Biases may influence both internal and external validity. *Internal validity* refers to the extent to which a design allows you to critically test the causal relationships between an intervention and an outcome. Threats to internal validity can be seen

EXHIBIT 5.1

EXAMPLES OF POTENTIAL BIAS IN RANDOMIZED CONTROLLED TRIALS

During Planning
    Choice of question bias
    Regulator bias (e.g., Institutional Review Board requirements)
    Selection bias

During Conduct
    Ascertainment bias (not blinded)
    Population choice bias (may be overly narrow)
    Intervention choice bias
    Comparison (or control) group choice bias
    Outcome choice bias (relevant and/or just easy to measure)

During Reporting
    Drop-outs not reported
    Protocol violations not reported
    Selective reporting of results
    Data dredging bias

During Dissemination
    Publication bias
    Language bias
    Time lag bias

During Uptake
    Careless reader bias (do not read key sections of a report)
    Rivalry bias (do not like author so ignore article)
    Personal habit bias (over- or underrate study because disagrees with personal beliefs)
    Clinical practice bias (disregard because disagrees with clinical experience)
    Prominent author bias (overrate value of studies by well-known authors)
    Printed word bias (overrate just because it is printed)
    Flashy title bias
    Geographic bias (judgment based on location)
    Favored design bias ("I do not like your design")
    Small trial bias (underestimate value of small trial)
    Vested interest bias (e.g., "Uptake will decrease my profits")
    Belligerence bias (underrate value for sake of being difficult)
    Institution bias ("We don't do things that way").

Source: Based on *Randomized Controlled Trials: Questions, Answers and Musings* (2nd ed.), by R. Jadad and M. R. Enkin, 2007, Malden, MA: Blackwell.

in Exhibit 5.2. Biases include *selection bias* (e.g., biased allocation to experimental and control groups), *performance bias* (unequal provision of care apart from the methods under evaluation), *detection bias* (biased assessment of outcome), and *attrition bias* (biased loss of participants to follow-up). Such biases are rival hypotheses to claims, for example, that a particular method resulted in observed outcomes. *Confounders* may occur—variables that are related to a causal factor and some outcome(s) that are not represented equally in two different groups. "Zero time bias" may occur in which people in a prospective study are enrolled in a way resulting in systematic differences between groups (as in prospective cohort studies). Well-designed RCTs contain more control for different kinds of biases compared to weaker studies, such as quasi-experimental studies. Many results based on a single study cannot be replicated (Baker, 2015).

External validity refers to the extent to which findings in a study can be generalized to other circumstances. Other circumstances may include other kinds of clients (e.g., age), settings (e.g., hospital compared to small agency), services

---

EXHIBIT 5.2
POSSIBLE CONFOUNDING CAUSES (RIVAL EXPLANATIONS) FOR CHANGE

1. *History:* Events that occur between the first and second measurement, in addition to the experimental variables, may account for changes (e.g., clients may get help elsewhere).
2. *Maturation*: Simply growing older or living longer may be responsible, especially when long periods of time are involved.
3. *Instrumentation*: The way something is measured changes (e.g., observers may change how they record).
4. *Testing effects*: Assessment may result in change.
5. *Mortality*: Different loss of people from different groups.
6. *Regression*: Extreme scores tend to return to the mean.
7. *Self-selection bias*: Clients are often self-selected rather than randomly selected. (They may differ in critical ways from the population they are assumed to represent and differ from clients in a comparison group.)
8. *Helper selection bias*: When certain kinds of clients are selected to receive certain methods.
9. *Interaction effects*: Only certain clients may benefit from certain services; others may even be harmed.

Source: Based on *Experimental and Quasi-Experimental Designs for Research*, by D. T. Campbell and J. C. Stanley, 1963, Chicago, IL: Rand McNally.

offered (e.g., timing, number of sessions, other concurrent services), kinds of outcomes reviewed, and length of follow-up. To what extent can you generalize the causal relationship found in a study to different times, places, and people and different operational definitions of interventions and outcomes? Cartwright and Hardie (2012) discuss complications that may arise in assuming an intervention tested with success in one setting "will work" in another. Farrington (2003) uses the term *descriptive validity* to refer to the adequacy of the presentation of key features of an evaluation in a research report.

The literature on experimenter and subject biases highlights the importance of research that controls for these. For example, we tend to give socially desirable responses—to present ourselves in a good light. Knowing a hypothesis creates a tendency to encourage the very responses that we are investigating. Experimenter effects are not necessarily intentional; even when we do not intend to skew results in a certain way, this may occur. Experimenter biases influence results in a number of ways. If the experimenters know the group a subject is in, they may change their behavior, for example, subtly leading the person in a certain direction. This is why it is vital in RCTs for raters of outcome to be blind—unaware of the group to which a person is assigned.

QUESTIONS TO ASK ABOUT ALL RESEARCH

Certain questions are important to raise across research methods because of the potential for flaws that may result in misleading conclusions. These include concerns about the size and source of samples used, whether there is a comparison group, the accuracy and validity of measures used, and the appropriateness of data analysis. Answers to these characteristics will shed light both on the internal and external validity of a study. External validity concerns the extent to which findings can be accurately generalized to other clients and situations. Methodological quality criteria include statistical conclusion validity, internal validity, construct validity, and external validity. The term *validity* refers to the accuracy of assumptions in relation to causes and effects. Classic criteria for assuming a causal relationship include (1) the cause precedes the effect, (2) the cause is related to the effect, and (3) other plausible alternatives of the effect can be excluded (Mill, 1911). Too often the limitations of studies are not mentioned, are glossed over, or are minimized. Flaws in traditional methods of knowledge dissemination such as peer-reviewed journals were one of the reasons for the origins of evidence-based practice (see Chapter 2). Poor reporting of research does not necessarily mean that it was poorly constructed; it may only be poorly reported.

The concept of levels of evidence is often used on the assumption that different kinds of research related to a certain kind of question offer different degrees of control regarding potential biases that may limit conclusions that can be drawn. Here is one suggested hierarchy regarding levels of evidence for studies of effectiveness:

1. Systematic review of RCTs
2. Experimental studies (e.g., RCT with concealed allocation)
3. Quasi-experimental studies (e.g., experimental study without randomization)
4. Controlled observational studies
   a. Cohort studies
   b. Case control studies
5. Observational studies without control groups
6. Expert opinion, for example, based on consensus

Such hierarchies can be misleading in obscuring the limitations of even well-designed RCTs and related systematic reviews, for example in generalizing use to other individuals/settings (Cartwright & Hardie, 2012). And, many questions are informed by more than one kind or research. Informative inquiry often requires a variety of types of research, and different questions require different types of exploration.

Is the Research Question Clear?

Do the authors clearly describe their research question? Examples of clear questions are: "What factors contribute to the reabuse of children returned to their biological parents?" or "Do substance abuse programs to which parents are referred help them to decrease alcohol consumption compared to no intervention?" Unclear questions do not allow for clear tests at the point of data analysis—set in advance so all are clear on key concerns.

What Kind of Question Is It?

Does the article concern the effectiveness of a practice method? Is it an assessment question? Does it describe a new risk assessment measure for depression in the elderly?

Is It Relevant to My Clients?

If you knew the answer, could you and your clients make more informed decisions? Does it concern outcomes of interest to your clients? Have any key outcomes been omitted? Is the setting similar to your practice setting? Are the clients similar?

Does the Research Method Used Match the Question Raised?

Can the research method used address the question? Different questions require different research methods. That is why discussing whether qualitative or quantitative research is best is unproductive—it depends on the question. Oxman and Guyatt (1993) suggest a scale ranging from 1 (*not at all*) to 6 (*ideal*) in relation to the potential that a research method can critically test a question.

Is There a Comparison Group?

Critically testing certain kinds of questions requires a comparison. A hallmark of RCTs is distributing clients to two or more different conditions. An intervention group (cognitive behavior therapy for depression) may be compared to a no-treatment group or to a comparison group (interpersonal therapy). Only if we have a comparison can we identify which might be better. In a pre–post test, there is no comparison with a group receiving no service or a different service. Thus, there could be a variety of other reasons for any changes seen (see Exhibit 5.2)

Is the Study Design Rigorous?

The general research method may be appropriate but be carried out in an unrigorous manner that allows the play of many biases. (See other questions in this section.)

What Is the Sample Size and Source?

Most research involves a sample that is assumed to be characteristic of the population from which it is drawn. Selection biases are one kind of bias related to how subjects were chosen. Does the sample used offer an opportunity to answer questions raised? (Some research deals with an entire population such as all graduates of the University of California at Berkeley's social work master's degree program in the year 2017.) A key question is "Can we accurately generalize from a sample to the population from which it is drawn or from one population to another

(other year)?" Does the sample represent the population to which generalizations will be made? Questions here include:

- Is the sample selection process clearly described?
- How was the sample selected?
- From what population was it selected?
- Is it representative of the population?
- Were subjects lost in follow-up?

The answers to these questions provide clues about biases that may limit the potential of a study to answer questions posed. For example, small samples drawn by convenience, rather than by random selection in which each individual has an equal chance of selection, may not provide information that reflects characteristics of the population of interest. Researchers may not clearly describe the source of their sample. CONSORT guidelines include a flow chart to describe samples used in RCTs (www.consort-statement.org). Readers can determine how many people were excluded at different points and for what reasons; they can see for themselves possible sources of bias in the final sample on which conclusions are based.

Sample size and the critical testing of hypotheses are closely related. That is, some studies do not find effects not because there are no effects to be found, but because the sample does not have the power to critically test whether there is an association or not. As Farrington (2003) notes, "A statistically significant result could indicate a large effect in a small sample or a small effect in a large sample" (p. 52). Use of a very large sample may yield many significant differences that may not be illuminating. Clear description of the source of samples is important both in qualitative and quantitative research.

Are Measures Used Reliable and Valid?

Measures of certain concepts, such as self-efficacy and substance abuse, are used in research. Do they measure what they purport to measure—are they valid? Are measures relevant to your clients? The validity of measures is of concern in all research. *Reliability* refers to the consistency of results provided by the same person at different times (test–retest reliability or stability), by two raters of the same events at the same time (interrater reliability), or by parallel forms or split halves of a measure (internal consistency or homogeneity). *Validity* refers to the extent to which a measure reflects what it is designed to measure. There are many different kinds. *Predictive validity* refers to the extent to which a measure accurately predicts behavior at a later time. For example, how accurately does a measure of suicidal potential predict suicide attempts? *Concurrent validity* refers to the extent to which a measure correlates with a valid measure gathered at the same time. For example, do responses on a questionnaire concerning social behavior correspond to behavior in real-life settings? The term *criterion validity* is used to refer to predictive and concurrent validity. *Content validity* refers to the degree to which a measure adequately samples the domain being assessed. For example, does an inventory used to assess parenting skills include an adequate sample of such skills? *Face validity* refers to the extent to which items included on a measure make sense "on the face of it." Given the intent of the instrument, would you expect the included items to be there? For example, drinking behavior has face validity as an outcome measure for decreasing alcohol use.

   Construct validity refers to the degree to which a measure successfully measures a theoretical construct—the degree to which results correspond to assumptions about the measure. For example, a finding that depressed people report more negative thoughts compared with nondepressed people adds an increment of construct validity to a measure designed to tap such thoughts. Different methods of assessing a construct (e.g., direct observation, self-report) should yield similar results. Do scores on a measure correlate in predicted ways with other measures? They should have positive correlations with other measures of the same construct (*convergent validity*) and negative correlations with measures that tap opposite constructs (*divergent validity*). Reliability places an upward boundary on validity; a measure cannot be valid if it is not reliable (cannot be consistently assessed). A measure may be reliable but invalid, perhaps because of shared biases among raters. Research using one kind of data (self-report) may present an inaccurate picture. For example, self-reports of parents regarding their children's behavior may not match reports based on observation of parent–child interaction.

Did Authors Report Attrition (Drop-Out Rates)?

Some subjects may drop out over the course of a study. This number should be reported and is reflected in "intention-to-treat" analysis. This is "an analysis of a study where participants are analyzed according to the group to which they were initially allocated. This is regardless of whether or not they dropped out, fully complied with the treatment, or crossed over and received the other treatment. It protects against attrition bias" (Center for Research and Dissemination, University of York, April 4, 2004).

Was There Any Follow-Up—If So, How Long?

An intervention may be effective in the short term but not in the long term. How long were subjects followed up?

Are Procedures Clearly Described?

Are interventions clearly described? If not, it will not be possible to replicate them. Only if methods are clearly described can readers determine whether methods used were offered in an optimal manner.

Are the Data Analyses Sound?

Statistics are often used to explore whether there is a relationship between two or more variables. Researchers ask, what is the probability of finding an association by chance in samples of different sizes; they estimate the probability of getting a result in a sample of a certain size. The null hypothesis (the assumption that there is no difference between two variables we think are associated or two groups that we think will differ) is tested. The term *statistical significance* refers to whether a test falls *at or* below certain *p* value. Statistical testing of this nature is controversial (e.g., Colquhoun, 2014; Oakes, 1986; Penston, 2010). "Gigerenzer (2018) argues that" good scientific practice has been replaced by an ill-advised statistical ritual" (p. 199). The inference from sample to population came to be considered the sine qua non of good research, and statistical significance came to be considered the means of distinguishing between true cause and mere chance. Common scientific standards such as minimizing measurement error, conducting double-blind experiments, replicating experiments, providing detailed descriptive statistics, and formulating bold hypothesis in the first place were pushed into the background" (pp. 200–201). Complex statistical methods will not correct major flaws in the design or conduct of a study. This is why care in planning studies is so important. Clinical significance may be ignored in promoting statistical significance.

Different statistical tests entail different assumptions about the underlying distribution of variables. A test may be used that requires interval data (reflecting continuous data in which points are separated by equal intervals) for ordinal data (in which differences are rank ordered but you do not have any idea how much difference there is between points)—it is like using a rubber ruler. Continuous variables may be treated as dichotomous. Consider drinking. One could have no drinks, one drink, or many drinks per day. This may be treated as a binary variable (categorically defined); either one is or is not an alcoholic; a continuous variable is transformed into a binary one. Data are lost in changing a continuous variable to a dichotomous one—individual variations are omitted. Inappropriate use of statistical tests include fishing (running scores of statistical tests to see if any would be significant). You may read an article that uses many different variables with a large sample in which authors claim that 15 significant differences were found. The question is: How many correlations were run? A certain percentage would be significant by chance. Has judgement about the quality of research been replaced with quantitative surrogates (Gigerenzer, 2018)?

Are Claims Accurate?

Problems in any of the previously described characteristics, including samples and measures used, may not allow clear conclusions. Inflated claims are common. That is why is it important to draw on high-quality systematic reviews and to know how to locate and critically appraise research findings for yourself. For example pre–post tests cannot tell us whether the intervention was responsible for the results because there is no comparison group. Yet the author may say, "Our results show that X was effective." This is a misleading claim. Claims that a practice or policy used in one location can be successfully used in others are often inaccurate (Cartwright & Hardie, 2012). Critical thinking skills, knowledge, and values are vital to critical appraisal of claims (Gambrill, 2012a, 2012b).

Are Findings Clinically Important?

Will research findings from a study help you to help your clients? For example, how many clients would have to receive a service for one to be helped? What is the number needed to treat (NNT)? People differ in their views about when there is "enough evidence" to recommend use of service or to recommend that a program not be used because it is harmful. What is the number needed to harm?

Who Sponsored the Study?

Special interests may bias results. Do authors have any conflicts of interest that may bias conclusions (Cosgrove, Bursztajn, Krimsky, Anaya, & Walter, 2009; Lexchin, 2012). Sponsorship of research by a company with vested interest in a product, such as a pharmaceutical company or child welfare training program offered to all staff in a state, may encourage biased material (Lundh, Lexchin, Mintzes, Schroll, & Bero, 2017).

QUESTIONS ABOUT EFFECTIVENESS AND PREVENTION

How can we discover if a practice or policy does more good than harm? An example of an effectiveness question is:

- In youth with antisocial behavior, is group cognitive behavioral training or individual counseling more effective in decreasing such behaviors and increasing positive behaviors?

A key concern with effectiveness questions is: Is there a comparison group that allows us to determine whether different results would be attained with different groups?

Randomized Controlled Trials

In experimental designs, such as randomized controlled clinical trials, there is a comparison between different groups, which may be an experimental group that receives a special treatment and a control group in which there is no special treatment. Or, a comparison group receiving a different service may be used. Two different services may be compared. Factorial experimental designs explore the effects of more than one independent variable. Interaction effects are often of interest here, for example, between personality, peer rejection of youth, and school environment. Random distribution of subjects to different groups using an effective randomization procedure is a key feature of rigorous experimental designs. Here are questions to raise:

- How were subjects selected?
- Were subjects properly randomized into groups using concealed assignment?
- Are subjects and their contexts similar to my clients?
- Are all subjects who entered the trial accounted for at its conclusion?
- Was everyone involved in the study (subjects and investigators) "blind" to treatment?
- Were the intervention and control groups similar at the start of the trial?
- Were groups treated equally (aside from the experimental intervention)?
- Are the results clinically as well as statistically significant? Are outcome measures clinically important?
- Were other factors present that might have affected the outcome?
- Are benefits worth potential harms and costs?

Without a comparison group (e.g., a group that did not receive an intervention), we do not know what would have happened in the absence of intervention. This is a key problem in pre–post studies. Baer (1982) argues that marker variable research (e.g., correlational research) is often continued when it is time to conduct more rigorous experimental tests, such as RCTs, where possible and relevant. Were subjects randomly selected? Were they randomly distributed to different groups (see CONSORT guidelines)? If so, how? Some methods of random distribution do not guard against biases that may skew the results. Blinding (single, double, triple, or more) may be needed to decrease bias.

> Blinding is used to keep the participants, investigators and outcome assessors ignorant about which interventions participants are receiving during a study. In single blind studies only the participants are blind to their group allocations, while in double-blind studies both the participants and investigators are blind. Blinding of outcome assessment can often be done even when blinding of participants and caregivers cannot. Blinding is used to protect against performance and detection bias. It may also contribute to adequate allocation concealment. However, the success of blinding procedures is infrequently checked and it may be overestimated. (Center for Research and Dissemination, University of York, April 4, 2004)

Farrington (2003) suggests that the SMS is the most influential methodological quality scale in criminology. This scale was used to rate prevention programs using 10 criteria on a scale from zero to 5: (1) adequacy of sampling, (2) adequacy of sample size, (3) pretreatment measures of outcome, (4) adequacy of comparison groups, (5) controls for prior group differences, (6) adequacy of measurement of variables, (7) attrition, (8) post-intervention measurement, (9) adequacy of statistical analyses, and (10) testing of alternative explanations.

It is difficult to carry out experiments in applied setting. However, many investigators do manage to carry out studies in real-life settings that provide rigorous tests of claims. Joan McCord (1978) investigated the effectiveness of special services to youth designed to prevent delinquency. Youth were randomly distributed to the usual services or to a special group receiving a variety of services. The program included youth with good as well as bad prognoses. The independent variable was the service program. The dependent variable was the outcome of interest. The program lasted five and one-half years, when the boys were between 10.5 and 16 years of age. These two groups were tracked over 30 years. Among the 253 matched pairs assessed for follow-up, 125 of the treatment boys had been sent to summer camp, and 128 were not. None of the treatment approaches showed measurable benefits, and some, such as repeated placement in summer camps, resulted in harm." Had there been no control group, evaluators might have concluded that the program was beneficial because so many of the treatment boys were better adjusted than anticipated. Or, because two thirds reported beneficial effects for themselves, evaluators might have considered the program effective. But these judgments would have been contrary to objective evidence that the program resulted in adverse outcomes for many participants. The Cambridge-Somerville Youth Study was effective. The intervention had lasting effects. The design showed that social interventions can have long-term (negative) effects". (McCord, 2003, pp. 22–23)

Effect size is one statistic used to describe the effects of an intervention in an experimental study. This indicates the strength of a relationship between, or among, two or more variables. Effect sizes range from zero to 1. There are many kinds. Cohen's d standardized differences between means is often used. An effect size of zero means there is no difference. An effect size above zero indicates a positive effect and a negative effect size indicates a negative effect. Larger effect sizes indicate stronger relationships. Cohen (1977) suggests that small effect sizes are about 0.2, medium ones about 0.5, and larger effect sizes about 0.8 or greater. Effect sizes should be reported. These can be calculated in different ways, all of which are designed to describe the relationship between the effect found in the intervention group and the effect found in a comparison group. One is to divide the mean difference between the experimental and control groups by the standard deviation of the control or alternative treatment group. The narrower the confidence interval, the stronger the effect size.

What may be true of a group may not be true of a given individual. Thus, aggregate studies must be interpreted with caution in relation to generalizing to different individuals and different settings. Otherwise you may make the "ecological fallacy"—assume that what is true of a group is true of an individual.

In quasi-experimental studies, allocation of participants to different groups is arranged by the researcher but there is no genuine randomization and allocation concealment, thus selection biases are of concern as well as a number of other biases depending on the design. Pre–post studies are one variety; they do not include a comparison group so we cannot determine causation. Time series designs are one kind of quasi-experimental study.

Observational Studies

In observational studies, assignment of subjects to different groups is not under the control of the investigator. Different groups are self-selected or are "natural experiments" (Campbell, 1969). Subjects are not randomly assigned to different services or exposed to different kinds of risks. Such exposure or intervention occurs by choice or circumstance. Examples include exposure to lead in houses and to family violence. Those who are exposed and those who are not exposed may differ in important ways, thus introducing selection biases.

> An observational study concerns treatments, interventions, or policies and the effects they cause and in this respect it resembles an experiment. A study without a treatment is neither an experiment nor an observational study. Most public opinion polls, most forecasting efforts, most studies of fairness and discrimination, and many other important empirical studies are neither experiments nor observational studies. (Rosenbaum, 2002, pp. 1–2)

Experimental studies may be impossible to conduct because of ethical or logistic reasons. They may not be unnecessary. They may be inappropriate, or inadequate. Important roles for observational methods suggested by Black (1994) include:

1. Some interventions have such a large impact that observational data are sufficient to show it.
2. Infrequent adverse outcomes would be detected only by RCTs so large that they are rarely conducted. Observational methods may be the only alternative.
3. Observational data provide a means of assessing the long-term outcome of interventions beyond the time-scale of many trials.
4. Many clinicians will be opposed to a RCT; observational approaches can be used to demonstrate clinical uncertainty and encourage a trial.
5. Some important aspects of care cannot be investigated in a RCT for practical and ethical reasons. (Adapted from Black, 1994)

Observational studies include (1) cohort studies, (2) case control studies, (3) pre–post studies, and (4) case series. This order reflects the level of evidence provided regarding effectiveness, although there are exceptions (e.g., see discussion of case control studies). Observational studies may be descriptive or analytical. Analytical studies include cohort and case control studies.

Observational studies differ in their *ecological validity*, that is, the extent to which the study is carried out in contexts that are similar or identical to the everyday life experiences of those involved. A variety of strategies are used to detect hidden biases in observational studies, such as inclusion of a number of control groups to try to identify hidden covariates (characteristics that influence the results other than the one focused on). And, as Rosenbaum (2002) suggests, "even when it is not possible to remove bias through adjustment or detect bias through careful design, it is nonetheless possible to give quantitative expression to the magnitude of uncertainties about bias, a technique called *sensitivity analysis*" (p. 11).

Cohort Studies

In cohort studies, a group of individuals that has experienced a certain situation (e.g., witnessed domestic violence) is compared with another group which has not been so exposed. Both groups are followed up at a later time to determine the association between exposure and an outcome of interest (such as subsequent abuse of one's own children). Cohort studies are prospective and analytical. Because of lack of random assignment, they are prone to a number of biases, such as lack of control over risk assignment and uneven loss to follow-up. Cohort studies are often used to describe different kinds of risk. Questions to ask about cohort studies include (see Gray, 2001a):

- Is there sufficient description of the groups (how they were recruited) and the distribution of prognostic factors?
- Are the groups assembled at a similar point for example in relation to disorder progression? (Were decisions made that could have included or excluded more severe cases?)
- Is the intervention reliably ascertained?
- Were the groups comparable on all important confounding factors?
- Was there adequate adjustment for the effects of these confounding variables?
- Were measures used valid?
- Was a dose-response relationship between intervention and outcome demonstrated?
- Was outcome assessment blind to exposure status?
- Was the presence of co-occurring disorders considered?
- Was follow-up long enough for the outcomes to occur?
- What proportion of the cohort was followed-up?
- Were drop-out rates and related reasons similar across intervention and unexposed groups? (CRD, University of York, Phase 5, p. 11, 2004)

Gray (2001a) notes that "the main abuse of a cohort study is to assess the effectiveness of a particular intervention when a more appropriate method would be an RCT" (p. 150).

Case Control (Case-Referent) Studies

In a retrospective case control study, we start with people who have a particular characteristic (a certain illness) and look back in time in relation to certain outcomes. Samples may be small in such studies yet suggest strong relationships. Consider the case-referent study reporting a relationship between the drug diethylstilbestrol (DES) given to pregnant women and vaginal cancer. Herbst, Ulfelder, and Poskanzer (1971) included 8 women who had vaginal cancer and 32 who did not in relation to use of DES during pregnancy. Seven had taken DES in the group with vaginal cancer, and none had taken it in the referent group. This study illustrates the value of case-referent studies regarding rare conditions or for risk factors that have long development phases. Criteria for reviewing case control studies are suggested as follows:

- Is the case definition explicit?
- Has the illness state of clients been reliably assessed and validated?
- Were the controls randomly selected from the source of population of the cases?
- How comparable are the cases and controls with respect to potential confounding factors?
- Were interventions and other exposures assessed in the same way for cases and controls?
- How was the response rate defined?
- Were the nonresponse rates and reasons for nonresponse the same in both groups?
- Is it possible that overmatching has occurred in that cases and controls were matched on factors related to exposure?
- Was an appropriate statistical analysis used (matched or unmatched)? (CRD, University of York, Phase 5, p. 11, 2004)

Cross-Sectional Study

In a cross-sectional study, a snapshot is taken of people at a particular time. Such studies may be used to describe the frequency or rate of a behavior or to try to identify the relationship between one or more factors and a problem, such as child abuse. Unfortunately, such research does not show which came first.

Pre–Post Study (Before and After)

Responses are compared before and after some intervention. Such designs do not provide information about the causal relationship between an intervention and an outcome unless perhaps the change is very large and is replicated. They do provide information about change.

Case-Series Study

Another kind of study consists of describing characteristics of a series of case examples. Because of the lack of comparison we cannot make assumptions about causes. Questions for reviewing case-series studies include:

- Is the study based on a representative sample selected from a relevant population?
- Are criteria for inclusion explicit?
- Did all individuals enter the study at a similar point in their progression of the problem?
- Was follow-up long enough for important events to occur?
- Were outcomes assessed using objective criteria or was blinding used?
- If comparisons of sub-series are being made, were there sufficient description of the series and the distribution of prognostic factors? (CRD, University of York, Phase 5, p. 11, 2004)

A case report is essentially an anecdotal report—a description of a single case. Such reports differ greatly in rigor.

N of 1 Studies

Here data are collected regarding an individual client over time allowing comparisons of baseline levels of concerns to intervention levels (e.g., Lillie et al., 2011). A variety of experimental designs may be used (Barlow, Nock, & Hersen, 2009). Questions Guyatt and Rennie (2002) suggest for deciding on the feasibility of such a study include "1) Is the client eager to collaborate? 2) Does the program have a rapid onset and offset? 3) Is an optimal duration of service feasible? 4) What important targets of service should be measured? And 5) What dictates the end?" (p. 278).

Questions about Harm

Just as we can ask about NNT, we can ask about number needed to harm (NNH). That is, how many people would have to receive a service for one to be harmed? Do studies offer information about possible harms of interventions, including assessment and diagnostic measures? (Examples of harmful interventions include Scared Straight program for juveniles [e.g., Petrosino, Turpin-Petrosino, Hollis-Peel, & Lavenberg, 2013] and brief psychological debriefing [Rose, Bisson, Churchill, & Wessely, 2002]).

SYSTEMATIC REVIEWS AND META-ANALYSES

In systematic reviews there is a search for all evidence related to a specific question (e.g., Littell, Corcoran, & Pillai, 2008). For example, Cochrane review groups search for published and unpublished research reports related to a specific question. Authors describe how they searched, where they searched, what criteria they used to appraise the quality of studies, and rigorous criteria are used to review studies. Such reviews "are designed to minimize the likelihood that the effects of interventions will be confused with the effects of biases and chance" (Chalmers, 2003, p. 22). As with all research, reviews may be rigorous or flawed. There are vast differences between haphazard (incomplete, uncritical) and rigorous, exhaustive reviews. Overlooking important methodological concern encourages inflated claims of effectiveness (Ioannidis, 2016). Criteria for assessing the rigor of reviews include (Oxman & Guyatt, 1993, p. 128):

- Did the review address a clear question?
- Were the search methods reported?
- Was the search comprehensive?
- Were inclusion criteria reported?
- Were criteria for inclusion appropriate?
- Was selection bias avoided?
- Were validity criteria reported?
- Was validity assessed appropriately?
- Do the conclusions match the data reported?
- Can the results be applied to my clients?
- Were all important outcomes considered?
- Are the benefits worth the harms and costs? (See PRISMA guidelines for more detail: www.prisma-statement.org.)

Little if any of the above is given in incomplete reviews. Without this information, readers cannot make an informed estimate concerning the evidentiary status of claims. Farrington (2003) suggests five methodological criteria: (1) *internal validity*—demonstrating that the intervention caused an effect on the outcome; (2) *descriptive validity*—without information about key features of research it is hard to include the results in a systematic review; (3) *statistical conclusion validity*; (4) *construct validity*; and (5) *external validity*. He suggests that these occur in order of importance, at least concerning systematic reviews of impact evaluations.

Critical appraisal of a study takes a great deal of time. That is probably why it is often not done. The abstract and discussion sections of reports become the least important, and the method and results sections are of key concern. Randomization procedures in RCTs are carefully reviewed. Measures used are critically appraised regarding their reliability and validity. Results are carefully reviewed, including the validity of outcome measures and the extent to which descriptions in the text match data presented in tables and figures. Statistical methods used are reviewed for their appropriateness. And, conclusions are appraised. Are they warranted? For example, an outcome measure of fewer hospital days may be a result of an administrative decision not to hospitalize clients in one group (Gomory, 2001). Conceptual critique is also important. For example, the influence of moderating variables may have been glossed over, for example, personal problems may be assumed to have a biomedical cause when little or no evidence exists for such an assumption. Counterevidence to assumptions may be available but not be mentioned. Reviews that claim to be systematic may not be rigorous in their methods of review. In a meta-analysis, a statistical summary is offered. Questions here include: Were the methods used to combine studies reported? Were the findings combined appropriately? Does it list, in tabular form, indices of effect size? Examples of criticisms of meta-analyses include retrievability bias, overlooking heterogeneity of outcomes and the potential contributions of moderating variables, inclusion of poorly designed studies that contain many sources of bias, and inclusion of multiple dependent variables (outcomes) with different effect sizes, perhaps due to variables, such as different laboratories (e.g., Littell, Corcoran, & Pillai, 2008).

A Forest Plot is a display in graph form of results from studies exploring the same question. The solid line running down the center indicates the point where there is no difference between treatment and control groups. Each horizontal line represents one trial and the length of each line shows the confidence interval (CI). The smaller this is, the less the variability in results in a study. The larger it is, the greater the variability in a study. If a CI crosses the vertical line, the range of estimated effects of intervention includes the possibility both of getting better and of getting worse. Generally, if the whole CI is on the left of the line, the intervention improves the situation, and if it is on the right of the line, it makes the situation worse. The CI also shows the precision of the estimate. The shorter the length of the CI, the more precise the estimate is. This visual description allows you to quickly see how many studies fall to the left or to the right of the midline.

A variety of other kinds of reviews are available (Grant & Booth, 2009) including realist reviews that focus on explanation in addition to outcomes (Apollonio, Wolfe, & Bero, 2016) and scoping reviews in which there is an interest in mapping key concepts related to a research area and sources and types of available evidence. Such a review may be conducted to determine whether a systematic review would be of value (Arksey & O'Malley, 2005).

QUESTIONS ABOUT CAUSES

Causality is of great interest in all helping professions. Consider Mindy, a school social worker who was asked by a teacher to help her with a second-grade student Robert whom she described as out of control; he shouts out in class and tears up his work. A well-formed question might be: "In elementary school children who are a classroom management problem, what are common causes?" We could draw on a variety of theories and assessment methods to try to identify related factors. Each theory may appeal to different factors. We could ask teachers what they think. We could compare this with results of a descriptive and functional analysis of behavior (Cipani & Schock, 2011). The latter form of investigation may show that being under- or overchallenged contributes to disruptive behavior in a classroom (problems in curriculum design) and/or that classroom contingencies maintain such behavior (desired behaviors are ignored, and inappropriate behaviors are followed by attention). We could intervene based on observational data suggesting that deficits in curricular design are responsible for concerning behaviors. If this is effective as shown by collection of $N-1$ data over time (six months), does this show we have identified the cause?

Causes differ in many ways including whether they are fundamental, whether they hold only if other things are equal, and whether they are deterministic or probabilistic (Cartwright & Hardie, 2012). Causality may be (incorrectly) assumed based on mere association. Understanding causes is integral to designing effective interventions. However, rarely is causality fully known and such knowledge may not be necessary for effective intervention. The influence of individual variations has long been noted (e.g., Williams, 1956). Cartwright and Hardie (2012) describe the many ways in which causality can differ in different situations and the implications of this for assuming effectiveness of an intervention tested with success in one setting with other individuals and in other contexts. (See also Deaton & Cartwright, 2016). They ask, 'What else has to be present for a practice or policy to work?" and argue that complexities have been greatly underestimated in mandating or recommending use of an intervention or policy with other individuals and in other settings. The less we understand causal variations and their influences, the less likely we are to make accurate generalizations about external validity (can we use this intervention in other settings with other individuals?). This highlights the importance of having a sound argument for evidence claims (see Chapter 7).

Surveys

Surveys are used for many purposes including describing the prevalence of certain conditions (such as depression) to gather people's views about quality of care and services and to try to identify causes using complex statistical tools, such as regression analysis. The purpose of correlational research is to investigate the relationship between two or more variables using statistical analysis. Pearson product moment correlation coefficients are typically used as the statistic to represent the degree of association. They range from –1 to + 1, both indicating a perfect correlation. For example, we may ask, "What is the relationship between college grade-point average (GPA), scores on the Graduate Record Examination (GRE), and performance in graduate school?" Correlational designs differ in their ecological validity (the extent to which findings can be generalized to other groups). Associations found do not necessarily reflect causal relationships. There may be some other variable that is responsible for the association. There could even be a reverse association. Gray (2001a) suggests the following questions to critically appraise a survey:

- How was the population surveyed chosen? Was it the whole population or a sample?
- If a sample, how was the sample chosen? Was it a random sample or was it stratified to include all sectors of the population?
- Was a valid questionnaire used? If interviewers were used, did the authors mention the possibility of different results from different interviewers?
- What procedures were used to verify the data?
- Were the conclusions drawn all based on the data or did those carrying out the survey infer conclusions? Inference is acceptable, but it must be clearly distinguished from results derived solely from the data. (p. 153)

QUESTIONS ABOUT PREVALENCE
AND INCIDENCE (FREQUENCY AND RATE)

Making informed decisions may require accurate information regarding the incidence and prevalence of a concern. Prevalence refers to the number of instances of an illness or other characteristic in a population at a given time. Incidence refers to the number of new events in a given population in a given time. Epidemiology is the study of the distribution and determinants of health-related states or events in specific populations and the application of this study to control of health problems (Porta, 2014).

Let us say that a parent seeks help because she is worried about her child being abducted by a stranger. She has read a report in the newspaper saying that stranger abduction is common and parents should be careful. Because of this, she rarely allows her children to go out unaccompanied. Her husband believes that his wife is overconcerned and, because of this, depriving her child of freedom and opportunities to learn and grow. As with other decisions, we can translate information needs into well-formed questions that allow us to search for related literature. The following question may guide a search: "In suburban neighborhoods, what is the incidence and prevalence of stranger abduction of young children?" Other relevant questions include: "For young children, are there effective preventative steps that can be taken to decrease stranger abduction?" and "Under what circumstances does stranger abduction occur?" Ecological studies are descriptive in nature and use data collected for a variety of purposes, including administrative needs. An example is comparison of the different rates of child abuse in different communities that have different levels of social support. Both cohort studies and cross-sectional studies may be used to gather information about frequency or rate.

QUESTIONS REGARDING EXPERIENCES: QUALITATIVE RESEARCH

Examples of questions that arise here include:

- Among child welfare staff, what are current sources of strain and perceived causes?
- In elderly clients, entering a nursing home, what are feelings and thoughts?

Qualitative research may be of many different kinds, including case studies, narrative analyses, focus groups, and participant observation. The concern in ethnographic research is to describe people's experiences as they see them. Case studies consist of detailed descriptions of individuals, groups, organizations, or neighborhoods. They differ in the method used to select the sample and thus how representative they may be to the larger population. Observational data differ in rigor, ranging from careful systematic observation including reliability checks reflecting degree of agreement between raters to unsystematic, anecdotal observation. Anecdotal research may be of value, for example, in suggesting more rigorous research (Aronson, 2003). As Becker (1996) notes, misinterpretations of people's experience and meanings are common; we may be wrong when we guess at what could be observed directly. Ethnographic research differs vastly from surveys. Consider the question "What kinds of risks (if any) do street addicts take?" In their article describing HIV risk among homeless heroin addicts in San Francisco, Bourgois, Lettiere, and Quesada (2003) argue that ethnographic methods in which people spend time on the street, with addicts, provide more accurate information than does information gathered through a survey. "Virtually all our network members have told us that they distort their risky behavior on questionnaires" (p. 270).

Qualitative research may have intervention implications. "The challenge is not merely to access, document and explain the dynamics of every day suffering; but also to translate it into meaningful interventions that do not unconsciously reproduce structures of inequality and discourses of subordination" (Bourgois et al., 2003, p. 272). The question is: "What kind of research will provide the most accurate answer to questions of interest?" Campbell (1996) agrees with Becker about overstretching quantitative research. "Quantitative data often represents low-cost, mass-produced research and is often wrong. The others' meanings as inferred from questionnaire averages are overly determined by the ethnocentric subjectivity of the researcher" (p. 161).

As Campbell (1996) notes, "questionnaires, fixed interviews, and experimental designs limit the dimensions of inquiry in advance. Often this precludes learning information that would have discredited the validity of the quantitative results and the hypotheses that guided the research" (p. 162). Campbell considers the "most ubiquitous source of error in efforts to know the other" to be "to interpret as a cultural difference what is in reality a failure of communication. . . ." (p. 165). A checklist for critically appraising a qualitative research paper follows (see other sources for additional descriptions of qualitative research methods):

1. Did the article describe an important clinical problem examined via a clearly formulated question?
2. Was a qualitative approach appropriate?

3. How were (a) the setting and (b) the participants selected?

4. What was the researcher's perspective, and has this been taken into account?

5. What methods did the researcher use for collecting data—and are these described in enough detail?

6. What methods did the researcher use to analyze the data—and what quality control measures were implemented?

7. Are the results [believable], and, if so, are they clinically important?

8. What conclusions were drawn, and are they warranted by the results?

9. Are the findings of the study transferable to other clinical settings? (Adapted from Greenhalgh, 2010, p. 227)

QUESTIONS ABOUT DIAGNOSIS AND SCREENING

Tests are used for many purposes, such as to make a diagnosis (to rule a condition or characteristic in or out). Diagnostic tests are used on symptomatic clients; screening tests are used on asymptomatic clients. Using a diagnostic test to screen a population will result in many false positives. Failure to critically appraise related research may result in imposing inaccurate labels on clients, scaring people about irrelevant risks, and overlooking important risks or protecting factors. Tests may be used to predict future behavior. They should be used to revise subjective estimates, that is, to change a decision. If there is nothing you would do differently, why have a test? Clinicians tend to overestimate the predictive accuracy of test results. One cause of this error is ignoring base rate data. The predictive accuracy of a test depends on the initial risk of a condition in the person receiving the test. The probability that a client with a positive (or negative) test result for dementia actually has dementia depends on the prevalence of dementia in the population from which the client was selected—that is, on the pretest probability that a client has dementia. Because there is little appreciation of this point, predictive accuracy often is overestimated.

Critically Appraising Reports of Diagnostic Accuracy

Like investigations of the effectiveness of an intervention method, a variety of biases as well as incomplete reporting of how a test was developed and tested can lead to problems in interpreting accuracy. Classification is involved in testing— placing people into categories. Surprisingly few reference standards are clear for making unequivocal classifications. The best type of evidence in relation to how test results relate to benefits of treatment is an RCT. If RCTs are not available, cohort studies may provide information. Guidelines provided in STARD (www.stard-statement.org) include a checklist and flow chart that can be used to estimate bias in a diagnostic study and to judge the usefulness of findings. Greenhalgh (2010) suggests the following points for critically appraising related articles:

1. The test is relevant to my practice.
2. The test has been compared with a true gold standard.
3. The validation study included an appropriate spectrum of clients.
4. Work-up bias was avoided.
5. Observer bias has been avoided.
6. The test has been shown to be reproducible both within and between observers.
7. The features of the test as derived from this validation study are described.
8. Confidence intervals are given for sensitivity, specificity and other features of the test.
9. A sensible "normal range" has been derived.
10. The test has been placed in the context of other potential tests in the assessment sequence for the problem. (Adapted from Greenhalgh, 2010, p. 225)

Is the false positive rate reported (the percentage of persons inaccurately identified as having a characteristic)? Is the false negative rate reported (the percentage of persons inaccurately identified as not having a characteristic)? Are sensitivity and specificity reported? These concepts can be illustrated by a four-cell contingency as shown in Exhibit 5.3. Key concepts in reviewing the validity of tests include:

- *Sensitivity*: Among those known to have a problem, the proportion whom a test or measure indicates as having the problem.
- *Specificity*: Among those known not to have a problem, the proportion whom the test or measure indicates as not having the problem.
- *Pretest probability (prevalence)*: The probability that an individual has the disorder before the test is carried out.
- *Posttest probability*: The probability that an individual with a specific test result has the target condition (posttest odds/[1+ posttest odds]).
- *Pretest odds*: The odds that an individual has the disorder before the test is carried out (pretest probability/[1—pretest probability]).
- *Posttest odds*: The odds that a client has the disorder after being tested (pretest odds × likelihood ratio).

EXHIBIT 5.3
CONTINGENCY TABLE

		Outcome	
		Improved	Not Improved
Participated In Intervention	Yes	A Successes	B Failures
	No	C Spontaneous recovery	D Untreated Unimproved

- *Positive predictive value (PPV)*: The proportion of individuals with positive test results who have the target condition. This equals the posttest probability given a positive test result.
- *Negative predictive value (NPV)*: The proportion of individuals with negative test results who do not have the target condition. This equals 1 minus the posttest probability given a negative test result.
- *Likelihood ratio (LR)*: Measure of a test result's ability to modify pretest probabilities. LRs indicate how many times more likely a test result is in a client with a disorder compared with a person free of the disorder. Small LRs indicate strong relationships. A LR of 1 indicates that a test is totally uninformative.
- *LR of a positive test result (LR +)*: The ratio of the true positive rate to the false positive rate: sensitivity/(1 – specificity).
- *LR of a negative test result (LR –)*: The ratio of the false negative to the true negative rate: (1 – sensitivity)/specificity. (Adapted from Pewsner, Pattaglia, Minder, Marx, Bucher, & Egger, 2004)

Only if a test increases accuracy of understanding should it be used. Often in social work, psychology, and psychiatry, there is no gold standard against which to compare a test. An example of a "gold standard" is reviewing an X-ray to detect pneumonia when someone has a bad cough.

Screening

Screening of nonsymptomatic individuals is a key public health strategy with recommendations to broaden screening to concerns such as depression and anxiety. The New Freedom Commission on Mental Health (2003) recommended universal screening. The benefits of screening should outweigh harms (Gigerenzer, 2014b; Lenzer, 2004). Is there an effective intervention? If not, why get screened? (See Welch, Schwartz, & Woloshin, 2011.) Requirements for a screening program include:

- The benefit of testing outweighs the harm.
- The disorder is serious with a high burden of suffering.
- The natural history of the disorder is understood.
- The disorder occurs frequently.
- Effective intervention exists, and early intervention is more effective than late intervention.
- The test is easy to administer.
- The test is inexpensive.
- The test is safe.
- The test is acceptable to participants.
- The sensitivity, specificity, and other operating characteristics of the test are acceptable (Gray, 2001a).

QUESTIONS ABOUT PROGNOSIS, RISK, AND PROTECTIVE FACTORS (PREDICTION)

Both prognosis and risk project into the future; related tests attempt to predict events in the future. Depending on a diagnosis (e.g., of depression) one has a certain prognosis, which, in turn, is related to certain protective and risk factors. Child welfare workers make predictions about future risk of abuse. Thus, both prognosis and prediction look into the future, and, as with all such looks, there will be errors. Errors in earlier stages (e.g., assessment) may result in errors at later stages (selection of plans). Examples of questions here are:

- In elderly, frail clients living alone, what is the risk of hip fracture?
- In young children abused by their parents, what is the risk of future abuse?
- In young adults who have unprotected sexual intercourse with multiple partners, what is the risk of developing AIDS?

Prognostic studies include clinical studies of variables that predict future events, as well as epidemiological studies of risk factors. This information may provide a guide for choice of service options. In ecological (aggregate) studies, secondary data are often used to identify associations in a population between risk factors and outcomes of interest, such as a certain illness. Generalization from aggregate data to individuals is problematic because of the likelihood of the *ecological fallacy* (assuming what is true for a group is true for an individual). Actuarial methods using the results of empirical investigations of the relationships between certain characteristics and an outcome have been found to be superior to intuitive methods for making accurate predictions in a number of areas (e.g., Cuccaro-Alamin, Foust, Vaithianathan & Putnam-Hornstein, 2017). Both cohort and case control studies have been used to try to identify and quantify risk factors. Problems in trying to describe risk include naturally occurring fluctuation of risks. Protective as well as risk factors are of importance in prevention (e.g., Jensen & Fraser, 2015). Miser (1999) suggests the following questions to raise concerning articles about risk:

1. Was a clearly defined comparison group of those at risk for the outcome of interest included?
2. Were the outcomes and exposures measured in the same way in groups compared?
3. Were observers blinded to the exposure of outcome and to the outcome?
4. Was follow-up sufficiently long and complete?
5. Is the temporal relationship correct? (Does exposure precede outcome?)
6. Is there a dose–response gradient? (As the quantity or duration of exposure to an agent increases, does the risk of outcome likewise increase?)
7. How strong is the association between exposure and outcome? (Is the relative risk or odds ratio large?)

Both absolute and relative risks should be given. Reduction in relative risk sounds impressive compared to absolute risk reduction and thus is very misleading. Let's say an oncologist tells a patient who enquires about the effectiveness of chemotherapy for her in reducing risk of cancer recurrence: "There are 50% fewer recurrences in ten years." This sounds very impressive. When asked about absolute risk reduction, the oncologist said, "Out of 100 people, there are 3 fewer recurrences of cancer in ten years." This represents 103 with chemo compared to 106 without. Providing absolute risk reduction is vital to help clients to make informed decisions.

EBPS/EBIS AND PRACTICE GUIDELINES

Many sources provide lists of evidence-based practices (EBPs) and evidence-based interventions (EBIs) according to assumed evidentiary status (see Exhibit

4.2). Best practices and "evidence-based practice" have become buzzwords (Cosgrove, Bursztajn, Erlich, Wheeler, & Shaughnessy, 2013; Gorman, 2017). Both practice guidelines and lists of EBPs differ in the process used to create them including rigor of critical appraisal of related research and attention to variations in circumstances and characteristics of individual clients, including their preferences. Terms such as *validated* and *well-established* used in lists of programs may mislead practitioners and policymakers about the evidentiary status of programs. In 1995 the American Psychological Association Task Force on Psychological Intervention Guidelines recommended that if two RCTs show the effectiveness of an intervention, then this method has been "established" as valid. Certainty is suggested by the term *established* when two RCTs, even though well-designed, cannot certainty make. The next two trials may show different results. And, generalization of results to other clients and communities may not be warranted.

Categories on the Scientific Rating Scale used by the California Evidence Based Clearinghouse for Child Welfare include (1) Well-supported by Research Evidence, (2) Supported by Research Evidence, (3) Promising Research Evidence, (4) Evidence Fails to Demonstrate Effect, (5) Concerning Practice and NR (not able to be rated). Research evidence is defined on their website as" research study outcomes that have been published in a peer-reviewed journal". Viewers can click on a related source in which we find no mention of the flaws in peer review such as inflated claims of knowledge. Uncritical promotion of EBPs and practice guidelines overlook flaws in related research and obstacles to generalizing results to other settings and individuals (Lenzer, 2013).

Guidelines

In the preparation of a guideline there should be a careful review of "all pertinent evidence, a critical appraisal of its quality, a synthesis of evidence, a balancing of benefits and harms, an assessment of feasibility and practicality, a clear statement of the recommendation and a detailed rationale" (Eddy, 2005, p. 12). Guidelines are prepared by small groups employing explicit rigorous criteria for analyzing related data and are designed to enable informed decision making on the part of individual practitioners. Rigorous guidelines contribute to informed decision making on the part of individual practitioners. GRADE (Grading of Recommendations: Assessment, Development, and Evaluation) is the standard of guideline development in reviewing quality of evidence and offering recommendations. This classifies the direction and strength of recommendations and offers the most rigorous, transparent, and nuanced approach, including considering how strength of evidence may affect client preferences and decisions about tradeoffs regarding benefits and harms (www.gradeworkinggroup.org). AGREE is a reporting checklist for guidelines (Brouwers, Kerkvliet, Spithoff, & AGREE Next Steps Consortium, 2016). Attention is paid to choosing critical and important outcomes to clients, rating the confidence in effect estimates for each outcome as well as across outcomes, considering resource use, and creating an evidence profile and summary of findings. GRADE guidelines can provide valuable guidance for construction of decision aids (Agoritsas et al., 2015). GRADE categories include:

1. *Strongly recommended* that clinicians provide the service to eligible patients. Good evidence that the service improves important outcomes and that benefits substantially outweigh harms.
2. *Recommended* that clinicians provide the service to eligible patients. There is fair evidence that the service improves important health outcomes and that benefits outweigh harms.
3. *Recommends selectively* offering or providing this service to individuals based on professional judgment and patient preferences. There is at least moderate certainty that the net benefit is small.
4. *Recommends against the service.* There is moderate or high certainty that the service has no net benefits or that harms outweigh benefits.
5. *Current evidence is insufficient to make a recommendation.* Evidence is lacking, of poor quality, or conflicting and the balance of benefits and harms cannot be determined.

Three levels of certainty are included in the GRADE definition: *high* (available evidence usually includes consistent results from well-designed, well-conducted studies in representative primary care populations); *moderate* (the available evidence is sufficient to determine the effects of the preventive service on health outcomes, but confidence in the estimate is lowered by factors such as the number, size, or quality of individual studies, inconsistency of findings across studies, limited generalizability of findings to routine primary care and lack of coherence in the chain of evidence), and *low* (the available evidence is insufficient to assess effects on health outcomes). Evidence may be insufficient because of the limited number or size of studies, important flaws in study design or methods, inconsistency of findings across individual studies, gaps in the chain of evidence, findings are not generalizable to routine primary care, and lack of information on important health outcomes).

CONTROVERSIAL ISSUES

People differ in the certainty with which they make claims based on given re-search. Judgments made about the evidentiary status of claims differ in their ac-curacy. The research design used to explore a question reflects the researchers' views about knowledge and how it can be gained as well as their views about being honest brokers of knowledge and ignorance. Inflated claims suggest a variety of possibilities: (1) being uninformed about the limitations of different research designs in critically testing a question; (2) being aware of this, but not caring; or (3) caring but need a publication. Claims may be inflated in a number of ways in-cluding claims of effectiveness or claims of no effectiveness. Just because a pro-gram has been found to be effective or ineffective in critical tests does not warrant claims of certainty. Also, other dimensions come into play in addition to eviden-tiary status, such as importance of outcomes to clients (see Chapters 2 and 4).

OBSTACLES

Both personal and environmental obstacles may impede critical appraisal of re-search related to life-affecting decisions and using this to enhance quality of services. Research courses are often given separately from practice courses in pro-fessional education programs, which may discourage integration of practice and research skills. Agencies may not provide a culture of inquiry including provision of needed training and tools and access to valuable databases. Exploration of how to address application problems in an active area of research (see Chapter 11).

SUMMARY

Different questions require different research methods to critically test them. Some are exploratory and descriptive; there is an interest in describing the relationships among different variables. A question may be: "What is the relationship between certain characteristics of a helper (e.g., warmth) and service outcome?" Some re-search (experimental studies) involves testing a hypothesis. An aim may be to identify causal relationships among variables. Research methods differ in the de-gree to which sources of bias are present. A key concern is the match between a question and the likelihood that the method used to test it can do so. Currently, literature in the helping professions abounds with poor matches (e.g., Gorman & Huber, 2009; Ioannidis, 2016).

Evidence-informed practice encourages attention to the limitations of research. Keep in mind that one of the key reasons for the origin of EBP was a concern about flaws in published research, such as inflated claims of knowledge. Bogus claims are problematic in a profession in which clients are affected by beliefs in such claims that may result in selection of ineffective or harmful methods. A variety of tools and entire enterprises, such as the Cochrane and Campbell collaborations, have been developed to help us to make informed decisions—informed about ignorance as well as knowledge. Each year brings new sources that can be used to enhance skills in critical appraisal of research such as testingtreatmens.org. These include user-friendly checklists for critically appraising the quality of different kinds of research.

6

Cultivating Expertise in Decision-Making

IN BARON'S SEARCH-INFERENCE framework, decision-making requires searching for possibilities, evidence, and goals. Options may differ in number, variety, and whether they include feasible options that will contribute to attaining valued goals. Lists differ in their noise level (number and vividness of irrelevant and misleading options). Clinical expertise is drawn on in making decisions including posing questions regarding information needs, gathering information, engaging clients in the helping process, integrating data, selecting interventions and examining outcomes. Multiple sources of information may have to be considered in making decisions including client characteristics and circumstances, external research findings, and local circumstances including available resources. Different sources of evidence must be weighed in terms of their importance. Clinical expertise includes interpersonal skills—common factors such as empathy and warmth, which contribute to forming an alliance with clients (see Chapter 10). Obstacles to decision-making are illustrated in Exhibit 6.1. They include the changing nature of situations, the unpredictability of behavior; limited opportunities for corrective feedback; lack of domain specific knowledge and skills, both avoidable and not; and infrequent occurrence of tasks. Review of the effects of emotion on decision-making, memory, and attention shows that emotion and cognition are closely related and influence behavior (LeBlanc, McConnell, & Monteiro, 2014).

Some barriers to decision-making are self-inflicted such as lack of active open-minded thinking in searching for possibilities. Dysfunctional management practices include lack of interest in gathering outcome data. Some are created by educational programs that fail to provide needed values, knowledge, and skills.

EXHIBIT 6.1

EXAMPLES OF OBSTACLES TO INFORMED DECISION-MAKING

1. *Limited knowledge about[a]:*
   causes of problems
   validity of assessment measures
   effectiveness of interventions
   empirically-informed theory (e.g., regarding behavior)
   valuable problem-solving strategies
   accuracy of evaluation measures

2. *Lack of knowledge and skills in critical thinking and problem-solving:*
   lack of active open-minded thinking
   a one-shot view of integration—integration continues (e.g., informed by outcomes)
   a limited view of relevant information (e.g., disciplinary blinders)
   prone to attentional biases
   poor skills in argumentation
   prone to myside bias

3. *Lack of skill such as:*
   interviewing
   observational
   offering high levels of common factors; allegiance building
   providing clear information
   critically appraising claims
   posing clear questions
   locating valuable research
   avoiding burnout (see Chapter 11).

4. *Lack of knowledge about clients:*
   characteristics and circumstances including client preferences, motivation, and goals; cultural differences; social support system; history; and recreational skills or opportunities

5. *Motivational and emotional obstacles:*
   myside bias
   low tolerance for uncertainty
   excessive fear of making mistakes
   arrogance
   lack of empathy
   lack of interest in making informed decisions

6. *Lack of knowledge about resources:*
    community settings
    services provided by other agencies
    clients' neighborhood characteristics

7. *Lack of resources including:*
    feedback regarding decisions
    coaching
    relevant databases for information retrieval
    time
    continuing education opportunities
    needed services

8. *Organization obstacles* (see Chapter 11).
9. *Political, social, and economic factors*

---

^aMay be due to personal and/or objective ignorance.

Variations in the rate of use of an intervention reflect the different decisions that may be made regarding a concern. For example, Gigerenzer (2002a) notes that, in Maine, "the proportion of women who have had a hysterectomy by the age of 70 varies between communities from less than 20 percent to more than 70 percent" (p. 101). Decisions differ in terms of how quickly they must be made, how experienced the person is in making the decision, the kind of feedback offered, and time available to consider choices and outcomes (Connelly & Beach, 2000).

PROBLEMS AND THEIR PROSPECTS

Problems involve gaps between a current and a desired situation. They range from routine ones that are easy to solve to those that are difficult or impossible to solve, even by experts, perhaps because of a lack of available knowledge. There are (1) clear problems with clear solutions; (2) clear problems with no solutions; (3) unclear problems with clear solutions; and (4) unclear problems with no solutions. Specialized knowledge may be required to distinguish among these possibilities. Let's say that Ms. Rivers is a social worker in a protective service program for the elderly and that she receives a call that Mrs. Rigly, age 75, who lives by herself seems to be disoriented and is having increasing trouble living on her own—she leaves the door to her apartment unlocked at times and sometimes leaves the gas burning on the stove. What reasons come to mind, and how could these be tested? Uncertainties abound in decision-making, including posing questions; what are the most important questions to pose in pursuit of a hoped-for outcome. What is the most important evidence to search for? Uncertainty may concern: (1) the nature of the problem; (2) the outcomes desired; (3) what is needed to attain valued outcomes; (4) the likelihood of attaining outcomes; and (5) measures that will best reflect degree of success. It may concern the likelihood that an assessment framework and related measures accurately represent the problem.

Success in problem-solving is related to readiness to recognize uncertainties, controversies, and related personal and objective ignorance. Uncertainties differ depending on experience and knowledge in an area. Problems that confront clients are often difficult, complex, unstructured ones that challenge the most skilled of helpers. Rarely is all relevant information available. We can consider only so much information at one time. Related consequences may include (1) selective perception (we do not necessarily see what is there); (2) sequential rather than contextual processing of information; (3) misleading reliance on heuristics to reduce effort (e.g., frequently occurring cues, vivid case examples); and (4) faulty memory. Time pressures often limit information gathered. General principles do not allow specific predictions regarding individuals (Dawes, 1994).

Different problem-solving phases and different kinds of problems entail different uncertainties and possibilities of error. The acquisition of information may be biased; how we direct our attention influences what we see (and what we miss). How we process information may be biased (we may not consider vital cues and may not question hunches). Bias may be introduced by how professionals are required to record information. Many errors result from lack of active open-minded thinking (see Exhibit 6.2). Information about options may be missing, and accurate estimates of the probability that different alternatives will result in desired outcomes may be unknown. Preferences may change in the very process of being asked about them.

Competing goals in a clinical context include saving time and effort, helping clients, performing well, and avoiding errors. Goal conflict is a concern in many areas. Competing goals in child welfare settings include providing services to parents and respecting their wishes, guarding the well-being of children, and protecting oneself from lawsuits. As one goal is pursued, another may be forgone. Goals may change in light of evidence regarding different possibilities (Baron, 2008). "Because local rationality revolves around how people pursue their goals, understanding performance at the sharp end depends on tracing interacting multiple goals and how they produce tradeoffs, dilemmas, and double binds" (Woods & Cook, 1999, p. 160). Failure to recognize uncertainties often results in harm to

EXHIBIT 6.2
PROBLEM-SOLVING PHASES AND COMMON ERRORS RELATED TO LACK
OF ACTIVE OPEN-MINDED THINKING

Step	Common Errors
1. Clarify the problem.	• Jump to conclusions (overlook alternative views).
	• Seek to justify views rather than critically evaluate them.
	• Ignore environmental causes.
	• Gather irrelevant data.
	• Ignore problem-related theory and research.
	• Overestimate personal problem-related knowledge.
	• Rely on invalid data (e.g., small biased samples).
	• Disregard conflicting evidence.
	• Stereotyping.
2. Search for solutions.	• Overlook options.
	• Look only for data that confirm assumptions.
	• Overlook constraints.
	• Overlook resources.
	• Fail to revise views based on new information.
	• See other items under Step 1.
3. Decide on a plan.	• Overlook options.
	• Overlook constraints.
	• Fail to fully inform clients about options and their potential costs and benefits.
4. Implement plans.	• The "dilution" effect (i.e., offer ineffective version of
5. Evaluate results.	plans).
	• Do not arrange for timely corrective feedback
	• Use vague outcome measures.
	• Use invalid measures (e.g., misleading surrogates).
	• Fail to plan for generalization and maintenance.
	• Do not gather both subjective and objective measures.
	• Post hoc fallacy (assume that because there is a change, services were responsible).
	• Overlook harmful effects.
6. Try again?	• Give up too soon.

Source: Adapted from *Social Work Practice: A Critical Thinker's Guide* (3rd ed.), by E. Gambrill, 2013, New York, NY: Oxford.

clients. They are so important to recognize that an Uncertainties Page has been initiated in the *British Medical Journal* to bring these to the attention of physicians (see also Database of Uncertainties about the Effects of Treatments; DUETS). Ignorance, both avoidable and not, is related to uncertainty. Vague descriptions may hinder problem-solving. Recognizing ignorance encourages questions such as "What background and foreground information do I need to make an informed decision?" and "What kind of errors may I be making?" Underestimating personal ignorance (what *you* do not know) or objective ignorance (what no one knows) may result in missing important uncertainties.

Different clinicians confront different problems. Features of situations that increase problem demands include time pressures, conflicting goals, and unanticipated variations in pacing (Woods & Cook, 1999). Understanding demands "can reveal a great deal about the knowledge activation, attentional control or handling of multiple goals that is needed for successful performance" (Woods & Cook, 1999, p. 161). The notion of rationality favored by authors such as Gigerenzer, Klein, and Simon emphasize the match between the problems we confront and the environments in which they occur (ecological rationality; see discussion in Chapter 3). The emphasis on the contextual nature of decision-making has implications for the extent to which a given decision-making procedure is generalizable with positive outcomes over different individuals, groups, and situations; it depends on the similarity and the nature of the decisions and the contexts to which they are made.

THE IMPORTANCE OF PROBLEM FRAMING

Problem framing is critical; clarifying and deciding how to structure a problem—considering different possibilities in light of related evidence and goals. Different theories involve different problem spaces (i.e., how a problem is represented). Consider homelessness. This could be viewed as (1) the client's own fault (he is lazy); (2) a family problem (relatives are unwilling to help); (3) lack of low-cost housing; (4) a problem with service integration; (5) due to a "mental disorder"; (6) a result of our basic economic structure (e.g., unskilled jobs have decreased); (7) discrimination based on racial prejudice; or (8) a mix of all these possibilities. Differences in how problems are framed (e.g., to avoid negative events or to achieve positive benefits), how questions are posed, and how responses are gathered (by either closed or open questions) influence judgments. New goals may emerge during the course of decision-making. Problem framing is often controversial as in viewing troubling or troubled behaviors as mental illnesses (Conrad, 2007; Speed et al., 2014; Szasz, 2007). Only by clarifying and restructuring a problem may it be solved or may you discover that there is no solution. Creative (bold guesses) and contextual thinking will often be needed to describe the "problem space" in a way that yields a solution. Only in this way may we discover the interrelationships among different levels of influence including related contingencies (e.g., individual, family, community, service system, policy).

DIFFERENCES BETWEEN EXPERTS AND NOVICES

Professionals are expected to have special expertise in a particular area reflected in professional licenses. Content knowledge without performance skills to put this to use is known as the *parroting problem*; we can describe what should be done to solve a problem but cannot put this knowledge into effect. Like any other term, the accuracy with which the term *expert* is applied varies. Jenicek (2006) includes understanding, correct decision-making, appropriate actions, their critical evaluation and self-improvement. There is a rich literature describing the differences between experts and novices and how expertise can be developed (e.g., Monteiro & Norman, 2017; Klein, 2011; Phillips, Klein, & Sieck, 2005; Rousmaniere, 2017; Schraagen, Militello, Ormerod, & Lipshitz, 2008). This indicates that:

- Expertise varies greatly.
- Domain-specific knowledge is important: both problem-related knowledge and self-knowledge influence success.
- Experts used different reasoning processes compared to novices (e.g., pattern recognition, mental simulations).
- Problem structuring is a critical phase: Some ways of structuring problems are better than others.
- Creative as well as critical thinking is required.
- Repeated practice providing corrective feedback is critical to developing informed intuition that allows us to respond effectively; skill in learning from experience is important, not experience per se, including learning from errors.
- Our goals influence our actions.
- We may fall into a number of "intelligence raps"; we jump to conclusions (decide on one option too soon); errors of omission and commission occur.
- Experts, compared to novices, organize knowledge in a different way; they approach problems on a more abstract level and can more readily identify anomalies and additional information that would be helpful.

- Situation awareness (local rationality) is important (attending to the problem context).
- The strategies we use influence our success.
- Monitoring progress is important, for example, to catch false directions.
- Beliefs about what knowledge is and how to get it (our personal epistemology) influence success.
- How we decide to allocate our resources influences success (e.g., time spent in planning).
- We can learn to become better problem solvers.

Good problem-solvers are more attentive to situational details and more tenacious compared to poor problem solvers. Ennis (1987) suggests that being sensitive to the feelings, level of knowledge, and degree of sophistication of others, as well as seriously considering other views, is important. Successful compared to unsuccessful problem solvers think more about their thinking. They engage in active open-minded thinking to critically review their assumptions and reasoning. They are their own best critics. They pay attention to data that contradict their assumptions. They ask questions about the accuracy of data, such as: What evidence supports this claim? What evidence contradicts it? Has it been critically tested? With what results? Are there other well-argued views?

Experts compared to novices possess domain-specific knowledge and can more rapidly identify information needed to solve a problem. They have valuable "scripts" that guide decision-making (Hamm, 2003; see Exhibit 6.3). The "possession of relevant bodies of information and a sufficiently broad experience with related problems to permit the determination of which information is pertinent, which clinical findings are significant, and how these findings are to be integrated into appropriate hypotheses and conclusions" were foundational components related to competence in clinical problem-solving (Elstein, et al., 1978, pp. x–xi; see also Elstein, 2009). Experts pay more attention to problem definition and structure problems at a deeper (more abstract) level compared to novices, who tend to accept problems as given. For example, helpers skilled in functional analysis look beyond the topography (form) of behavior to examine its functions (Gambrill, 2014a; Madden, 2013; Staats, 2012). Situation awareness enables more rapid recognition of anomalies and false directions. Experts:

- Know more (what, how, and when to do what).
- Demonstrate superior performance, mainly in their own areas of expertise.
- Are motivated to do well.

EXHIBIT 6.3
EXAMPLES OF VALUABLE EXPERTISE

1. Use specialized content knowledge and related skills allowing recognition of important patterns, anomalies, uncertainties, and missing information.
2. Help clients to clearly describe and prioritize hoped-for outcomes and discover related circumstances, drawing on relevant theory and research.
3. Identify important information needs, pose related clear questions and locate related research.
4. Accurately weigh evidence regarding possibilities and goals using effective skills in argumentation.
5. Use valid assessment theories and related tools and accurately interpret information gathered.
6. Effectively integrate different kinds of information.
7. Suggest interventions most likely to be effective that are compatible with assessment information and client preferences.
8. Use effective argumentation skills.
9. Help clients to make informed decisions including trade-offs between benefits and harms of an intervention.
10. Arrange valuable learning opportunities.
11. Identify and avoid common biases, influence of fallacies, and propaganda ploys (e.g., glittering generalization).
12. Recognize when individual/cultural differences require deviations from recommended guidelines.
13. Offer high levels of common factors such as empathy and warmth (see Chapter 10).
14. Recognize and correct important gaps in knowledge and skill.
15. Arrange ongoing monitoring of relevant outcomes.
16. Involve clients as informed participants in decision-making.
17. Seek help when needed.
18. Recognize influence of stress and fatigue on decisions.
19. Revise views and strategies when needed.
20. Help clients to attain hoped-for outcomes.
21. Acquire needed resources.
22. Troubleshoot; overcome obstacles.
23. Identify and minimize errors.
24. Arrange effective "handovers" (e.g., referrals).

Source: Based on *Critical Thinking for Helping Professionals: A Skills-Based Workbook* (4th ed.), by E. Gambrill and L. Gibbs, 2017, New York, NY: Oxford University Press.

- Know better how to use what they know (procedural knowledge); are faster at solving problems and making satisfactory trade-offs among different options.
- What they know is better organized, enabling speedy recognition of patterns and disregarding of irrelevant information (e.g., mental models, schemas, logical competitor set).
- Represent problems at a deeper level compared to novices.
- What they know is more accessible; they have superior short- and long-term memory.
- Have better learning skills.
- Are more likely to carry out an executive review of their reasoning—to assume simultaneously the roles of doer and observer; if there is time to do so.
- Are better at identifying leverage points and managing uncertainty constructively.
- Are more attentive to the importance of ongoing monitoring of progress.
- Are better at gathering, interpreting, and appropriately applying relevant information.
- Are better at spotting anomalies and detecting problems (see Exhibit 6.3).

Novices, because of lack of experience in an area offering corrective feedback and other relevant knowledge, may fail to recognize important features and unexpected anomalies or may attend to irrelevant ones. We make decisions about where to focus our attention. Woods and Cook (1999) use the term *mindset* to refer to loss of situational awareness, framing effects, and juggling multiple lines of thought and activity in time. Not only is it important to have relevant information, but it must also be organized so that we can take advantage of it when needed in real time. New goals may emerge during the course of decision-making (Baron, 2008; Klein, 1998).

Based on interviews with experienced firefighters, nurses, and paramedics, Klein (1998) argues that expert decision makers quickly size up a situation based on informed intuition; they identify important cues relying on the similarity of the new situation to others previously experienced. Klein calls this "primed decision-making." Interviews with experts show that it is difficult for them to identify the cues they use. For example, an experienced pediatric nurse looked at a baby and said, "This baby is in trouble" (which was true). When asked why, she said, "I just knew it." It took a while for her to identify specific characteristics of the baby's features she used as cues. Such research highlights the importance of *situation awareness*—accurate understanding of what is occurring in a situation from moment to moment as circumstances change. Experts are better at critiquing themselves when things are slipping away. Because their content knowledge is greater and is better organized, they have more free time compared to novices who still struggle to integrate different kinds of information and therefore lack time to look ahead and backward in ways that facilitate decision-making.

Expert problem-solving takes advantage of new possibilities as they arise; it is opportunistic (Lesgold et al., 1988). When specialized knowledge is needed and available, its use gives the edge to professionals familiar with this knowledge who also possess and use effective interpersonal skills (Wampold & Imel, 2015). Because experts are better informed in their area of expertise, they are less likely to make diagnostic or assessment errors (Norman et al., 2011). They are more likely to use valid assessment measures and effective interventions and to recognize when resources are lacking and problems are not possible to solve. They are more likely to be data focused, to focus on relevant data, to be aware of their ignorance, to understand probabilities, and to avoid misleading influence of redundant data and false dilemmas. Awareness of knowledge gaps, both personal and objective, is an ingredient of expertise. The role of self-knowledge and active open-minded thinking has been emphasized by scholars in the area of decision-making (e.g., Baron, 2008; Nickerson, 1986; Paul, 1993; see Chapter 1). Socrates was the preeminent advocate of self-knowledge—particularly in relation to one's own vast ignorance (Plato, 1983). Experts do not necessarily perform better than novices in unstructured problem areas such as psychology and psychiatry (Tracy, Wampold, Lichtenberg, & Goodyear, 2014), and experts do not necessarily make sound decisions outside of their area of expertise.

Research concerning naturalistic decision-making shows that steps presumed to be of value in a rational model of problem-solving and decision-making, in which we identify alternatives, estimate the probability that each will yield hoped-for outcomes, assign values to different options, and select the alternative with the greatest value, are often impossible to satisfy and are not needed to solve problems (Salas & Klein, 2001; Zsambok & Klein, 1977). We "satisfice" rather than optimize. Those with experience in an area that provided corrective feedback are able to quickly recognize important cues. The view that we do not try to optimize—we exploit characteristics of particular environments to make decisions—is a continuation of Simon's (1982) bounded rationality that satisficing is sufficient in many situations and that the time and effort required to identify alternatives and evaluate their soundness is not only unnecessary in many situations to arrive at sound decisions, it may result in more errors perhaps because cues that are valuable are lost in a sea of data. Gigerenzer and his colleagues argue that optimization is not possible, let alone necessary; we rarely know all the factors influencing a behavior or event. There is a trade-off between accuracy ("good enough") and effort and time. The key question is "Are decisions made most likely to help clients attain outcomes they value?"

HOW IS EXPERTISE DEVELOPED?

Study of decision-making in real-life circumstances shows that skill in solving problems often requires special knowledge in a particular area such as emergency care and a great deal of experience in applying this in settings in which *corrective feedback* is gained and used to enhance the quality of future decisions and future actions via deliberate practice (Klein, 1998, 2011). This permits the building of a "library" of distinguishable situations, enabling recognition-primed decision-making. Enhancement of knowledge requires thinking, and thinking involves skill in applying knowledge (Nickerson, Perkins, & Smith, 1985, p. 99). Thus, knowledge and thinking are highly related. Experience alone does not result in enhanced expertise (Rousmaniere, Goodyear, Miller, & Wampold, 2017). Deliberate practice enhances expertise, especially of *in*experienced practitioners. This involves a focused and systematic effort to improve performance over an extended period; involvement of and guidance from a coach, teacher, or mentor; immediate, ongoing feedback; and successive refinement and repetition via practice (Miller, Hubble, & Chow, 2017, p. 26). Content knowledge including a sound theory and practice in applying it to diverse situations together with corrective feedback contributes to rapid pattern recognition that may suggest how to attain hoped-for outcomes. It allows experts, compared to novices, to "see" different things, such as opportunities for problem solution. Strategies that encourage attention to context are especially important in our therapeutic state in which the cause of troubled and troubling behavior is assumed to be brain diseases and thoughts, overlooking the role of environmental circumstances including lack of employment opportunities, lack of healthcare, and environmental pollution (e.g., Case & Deaton, 2015; Mirowsky & Ross, 2003; Whitaker & Moncrieff, 2015).

Values, skills, and knowledge related to critical thinking, such as contextual awareness and questioning assumptions, contribute to expertise in decision-making including use of *meta-cognitive skills* (thinking about our thinking), which decrease premature closure on misleading views (see discussion of active open-minded thinking in Chapter 1). Examples include seeking counterevidence to preferred views, asking questions such as "Could I be wrong?" and "Is there a better alternative?" Possibilities and goals are reviewed in relation to evidence at hand. Elstein, Shulman et al. (1978) found that the difference between expert diagnosticians and those who were not as accurate were that experts held hypotheses tentatively and were open to revising them as new information they sought emerged.

PROBLEM-SOLVING KNOWLEDGE AND SKILLS OR PROCESSING STRATEGIES?

Some views of expertise such as the dual process model of reasoning and a concern with cognitive biases focus on process. Other views emphasize the importance of specialized knowledge and experience (Monteiro & Norman, 2013). Dual process models focus on the importance of using controlled, reflective thinking (Type 2) as a check on (to override; Type 1; Evans & Stanovich, 2013; Kahneman, 2011). System 1 (intuition) is fast, parallel, automatic, effortless, and associative. Intuition (our "gut reaction) involves a quick judgment. Type 1 processes include implicit learning as well as well-practiced discriminations and decision-making principles that have become automatic (Kahneman & Klein, 2009). System 2 (analytic) is slow, serial, controlled, effortful, rule-governed, and flexible. It is argued that the need to override Type 1 processes is illustrated by our irrational responses in many situations encouraged by biases.

In active open-minded thinking we search for disconfirming evidence regarding preferred views. Baron (2017) argues that active open-minded thinking (AOT) differs from Type 2 thinking in emphasizing "the direction of thinking with respect to conclusions that are in force at the moment" (p. 2). "AOT is intended as the antidote to myside bias" (p. 5)—looking for reasons why a belief may be incorrect. He notes that "if you have not looked for reasons why your favored belief might be incorrect you should not have so much confidence that it is correct. . . . Fairness in direction is possible even when time is limited" (p. 5). The goal is to yield "beliefs that are most warranted, confidence that is justified, and decisions that are as close to optimal as time permits" (p. 6).

Analytical approaches are often inferior to system 1 methods especially among experts in an area; "novices may need a different approach" (Norman, 2009, p. 46). Monteiro and Norman (2013) argue that there is little evidence that process is central to diagnostic expertise" (p. S26). Rather, knowledge representations are viewed as "central to expertise" (see discussion of informed intuition in Chapter 3). They argue that the assumption that faster responses are more error prone than slower ones is not supported and that removing biases does not make up for a lack of content knowledge. For example, Norman (2009) describes the failure of just teaching the error-creating role of representativeness rather than teaching how making decisions based on similarity may help or hinder accurate guesses about what may be true. He argues that the focus of teaching should be on helping students to reflect on their own performance and identify where their reasoning may have failed rather than describing and defining a list of biases. Here again we see an emphasis on the importance of active open-minded thinking in which we search for disconfirming evidence regarding preferred views.

Complex tasks are made easier by informed experience. Experiential and affective processes dominate rather than deliberation (consideration of many alternatives) (Strough, Karns, & Schlosnagle, 2011):

(a) strategies directed at increasing analytical (System 2) processing, by slowing down, reducing distractions, paying conscious attention, and (b) strategies directed at making students aware of the effects of cognitive biases, have no impact on error rates. Conversely, strategies based on increasing application of relevant knowledge appear to have some success and are consistent with basic research on concept formation. (Monteiro and Norman, 2013, p. S26)

They suggest that diagnosis/assessment is a categorization and memory task dependent on analytical and experiential knowledge. From this perspective, "diagnoses are not reasoned so much as they are recognized" (p. S27). (See earlier discussion of pattern recognition.) "Experts generate better hypotheses. In short, expertise resides in content knowledge, not process" (p. S26). If "effective reasoning based on a memory model is largely derived from an extensive experiential and analytic knowledge base, the emphasis for strategies to improve reasoning skills changes from practicing a process to acquiring examples" (p. S30). We can concentrate on learning errors or concentrate on "learning the prerequisite knowledge to avoid errors" (p. S30)- focus on gaps in knowledge rather than cognitive errors.

As discussed in Chapter 3, intuition may be informed, for example, by extensive knowledge in an area and experience in applying it in contexts providing corrective feedback, or uninformed, for example, on the part of novices. This illustrates the vast differences between a novice in an area depending or her intuition, compared to a seasoned practitioner who has years of experience in an area making judgements and gaining corrective feedback. We all use heuristics, and we all use system 1 thinking (intuition), for example, to generate possible solutions to problems. The greater the background knowledge and experience, the more system 1 thinking can be relied on. Norman (2009) argues that accurate assessment/diagnosis "involves two distinct thinking modes, which are complimentary in many aspects, and which act in harmony to deal with the limitations of human memory" (p. 47__). Errors may occur because "normally adaptive heuristics operating on usually adequate knowledge fail" (p. 47).

THE ROLE OF SIMPLIFYING STRATEGIES (HEURISTICS)

The term *heuristic* refers to a rule of thumb (strategy). Nisbett and Ross (1980) and others such as Tversky and Kahneman (1973) focused on circumstances in which we violate probability rules and principles of "rational" decision-making, emphasizing errors that result from reliance on simplifying heuristics such as availability (e.g., vivid case examples, a preferred theory) and representativeness (e.g., assuming that causes resemble their effects). Gigerenzer (2005) argues that many events that have been viewed as cognitive illusions are reasonable judgments given the environmental structure. He argues that the heuristics and biases approach taken by scholars such as Nisbett and Ross (1980) views rationality as logical instead of *ecological* and that problems posed in laboratory experiments do not reflect real-life situations. He and his colleagues emphasize the adaptive nature of decision-making as it fits certain environments (Gigerenzer, 2005; Hertwig & Patcher, 2011). "Heuristics are not good or bad, rational, or irrational, per se, but only relative to an environment. . . ." (p. xix). When "ecologically relevant," such strategies may surpass more deliberate approaches. Advocates of this approach argue that our limited information-processing capabilities may be an advantage because they facilitate rapid decisions based on recognition of relevant environmental cues. They encourage attention to the most relevant cues, so avoiding errors introduced by too much information, including misleading and irrelevant data. Stanovich (2012) argues that heuristics depend on benign environments that contain useful data such as accurate anchors. In hostile environments, there are few valuable cues (and lack of corrective feedback; Hogarth, 2001). However, the vast content knowledge of experts offers a guard against cues in hostile environments.

THE ROLE OF COGNITIVE BIASES

There is an extensive literature describing biases and fallacies that hinder sound decisions as well as suggestions for minimizing them (e.g., Croskerry, 2009; Croskerry, Singhal, & Mamede, 2013; Gambrill, 2012b; Jenicek & Hitchcock, 2005;

see Exhibit 6.4). Such biases and fallacies hinder discovery of important information (e.g., that your original assumption is incorrect). They can intrude at any point
in the reasoning process and include gender, racial, and ethnic biases (Fitzgerald &
Hurst, 2017). And, as emphasized in earlier chapters, intelligence is not correlated
with susceptibility to biases (West, Meserve, & Stanovich, 2012; see Chapter 8 for
discussion of fallacies). Literature in four major areas contribute to understanding
fallacies and biases: (1) philosophy including critical thinking and informal logic;
(2) psychology including relevant social-psychological studies as well as research on
judgment, problem-solving, and decision-making; (3) sociology (the study of political, social, and economic influences on problems selected for attention and how
they are defined); and (4) studies of clinical reasoning, decision-making, and judgment in the helping professions, including corrupting influences such as conflicts
of interest. Many biases impede accurate decision-making by misdirecting attention and so could be called "attentional biases" (Baron, 2008, p. 56.) We are most
likely to miss fallacies and biases in situations in which we are biased for (or against)
a certain point of view and fail to engage in active open-minded thinking.

Representative thinking is mainly an associative process in which the
associations we have with a certain characteristic influence our judgments. We
may incorrectly assume that because a homeless child is similar to someone we
just saw, similar causes are involved. We may ignore sample size; we may assume
that causes resemble their effects when this is not so. We often rely on what is
available in making decisions such as a preferred practice theory or a vivid example
(Tversky & Kahneman, 1973; see Exhibit 6.5). We are influenced by the vividness
of material in collecting, organizing, and interpreting data. Vivid information is
more likely to be remembered than pallid information; it is more available (Nisbett
& Ross, 1980). Vivid information can be misleading, especially when duller but
more informative material is not considered. Our preconceptions and theories affect which concepts and beliefs are available; they influence what events we notice
or inquire about. Preconceptions can lead to incorrect inferences when (1) a theory
is held on poor grounds (there is not adequate reason to believe that it is relevant);
(2) a theory is used unconsciously; and (3) use of the theory "preempts examination of the data" (Nisbett & Ross, 1980, p. 71). Overconfidence in and availability
of a theory increase the likelihood of biased preconceptions. The more ambiguous
the data, the more descriptions are influenced by preconceptions.

We tend to exaggerate our own contributions to tasks and to overestimate the
prevalence of events that receive a great deal of media attention and underestimate
the prevalence of illnesses that receive little media attention (Slovic, 2010). We
tend to believe in initial judgments, even when we are aware that the knowledge
we have access to has been arbitrarily selected (e.g., by the spin of a roulette wheel).

EXHIBIT 6.4
EXAMPLES OF BIASES

- *Affective bias*: arguing from emotion, appeal to pity or anger, using emotional language.
- *Anchoring*: focus on certain features and fail to adjust.
- *Availability*: overestimating the likelihood of events with greater "availability" (e.g., in memory; see hindsight and outcome bias).
- *Base rate neglect*: ignore prevalence.
- *Clustering illusion*: tendency to see patterns where there are none.
- *Commission bias*: tendency toward action rather than inaction.
- *Confirmation bias*: searching only for confirming evidence; focusing on successes only (cherry-picking).
- *Contrast effect*: the enhancement or reduction of a stimuli when compared with a recently observed, contrasting object.
- *Diagnostic momentum*: once a diagnosis or label is attached to clients, it tends to "stick" and other possibilities are ignored (Croskerry, 2003).
- *Empathy gap*: tendency to underestimate the influence or strength of feelings in either oneself or others.
- *Framing effects*: drawing different conclusions depending on how the same information is presented.
- *Gambler's fallacy*: belief that future probabilities are altered by past events.
- *Groupthink*: premature closure on one possibility.
- *Hawthorne effect*: the tendency of people to perform or perceive differently when they know that they are being observed.
- *Hindsight bias*: "I knew it would be so"; hindsight does not equal foresight.
- *Illusion of control*: overestimation of one's degree of influence over external events.
- *Illusion of validity*: belief that further information offers additional relevant data when it does not.
- *Information bias*: tendency to seek information when it is not needed to make informed decisions.
- *Illusory correlation*: beliefs that inaccurately suppose a relationship between a certain type of action and an effect.
- *Omission bias*: judging harmful actions as worse than equally harmful omissions (inactions).
- *Outcome bias*: judging a decision by its eventual outcome instead of on the quality of the decision when it was made.
- *Overconfidence*: excessive confidence in one's own views.
- *Overlooking* regression effect.
- *Premature closure*: accepting a view before carefully examining it.
- *Representativeness*: making decisions based on similarity (e.g., assuming causes are similar to their effects).

- *Semmelweis reflex*: the tendency to reject new evidence that contradicts a belief.
- *Social desirability bias*: overreporting socially desirable characteristics or behaviors in oneself and underreporting socially undesirable characteristics or behaviors.
- *Status quo bias*: the tendency to like things to stay the same (related to loss aversion, endowment effect, and system justification).
- *Stereotyping*: expecting a member of a group to have certain characteristics without information about that person.
- *Sunk costs:* the more we invest in a particular view, the less likely we may be to consider alternatives.
- *Wishful thinking:* assuming there's something true makes it so.

Social Biases
- *Egocentric bias*: people claim more responsibility for themselves for the results of a joint action than an outside observer would.
- *False consensus effect*: the tendency for people to overestimate the degree to which others agree with them.
- *Forer effect (or Barnum effect)*: the tendency to give high accuracy ratings to descriptions of their personality that supposedly are tailored for each individual.
- *Fundamental attribution error:* the tendency for people to overempha-size personality-based explanation for behavior observed in others while underemphasizing the role and power of situational influences on the same behavior (see *actor-observer bias, group attribution error, positivity effect,* and *negativity effect*).
- *Group-serving bias*: identical to *self-serving bias* except that it takes place between groups rather than individuals, under which group members make dispositional attributions for their group successes and situational attributions for their group failures, and vice versa for outsider groups. Also called *parochialism*.
- *Halo effect*: the tendency for people's positive or negative traits to "spill over" from one areas of their personality to another in others' views of them (see also *physical attractiveness stereotype*).
- *Herd instinct*: common tendency to adopt the opinions and follow the behaviors of the majority to feel safer and to avoid conflict.
- *Illusion of asymmetric insight*: people perceive their knowledge of their peers to surpass their peers' knowledge of them.
- *Illusion of transparency*: people overestimate others' ability to know them and overestimate their ability to know others.

- *Illusory superiority*: perceiving oneself as having desirable qualities to a greater degree than other people. Also known as superiority bias (see also Lake Wobegon effect).
- *In-group bias*: the tendency for people to give preferential treatment to others they perceive to be members of their own groups.
- *Just world phenomenon*: the tendency for people to believe that the world is "just" and therefore people "get what they deserve.
- *Lake Wobegon effect*: the phenomenon that most people report themselves as above average in desirable qualities (see also *worse-than-average effect, illusory superiority*, and *optimism bias*).
- *Outgroup homogeneity bias*: individuals see members of their own group as being more varied than members of other groups.
- *Physical attractiveness stereotype:* the tendency to assume that people who are physically attractive also possess other socially desirable personality traits.
- *Projection bias*: the tendency to unconsciously assume that others share the same or similar thoughts, beliefs, values, or positions.
- *Self-serving bias*: the tendency to claim more responsibility for success than failures; tendency for people to evaluate ambiguous information in a way beneficial to their interests (see also *group-serving bias*).
- *Self-fulfilling prophecy*: the tendency to engage in behaviors that elicit results that (consciously or not) confirm our beliefs.

Memory
- *Consistency bias*: incorrectly remembering one's past attitude and behavior as resembling present attitudes and behavior.
- *Egocentric bias*: recalling the past in a self-serving manner (e.g., remembering one's exam grades as being better than they were).
- *False memory*: confusion of imagination with memory or the confusion of true memories with false ones.
- *Hindsight bias*: filtering memory of past events through present knowledge so that events look more predictable than they actually were, the "I-knew-it-all-along effect."
- *Self-serving bias*: perceiving oneself responsible for desirable outcomes but not responsible for undesirable ones.
- *Suggestibility*: a form of misattribution where ideas suggested by a questioner are mistaken for memory.

Source: See Wikipedia.com.

Adjustments from initial values are often inadequate as in *anchoring effects*. We are influenced by recency—what we last see or hear. All these tendencies highlight the importance of active open-minded thinking (see Chapter 1). *Confirmation biases* are common (seeking only data that support favored views) (Nickerson, 1998; Nyhan & Reifler, 2010). We tend to seek and overweigh evidence that supports our beliefs and ignore and underweigh contrary evidence. That is, we try to justify (confirm) our assumptions rather than to falsify them (seek counterexamples and test them as rigorously as possible). This is an example of *partiality in the use of evidence* that can result in avoidable errors. Tufte (2007) refers to this as *cherry-picking*.

We may assign exaggerated importance to some findings to protect a favored hypothesis. Studies of medical reasoning show that *overinterpretation* is a common error (Elstein et al., 1978). This refers to assigning new information to a favored

---

EXHIBIT 6.5
EXAMPLES OF BIASES RELATED TO AVAILABILITY (ACCESSIBILITY OF DATA)

Preconceptions and preferred theories	Influence by assumptions about behavior/people.
Vividness	Concrete and salient data stand out more and are given more weight than are abstract data (e.g., statistical reports) or events that do not occur.
Behavior confirmation	We seek data that confirm favored views and ignore contradictory data.
Anchoring and insufficient adjustment	Influence by initial judgments or data and underadjustment based on new information.
Recency effects	Influence by data seen, heard, or read most recently.
Fundamental attribution error	Attribute behavior to personal characteristics and overlook environmental influences.
Resources available	Base decisions on resources available rather than client need.
Emotional influences	Influence by our mood or feelings about a person/event.
Motivational influences	Influence by our preferences for certain outcomes.

hypothesis rather than exploring alternative accounts that more effectively explain data or remembering this information separately. Data that provide some support for and against views increase confidence for holders of both views (Lord, Ross, & Lepper, 1979). The tendency of clinicians to attribute problems to the person and to overlook the role of environmental factors (the *fundamental attribution error*) has been a topic of interest for some time (e.g., Batson, O'Quin, & Psych, 1982). It is during initial case formulation that cognitive biases and fallacies may play their most harmful role in taking us down false paths and not recognizing when we are on them. Failure to revise our views when needed is a key source of poor decisions. Our moods and affective reactions to different people or events influence our decisions (Bless, 2001). Slovic Finucane, Peters, and MacGregor (2002) refer to reliance on feelings of goodness and badness in guiding judgments as the *affect heuristic*.

We are subject to *framing effects*—different presentations of information (McNeil, Pauker, Sox, & Tversky, 1982). These include how a problem is viewed (e.g., is anxiety a mental disorder or a learned reaction?) and how a decision is posed, for example, in terms of gains or losses (Peng, Li, Miao, Feng, & Xiao, 2013). Focusing on losses result in different decisions compared to focusing on gains (Akl et al., 2011). We tend to be risk adverse; overweigh risk of loss and underweigh risk of lost gain. In *hindsight bias,* we mistakenly assume that we could have known at time 1 what we only knew at time 2. Cognitive-biases include influence by vivid material such as case examples and testimonials as well as our tendency to believe that causes are similar to outcomes. We may jump to conclusions (decide on one option too soon) and overlook promising alternatives. Judgmental strategies are not necessarily consciously used. An interest in understanding and predicting our environment encourages a readiness to overlook uncertainty and offer explanations for what in fact, are chance occurrences. We are prone to making *oversimplifications* such as:

1. Seeing different entities as more similar than they actually are.
2. Treating dynamic phenomena as static.
3. Assuming that some general principle accounts for all of the phenomena.
4. Treating multidimensional phenomena as unidimensional or according to a subset of dimensions.
5. Treating continuous variables as discreet.
6. Treating highly interconnected concepts as separable.
7. Treating the whole as merely the sum of its parts. (Feltovich, Spiro, & Coulson, 1993, cited in Woods & Cook, 1999, p. 152; see also Woods & Hollnagel, 2006)

We are subject to *wishful thinking* (i.e., preference for an outcome increases our belief that it will occur) and the *illusion of control* (simply making a prediction may increase our belief that it may come true).

Social Biases

Examples of social biases include the *actor-observer bias* (our tendency to attribute the behavior of others to their personality and to underplay the role of environmental variables and to do the opposite for our own behavior), *the false consensus effect* (we overestimate the extent to which others agree with our views), *the halo effect* (generalizing positive views from one area regarding an individual to others), and the *self-serving bias* (claiming greater responsibility for successes than for failures; see Exhibit 6.6). The influence of *illusory correlations* on clinical

---

EXHIBIT 6.6

KINDS OF ERROR

Knowledge-based: For example, ignorance regarding the science of behavior (Madden, 2013).

Rule-based: Misapplying a good rule; using a bad rule or failing to use a good rule.

Memory-based: Memory failure (e.g., forgetting a patient's allergy to an antibiotic).

Medication: Any preventable event that may result in inappropriate harmful medication use (see Dovey et al., 2002).

System error: Error due to technology and the environment of care and its interaction with users (professionals) and recipients (e.g., patients).

Skill-based: Slips and lapses; errors in execution of correctly planned actions including both action-based errors (slips) and memorybased errors (lapses).

Evidence-based: Errors due to a lack of best evidence, failure to use it, use of poor, unsupported, or inappropriate evidence in argumentation otherwise good or flawed, leading to incorrect claims and decisions. Ignoring or misusing evidence and ignoring alternatives are the most significant fallacies as sources of error.

Argument-based: Misusing or omitting valid argument components or using them inappropriately (e.g., grounds, backing, warrants) and linking them poorly in decision-making.

Source: Adapted from *Medical Error and Harm: Understanding, Prevention, and Control,* by M. Jenicek, 2011, New York, NY: CRC, pp. 60–70.

observation was explored in the late sixties (e.g., Chapman & Chapman, 1969). Individual differences influence susceptibility to errors and biases. Tetlock (2003) found

> Respondents who valued closure and parsimony highly were more prone to biases that were rooted in excessive faith in the predictive and explanatory power of their preconceptions—biases such as overconfidence, cognitive conservatism, certainty of hindsight and selective standards of evidence and proof . . . more "open-minded," lower-need-for-closure respondents . . . would end up being too imaginative and assigning too much subjective probability to too many scenarios. . . . (p. 234)

The *fallacy of stereotyping* (Scriven, 1976, p. 208) consists of treating a description as if it represents all the individuals in a group of which it may (or may not) be a typical sample. A focus on cultural differences may result in lack of attention to individual differences within a culture. If we search only for evidence that supports a stereotype, we may miss more accurate accounts. As Ceci and Bruck (1995) note, "failure to test an alternative to a pet hunch can lead interviewers to ignore inconsistent evidence and to shape the contents of the interview to be consistent with their own beliefs" (p. 80). We tend to overestimate the variability of in-groups (groups of which we are a member) and underestimate the degree of variability in "out-groups" (groups of which we are not a member). De-biasing strategies include questioning assumptions (thinking about our reasoning process), ongoing training, arranging feedback regarding decisions, and altering the task environment (e.g., using a checklist; Gawande, 2009). Other options include using decision aids such as apps and decision algorithms (e.g., Informed Medical Decisions Foundation; Croskerry, Singhal, & Mamede, 2013).

ERRORS: THEIR NATURE, CAUSES, CONSEQUENCES, AND POTENTIAL REMEDIES

Errors have received a great deal of attention in medicine, aviation, and nuclear power, and there is an extensive literature in all three areas. Medical errors are the third leading cause of death in the United States (James, 2013; Makary & Daniels, 2016). Research regarding errors in social work, psychology, and psychiatry is very limited. Jenicek (2011) defines human error in medicine as a flaw in reasoning, understanding, and decision making made by a creator or operator regarding the solution of a health problem or in the ensuing sensory and physical execution of a task in clinical or community care. . . . The error is committed at the level of reasoning, critical thinking, and decision making or at the level of sensory or motor execution of the decided task and action and their evaluation. . . . This also includes the failure of a planned action to be completed as intended (i.e., error of execution) or the use of the wrong plan to achieve an aim (i.e., error of planning). (p. 66)

Research shows that the causes of errors are typically systemic (Reason, 1997, 2001; Vincent, 2010); they are usually not caused by one person or one environmental characteristic. Rather, they are related to a number of characteristics. Motivational and informational sources of error interact in various ways. We are most likely to miss biases in situations in which we are biased for (or against) a certain point of view and the informational source contains the same bias.

Bias can intrude at any point in the judgmental process and may also occur because of interactions between different stages of data processing (Hogarth, 2001).

First, the acquisition of information from both the environment and memory can be biased. The crucial issue here is how certain information does or does not become salient. How we direct our attention influences what we see and what we miss). Second, the manner in which we process information can be biased; for example, we may attempt to simplify a situation by using a misleading strategy. Third, the manner in which we are required to respond can introduce bias. Finally, the outcomes of our judgments can create bias in both: (1) interpretation of their significance for example, is the outcome attributable to one's actions or simply a chance fluctuation?); and (2) learning relationships for predictive validity. (Hogarth, 2001, p. 158)

Reason (2001) distinguishes among mistakes, violations, lapses, and slips that may occur during planning, recalling intentions, carrying out a task, or monitoring. A violation entails knowingly omitting an important step. A lapse involves not recalling an intention to carry out an important task at the needed time. A slip entails unwittingly omitting an important task in a sequence and/or not detecting it.

Norman et al. (2017) emphasize the role of knowledge deficits in making errors. "Educational strategies directed at the recognition of biases are ineffective in reducing errors; conversely, strategies focused on the reorganization of knowledge to reduce errors have small but consistent benefits" (p. 23). They argue that errors arise from both Type 1 and Type 2 reasoning (p. 24). They describe research showing that errors do not arise from cognitive biases, one being that decreasing bias does not make up for lack of important knowledge. "Knowledge matters. Even if some proportion of errors arise from cognitive biases, the resolution of errors also involves the application of clinical knowledge, which may underlie the initial mistake" (p. 28). (See also earlier related discussion in this chapter.) Research regarding expert political judgment concerning real-world events within an individuals' domain of expertise shows that they often fall prey to five errors or biases:

1. *Overconfidence.* There are large gaps between the subjective probabilities assigned to outcomes and the objective probabilities of those outcomes occurring (e.g., the illusion of knowledge).
2. *Cognitive conservatism.* Experts are slow to update their beliefs.
3. *Certainty of hindsight.* Mistakes may be denied. "They tend to recall assigning higher subjective probabilities to those . . . outcomes that occur than they actually assigned before learning what occurred."
4. *Theory-driven standards of evidence and proof.* They "generally impose higher standards of evidence and proof on dissonant claims than they do on consonant ones." They use a double standard.
5. *Systematic evidence of incoherence in subjective probability judgments.* They "often judge the likelihood of the whole to be less, sometimes far less, than the sum of its parts." (Tetlock, 2003, pp. 233–234; see also Tetlock, 2005).

Faulty communication and lack of knowledge (both background and foreground), may result in errors in assessment (e.g., overlooking environmental circumstances or client assets), intervention (selection of ineffective or harmful services), and evaluation (e.g., focusing on irrelevant outcomes). Kinds of errors are illustrated in Exhibit 6.6. They may be errors of commission or omission. They usually reflect deficiencies in the *system of* care. Research regarding error highlights its inevitability and the many related causes:

- Human fallibility can be moderated up to a point, but it can never be eliminated entirely—partly because errors, in many contexts, serve a useful function (e.g., trial-and-error learning in knowledge-based situations).
- Different error types have different psychological causes, occur in different parts of organizations, and require different methods of management.

- Safety-critical errors occur at all levels of the system, not just at the sharp end.
- Measures that involve sanctions, threats, and appeal to fear and have limited effectiveness; in some cases, they can do more harm—to morale, self-respect, and a sense of justice—than good.
- Errors are a product of a chain of causes in which the precipitating psychological factors—momentary inattention, misjudgment, forgetfulness, and preoccupation—are often the last and least manageable links in the chain (for a discussions of cascade effects, see Woods & Hollnagel, 2006).
- Negative events are more often the result of error-prone situations and activities than of error-prone people (Reason, 1997, p. 129; see also Jenicek, 2011; Vincent, 2010).

Errors reported in family medicine include administrative errors (e.g., information in wrong place), errors in the process of exploring a client's condition (e.g., errors in the process of laboratory investigations such as wrong test ordered, incorrect reports, or important test not ordered), errors in treating a patient's condition (e.g., wrong medication or dose), errors in communication, and errors due to incorrect performance of a procedure and lack of knowledge or skills (Dovey et al., 2002).

Given that feedback is vital for learning, we miss valuable opportunities if we do not attend to errors and their causes and plan how to minimize them. Some errors are unavoidable because of lack of information. Many are avoidable. For example, they may be related to failure to acquire knowledge needed for accurate understanding of concerns (e.g., observation of parent–child interaction). Mistakes include failure to recognize a problem, collection of misleading information, incorrect problem framing, premature closure, and harmful delay in making decisions (Caruth & Handlogten, 2000). Types of medical mistakes include misdiagnoses, medication errors, procedural errors, administrative errors, communication errors, incorrect lab results, and equipment malfunction (National Patient Safety Foundation Survey, 2015). Related reasons include carelessness or negligence, lack of training, incompetence, miscommunication (e.g., misreading prescriptions), and excessive workloads.

Factors that influence how safety is handled include *safety-specific factors*, such as policies concerning incident and accident reporting and emergency resources, and *management factors,* including how change is handled, quality of leadership and communication, policies regarding hiring and placement, purchasing, and degree of control over purchasing. *Technical factors* also influence how safety is handled, such as compatibility of human and system interfaces. *Procedural factors* include standards, rules, and operating procedures. *Training characteristics* influence safety (Reason, 1997; see also Vincent, 2010.) For example, is there a close match between training offered and competencies required? If reporting mistakes is punished, few will do it. On the other hand, if agency policy recognizes that mistakes will be made and that they are vital for learning how to do better in the future and staff are encouraged to discuss them with their supervisors at an early point, they are less likely to result in further negative effects and can provide an opportunity to learn how to decrease avoidable mistakes (e.g., see classic study by Bosk, 1979).

Strategies suggested to make incident reporting work are illustrated in Exhibit 6.7. A key reason errors and mistakes continue is that no one identifies them, brings them to people's attention, searches for their causes, and involves others in trying to minimize avoidable ones.

THE ETHICS OF EXPERTISE

The ethical obligations of professionals to help, not to harm, and to involve clients as informed participants in decisions that affect their lives suggest an ethics of expertise. As emphasized throughout this book, ethical and evidentiary issues are closely intertwined. Special skills and knowledge are often required to help clients. A clinician may or may not possess these competencies and may or may not be aware of her own ignorance. There is a duty to be informed about important uncertainties about decisions made, to share ignorance as well as knowledge with clients in a supportive manner, and to reveal and advocate for needed changes in circumstances that affect individual clients, such as lack of needed resources. This will require active open-minded thinking. To present oneself as an expert when this is not the case is an ethical lapse—it misleads people. The greater the knowledge and skill needed to help clients attain hoped-for outcomes, the more important it is to possess these and the greater the ethical lapse of misleading clients concerning this issue. Both epistemic values (to accurately represent the world) as well as skills in self-regulation contribute to enhancing expertise (e.g., Stanovich, 2012) (See Chapters 2 and 11).

EXHIBIT 6.7

MAKING ADVERSE INCIDENT REPORTING WORK

1. Training all staff on risk management and incident reporting.
2. Continuing education on the aims and importance of risk management and incident reporting.
3. A clear statement that all staff are responsible for reporting.
4. A clear description of reportable incidents and indicators developed in consultation with staff.
5. User-friendly incident reporting forms.
6. Clear description of reporting procedures.
7. Encouragement of staff to report an incident even if they are not sure whether it is necessary to do so.
8. A designated person who is responsible for making sure that any incident that occurs during that time is reported.
9. A policy of no blame and no disciplinary action except in cases of gross misconduct, repeated errors despite retraining, or criminal negligence.
10. Regular feedback to staff describing action taken as a result of their reports.
11. Design of corrective strategies to reduced undesirable incidents in the future.
12. Inclusion in clinical practice of specific corrective strategies by general consensus.
13. Evaluation of the efficacy of corrective strategies.

Source: Adapted from "Clinical Incident Reporting," by J. Secker-Walker and S. Taylor-Adams, 2001, in *Clinical Risk Management: Enhancing Patient Safety* (2nd ed.), edited by C. Vincent, London, UK: BMJ, p. 434. See also M. Jenicek, 2011, *Medical Error and Harm: Understanding, Prevention, and Control.* New York, NY: CRC, and Vincent (2010).

SUMMARY

Professionals are assumed to have special expertise that contributes to achieving hoped-for outcomes. This is the reason there are special licenses for specific kinds (e.g., psychiatrists, social workers, dentists). Literature on decision-making and expertise highlights how decision-making may go wrong, including lack of needed content knowledge and failure to correct biases by active open-minded thinking. Literature on medical decision-making emphasizes content—specialized knowledge as a result of years of acquiring content knowledge and experience in a field allowing rapid recognition of patterns. Errors and omissions in earlier steps may combine with lack of knowledge and skill in integrating multiple kinds of information resulting in decisions that are not optimal. Experience alone does not increase expertise. Developing, maintaining, and enhancing expertise requires enhancing knowledge and skills facilitated by repeated opportunities to gain corrective feed-back and learning from this. The process of evidence-based practice encourages AOT including attention to gaps in knowledge and efforts to decrease them. This increases the likelihood that decisions will be well-reasoned.

7

Argumentation

ITS CENTRAL ROLE IN DELIBERATIVE DECISION-MAKING

MAKING DECISIONS INVOLVES consideration of possibilities, evidence and goals (see Chapter 1). Reasoning, problem-solving, and decision-making are closely related and the tasks they involve overlap. We make decisions to address problems. As Baron (2008) suggests, the whole point of thinking is to make decisions that contribute to achieving valued goals. Consideration of possibilities will require making arguments for and against different views in light of related evidence. Consider:

> Mrs. Z, 70 years old, a retired school teacher presented with an intense fear of water. She would not sit down in my office because there was a water basin in the office and she said that water may come out. She was worried that she would become a "dirty old lady" because she had to use such small amounts of water to clean herself. Assessment questions included: (1) Is this a simple phobia; (2) does this phobia serve another function, and, if so, what would it be; and (3) how can I find out?

We can decrease our vulnerability to misinformation by enhancing our skills in argumentation as well as by cultivating intellectual dispositions that contribute to sound decisions such as fair-mindedness to possibilities. "An argument is a sequence of reasoning used to remove doubt about some unsettled proposition, namely the conclusion that is claimed to be true but is not known to be true

186

by both parties to the discussion" (Walton, 2015, p. 104). Considering clashing perspectives (controversies) regarding an issue or question is vital to explore the cogency of different views; it is necessary for learning—for example, correcting background knowledge about an issue by discovering our ignorance (Johnson, 2015). Consider the following claims: (1) Our services work; (2) social anxiety is a mental disorder; (3) inability to concentrate can be remedied by taking Ritalin; and (4) full-body CT scans save lives. Are these claims accurate? What evidence is needed to evaluate the claim? Is this described? If someone makes a claim and is asked for evidence, he may describe this, acknowledge that no evidence was given or is available, or engage in palaver (vague responses designed to mislead (see Chapter 9).

The term *argument* has a different meaning in everyday use in which it refers to a disagreement between two people as in an argument about who should go to the store. An explanation differs from an argument. An explanation is offered by one party in a discussion to help another party understand something (Walton, 2015, p. 104). Skill in reasoning including avoiding myside bias and distinguishing between evidence and pseudoevidence is vital to constructive controversy. Argumentation is based on reasoning, but unlike reasoning (which Walton views as control free). it "is a dialectical notion." It is a matter of how reasoning is used for some purpose in a conversational exchange between two parties" (p. 251). (See Exhibit 7.1)

EXHIBIT 7.1
DIALOGUE TYPOLOGY

Type of Dialogue	Initial Situation	Participant's Goal	Goal of Dialogue
Persuasion	Conflict of opinions	Persuade other	Resolve issue
Inquiry	Need to have proof	party	Prove hypothesis
Discovery	Need an	Verify evidence	Support hypothesis
Negotiation	explanation	Find a hypothesis	Settle issue
Information	Conflict of interests	Get what you want	Exchange
Deliberation	Need information	Acquire information	information
Eristic (quarrel)	Practical choice	Fit goals and actions	Decide what to do
	Personal conflict	Hit out at opponent	Reveal deep conflict

Source: Goal-Based Reasoning for Argumentation, by D. Walton, 2015, New York, NY: Columbia University Press, p. 41.

REASONING, ARGUMENTS, DECISION-MAKING, AND EVIDENCE

Reasoning involves thinking critically about beliefs and claims. It involves argumentation, with yourself and others. We must be able "to reflect on [our] own theory as an object of cognition to an extent sufficient to recognize that it could be wrong. Second, [we] need to recognize evidence that would disconfirm the theory" (Kuhn, 1993, p. 93). That is, we must distance ourselves from our beliefs to critically evaluate them. We must recognize when a theory may be incorrect by seeking evidence that disconfirms it (Kuhn, 1993). Valuable skills include identifying assumptions and their implications (consequences), suspending judgment in the absence of sufficient evidence to support a claim/decision, understanding the difference between reasoning and rationalizing, and stripping an argument of irrelevancies and phrasing it in terms of its essentials. Consider this example: "Ms. Conner hears voices. She is schizophrenic." What are underlying assumptions? What is missing? Or, let's say that a social worker states that a parent uses abusive parenting methods because she is not skilled in the use of positive methods of managing her child's behavior. She finds during arranged role plays that the mother does have such skills. Her prior belief is disconfirmed because she questioned this and arranged a test of its accuracy. How often do we seek evidence that disconfirms a belief including "thought experiments"? This depends in part on our theory of knowledge:

- belief in what the experts say (knowledge is certain and accumulates)
- "knowledge is subjective, dictated by personal tastes and wishes of knower" (Kuhn, 1993, p. 169)
- "knowledge is an open ended process of continuing evaluation and judgement" (p. 169)

In the first instance, we depend on what the experts say. In the second we depend on feelings. The third reflects a scientific approach. As Kuhn notes, why people believe a certain thing is often more interesting and important than the beliefs themselves because this reveals *how* they think about beliefs/theories. For example, what kinds of evidence do they seek and use? Lack of evidence for a claim does not mean that it is incorrect. Nor does lack of evidence discourage people from believing a claim and promoting it as true. Indeed, if some scientists had not persisted in their explorations of claims dismissed as impossible or not critically tested, we would have missed out on many discoveries.

Partiality in the use of evidence such as hiding adverse effects of a drug is a hallmark of propaganda. Unless we are familiar with an area (such as social anxiety), we probably will not detect what is missing, such as an accurate description of well-argued alternative views. Propagandists often give an *illusion of argument*—pieces are missing, hoped-for actions ("Fight terror") and effects ("Be safe") are vague and critical appraisal is discouraged. Certain views may be encouraged and claims implied via visual images such as pictures of brains (McCabe & Castel, 2008) as well as described verbally. Our own biases often cloud our judgments and propagandists take full advantage of this.

In an article titled "Thinking as Argument" Kuhn (1992) describes different kinds of evidence. *Genuine evidence* includes evidence external to the asserted cause such as evidence of covariation and various kinds of indirect evidence such as disconfirming alternatives. Successful counterarguments may include those against causal necessity. Rebuttals may involve appeal to well-argued alternative theories. In *pseudoevidence*, there may be a simple restatement of the phenomenon in the context of a specific instance; evidence is "simply assimilated to a theory losing opportunities to use it to critique the theory" (p. 170). When asked to describe why they held a certain belief, some people in Kuhn's (1993, p. 93) studies mixed theory-based and evidence-based reasons. There is a mixing of beliefs with evidence. There is an absence of exclusion reasoning that allows the elimination of factors from consideration (and thereby simplifies analysis (p. 93). There is a focus only on positive cases. As Kuhn (1992) notes, these kinds of errors may be related to one's theory of knowledge, ranging from the belief that knowledge is certain to the view that knowledge requires continued evaluation. This discussion highlights the importance of an active search for evidence that does *not* support your beliefs—active open-minded thinking: What are counterexamples? What data would disprove this belief?

Reference may be made to imaginary evidence. Thousands of retractions have been made from peer-reviewed publications, many because of fabrication (data were just made up; see retractionwatch.com). A psychologist may report that he has seen many clients with anorexia and so he can speak with authority about this disorder, when, in fact, he has seen one such client. The fabrication of data seems to be becoming more common as pressures mount to publish and competition for funding becomes keener. Research findings may be misrepresented. Lists of alleged "best practices" may contain programs no better than those not included (Gandhi, Murphy-Graham, Petrosino, Chrismer, & Weiss, 2007; Gorman & Huber, 2009).

ARGUMENTS

Toulmin and his colleagues (1979) use the term *argumentation* to refer to the process of "making claims, challenging these, backing them with reasons, criticizing
these reasons and responding to the criticism offered" (p. 13). Arguments involve
a set of assertions, one of which is a conclusion and the rest of which are offered
to support that conclusion. A psychiatrist may argue that, because a client has a
history of being hospitalized for compulsive hand-washing, current complaints
indicate that another episode is imminent. Arguments consist of parts; they can
be taken apart as well as put together. They may be strong (convincing) or weak
(unconvincing), simple or complex. Claims may involve statements of fact ("a belief for which there is enough evidence to warrant a high degree of confidence";
Nickerson, 1986, p. 36), assumptions, or hypotheses. For example, there may be
no doubt that someone was hospitalized. The term *assumption* refers to "an assertion that we either believe to be true in spite of being unable to produce compelling evidence of its truth, or are willing to accept as true for purposes of debate
or discussion" (Nickerson, 1986a, pp. 36–37). A hypothesis is an assertion that we
do not know to be true but that we think is testable. Assumptions, hypotheses,
or statements of fact may be used as premises in an argument, or they may serve
as conclusions; that is, an assertion may be a conclusion that is drawn from what
precedes it and can also be a premise with respect to what follows it.

> The credibility of a conclusion can be no greater than the least credible of
> the premises from which it is drawn, so a conclusion cannot be considered
> a statement of fact unless all of the premises are statements of fact. . . . If
> the conclusion follows from two premises one of which is considered to be a
> fact and the other an assumption, the conclusion should not be considered a
> statement of fact. (Nickerson, 1986, p. 7)

A key part of an argument is the claim, conclusion, or position that is put forward (see Exhibit 7.2). What kind of claim is made? What evidence is needed to
evaluate the claim? Is this described? Is anything left out? Domain-specific knowledge including both content (knowing what) and procedural knowledge (knowing
how to apply content knowledge), may be needed to make and implement sound
decisions. For example, what knowledge would be important in determining the
quality of parenting skills? Excessive wordiness may make the premises or conclusion difficult to identify. Claims or conclusions are often qualified—that is,
some probability is expressed as in "I think it is likely that Mary Walsh abused
this child." Conclusions may be qualified by describing conditions under which

EXHIBIT 7.2

TOULMIN'S SIX TYPES OF STATEMENT IN A RATIONAL ARGUMENT

Label	Name(s)	Logical Function
C	Claim or conclusion	States a claim or a conclusion.
D	Data, evidence	Offers data or foundations such as relevant evidence.
W	Inference warrant	Warrants the connection between data (D) and claim (C) for example by appealing to research or experience.
Q	Qualifier	Qualifies a claim or conclusion by expressing degree of confidence and suggesting possible errors.
R	Rebuttal	Rebuts a claim or conclusion by describing conditions under which it does not hold; or introduces reservations showing the limits within which the claim (C) is made.
B	Backing	Backs up, justifies, or otherwise supports an inference warrant by appealing to further evidence such as empirical data.

Colloquially speaking:

C	answers "What are you claiming?" "What is your conclusion?"
D	answers "Where is your evidence?" "What data do you have?"
W	answers "What is the connection?" "Why are you entitled to draw that conclusion?"
Q	answers "How sure are you?" "What confidence do you have in your claim?" "How likely is it that what you say is correct?"
R	answers "What are you assuming?" "Under what conditions would your argument break down?" "What reservations would you make?"
B	answers "Is there support for the connection you are making?"

Source: Adapted from *The Case-Study Method in Psychology and Related Disciplines,* by D. B. Bromley, 1986, New York, NY: Wiley, p. 195. Copyright 1986 by John Wiley & Sons.

they may not hold as in the statement: "She would only abuse the child if she were under extreme stress."

The reasons or premises offered to support a claim is a second critical feature of an argument. Sound reasons consist of those for which sound arguments can be offered. Premises can be divided into two parts: grounds and warrants. The grounds (data or evidence) must be relevant to the claim as well as sufficient to support the claim. Warrants concern the inference or justification of making the connection between the grounds and the claim. Do the grounds provide support for the claim? Warrants may involve a variety of appeals including to common knowledge, empirical evidence, or theory. Consider the claim that Mary Walsh is responsible for the abuse of a child. The ground is that she had opportunity. The warrant may be that opportunity is sufficient to yield abuse. However, there is no firm backing for this warrant; opportunity does not an abuser make. Warrants purport to offer evidence for making the step from the grounds to the claim; the strength of the support should be evaluated. Does the warrant provide required evidence? Are the grounds necessary or sufficient? For example, opportunity to commit a crime is necessary but not sufficient to determine guilt. Can the premises be established independently of the conclusion? Is the argument convincing? Possible combinations of false or true premises and conclusions are shown in Exhibit 7.3.

An argument may be unsound for one of three reasons. There may be something wrong with its logical structure: (1) all mental patients are people; (2) John is a person; (3) therefore, John is a mental patient. It may contain false premises: (1) all battering men were abused as children; (2) Mr. Smith batters his wife; (3) therefore, Mr. Smith was abused as a child. It may be irrelevant or circular: (1) kicking other children is a sign of aggression; (2) Johnny kicks other children;

EXHIBIT 7.3

COMBINATIONS OF TRUE OR FALSE PREMISES AND CONCLUSIONS IN A
VALID LOGICAL ARGUMENT

		Conclusion	
		True	False
Premises	True	Necessary (If premises are true, conclusion must be true)	Impossible (If premises are true, conclusion cannot be false)
	False	Possible (Even if premises are false, conclusion *may* be true)	Possible (If premises are false, conclusion *may* be false)

Source: Adapted from *Reflections on Reasoning*, by R. S. Nickerson, 1986, Hillsdale, NJ: Erlbaum, p. 90.
Copyright 1986 by Lawrence Erlbaum Associates.

(3) therefore, Johnny is aggressive. The last two arguments contain informal fallacies; they have a correct logical form but are still incorrect. Arguments often contain unfounded premises; they give the impression they are valid, but, because relevant facts are omitted or distorted, they are not. Consider the logical error of *affirming the consequent*: (1) if he has measles, he should have red spots; (2) he has spots; (3) therefore, he has measles. *Denying the antecedent* also involves a logical error: (1) if we don't conserve our resources, the supply will run out; (2) we will not waste resources; (3) therefore, our supply will not run out. In neither case does the conclusion follow from the premises. These errors involve a confusion between one-way and bidirectional implication. The *premise conversion error* occurs when the claim "all X are Y" (all clinicians are human) is assumed to be the same as "all Y are X" (all humans are clinicians). Some arguments are false even though they are valid. A valid argument is one whose premises, if true, offers good or sufficient grounds for accepting a conclusion. The incorrectness of premises may be overlooked resulting in poor decisions.

Deductive arguments involve a sequence of premises and a conclusion; if the premises are true, the conclusion necessarily follows (although it may not be true because one or more of the premises may be false). Deductive arguments can produce false conclusions either when one of the premises is false or when one of the rules of deductive inference is violated, as in the fallacy of affirming the consequent. The conclusion may be true, but it is invalid because it is arrived at by an illogical inference. Seldom are the major premises as well as the conclusion clearly stated in deductive arguments; more typically, at least one premise is missing. Logical (deductive) arguments use deductive inferences. Objective criteria can be used to evaluate such arguments.

Inductive reasoning involves generalizing from the particular to the general. Related arguments are *defeasible* (subject to being overturned as new evidence is collected). It may be assumed that what is true of the sample is true of all cases. For example, if a psychologist sees three young successful professional men who use cocaine and who complain of stress in their work life, she may conclude that all such men experience stress. In inductive reasoning, we go beyond the data at hand in drawing a conclusion that we cannot affirm with certainty (see Popper's, 1972, critique of induction). Kinds of inferences that may be involved in an argument include:

abductive: This goes backwards from an observation to explore possible reasons (inference to best explanation

deductive: In a valid deductive inference it is (logically) not possible for the premises to be true and the conclusion false.

inductive: Generalizing from a number of particular circumstances.

plausible: Based on apparent facts in a case suggesting a conclusion that appears to be true.

presumptive: This refers to a proposition proposed by one person for acceptance by both parties in a discussion. It is subject to later retraction or acceptance by the other person.(See Nickerson, 1986; Walton, 2005).

WALTON'S PRAGMATIC APPROACH TO ARGUMENT: THE IMPORTANCE OF CONTEXT

Arguments occur in different contexts, including articles in professional journals, courts of law, and case conferences, which influence norms, values, procedures, and types of evidence that are acceptable or unacceptable (see Exhibit 7.1). Consider the excerpt Walton (2008) gives of a dialogue:

A. I have a fourteen-year-old son.
B. Well that's all right.
A. I also have a dog.
B. Oh, I'm sorry (p. 2).

As Walton notes, viewed without information about the context of this conversation, it seems very odd. The context concerns apartment rental. "From the pragmatic point of view, any particular argument should be seen as being advanced in the context of a particular dialogue setting. Sensitivity to the special features of different contexts of dialogue is a requirement for the reasoned analysis of an argument" (Walton, 2008, p. 2; see Exhibit 7.4). Different contexts determine appropriate and inappropriate "moves" by participants. Different goals are pursued in different contexts. "Practical reasoning can be used in all seven types of dialogue, but it needs to be evaluated differently depending on the type of dialogue in which it was used in a given case" (Walton, 2015, p. 41). Such reasoning involves deliberation in which we reason from a goal to an action (Baron, 2000; Walton, 2015).

Does intent matter? If two people are in a discussion and one uses a deceptive tactic but is not aware that it is deceptive, does it make a difference? It depends in part on whether both participants share the same goal. For example, if participants share the goal of arriving at the truth, there is an inquiry argument: one will thank the other for noting flaws because both share the same goal, for example, of helping a client receive quality services. If participants have different goals (the

---

EXHIBIT 7.4

WALTON'S ARGUMENT-BASED THEORY OF RATIONALITY

1. It analyzes and evaluates argumentation for a claim on a balance of evidence where there is evidence for as well as against it, using sound standards.
2. Rational argumentation is viewed as a dialogue, implying that two heads are better than one when assessing claims regarding what to accept based on evidence.
3. Critical questioning is used as a way to discover weak points in an argument, and it can represent critical questions as special types of premises in an argument map.
4. Argumentation is viewed as procedural; proving something is viewed as a sequence with a start point and end point, as depicted on an argument map.
5. It is commitment-based. It uses a database of commonly accepted knowledge that includes previous arguments and the commitments expressed in them.
6. It is dynamic; it continually updates its database as new evidence is discovered that is relevant to the argument under consideration.
7. It is defeasible; an argument being considered is subject to defeat as new relevant evidence is discovered that refutes the argument.
8. It is presumptive; in the absence of evidence sufficient to defeat it, a claim that is the conclusion of an argument can be tentatively accepted, even though it may be withdrawn later.
9. It has the capability to model explanations and to use this model to depict how argument, explanation, and evidence are combined.
10. It does not see knowledge as a set of fixed propositions that must be accepted beyond all doubt, but recognizes the fallibility of evidence-based scientific knowledge (Adapted from Walton, 2015, pp. 244–245).

---

other person may just want to get through the situation and is not interested in the "truth," as in palaver and Frankfurt's view of "bullshit"; see Chapter 9) or believe they already know the answer so can learn little or nothing from others, deceptive tactics may be used such as introducing a red herring (irrelevant content) or irrelevant ad hominum (noting that someone does not have a degree).

Inquiry

"The goal of *inquiry* is to [determine] whether a particular proposition is true [or false] or, alternatively, to show that, despite an exhaustive search uncovering all the available evidence, it cannot be determined that a proposition is true [or false]" (Walton, 1995, p. 106). The goal is an increase in knowledge. It is a cooperative endeavor. Glib answers to relevant questions are out of order as are "moral political denunciations of ideas, rather than assessment of their logical structure" (Webster, 1987, p. 194). The stages include collecting pertinent data, discussing possible conclusions, and presenting what has been decided, perhaps in a report. Evidentiary status (the premises are more sound or are more reliable as evidence than the conclusion they were used to determine) is a key concern in inquiry. Different types of inquiry have different standards of evidence (e.g., legal, governmental). A debate differs from inquiry because people can be won over using flawed arguments in an adversarial context (Walton, 1995).

Discovery

In a *discovery dialogue*, there is an interest in discovering and critically appraising claims or views. There is a commitment to sharing information.

Negotiation

In *negotiation,* the key goal is self interest, and the method is bargaining. (See Walton, 2005). There is a conflict of interest. As Walton (1997) suggests, at stake is not truth but goods or economic resources. Thus, argumentation may occur, but the goal may not be to discover the truth.

Information-Seeking

In i*nformation-seeking,* one party has some information that another party wants to find out about. This kind of discussion is asymmetrical. The role of the one party is to give information that he possesses, and the role of the other is to receive or gain access to it. Walton (1995) notes that this kind of dialogue is different from the inquiry in which all parties are "more or less equally knowledgeable or ignorant and their collective goal is to prove something" (Walton, 1995, p. 114).

Deliberation

In *deliberation,* there is a dilemma or practical choice that must be made. Questions may be "How do I do this?" or "Which of two possibilities are best?" Deliberative reasoning is integral to making informed decisions.

The Quarrel

The *quarrel* involves personal conflict. The goal is to share, acknowledge, and deal with "hidden grievances," often to facilitate continuation of a personal relationship.

Persuasion

Here there is a conflict of opinion. The goal is to persuade the other party of a conclusion or point of view using premises to which the other party is committed. The respondent may "have (1) the role of casting doubt on the proponents' attempts to prove his thesis or (2) the role of arguing for the opposite thesis" (Walton, 2013, p. 9). The goal "is to reveal the strongest arguments on both sides by pitting one against the other to resolve the initial conflict posed at the opening stage" (p. 9). There is an obligation to co-operate with the other person's efforts to support his view.

GRICE'S MAXIMS

Walton draws on Grice's maxims of conversation in his pragmatic approach. The *maxim of quantity* includes making your contribution to a conversation as informative as necessary and not making your contribution more informative than necessary. The *maxim of quality* includes not saying what you believe to be false and not saying that for which you lack adequate evidence. The *maxim of relevance* includes an expectation to be relevant (i.e., say things related to the current topic of the conversation), and the *maxim of manner* includes avoiding obscurity of expression and ambiguity, being brief (avoid unnecessary wordiness), and being orderly. This means that certain moves in an argument are "out of order"—they deflect from rather than contribute to the achievement of the goal of a certain kind of argument, for example, failing to respond to critical questions in inquiry dialogues (see Exhibit 7.5).

IMPLICATIONS OF WALTON'S PRAGMATIC VIEW OF ARGUMENTATION FOR UNDERSTANDING FALLACIES

In Walton's theory of argumentation, discourse traditionally viewed as a fallacy such as an abusive ad hominem (attacking the person rather than points in an argument) may be sound; someone may have low credibility. The term *argumentation scheme* refers to "forms of argument (structures of inference) that represent common types of arguments used in everyday discourse, as well as in special contexts like those of legal argumentation and scientific arguments (Walton, Reed, & Macagno, 2008, p. 1). All are *defeasible* (open to refutation; see Exhibit 7.6). Walton describes a set of questions to review each type of "argument scheme." This pragmatic view of fallacy emphasizes the importance of context. What is a fallacy in one context such as scientific inquiry may not be

EXHIBIT 7.5

NEGATIVE RULES IN DIFFERENT STAGES OF A PERSUASION DIALOGUE

Opening
1. Unlicensed shifts from one type of dialogue to another are not allowed.

Confrontation
1. Unlicensed attempts to change the agenda are not allowed.
2. Refusal to agree to a specific agenda of dialogue prohibits moving to the argumentation stage.

Argumentation
1. Not making a serious effort to satisfy an obligation. Examples include not meeting a burden of proof or not defending a commitment when challenged.
2. Trying to shift your burden of proof to the other party, or otherwise alter the burden of proof illicitly, is not allowed.
3. Purporting to carry out an internal proof by using premises that are not commitments of the other party is not permitted.
4. Appealing to external sources of support without backing up an argument properly can be subject to objection.
5. Failures of relevance include offering the wrong thesis, moving away from the point of concern, or answering the wrong question.
6. Both failure to ask questions appropriate for a given stage of dialogue and asking inappropriate questions should be prohibited.
7. Failure to reply appropriately to questions should not be allowed, including evasive replies.
8. Failure to define, clarify, or support the meaning or definition of a key term, in accord with standards of precision appropriate to the discussion, is a violation, if use of this term is challenged.

Closing
1. A participant must not try to force closure except by mutual agreement or by meeting the goal of dialogue.

Source: Adapted from *Informal Logic: A Pragmatic Approach* (2nd ed.), by D. N. Walton, 2008, New York, NY: Cambridge University Press, pp. 16–17.

in another such as a quarrel. "A fallacy is defined as an argument that not only does not contribute to the goal of a dialogue but actually blocks or impedes the realization of that purpose" (Walton, 1995, p. 255). Fallacies may or may not be used deliberately to gain some advantage unfairly.(See also Chapter 8.) A fallacy falls short of some standard of correctness although it may appear correct.

EXHIBIT 7.6
EXAMPLES OF ARGUMENT "SCHEMES"

- Argument from analogy
- Argument from a verbal classification
- Argument from rule
- Argument from exception to a rule
- Argument from precedent
- Practical reasoning
- Lack of knowledge arguments
- Arguments from consequences
- Fear and danger appeals
- Arguments from alternatives and opposites
- Pleas for help and excuses
- Composition and division arguments
- Slippery slope arguments
- Arguments from popular opinion
- Argument from commitment
- Arguments from inconsistency
- Argument from bias
- Abusive ad hominem strategies
- Argument from cause to effect
- Argument from effect to cause
- Argument from correlation to cause
- Argument from evidence to a hypothesis
- Abductive reasoning (reasoning from observation to hypothesis to testing)
- Argument from position to know
- Argument from expert opinion

Source: Adapted from *Methods of argumentation*, by D. N. Walton, 2013, New York, NY: Cambridge University Press, pp. 94–95. See also D. N. Walton, C. Reed, and F. Macagno, 2008, *Argumentation Schemes,* New York, NY: Cambridge University Press.

It may be an error or blunder or a tactic to get the best of the other person unfairly.

Walton (2015) views irrationality as being closed to critical questions and counter-arguments.

ARGUMENTS FROM AUTHORITY

Appeals to authority include reference to popular views, titles, tradition, and consensus. Someone may encourage you to accept a claim simply because many people believe it is true; they may appeal to popular sentiments to support a conclusion that is not supported by sound evidence (Walton, 2008). Walton (1997) emphasizes the importance of distinguishing between cognitive authority (always subject to critical questioning), and institutional or administrative authority:

> The second form of the appeal to authority invests some sources with infallibility and finality and invokes some external force to give sanction to their decisions. On questions of politics, economics, and social conduct, as well as on religious opinions, the method of authority has been used to root out, as heretical or disloyal, divergent opinions. Men have been frightened and punished into conformity in order to prevent alternative views from unsettling our habitual beliefs. (Cohen & Nagel, 1934, p. 194; quoted in Walton, 1997, p. 251).

Treating an expert opinion that should be open to critical questioning as if it were infallible represents a shift from one type of "authority" to another (Walton, 1997;2008). As Walton highlights, authority based on intellectual or cognitive grounds is *always* provisional and subject to change, for example as new evidence appears.

> In contrast administrative or institutional authority is often final and enforced coercively so that it is not open to challenge in the same way. Thus treating the authority backing an argument as though it were of the latter sort, when it is really supposed to be of the former sort, is a serious and systematic misuse of argument from authority. It can be a bad error or, perhaps even worse, it can be used as a sophistical tactic to unfairly get the best of a partner in argumentation. (Walton, 1997, p. 252)

Consider this example:

RESPONDENT: Why A?
PROPONENT: Because E asserts that A, and E is an expert.
RESPONDENT: Is E's assertion based on evidence?
PROPONENT: How could you evaluate such evidence? You are not an expert in this field of scientific knowledge.
RESPONDENT: No, I am not an expert but surely I have the right to ask what evidence E based her opinion on.
PROPONENT: The assessment of this kind of clinical evidence is the solemn responsibility of the scientists. You are not even a scientist! (Walton, 1997, p. 254)

Here are critical questions related to an appeal to expertise.

Expertise question	How credible is E as an expert source?
Field question	Is E an expert in the field that A is in?
Opinion question	What did E assert that implies A?
Trustworthiness question	Is E personally reliable as a source?
Consistency question	Is A consistent with what other experts assert?
Backup evidence question	Is A's assertion based on evidence? (Walton, 1997, p. 258).

The key marker of the *ad verecundiam* fallacy consists of efforts to close off, block, or preempt appropriate critical questions. This is inappropriate in many kinds of dialogue (e.g., inquiry). As Walton suggests, evidence of this dogmatic stance can be found in "dialogical clues":

> If the experts or their advocates who are using expert opinions to sup-
> port their arguments refuse to countenance any critical questioning of
> a kind that would be appropriate in the case, then that is contextual evi-
> dence of the committing of an *ad verecundiam fallacy*. To gather this con-
> textual evidence, one has to study the profile of dialogue as applied to
> the sequence of argumentation used by the arguers and their dialogue
> exchanges, showing how each reacted to the moves of the other in a given
> case. In particular, you need to look for repeated attempts to block off the
> asking of critical questions by saying that such questioning is not appro-
> priate in the dialogue the participants are said to be engaged in. (Walton,
> 1997, p. 259)

Weasel words such as *well validated, obviously, established,* and *firmly established,* widely used in the professional literature, suggest that it is not appropriate to question a speaker (see Chapter 9).

Walton (1997) suggests that fallacious appeal to an authority can occur in three ways. Common to all "is the suppression of critical questioning by making the appeal to authority seem more absolute than it really is" (p. 252).

> (1) an appeal to institutional authority can be presented in such a way that it
> appears to be more absolute [less open to critical questioning] than it really
> is; (2) the same thing can happen with an appeal to expert opinion [an ap-
> peal to cognitive authority]; or (3) the two types of appeals can be confused.
> In particular, the most common type of fallacy occurring here is the kind

of case where an appeal to expertise [cognitive authority] is confused with an appeal to institutional authority, particularly when the institutional authority is portrayed as having a finality or absolute authority that admits of no critical questions. (p. 252)

Only by looking at the different moves in an argument can we distinguish among the three kinds of fallacies: "The mark of the fallacious type of case is the dogmatic or 'suppressing' way of putting the argument by the proponent that interferes with the respondent's asking of appropriate critical questions at the next move or moves, appearing to leave the respondent no room to pose critical question(s)" (Walton, 1997, p. 253). Walton (1997) suggests that both the halo effect and obedience to authority (conformity) contribute to the appeal of the ad verecundiam argument as a "device of deceptive persuasion."

There is a powerful institutional halo effect that seems to exclude critical questioning by a non-scientist, and make the claim seem to be unchallengeable by reasoned argumentation. The setting, or way the argument is presented in context, makes it seem impolite and socially inappropriate— here the halo effect explains Locke's notions of 'respect' and "submission"— to question the say-so of an authority. (p. 260)

An authority in one area is not necessarily an authority in other areas. Experts often disagree, or little may be known in a field. Appeal to an expert is not a fallacy. When experts disagree, we should examine related evidence, reasons, and arguments. We can review the track record of an expert. The key basis of the fallacy of argument from authority "is the suppression of critical questioning by making the appeal to authority seem more absolute than it really is" (Walton, 1997, p. 252). (See earlier example.)

ENHANCING YOUR SKILLS IN ARGUMENTATION

Skill in analyzing arguments will help you to make informed decisions. A key part of examining an argument is filling in missing parts. Premises or conclusions may be missing. Seldom are the major premises as well as conclusions clearly stated in deductive arguments; one or more premise is missing. Questions in evaluating an argument include: (1) Is it complete? (2) Is its meaning clear? (3) Is it valid (does the conclusion follow from the premises? and (4) Do I believe the premises? (Nickerson, 1986, p. 88). (See descriptions of argument mapping; e.g., Walton, 2015, p. l; http://compendium.open.ac.uk-arg-schemes.html). An argument may be worthy of consideration even though it has some defects. The following steps are helpful in analyzing incomplete logical arguments:

- Identify the conclusion or key assertion (claim).
- List all the other explicit assertions that make up the argument as given.
- Add any unstated assertions that are necessary to make the argument complete. (Put them in parentheses to distinguish them from assertions that are explicit in the argument as given)
- Order the premises (or supporting assertions) and conclusion (or key assertion) to show the structure of the argument." (Nickerson, 1986a, p. 87)

General rules for composing arguments suggested by Weston (1992, p. v) include (1) distinguish between premises and conclusions, (2) present ideas in a natural order, (3) start from accurate premises, (4) use clear language, (5) avoid fallacies including loaded language, (6) use consistent terms, and (7) stick to one meaning for each term. Visual depictions of the relationship among premises, warrants, and conclusions, as in argument mapping and flow charts, can be helpful. Goals of argument visualization include automatic description of human reasoning from text and corroborating evidence in courts of law. Argument skills can be developed in collaborative peer dialogues (Johnson, 2015; Kuhn & Udell 2003). Questions to raise when evaluating inductive arguments include:

- Are the facts accurate?
- Do the examples consist of isolated or universal instances?
- Do the examples used cover a significant time period?
- Are the examples given typical or atypical?
- Is the conclusion correctly stated?
- Is the argument really of concern—the "so what" and "what harm" questions? (Huber, 1963, p. 140)

Claims based on statistical analyses may be misleading in a number of ways related to the size and representativeness of the samples on which they are based

(Penston, 2010). Groups with a special interest in a problem may inflate the number of people affected by a problem (Best, 2004). The importance of seeking clarity is illustrated by the varied meanings of words such as *sometimes, often* or *rarely*. A drug company may claim that more people improved using drug X than any other drug. However, the best drug on the market may only be effective five percent of the time. Drug X may be effective six percent of the time. Tables and charts may mislead rather than inform (Tufte, 2006). Giving specific numbers may offer an illusion of accuracy (Seife, 2010). Relative rather than absolute risk may be given which is very misleading (Gigerenzer, 2002a, 2014a). (See also Harding Center for Risk Literacy, www.harding-center.mpg.de). Our tendency to be influenced by vivid material makes us vulnerable to distortions created by photographs, charts, and graphs (Huff, 1954; Tufte, 2007). Graphic displays often lie by omission—by what is left out. They may omit data relevant to the question: "Compared with what?" Only a portion of a graph may be shown, resulting in a distorted view (Tufte, 1983).

Objective evaluation of inductive arguments is more difficult than it is with deductive arguments. As with all arguments, the accuracy of premises is vital to assess (see Socratic questions in Exhibit 1.2). However, even if these are assumed to be true, people may disagree as to whether they provide evidence for a conclusion. Questions of value in evaluating an argument include: Is it complete? Is its meaning clear? Are the premises accurate? Is it valid (does the conclusion follow from the premises; Nickerson, 1986, p. 88)? An argument may be worthy of consideration even though it has defects. Counterarguments should be considered; are there arguments on the same issue that point to an opposite or somewhat different conclusion? Principles Damer (2005) suggests for effective rational discussion include:

Fallibility: A willingness to admit you could be wrong.

Truth seeking: A commitment to search for the truth or best argued position—to examine alternative positions and to welcome objections to your view.

Burden of proof: This rests on the person who presents it.

Charity: The other person's arguments should be presented in their strongest version.

Clarity: Positions, defenses, and challenges are clearly described.

Relevance: Only reasons or questions directly related to the merit of the position at issue are offered.

Acceptability: The premises or reasons relied on meet standard criteria of acceptability.

Sufficient grounds: Those who present an argument for or challenge a position should attempt to provide reasons sufficient in number, kind, and weight to support the conclusion.

Rebuttal: The person who presents an argument for or challenges a position should attempt to provide effective responses to all serious challenges or rebuttals.

Resolution: An issue should be considered resolved if the proponent for a position presents an argument that uses relevant and acceptable premises sufficient in number, kind, and weight to support the premises and the conclusion and provides an effective rebuttal to all serious challenges.

Suspension of judgment: If no position can be successfully defended, or if two or more positions can be defended with equal strength, you should suspend judgment or, if practical considerations require a decision, proceed based on preferences.

Reconsideration: Parties are obligated to reconsider the issue if flaws are found in an argument.

EXAMPLES OF DIFFERENT KINDS OF REASONS

Many kinds of reasons are appealed to in arguments; see discussion of evidence in Chapter 3). These influence what information we seek. Consider:

1. Bill drinks because he is an alcoholic; he has a disease.
2. Mary's hallucinations are caused by a mental disorder—schizophrenia.
3. Joe's antisocial behavior at school is related to ineffective curriculum planning and ineffective classroom management skills on the part of the teacher and few recreational activities.
4. HIV risk behaviors are due to a variety of causes, all of which must be addressed.

In examples 1 and 2, we see appeals to biomedical causes. In the third example, a social learning view is emphasized, and, in the fourth, a multicausal view is proposed. Tesh (1988) argues that multicausal views allow planners to focus on only one cause, ignoring the rest so misleading the public that a problem has been addressed when it has not.

Reasoning from Analogy

We often reason from analogy. We look to what has happened before to discover what to do in new situations; we seek and draw conclusions from a comparison of experiences. Analogies may be literal or figurative. The view that common difficulties are "mental illness" identical to physical illnesses such as diabetes is the best-known analogy in the helping professions and is widely accepted. Arguments based on analogy depend on the similarity of cases compared. Questions here are: How many respects are similar? How many are dissimilar? Are the bases of comparison relevant to the issue? Advertisements make heavy use of symbols, words, and illustrations designed to transfer feelings from the material to the product promoted.

Reasoning from Samples

Here we generalize from samples to populations. A psychiatrist may interview three Vietnamese families and make assumptions about all Vietnamese families. The accuracy of a generalization depends on the size and representativeness of the sample and the degree of variability in a population. Questions here include: Do the examples accurately reflect characteristics of the population? What variations occur? Propagandists use vague terms to describe samples such as "many people."

Reasoning from Signs and Symptoms

Observed signs (such as slumped shoulders, downcast eyes, and tears) are used to infer emotional states such as depression. Signs are used as indicative of a certain history. Are the signs accurate indicators of the state assumed? In medicine, there are signs as well as symptoms, although here, too, this distinction may be obscured. If you feel hot (a symptom), your physician can take your temperature (a sign). Are there "signs" in other helping professions? Many argue that technology in neuroscience such as MRI imaging has revealed brain differences between those viewed as having a mental disorder and those not so labeled. Others argue that related research is flawed (e.g., Vul, Harris, Winkielman, & Pashler, 2009). Are there alternative well-argued explanations such as a history of taking medication?

Reasoning from Emotion

Accounts may be emotionally compelling but weak from an evidentiary standpoint. For example, astrological views give many people the feeling of understanding; this does not mean that these views are accurate. Politicians and advertisers may appeal to self-pity, fear, and self-interest. Vivid testimonials and case examples play on our emotions. Words, music, and pictures in a commercial may contribute to an emotive effect. Because of the commercial's emotional appeal, we may overlook the lack of evidence for claims made. Arguments should not be dismissed simply because they are presented emotionally or because we dislike the conclusion. And, the emotion with which a position is presented is not necessarily related to the soundness of an argument; in many cases, appeal to emotion is rational, as in value conflicts; "... sentiment is not necessarily the enemy of reason, only certain sentiments, namely, those that encourage an unwillingness to think, to consider alternatives, to evaluate evidence correctly, and so on" (Baron, 1985, p. 238). As with other defeasible argumentation strategies that are open to refutation, appeal to emotion may or may not be used as a ploy to deflect attention from lack of evidence for a claim. Creating or avoiding emotional reactions may be one goal in making a decision, for example, to decrease postdecision regret.

Reasoning by Cause

We also reason by cause; we have assumptions about the causes of anxiety, substance abuse, and domestic violence. We may appeal to biological, psychological, or sociological causes. Different theories suggest different causes. The question is: "How much *real* understanding, as opposed to *feeling* of understanding, do they provide?" (Scriven, 1976, p. 219). Examples of fallacies related to causal reasoning include inferring cause from correlation, confounding necessary and sufficient cause, confusion of cause and effect, the "domino" or "slippery slope" fallacy, false dilemma, and fallacies of accident, composition, or division (see Chapter 8). Post-hoc reasoning may lead us astray as when assuming that feeling better after taking a pill means that the pill caused the effect. Other possibilities include spontaneous remission—you were just about to feel better anyway.

Most complex events are related to multiple causes. This illustrates the oversimplistic nature of the assumption that there is one cause when there are many. It seems that the less that is known, the more flagrant the claims of knowledge. Some authors have criticized descriptions of causal factors in the social sciences as an uninformative potpourri. Consider the term *biopsychosocial*, which implies that biological, psychological, and social factors all contribute to a problem. Aren't some factors more important than others? (See Tesh, 1988, for a critique of multicausal accounts.) Questions Walton suggests for distinguishing between correlation and causation include:

1. Is there is a positive correlation between A and B?
2. Are there a significant number of instances of the positive correlation between A and B?
3. Is there good evidence that the causal relationship goes from A to B, and not from B to A?
4. Can a third factor be ruled out that accounts for the correlation between A and B (a common cause) that causes both A and B?
5. If there are intervening variables, can it be shown that the causal relationship between A and B is indirect (mediated through other causes)?
6. If the correlation fails to hold outside a certain range of cases, then can the limits of this range be clearly indicated?
7. Can it be shown that the increase or change in B is not solely due to the way B is defined, the way entities are classified as belonging to the class of Bs, or changing standards over time in the way Bs are defined or classified? (adapted slightly from Walton, 2005, pp. 166–167).

Reasoning by Exclusion

This involves a search for rival explanations. Alternative accounts for a given event or behavior are identified, the adequacy of each is examined, and those found wanting are excluded.

INDIVIDUAL AND CULTURAL DIFFERENCES

People differ in their intellectual dispositions and values (e.g., fair-mindedness). They differ in the quality of their thinking skills, in their background knowledge, and in the kinds of accounts that satisfy their curiosity. As Baron (1987) notes, "if people do not believe that thinking is useful, they will not think" (p. 259). As discussed in earlier chapters, intelligence is only moderately associated with dispositions such as active open-minded thinking and uncorrelated with others (Stanovich, 2012). Paul (1993) has long emphasized the vital role of intellectual traits in critical thinking such as fair-mindedness (www.criticalthinking.org) as has Baron (1987, 2008). Some people prefer empathic accounts. Techniques of empathy building include telling a history and describing an individual's circumstances, intentions, and feelings. Nettler (1970) suggests that "the heart of empathy is imagined possibility" (p. 34). The empathizer thinks, "Under these circumstances I, too, might have behaved similarly." Empathic views often involve appeal to concepts that are only variant definitions of the behavior to be explained. Consider:

> PROBATION OFFICER: Why, doctor, does our client continue to steal?
> PSYCHIATRY OFFICER: He is suffering from antisocial reaction.
> PROBATION OFFICER: What are the marks of "antisocial reaction"?
> PSYCHIATRIST: Persistent thievery is one symptom. (Nettler, 1970, p. 71)

In scientific accounts, critical appraisal of claims is emphasized; there is an active effort to seek out errors in assumptions as described in Chapter 3. Scientific inquiry is designed to eliminate errors, not to claim final accounts. Premature claims of knowledge or ignorance stifle inquiry. Popper (1994) suggests they function as prisons that limit our vision. Ideological accounts are distinguished from scientific ones by their rejection of objectivity, their ready acceptance of sound and unsound premises, and their reliance on ethical judgments. They "became operative as they are believed, rather than as they are verified" (Nettler, 1970, p. 179). Depending on who is talking and what they are talking about, ideology is a virtue or a sin. Thompson (1987) distinguishes between two uses of the term *ideology*. One is as a purely descriptive term. For example, we can describe views central to an approach. In the second use, the term refers to maintaining power. It is this use of ideology that has negative connotations, and it is in this sense that language is used as a medium of influence. "Ideological views are used to account for 'collective' behavior as empathetic ones do in the clarification of individual actions—they fill the needs of curiosity left by the gaps in knowledge" (Nettler, 1970, p. 187).

William James (1975, p. 13) suggested that temperamental differences (tender vs. tough-minded) account for preference for different kinds of explanations. Differences are related to educational and socialization experiences (Stanovitch & West, 2002). Such differences may be attributed inaccurately to inherent style differences, for example, that women are naturally more subjective and intuitive in their approach in contrast to men who are more objective. Encouraging intuitivism and emotional reasoning helps to protect those who offer dubious services by discouraging critical appraisal of claims. As many such as Freire (1973) have argued, the economically privileged benefit most from an anti-intellectual bias in protection of their privileges.

Cultural differences include norms regarding questioning authority figures (Tweed & Lehman, 2002). A focus on arriving at sound decisions rather than protecting the status of authority figures encourages a culture in which claims are questioned (see also Chapter 11).

> Cultures that encourage rational thinking are those that value questioning, inquiry, the satisfaction of curiosity, and intellectual challenge. Cultures that oppose such thinking are those that value authority, quick decision-making, correctness (even from guessing) rather than good thinking, and constancy of opinion to the point of rejecting new evidence. (Baron, 1987, p. 259)

SUMMARY

Skill in offering and critiquing arguments as well as dispositions that encourage their use such as fair-mindedness are integral to informed decision-making including countering attempts to block critical appraisal of possibilities, evidence, and goals. Considering clashing perspectives regarding an issue or question is needed to explore the cogency of different views. Grappling with differences between our beliefs and new ideas is necessary for learning—for correcting background knowledge and discovering our ignorance. Reasoning requires a certain attitude toward the truth—a questioning attitude and an openness to altering beliefs in light of evidence offered—a willingness to say 'I don't know"—a willingness to seek counterevidence to preferred views. Valuable attitudes include recognizing the fallibility of our opinions and the probability of bias in them and valuing the discovery of ignorance as well as knowledge. Important skills include identifying assumptions and their implications (consequences), suspending judgment in the absence of sufficient evidence to support a claim or decision, understanding the difference between reasoning and rationalizing, and stripping an argument of irrelevancies and phrasing it in terms of its essentials.

Doman-specific knowledge including both content (knowing what) and procedural knowledge (knowing how to apply content knowledge to make informed decisions) may be needed. And, reasoning does not necessarily yield the truth, nor does the accuracy of a conclusion necessarily indicate that the reasoning used to reach it was sound. Walton's pragmatic theory of argumentation is valuable for those in the helping professions. The context and related goal of a discussion (e.g., negotiation compared to inquiry and critical discussion) suggest appropriate and inappropriate moves. Being reasonable involves active open-minded thinking. Being reasonable also "takes courage, because it seldom corresponds to being popular" (Scriven, 1976, p. 50). Not everyone values criticism; self-interest may result in attempts to block critical appraisal of views.

8

Avoiding Fallacies

MAKING INFORMED DECISIONS may be hindered by fallacies in reasoning. Becoming familiar with fallacies and acquiring effective ways to avoid them will enhance the quality of decisions (See Exhibit 8.1.). Consider the following examples (Gambrill & Gibbs, 2017). Can you spot the fallacy?

> *Situation 1*: An interdisciplinary case conference in a nursing home.
> *Psychology intern*: I don't think you should use those feeding and exercise procedures for Mrs. Shore. They don't work. Since she has Parkinson's, she'll spill her food. I also don't think you should walk her up and down the hall for exercise. I have read reports that argue against everything you're doing.
> *Nurse*: I am not sure you are in the best position to say. You have not completed your degree yet.
> *Situation 2*: Monthly meeting of agency administrators.
> *Administrator*: I think your idea to give more money for work with the elderly is not a good idea because we would then have to allot more money to services for other groups.
> *Situation 3*: Client treated by a chiropractor. Mrs. Sisnero was experiencing lower back pain. She saw her chiropractor, felt better afterward, and concluded that the chiropractor helped her back.
> *Situation 4*: Continuing education course at the University of California Extension given by Dr. Presti on alcohol abuse.

EXHIBIT 8.1
EXAMPLES OF FALLACIES

- Abusive *ad hominem*: Attacking the person rather than critically appraising argument (genetic fallacy).
- *(Irrelevant) appeal to emotions:* Using flattery and transfer effects, such as associating preferred views with good things and disliked views with bad ones.
- *Appeal to unfounded authority*: This may apply to popularity, status, newness, tradition, and "plain folks"; uncritical documentation (relying on citation alone).
- *Arguing from ignorance:* Assuming that an absence of evidence for an assumption indicates that it is not true.
- *Begging the question:* Assume what must be argued.
- *Case example fallacy*: Attempted proof by one case.
- *Confusing cause and effect*: Does depression cause drinking, or does drinking cause depression?
- *Confusing correlation and causation*: Assuming that correlation reflects causation.
- *Ecological fallacy*: Assuming that something true for a group is true of an individual.
- *Either/or*: Incorrect assumption that there are only two alternatives, false dilemma.
- *False analogy*: A is like B; B has property P; therefore, A has property (www. fallacyfiles.org).
- *Fallacy of accident*: Applying a general rule when it does not apply.
- *Fallacy of composition*: Assuming that what is true of the parts is true of the whole.
- *Fallacy of division*: Assuming that something is true of one or many parts because it is true of the whole.
- *Fallacy of the single cause*: Assuming there is one cause when there are many.
- *Hasty generalization*: Biased sample, sweeping generalization.
- *Illusory correlation*: Inaccurately perceiving a relationship between two unrelated events.
- *Is/ought fallacy*: Assuming that because something *is* the case, it *should* be the case.
- *Language-based fallacies*: Repetition, fallacy of labeling, inappropriate vagueness, leading questions, innuendo; jargon; double-barreled question, ambiguous (see Chapter 9).
- *Overlooking regression effects*
- *Post hoc ergo propter hoc*: Assuming after this; therefore, because of this.
- *Red herring*: Effort to distract others by irrelevant content.
- *Slippery slope*: Assuming (mistakenly) that if one event occurs, others will follow when this is not necessarily true.
- *Straw man argument*: Distorting a position.
- *Testimonial*: Attempted proof by an example.

Note: See Wikipedia.com.

Me: You use the term *alcohol disorder* often. Can you tell me what this means?

Dr. Presti: A lack of order.

Walton's (1995) pragmatic view of fallacy highlights their role in blocking critical appraisal. They may do so by creating diversions or avoidable confusions, by censorship, or intimidation (Gambrill, 2012a). Walton (1995) views a fallacy as "not just any error, lapse, or blunder in an argument," but as "a serious error or tricky tactic" to get the best of one's speech partner illicitly" (p. 15). One party moves ahead too fast or tries to silence the other party by ending dialogue prematurely or by shifting to a different kind of dialogue (Walton, 1997). Walton's pragmatic theory of fallacy shares six characteristics:

" 1. A fallacy is a failure, lapse, or error, subject to criticism, correction or rebuttal.
2. A fallacy is a failure that occurs in what is supposed to be an argument.
3. A fallacy is associated with a deception or illusion.
4. A fallacy is a violation of one or more of the maxims of reasonable dialogue or a departure from acceptable procedures in that type of dialogue.
5. A fallacy is an instance of an underlying, systemic kind of wrongly applied technique of reasonable argumentation.
6. A fallacy is a serious violation, as opposed to an incidental blunder, error or weakness of execution." (Walton, 2013, pp. 213–214).

Paul and Elder (2004) use the term *trick* or *stratagem* to refer to foul ploys used deliberately as persuasion strategies (see Exhibit 8.2).

The Skeptics Dictionary (www.skepdic.com) and fallacyfiles.org are valuable sources that describe fallacies including *the divine fallacy* (the assumption that if you can't understand some phenomena, God must have created it) and the *pragmatic fallacy* (arguing that something is true because it works, for example, "therapeutic touch"—but does it? What does "work" mean?). Examples from *Follies and Fallacies in Medicine* (Skrabanek & McCormick 1998) include *the ecological fallacy* (assuming that relationships in populations occur in an individual), *the fallacy of obfuscation* (use of language to mystify rather than clarify), *the "hush hush" fallacy* (ignoring the fact that mistakes are inevitable), and *the fallacy of the golden mean* (assuming that the consensus of a group indicates the truth). Examples of faulty reasoning from *Biomedical Bestiary* (Michael, Boyce, & Wilcox, 1984) include *the grand confounder* (what is claimed to be a causal relationship is due to another factor) and the *numerator monster* (information concerning the health of someone

---

EXHIBIT 8.2
EXAMPLES OF FOUL WAYS TO WIN AN ARGUMENT

- Accuse your opponent of doing what he accuses you of
- Call for perfection (the impossible)
- Use vivid analogies and metaphors to support your view even when misleading
- Create misgivings (dirty the water)
- Use double standards (e.g., for evidence)
- Attack only evidence that undermines your case
- Demonize the opposing side and sanitize yours (Rank, 1984)
- Evade questions
- Flatter your audience
- Hedge what you say
- Ignore the evidence
- Ignore the main point
- Focus on a minor point
- Use glittering generalizations
- Make an opponent look ridiculous
- Raise only objections
- Shift the ground
- Introduce distracting jokes
- Focus on a vivid case example
- Shift the burden of proof
- Use double talk (see Chapter 9)
- Tell lies
- Reify concepts (treat abstract words as if they are real)
- Use bogus statistics
- Claim the point is "old hat"
- Use "faint praise"

Source: Adapted from *Critical Thinking: Tools for Taking Charge of Your Professional and Personal Life*, by R. W. Paul and L. Elder, 2004, Upper Saddle River, NJ: Prentice Hall, and "Factifuging," by N. Kline, 1962, *The Lancet, 279*, pp. 1396–1399.

with no reference to the population from which this individual came). Gambrill and Gibbs (2017) include reasoning-in-practice games designed to increase awareness of fallacies in reasoning when making clinical decisions.

Many different schemes have been suggested to classify fallacies. We could, for example, examine causal fallacies including inferring cause from correlations, post hoc ergo propter hoc, confusing necessary and sufficient causes and confusion of causes and their effects. Fallacies of definition include using definitions that are too narrow or too broad. Statistical fallacies include faulty generalizations (Penston, 2010). The following discussion views fallacies under the categories of irrelevant appeals, evading the facts, overlooking the facts, distorting facts/positions, diversions, use of confusion, and the allure of authority.

IRRELEVANT APPEALS

Irrelevant appeals include fallacies of relevance in which the wrong point is supported or when a conclusion established by premises is not relevant to the issues being discussed. These are informal fallacies; that is, none involve a formal mistake. Many achieve their effect by taking advantage of one or more of our natural tendencies, such as wanting to please others or going along with what others think (the principle of social proof).

Irrelevant Emotional Appeals

Emotional appeals include appeal to pity, force or threat, flattery, guilt, and shame. Propaganda appeals to our deepest motivations—to avoid danger (fear), to be one of the boys/girls (acceptance and emotional support), or to be free to hate our enemies (Ellul, 1965). However, the emotion with which a position is offered does not mean that the argument is poor. Good arguments can be (and often are) offered with emotion. Appeal to emotions such as pity and sympathy may be reasonable in some kinds of arguments (Walton, 2008).

Irrelevant Ad Hominems

Here, the background, habits, associates, or personality of an individual are attacked or appealed to, rather than her argument. Rather than arguing ad rem (to the argument), someone argues ad hominem, to the person proposing it. (See Situation 1.) There are many forms of this "genetic fallacy"—the view that the source of an idea indicates its soundness. Ad hominem appeals may function as diversions. Improper appeals to authority to support a position are a kind of ad hominem argument. The effectiveness of ad hominem arguments depends partly on the principle of liking (disliking), as well as the principle of authority (see Chapter 7). Is an ad hominem attack or appeal ever relevant? If an attack on the presenter of the argument is related to the issue at hand, then in some cases it may be relevant. For example, someone could be shown to offer unreliable accounts on most occasions. However, this person may be offering a correct account this time.

Ad hominem arguments are surprisingly effective for a variety of reasons, only one of which is failure to identify the usually fallacious nature of the argument. Others include (1) implicit agreement with the implications about the individual; (2) agreement with the conclusion of the argument with little concern for its correctness; (3) unwillingness to raise questions, cause a fuss, or challenge authorities who may counterattack; and (4) social pressures in group settings—not wanting to embarrass others. The remedy in relation to ad hominem arguments is to point out that the appeal made provides no evidence for or against a claim.

Guilt (or credit) by association is a variation of an ad hominem argument—judging people by the company they keep. An attempt to discredit a position may be made by associating it with a disliked institution, value, or philosophy, as in the statement that behavioral methods are antihumanistic or psychoanalytic methods are antifeminist. "Imposter terms" or "euphemisms" may be used to make an unpopular view or method appear acceptable (see Chapter 9). As Nickerson (1986) points out, we are more likely to agree with institutions and philosophies we favor; however, it is unlikely that we will agree with every facet, and, similarly, it is unlikely that we would disagree with every aspect of a disliked view.

> Credit or discredit by association becomes a fallacy when it is applied in a
> blind and uncritical way. Whether or not a particular view is one that is held
> by a specific individual, institution, or philosophy that we generally support (or oppose) is very meager evidence as to the tenability of that view.
> (Nickerson, 1986, p. 116)

In the bad seed fallacy, it is assumed that a person's character or habits are passed on to his descendants (Michalos, 1971). Genetic factors do play a role in influencing behavior; however, the correlations presented are typically far from perfect and, in any case, may not support a causal connection. An argument may be made that a position is not acceptable because the person's motives for supporting the issue are questionable. For example, a proposal that a new suicide prevention center be created may be denied on the grounds that those who propose this will profit from such a center. The accuracy of the view proposed cannot be determined from an examination of the motives of those who proposed it, but only from an examination of the related evidence. It may be argued that because our intentions or motives are good, a claim is true. A psychologist may wish to place a child on Ritalin even though there is little evidence that this is indicated.

He may protest that his intent is to help this child. Appeals to good intentions are the opposite of the assumption of suspect motives. In both cases, evidence is needed that the claim is correct; motives, whether altruistic or otherwise, are not evidence.

Claims of inconsistency may be made to distract others from considering evidentiary issues. A discrepancy between a person's behavior and his principles may be invalidly used against him. A clinician who is not sympathetic to behavioral methods may say to her behavioral friend, "If behaviorists know so much about how to change behavior, why are you still smoking when you want to stop?" Another kind of false claim of inconsistency is when a charge is made that a person's behavior is not consistent with his principles when his principles have changed.

Appeal to Common Practice

It may be argued that because other people do something, it is all right to do the same. It may be argued that because few clinicians keep up with practice-related literature, this is OK. Standard practice may be (and often is) of poor quality.

Fallacy of Ignorance

Here, it is asserted that a claim is true because it has not yet been proven false or a claim is false because it has not been shown to be true (Wikipedia). A clinician may argue that because there is no evidence showing that "directed aggression" (hitting objects such as pillows) does not work, it is effective and should be used. The fact that no one can think of a course of action that is better than one proposed may be used as an argument that the proposed course is a good one. In fact, they could all be bad. It is hard to believe that this fallacy would ever work (i.e., influence people), but it does, as do some other weak appeals—such as simply asserting that a position is true.

Fallacy of Special Pleading

The fallacy of special pleading involves favoring our own interests by using different standards for different people, as in "I am firm, thou art obstinate, he is pigheaded" (Thouless, 1974, p. 11). A clinician may claim that she does not have to evaluate her work as carefully as other clinicians because of her lengthy experience.

Attacking the Example

The example offered might not be an apt one. A remedy is to point out that a successful attack on the example does not take away from the possible soundness of a position and to offer a better example. This fallacy is the opposite of the use of a suspect particular case as proof for a generalization.

EVADING THE FACTS

Fallacies that evade the facts, such as begging the question, appear to address the facts but do not: "Such arguments deceive by inviting us to presume that the facts are as they have been stated in the argument, when the facts are quite otherwise" (Engel, 1982, p. 114). Simply ignoring a question is a common tactic. This tactic can be successful if no one is present who will object, perhaps because everyone agrees with the original position. One form of ignoring the issue is to claim there is no issue. The question may be swept aside as irrelevant, trivial, or offensive.

Begging the Question

This refers to assuming the truth or falsity of what is at issue, that is, trying to settle a question by simply reasserting a position. Variants of question begging include use of alleged certainty, circular reasoning, and unfounded generalizations to support a conclusion, complex, trick, or leading questions and ignoring the issue. This tactic is surprisingly effective often because it is accompanied by appeals to authority. Such appeals take advantage of persuasive biases, such as liking (we are less likely to question poor arguments of people we like), authority (we accept what experts say), and social proof (we are influenced by what other people do). Consider the statement, "The inappropriate releasing of mentally ill patients must be ended." The speaker assumes that releasing mentally ill patients is inappropriate, instead of offering evidence to show that it is. Presenting opinions as facts is a common variant of this fallacy. Someone may say, "Offering positive incentives for desired behaviors is dehumanizing because it is behavioral." The assumptions are that behavioral methods are dehumanizing and that offering positive incentives for desired behaviors is behavioral. Since the truth of the wider generalizations is questionable, the particular example is questionable. Use question-begging as a clue that relevant facts are being evaded.

220 Critical Thinking and the Process of Evidence-Based Practice

Apriorism is a form of question-begging in which a position is claimed as true (prior to any investigation) because it is necessary according to a particular view of the world (or of clinical practice). Consider an assertion that psychiatrists should supervise treatment of patients implying that other kinds of mental health professionals should work under their supervision. What is needed is a description of evidence for and against the position advanced. Bold assertions are a common form of question begging. Alleged certainty is used to encourage readers or listeners to accept a claim without any evidence that the claim is accurate. The claim is presented as if it were obvious, in the hope that our critical senses will be neutralized. Examples are (1) "No one doubts the number of alcoholics in the United States today" and (2) "It is well accepted that therapy works."

Appeals to consensus may be made with no evidence provided that there is a consensus concerning a position as in "Everyone knows it's in the genes." This appeal, as well as the appeal of alleged certainty, takes advantage of the principle of social proof (our tendency to believe that what most other people think or do is correct). A clinician may say that "use of play therapy with autistic children is the accepted method of choice." Even if evidence for a consensus is offered, that does not mean that the position is correct. Consensus is a notoriously unreliable ground on which to believe a claim.

Wishful thinking involves the assumption that because some condition ought to be, it is the case—without providing any support for the position. Statements made about declassification (hiring staff without advanced clinical degrees) are often of this variety; it is assumed (proclaimed) that declassification is bad; no evidence is presented. Speakers or writers are guilty of using question-begging epithets when they add evaluative terms to neutral descriptive terms—the aim is to influence through emotional reactions. For example, "Fairview Hospital opened today" is a simple declarative statement. "The long-needed Fairview Hospital opened its doors today" includes evaluative epithets. Variations of this fallacy include the use of emotive language, loaded words, and verbal suggestion. Emotional terms may be used to attempt to prejudice the facts by using evaluative language that supports what we want to demonstrate but have not shown. "By overstatement, ridicule, flattery, abuse and the like, they seek to evade the facts" (Engel, 1982, p. 120).

Circular arguments are another form of question begging, as in the following example (Engel, 1982, p. 142).

People can't help what they do.
Why not?
Because they always follow the strongest motive.

But what is the strongest motive?

It is, of course, the one that people follow.

The conclusion that a speaker or writer is trying to establish is used as a premise or presupposed as a premise. Such circular arguments may seem so transparent that they would never be a problem. However, they occur in clinical practice. Consider the following dialogue.

Mr. Levine can't control his outbursts.

Why is that?

Because he is developmentally disabled.

Why do you say that he is developmentally disabled?

Well, because he has outbursts when he is frustrated.

Attributing the cause of outbursts to the developmental disability offers no information about how to alter the frequency of the outbursts. Facts cannot challenge the generalization because the truth is guaranteed by definition (Michalos, 1971).

Complex, leading, or trick questions with indirect assumptions may be used. A question may be asked in such a way that any answer will incriminate the speaker (e.g., "Where do you keep your cocaine?"). This is the interrogative form of the fallacy of begging the question; the conclusion at issue is assumed rather than supported. "Complex questions accomplish this by leading one to believe that a particular answer to a prior question has been answered in a certain way when this may not be the case" (Engel, 1982, p. 122). The remedy is to question the question. Such questions are also fallacious "because they assume that one and the same answer must apply to both the unasked and the asked question as in the example of 'Isn't Dr. Green an unthinking feminist?'" (p. 124). If the question is divided into its parts, different answers may apply: Is Dr. Green a feminist? Is she unthinking? Thus, the remedy is to divide the original question into its implied components and answer each one at a time. Another variation of complex questions is requesting explanations for supposed facts that have not been supported, as in "How do you account for extrasensory perception (ESP)"? Since there is controversy about whether ESP exists, and many people believe that research exploring such phenomena has yielded negative results, there may be no extraordinary effects to explain, perhaps just fallacies or questionable experimental designs to be uncovered.

OVERLOOKING THE FACTS

Relevant facts are often neglected, as in *the fallacy of the sweeping generalization*, in which a rule or assumption that is valid in general is applied to a specific example to which it is not valid (Engel, 1982, 1994). It might be argued that since expressing feelings is healthy, Susan should do it more, because it will increase her self-esteem and make her happier. However, if expressing feelings will result in negative consequences from significant others (such as work supervisors and her husband), the general rule may not apply here. This kind of fallacy can be exposed by identifying the rule involved and showing that it cannot be applied accurately to the case at hand.

The *fallacy of hasty generalization* is the opposite of the fallacy of the sweeping generalization; here, an example is used as the basis for a general conclusion that is not warranted. For example, if a psychologist has an unpleasant conversation with a social worker and says, "Social workers are difficult to work with," the generalization to all social workers might be inaccurate. This fallacy is also known as the *fallacy of hasty conclusion,* and it has many variants. Common in all are unwarranted generalizations from small or biased samples. This fallacy entails a disregard for the law of large numbers. (See also discussion of suppressed evidence and of either/or thinking.)

In the *fallacy of composition*, it is assumed that what is true of a part is also true of the whole. An example is the assumption that because each staff member in a psychiatric hospital is skilled, the hospital as a whole is an effective treatment center. In the *fallacy of division*, it is assumed that what is true of the whole is true of all the parts. A client may assume that because a clinic has a good reputation, every counselor on the staff is competent, but this is not necessarily true.

DISTORTING FACTS AND POSITIONS

A number of informal fallacies distort positions. Famous people may be misquoted, or views misrepresented.

Straw Man Arguments

In straw man arguments, a position similar to but different from the one presented is attacked; an argument is distorted, and the distorted version is then attacked (see discussion of avoidable misrepresentations of the process of evidence-based practice in Chapter 2).

Forcing an Extension

Forcing an extension may be intentionally used by someone aware of the fact that it is usually impossible to defend extreme positions; that is, most positions have some degree of uncertainty attached to them, like the statement that insight therapy is useful with many (not all) clients. The original position may be misstated in an extreme version (insight therapy is effective with all clients) and this extreme version then criticized. The original, less extreme position should be reaffirmed.

The Fallacy of False Cause

The fallacy of false cause involves arguments that suggest that two events are causally related when no such connection has been demonstrated. It may be argued that because one event followed another, it was caused by that event. A client may state that because she had a bad dream the night before, she made a bad mistake the next day.

Irrelevant Conclusion

An argument may be made for a conclusion that is not the one under discussion. While seeming to counter an argument, irrelevant statements advance a conclusion that is different from the one at issue. Other names for this fallacy include *red herring, irrelevant conclusion, ignoring the issue,* and *diversion.* This fallacy can be quite deceptive because the irrelevant argument advanced often does support a conclusion and so gives an impression of credibility to the person offering it and the illusion of a lack of cogency for the original argument, but the argument does not address the conclusion at issue (Engel, 1994). An example is, "The advocates of reality therapy contend that if we adopt their practice methods, clients will be better off. They are mistaken, for it is easy to show that reality therapy will not cure the ills of the world." There are two different points here: (1) whether reality therapy is effective and (2) whether it will "cure the ills of the world." Showing that the latter is not true may persuade people that the first point has also been shown to be untrue. The fallacy of irrelevant thesis is a version of forcing an extension. Notice that distortion of a position can make it look ridiculous and so easily overthrown. If the presenter of the original, more modest view is duped into defending an extreme version, he will likely fail.

Inappropriate Use of Analogies

Analogies can be helpful if they compare two phenomena that are, indeed, similar in significant ways; the more familiar event can be helpful in highlighting aspects of the less familiar event that should be considered. However, if the two events differ in important ways, then the analogy can interfere with understanding. Two things may bear a superficial resemblance to each other but be quite unlike in important ways. Consider the question "Should couples have sex before marriage?" A response might be "You wouldn't buy a car without taking it out for a test drive, would you?" (Bransford & Stein, 1984, p. 88). Some people who hear this argument simply say, "Oh, yes, you have a point there." Others will see that the analogy is inappropriate; marriage is significantly different from buying a car. The soundness of the analogy must always be explored. Does "mental illness" (disease/disorder) match the characteristics of a disease? Does it have a known etiology, a predictable course, and get worse without treatment?

Argument by mere analogy refers to the use of an analogy "to create conviction of the truth of whatever it illustrates, or when it implies that truth in order to deduce some new conclusion" (Thouless, 1974, p. 169). When an argument from analogy is reduced to its bare outline, it "has the form that because some thing or event N has the properties a and b which belong to M, it must have the property c which also belongs to M" (p. 171). Arguments from analogy may sometimes be difficult to recognize; that is, the analogy may be implied rather than clearly stated. The mind of a child may be likened to a container that must be filled with information. This analogy carries implications that may be untrue, such as that we have sharply limited capacities. So "the use of analogy becomes crooked argumentation when an analogy is used not as a guide to expectations, but as proof of a conclusion" (Thouless, 1974, p. 176).

Analogies create vivid images that are then readily available. They may oversimplify concerns in a misleading manner. Their vividness may crowd out less vivid but more accurate analogies and discourage a review of possible limitations of the analogy. There is thus an emotional impact; analogies play upon our emotions. We may forget that, although they may be a useful guide to what to look for, "they are never final evidence as to what the facts are" (Thouless,

1974, p. 175). They are one of many devices for creating conviction, even though there are no rational grounds for the conviction. Arguments from mere analogy can be dealt with by noting at what point the analogy breaks down.

In *argument from forced analogy*, an analogy is used to advance an argument when there is so little resemblance between the things compared to ever expect that they would resemble each other in relation to the main point under discussion. The remedy consists of examining just how closely the analogy really fits the matter at hand. Thouless (1974) recommends trying out other analogies and noting that these carry as much force as the original one.

DIVERSIONS

Many informal fallacies succeed by diverting attention from the main points of an argument such as ad hominem arguments in which attention may be focused on the person making the argument rather than the argument itself. Trivial points or irrelevant objections may be focused on. Witty comments and jokes can be used to divert attention from the main point of an argument or from the fact that little evidence is provided for a position. A joke can be made that makes a valid position appear ridiculous or poorly conceived. Attempts to defend a position in the face of such a response may seem pedantic. The remedy is to point out that, although what has been said may be true (or humorous), it is irrelevant.

Answering a Question with a Question

Hypothetical questions may be introduced to distract from important points. Questions are vital to evaluation of arguments. However, in arguments, they are never an end in themselves. (In other contexts, such as an exchange between Buddhist monks, another end may be sought.)

Appeal to Emotion

Emotional language can be used to create anger, anxiety, or blind adherence to a position and to distract us from noticing flaws in an argument. Appeals to anxiety and fear are widely used to distract listeners and readers from the main issues. Social psychological persuasion strategies may be used (see Chapter 9).

Red Herring

Here someone tries to distract you from the main point of an argument by introducing irrelevant content. The point is to divert others from the central issue.

THE USE OF CONFUSION

Some fallacies work by confusion. Raising doubt is a key strategy used by deniers of climate change. People may attempt to create confusion by citing a counterexample to a position, saying that "the exception proves the rule." Finding an example that does not fit a rule may be informative about the boundaries within which a rule is applicable but may say nothing about the truth or falsity of the rule in question. Excessive verbiage is a common means of creating confusion as described by Orwell (1958). Someone may talk about many different things and then state a conclusion that supposedly stems from all of them. If excessive verbiage is complemented by prestige, the use of pseudoarguments is even more likely to confuse and mislead. We are misled by our tendency to go along with what authorities say. Another persuasive influence at work here may include liking—if we like someone, we are more prone to agree with what they say and to think they are saying something of value.

Equivocation involves playing on the double meaning of a word in a misleading or inaccurate manner. The fallacy of equivocation is committed if someone begins with a premise attributing independence in one sense to a person and concludes that she possesses independence of an entirely different kind (Michalos, 1971).

Someone may claim a lack of understanding to avoid coming to grips with an issue or try to confuse issues by repeatedly asking for alternative statements of a position (Michalos, 1971, p. 75). Feigned lack of understanding may be combined with use of power, as when an instructor tells a student that he does not understand the point being made.

THE ALLURE OF AUTHORITY

The essence of pseudoscience is using the trappings of science without the substance. These "trappings" can fool us because of the allure of the "authority" of science and scientific experts. We may assume (incorrectly) that because an article appeared in the peer-reviewed literature, claims made are accurate, when they may be false. McCabe and Castel (2008) presented university students with 300-word news stories about fictional findings that were based on flawed scientific reasoning. One story claimed that watching TV was linked to math ability because both TV viewing and math activated the temporal lobe. Students rated stories accompanied by a brain image to be more scientifically sound than the same story accompanied by equivalent data presented in a bar chart or when there was no graphical illustration at all. The authors argue that "brain images are influential because they provide a physical base for abstract cognitive processes, appealing to people's affinity for reductionist explanations of cognitive phenomena" (p. 343).

SUMMARY

Both formal and informal fallacies may dilute the quality of clinical decisions. Most fallacies are informal ones; that is, they do not involve a formal mistake. Irrelevant ad hominem arguments may be used, in which the background, habits, associates, or personality of the person (rather than the arguments) are criticized or appealed to. Variants of ad hominem arguments include guilt (or credit) by association, the bad seed fallacy, appeals to faulty motives or good intentions, special pleading, and false claims of inconsistency. Vacuous guarantees may be offered, as when someone assumes that because a condition ought to be, it is the case, without providing support for the position. Fallacies that evade the facts (such as begging the question) appear to address the facts, but do not. Some informal fallacies overlook the facts, as in the fallacy of the sweeping generalization, in which a rule or assumption that is valid in general is applied to a specific example for which it is not valid.

Other informal fallacies distort facts or positions; in straw man arguments, a position similar to (but significantly different from) the one presented is described and attacked. The informal fallacies of false cause, forcing an extension, and the inappropriate use of analogies also involve the distortion of facts or positions. Diversions may be used to direct attention away from a main point of an argument. Trivial points, irrelevant objections, or emotional appeals may be made. Some fallacies work by creating confusion, such as feigned lack of understanding and excessive talk that obscures arguments. Knowledge of formal and informal fallacies decreases the likelihood that decisions will be influenced by these sources of error.

9

The Influence of Language and Social-Psychological

Persuasion Strategies

MANY CRITICAL THINKING skills involve recognizing how language affects decisions; language is closely related to thought (Hayakawa, 1978). Just as thought may corrupt language, language may corrupt thought (Orwell, 1958). Unless we are skilled in avoiding the misleading influence of language, decisions may be shaped by the words we use in ways that harm rather than help for example using misleading negative labels regarding clients. Language may mislead us because of lack of skill in writing and thinking, lack of caring, or deliberate intent to mislead on the part of a speaker or writer. Combs and Nimmo (1993) describe palaver as a kind of discourse in which truth and falsity are irrelevant—in which a variety of nonrational methods are used as criteria including slogans, jingles, myths, intuitions, images, and symbols, which are self-serving. It includes rambling speech and digressive claims presented in appealing ways. They note the similarity of palaver to Frankfurt's (1986) notion of "bullshit." In both palaver and bullshit, truth is irrelevant. There is no concern for truth, only to create credibility and for guile and charm. As Frankfurt (1986; 2005) suggests, the purveyor of bullshit does not reject the authority of truth as the liar does, he pays no attention to it. Frankfurt (1986) suggests that faking is inevitable whenever circumstances require that we speak without knowing what we are talking about.

Carelessness is often responsible for foggy writing and speaking—not taking the time and thought to clearly describe inferences and reasons for them. Our blind spots (biases) may impede careful use and review of influence by language including illusions of transparency. Misuse of language may or may not be intentional. Sources of error related to use of language can be seen in Exhibit 9.1.

These examples may be used to hide (censor), distort, divert, or confuse issues under consideration. The varied functions language serves complicates understanding of spoken or written statements. These include description, attempts to persuade others to believe or act differently, and statements that direct or guide us, as in "call the crisis hotline."

CONFUSING DIFFERENT LEVELS OF ABSTRACTION

Words differ in their level of abstraction. Many words have no extensional meaning—that is, there is nothing we can point to in the physical world. Words

---

EXHIBIT 9.1
SOURCES OF ERRORS RELATED TO USE OF LANGUAGE

1. Assumption of one word, one meaning
2. Misleading use of scientific terms
3. Misleading metaphors
4. Use of vague terms
5. Shifting definitions of terms
6. Reification (acting as if an abstract concept actually exists)
7. Influence by semantic linkages and cuing effects
8. Predigested thinking
9. Confusing verbal and factual propositions
10. Use of pseudotechnical jargon
11. Misuse of speculation (assuming what is can be discovered by merely thinking about a topic)
12. Conviction through repetition
13. Insistence on a specific definition that oversimplifies a situation
14. Influence through emotional words
15. Use of a confident manner and bold assertions
16. Order effects
17. Newsspeak
18. Excess wordiness
19. Misuse of labels (e.g., vague, focus on negatives)
20. Confusion of different levels of abstraction
21. Careless use of language
22. Eloquence without clarity

may suggest differences that do not exist. The intentional meaning of a word refers to what is connoted or suggested. Not recognizing that words differ in level of abstraction may create confusion and needless arguments. Both the one word-one meaning fallacy and the assumption that definitions are things reflect a confusion among (or ignorance of) different levels of abstraction.

MISUSES OF CITATIONS (UNCRITICAL DOCUMENTATION)

References that provide little or no evidence for related claims are common (Greenberg, 2009; Ioannidis, 2005, 2016). In such instances, an illusion of knowledge is created.

OVERSIMPLIFICATIONS

The term *oversimplication* refers to the tendency to oversimplify complex topics, issues, or perspectives into simple formulas that distort content. Stereotyping is a form of oversimplified thinking. Referring to hundreds of behaviors, feelings, and thoughts as "mental disorders" (diseases) ignores the continuous nature of the vast majority of related behaviors as well as contextual influences. Slogans are a form of oversimplification.

MISSING LANGUAGE (CENSORSHIP)

Missing language is one of the most deceptive misuses of language. For example an article may state that "We measured how doctors treat low back pain", when what the researchers really did was ask them what they did (use self report).

We are less likely to make sound decisions if we do not have access to relevant information such as well-argued alternative views. The abundance of terms for alleged "psychological disorders" is far greater than terms for positive states of behavior and being. This is a prime example of missing language. Physicians often fail to communicate information that would enable informed decisions such as potential harms of proposed interventions (Gotzsche, 2013). Advertisements may deceive by what is not described such as equivalent results of competitive products and potential harms.

PSEUDOTECHNICAL JARGON AND BAFFLEGARB

Jargon can be useful in communicating in an efficient manner if listeners (or readers) share the same meaning of technical terms. However, jargon may be used to conceal ignorance and "impress the innocent" (Rycroft, 1973, p. xl). *The fallacy of the alchemist* refers to influence by vague terms and thinking that you have gained some knowledge about a topic (when you have not). We tend to be impressed with things we cannot understand. Professors tend to rate journals that are hard to read as more prestigious than journals that are easier to read (Armstrong, 1980). Obscurity may be desirable in some circumstances, such as when exploring new possibilities. However, obscurity is often a cloak for ignorance. "Bureaucratese" (unnecessarily complex descriptions) abounds. Examples include "mumblistic" (planned mumbling) and "profundicating" (translating simple concepts into obscure jargon; Boren, 1972). The potential for obscure terms to become clear can be explored by asking questions such as "What do you mean by that?" and "Can you give me an example?"

Obscure language may remain unquestioned because of fear that the questioner will look ignorant or stupid. Consider the risks of lack of clarification, for example to clients, as well as the risks of revealing a lack of knowledge. Writers and speakers should clarify their terms, bearing in mind appropriate levels of abstraction. If they don't, it may be because they cannot. Not all people will be open to questions, especially those who use vague language to hide aims or lack of knowledge. "The great enemy of clear language is insincerity. When there is a gap between one's real and one's declared aims, one turns as it were instinctively to long words and exhausted idioms like a cuttlefish squirting out ink" (Orwell, 1958, p. 142). Others may become defensive and try to "neutralize" those who pose questions, perhaps using their prestige to do so. They may share Humpty Dumpty's attitude:

> "When I use a word" Humpty Dumpty said, in a rather scornful tone, "it means just what I choose it to mean neither more nor less."
>
> "The question is," said Alice, "whether you can make words mean so many different things."
>
> "The question is," said Humpty Dumpty, "who is to be master, that's all." (Carroll, 1871/1946, p. 229)

A question could be asked in such a straightforward manner that if the person still cannot understand it, his own lack of astuteness is revealed (Thouless, 1974).

The discourse of science is often used to create a false impression of objectivity and rigor, for example, by using specialized terminology that is unfamiliar to others (see discussion of pseudoscience in Chapter 3). Narratives of progress may be used to imply that advances are being or soon will be made (Boyle, 2002). Boyle (2002) suggests that use of the language of medicine combined with the language of science is a potent rhetorical mix that may create illusions of objectivity, knowledge, and progress.

USE OF EMOTIONAL WORDS

Professionals, as well as advertisers and politicians, make use of emotional words and images. We may act toward people, objects, or events in accord with the affective connotations associated with a name. Being aware of the potential biasing effects of emotional terms and using more neutral ones may increase the quality of decisions.

METAPHORS

Proverbs, similes, or metaphors that have emotional effects may be used to describe or support a position. They may be of value in developing new ideas. On the other hand, they may obscure rather than clarify a problem or issue; they may create a feeling of understanding without an accompanying increase in real understanding.

NAMING/LABELING

Labels that have few if any implications for selection of effective interventions but which are stigmatizing are often applied to clients (Watson & Eack, 2011). Naming hundreds of everyday behaviors and feelings (or their lack) as "mental illnesses" in need of treatment transfers our associations with physical illness onto behaviors, thoughts, and feelings now labeled "mental illnesses" as Szasz (1961, 2007) has long argued in his rhetorical analysis of this concept. Such labels are used as explanations for life's travails (Herzberg, 2009). Labels may be applied incorrectly as discussed in Chapter 2 regarding the term *evidence-based practice*.

Pseudoexplanations are one result of the unexamined use of labels. Such labels give an illusion of understanding client concerns and thus interfere with needed assessment. And, as argued by Williams (2017), negative labels may create negative views of clients. The term *aggressive,* used as a summary term for specific actions, may also be used to refer to an aggressive disposition, which is believed to be responsible for these actions. This disposition then comes to be thought of as an attribute of the person, ignoring environmental influences. The circularity of such discourse reveals that no new information is offered.

THE ASSUMPTION OF ONE WORD, ONE MEANING

Words have different meanings in different contexts. Differences that exist in the world may not be reflected in different use of words, or differences in language may not correspond to variations in the world. Misunderstandings arise when different uses of a word are mistaken for different opinions about a topic of discussion. "Unless people mean the same thing when they talk to each other, accurate communication is impossible" (Feinstein, 1967, p. 313). Two people discussing "addiction" may not have the same definition of this term, and a muddled discussion may result. Confusion can be avoided by checking definitions of key concepts.

USE OF VAGUE TERMS

Barnum believed that you can sell anything to anybody. He documented this in *Humbugs of the World* (Barnum, 1865). The Barnum Effect, also called the Forer Effect, refers to our tendency to rate vague statements as highly accurate of ourselves even though the statements could apply to many people. This is also known as the *subjective validation effect* (searching for personal meaning in ambiguous statements). Astrologers and psychics take advantage of our tendency to believe vague descriptions about ourselves. Vague terms are common in clinical contexts such as *uncommunicative, aggressive, immature,* and *drug dependency.* Results of assessment are often presented in vague terms, such as *probable* or *cannot be excluded,* which may have different meanings to different people. Vague descriptions regarding risk include: "Risk of violence is high," "risk of violence is low," "risk changes over time," "your risk is high," and "fifty-percent less risk of recurrence of cancer." There is an illusion of information being provided. (See discussion of the importance of distinguishing between absolute and relative risk in Chapter 5.) If terms are not clarified, different meanings may be used, none of which may reflect the real world. Weasel words provide an illusion of argument or accuracy. Examples include:

- "Many people say . . ." How many? Who says so? On what basis?
- "Some people argue that . . ." Who? On what basis?
- "Studies show . . ." What studies? On what basis?
- "Expert suggests . . ." What experts? On what basis?
- "It is notable that . . ." On what basis is it notable?

Weasel words such as "well validated," "established," "and firmly established," are widely used in the professional literature. Such words may be designed to influence without informing. Vagueness of terms may be an advantage in the early stages of thinking about a topic to discover approaches that otherwise may not be considered.

REIFICATION, WORD MAGIC

Here it is mistakenly assumed that a word corresponds to something real. (See also discussion of labeling.) As Boyle (2002) notes, it is easy to believe that what is referred to by a word actually exists—particularly if authority figures such as psychiatrists use the term and act as if it is unproblematic. Our tendency to rely on "experts" and to believe that if there is a word, it refers to some entity in the world (reification) combines with other factors, such as lack of time, a disinterest in digging deeper, laziness, and an interest in avoiding responsibility for behavior or troubles by attributing them to a brain disease. This is a powerful mix.

CONFUSING VERBAL AND FACTUAL PROPOSITIONS

Questions (such as "What is a borderline personality?") often involve disputes about use of words, as if they were questions of facts. (See also discussion of reification.) What must be established by critical inquiry is presuming as fact, as in the fallacy of begging the question (see Chapter 8). Questions of fact cannot be settled by arguments over the use of words. The problem of how to use a word is different from the problem of what is a fact. Pointing out the lack of objective criteria is helpful when there is a confusion between verbal and factual propositions.

INFLUENCE OF SEMANTIC LINKAGES AND CUING EFFECTS

An example is the tendency to think in terms of opposites, such as *good/bad* or *addicted/nonaddicted*. Manufacturers of drugs select names for drugs, such as chemotherapies, to encourage sales (Abel & Glinert, 2008). Decisions concerning degree of responsibility for an action differ depending on whether a person is the subject of the sentence, as in "Ellen's car hit the fireplug," compared to "The fireplug was hit by Ellen's car" (Loftus, 1980; see also Loftus, 2005). Familiarity with the influence of semantic linkages and cuing effects may help us to avoid related errors. Statements can be rearranged to see if this yields different causal assumptions. (See also critique of eyewitness testimony; e.g., Skeem, Douglas, & Lilienfeld, 2009).

MISUSE OF VERBAL SPECULATION

This refers to the use of "speculative thinking to solve problems which can only be solved by the observation and interpretation of facts" (Thouless, 1974, p. 78). Speculation is valuable in discovering new possibilities, but it does not offer information about whether these insights are correct.

CONVICTION THROUGH REPETITION

Repetition of ideas and images is one of the most popular means of influence. Simply hearing, seeing, or thinking about a claim or idea many times may increase belief in this. As Thouless (1974) notes, we tend to think that what goes through our mind must be important. Repeating a position increases the likelihood of its acceptance, especially if the statement is offered in a confident manner by a person of prestige and has a slogan quality that plays on our emotions. A willingness to challenge even cherished beliefs helps to combat this source of error. "If our examination of the facts leads to a conclusion which we find to be inconceivable, this need not be regarded as telling us anything about the facts, but only about the limits of our powers of conceiving" (Thouless, 1974, p. 80).

BOLD ASSERTIONS

People may confidently assert a position with no attempt to provide any evidence for it. A clinician may say, "Mr. Greenwood is obviously a psychopath who is untreatable." A confident manner and bold assertions often accomplish what should be achieved only by offering sound reasons for a position. Words and phrases that are cues for this tactic include *unquestionable, indisputable, the fact is, the truth is,* and *everyone knows.* Bold assertions are a form of *begging the question*; the truth or falsity of the point is assumed (Walton, 2008). Evidence should be provided for the position asserted.

ORDER EFFECTS

What we hear or see first may influence what we attend to and our causal attributions. It narrows the range of data that is attended to (see Chapter 6).

NEWSSPEAK

Newsspeak refers to the intentional abuse of language to obscure the truth—"language that distorts, confuses, or hides reality" (MacLean, 1981, p. 43). Examples include *neutralized* (meaning, killed), *misspoke* (meaning, lied), and *air support* (meaning, bombing and strafing). Orwell (1958) wrote, "In our time, political speech and writing are largely in defense of the indefensible . . . political language has to consist of euphemisms, question begging, and sheer cloudy vagueness" (p. 136). Here are examples of newsspeak:

Statement or Term	Translation
Fiscal constraints call for retrenchment.	Some people are going to be fired; clinics will be closed.
New policies have been put in place to ensure better services for clients.	All services will be provided by psychiatrists.
Improve your practice tenfold.	Attend Dr. X's workshop.
Pregnancy crisis center.	Prolife centers, which are anti-abortion.
Community care in place of warehousing.	Patients will be discharged from mental hospitals even though no adequate community care is available.

Readers, unless they are an expert in an area, rarely are aware of what is not discussed in a report such as alternative well-argued views. Too seldom are the pros and cons concerning an issue reviewed. Unacknowledged conflicts of interests may result in the cherry-picking of research reports, bias in placement, misleading words and selection of photographs, and hidden editorials (content presented as disinterested descriptions that give biased accounts). Use of these devices may or may not be deliberate.

MANNER OF PRESENTATION

The eloquence with which an argument is presented, whether in writing or in speech, is not necessarily related to its cogency; words that move and charm may not inform. To the contrary, eloquence may lull our critical powers into abeyance. Consider the Dr. Fox lecture. An actor who could convincingly present a "professional" manner was hired to give a lecture to psychiatrists, psychologists, social worker educators, psychiatric social workers, and other educators and administrators on the application of mathematics to human behavior (Naftulin, Ware, & Donnelly, 1973). Dr. Fox was introduced with an impressive list of qualifications and gave an eloquent lecture. Indeed, he knew nothing about the subject, but no one detected the ruse. Thus, a confident manner may accompany nonsense.

EUPHEMISMS

The term *euphemism* refers to use of words designed to be less distasteful or offensive than others often to hide what is actually going on. Examples include calling enforced incarceration "treatment for the benefit of the client." Rogowski (2011) suggests that phrases such as the "mixed economy of care" and the "independent sector" are deliberately obscure and misleading (p. 156).

OTHER SOURCES OF FALLACY RELATED TO LANGUAGE

Insisting on a specific definition of a term is inappropriate if this obscures the complexity of a situation. Ferreting out the nature of an argument is often difficult because of excessive wordiness.

MAKING EFFECTIVE USE OF LANGUAGE

Tips for making effective use of language include:

- Be alert for special interests. Is someone trying to sell you something?
- Recognize the influence of emotional language.
- Clearly describe arguments.
- Be on the lookout for reification and palaver(bullshit).
- Be wary of analogies and metaphors; examine their similarity and claimed relationships to conclusions.
- Keep the context of a dialogue in mind (e.g., is the goal to discover what is true or false?)
- Use different examples when thinking about intances of a category to avoid stereotypes.
- Recognize when an anchor may bias judgments; consider alternative anchors.
- Ask questions to enhance comprehension.
- Use displays such as graphs and flow charts.

THE INFLUENCE OF SOCIAL-PSYCHOLOGICAL PERSUASION STRATEGIES

Persuasive attempts are common in clinical contexts. Clinicians try to persuade clients to carry out agreed-on tasks and to convince other professionals to offer needed resources. Conversely, clinicians are the target of persuasive attempts by clients, colleagues, the peer reviewed literature, the media, and related industries such as the pharmaceutical industry. The essence of persuasion is influencing someone to think or act in a certain manner. It may occur intentionally or unconsciously. Being informed about social-psychological persuasion strategies will help you to resist effects that dilute the quality of decisions. Competence in the use of social influence is a key component of "practical intelligence."

In the elaboration likelihood model, it is suggested that a given variable may serve as a clue as to what to believe by influencing the amount of elaboration we engage in, or it may bias the direction of elaboration (Fabrigar, Smith, & Brannon, 1999). This model suggests a continuum of persuasion and how attitudes are created (Petty & Cacioppo, 1986; Petty & Hinsenkamp, 2017) ranging from influence via emotional associations or inferences based on peripheral cues such as our mood or the status of those trying to persuade us, to thoughtful consideration of arguments related to a topic—there is a deliberative process; we think about arguments for and against a position. *Persuasion by affect* (the "affect heuristic") comes into play when we do not engage in elaboration and are influenced not so much by what people say but by extraneous variables, such as how attractive they are or how confidently they present their views (e.g., Slovic, Finucane, Peters, & MacGregor, 2002). Persuasion strategies based on liking and authority attain their impact largely because of affective associations. The elaboration likelihood model suggests that we must be both motivated and able to engage in the cognitive effort to critique information regarding a topic, person, or idea (see Petty, Cacioppo, Strathman, & Priester, 2005). Here we have yet another example of different ways to reach a decision—quickly based on emotions, for example, or in a more deliberative manner using active open-minded thinking (see Chapters 1 and 6).

The *principle of liking* is a frequently used persuasive strategy. We like to please people we know and like. The liking rule is often used by people we do not know to gain our compliance. Factors that encourage liking include physical attractiveness, similarity, compliments, familiarity, and cooperation. We are more receptive to new material if way like the person presenting it. Associating "pitches" with food, as in the "luncheon technique," is a well-known strategy designed to create liking and loyalty (Razran, described in Cialdini, 2001, p. 167). (See also Cialdini, 2008.) Big Pharma wines and dines opinion leaders to gain their loyalty to a product (Brody, 2007). Concerns about disapproval are often responsible for a reluctance to offer counterarguments to popular views in case conferences.

Another persuasion strategy is based on a *desire to be (and appear) consistent* with what we have already done. Being consistent usually works for us. "But because it is so typically in our best interests to be consistent, we easily fall into the habit of being automatically so, even in situations where it is not the sensible way to be" (Cialdini, 1984, pp. 68–69).

Obtaining an initial concession or offering a favor may be used to gain compliance through the influence of *the reciprocity rule*; we feel obliged to return favors. The reciprocity rule lies behind the success of the "rejection-then-retreat technique," in which a small request follows a large request—the small request is viewed as a "concession" and is likely to be reciprocated by a concession from the other person.

Informal fallacies *appealing to pseudoauthority* take advantage of our tendency to go along with authorities. Many appeals to authority are symbolic, such as certain kinds of titles; they connote rather than offer any content supporting the accuracy of the authority. Some appeals to authority attempt to influence through fear and neutralization of counterarguments.

The *scarcity principle* rests on the fact that opportunities seem more valuable when their availability is limited (Cialdini, 1984, p. 230; see also Bruch & Feinberg, 2017.) A nursing home intake worker may say, "If you don't decide now, space may not be available" (which may not be true).

Actions are often guided by the *principle of social proof*—that is, finding out what other people are doing or think is correct. This principle also provides a convenient shortcut that often works well; however, if it is accepted automatically, it can result in errors. The danger in appealing to the principle of social proof is the "pluralistic ignorance phenomenon" (Cialdini, 1984, p. 129). This principle operates most powerfully when we observe the behavior of people who are similar to ourselves. False evidence may be provided to influence people through the principle of social proof, such as claiming (without evidence) that hundreds have benefited from use of a new therapy.

We are also influenced by the *contrast effect*. A client who is fairly cooperative may be viewed as extremely cooperative following an interview with a very resistant person.

In everyday life, the principles on which these strategies are based provide convenient shortcuts that often work for us. We don't have time to fully consider the merits of each action we take or "pitch" we hear—we take shortcuts that often work for us as described in Chapter 3. These compliance-induction strategies take advantage of our natural human tendencies. However, others can exploit them for their own purposes; our automatic reactions work in their favor. "All the exploiters need do is to trigger the great stores of influence that exist in a situation and direct them toward the intended target" (Cialdini, 1984, p. 24). These strategies offer others an opportunity to manipulate without appearing to do so (see also Cialdini & Sagarin, 2005).

Ploys related to language and social psychological persuasion strategies are so common in pharmaceutical advertising that some professional education programs now pay attention to this source of persuasion. For example, guides for "Talking with a drug Rep" have been developed (see ProvenEffective.org). Drug reps are trained in scripts for dealing with particular types of physicians to maximize influence. Physician categories include "Aloof and Skeptical," "Thought Leader," and "Prescribing a Competitive Drug" (Fugh-Berman, & Ahari, 2007). Becoming familiar with persuasion strategies and decreasing automatic influence by these tactics should upgrade the quality of decisions.

SUMMARY

Misuse of language contributes to inaccurate decisions. Careless use of language is a source of error. Confusion about the different functions of language may result in muddled discussions, as may confusion among different levels of abstraction. If terms are not clarified, confused discussions (or thinking) may occur, due to the assumption of one word, one meaning. Reification (using a descriptive term as an explanatory term) offers an illusion of understanding without providing any real understanding. Technical terms may be carelessly used, resulting in "bafflegarb" or "psychobabble"—words that sound informative but are empty and not helpful for making sound decisions. Labels have emotional connotations that influence us in ways that do not necessarily enhance the accuracy of decisions. Knowledge of fallacies related to use of language and care in using language while thinking, listening, writing, or reading should improve the quality of decisions.

Both clinicians and clients use and are influenced by social-psychological persuasion appeals. A knowledge of these strategies is of value in avoiding influences that decrease the accuracy of decisions. Learning to recognize and counter persuasion strategies (such as attempted influence based on liking and appeals to consistency, authority, or scarcity) should increase the likelihood of well-reasoned decisions.

10

Communication Skills (Continued)

DECISION-MAKING IN THE helping professions takes place within exchanges with clients, their significant others, fellow workers, administrators, and various others involved in the system of care. The quality of communication between clients and helpers is important in all helping professions including offering positive reactions and avoiding negative ones (Norcross & Wampold, 2011). Poor communication skills may result in lost opportunities to help clients, for example, to gain or transmit important information (Katz, 2002). Examples include poor attending skills and eye contact, frequent interruptions, appearing cold and aloof, and being aggressive or punitive. Behaviors in team meetings such as discounting, name calling, and harsh criticism may discourage critical appraisal of options. Vague instructions, a failure to raise important questions, and defensive reactions to corrective feedback contribute to avoidable errors.

Interpersonal skills that contribute to evidence-informed decisions include providing clear explanations, engaging participants in a process of shared decision-making, and empathy and warmth that contribute to positive outcome (e.g., Wampold & Imel, 2015a, 2015 b). Communication skills such as friendliness and empathy influence client options including obtaining needed resources from other agencies. Related skills include:

- Observing and accurately translating social signals; recognizing attitudes and feelings.
- Raising questions about the evidentiary status of claims that affect client well-being.

- Prompting, modeling, and reinforcing helpful behaviors.
- Requesting behavior changes (e.g., regarding ineffective or harmful methods).
- Offering empathic responses.
- Avoiding negative reactions (e.g., blaming, eye-rolling, smirking).
- Using nonverbal signals consistent with your intent.
- Selecting appropriate goals.
- Conveying a friendly attitude.
- Providing constructive feedback.
- Minimizing negative reactions such as signs of disinterest.
- Offering compliments/expressing appreciation.
- Conveying respect.
- Offering encouragement.
- Making amends as appropriate (e.g., apologizing).

You may have to "problem solve" to decide what to do. The following steps can be helpful:

1. Stop, calm down, and think.
2. Describe the problem and how you feel.
3. Select a positive goal.
4. Identify options and consider the consequences.
5. Try the best plan.
6. Evaluate the results.

Helpful rules for keeping interfering emotional reactions in check include considering other people's perspectives, focusing on service goals (shared interests), and reinforcing behaviors you want to encourage. In some situations, direct action (requesting or negotiating changes) may be most effective. In others, indirect methods may be best such as calming self-talk or delaying a reaction. What will be effective in one situation may not be in another. What exactly do you want? Clearly describe the five Ws: who, where, when, what, and why. What would have to be different for a problem to be solved? Use emotional reactions such as anger or anxiety as cues to what you want. Identify your "emotional allergies" (incidents that "get under your skin). The more clearly you describe what you want, the more information you can offer to others. Focus on positive goals. Rather than telling your supervisor, "I was dissatisfied with our last meeting," say, "I'd like more specific feedback from you about how I'm evaluating progress with Mrs. L."

Knowledge about cultural differences will contribute to responding effectively. For example, although saving face is important in all cultures, the particular situations that result in "loss of face" may differ in different groups. Nonverbal behaviors such as eye contact or smiling at certain times may have different meanings in different cultures. Laughter may reflect embarrassment; lack of eye contact may reflect deference (not disinterest). Indirectness is highly valued in some cultures. Developing effective communication skills will help you to acquire needed resources for clients. Drury (1984) recommends building a strong case for change (the more specific the better) and recognizing norms and power dynamics in organizations (p. 255). Consider both personal (effects on yourself) and social outcomes (effects on others) as well as what you may lose by not doing anything. For example, if you do not ask your supervisor for more specific feedback, you may lose valuable learning opportunities.

ASSERTIVE, PASSIVE, AND AGGRESSIVE BEHAVIOR

Making informed decisions requires critical appraisal of claims and related arguments, your own as well as those of others including "experts". This will require speaking up rather than remaining silent in the face of questionable claims and practices and policies that may harm clients. You may ask colleagues to clarify points they view as self-evident (when they are not). Raising questions that affect clients' lives is vital in a learning organization (see Chapter 11). Some people are passive (e.g., say nothing) when they must speak up to attain valued outcomes. Others are aggressive; they put people down and harshly criticize them. Assertive behavior involves expressing preferences in a way that encourages others to take them into account and does not infringe on their rights, for example, to disagree with you (Alberti & Emmons, 2008). There is a focus on the situation or behavior rather than the person. Alternatives to aggressive reactions include clear requests and emphasizing common interests such as helping clients.

Behaviors and outcomes associated with passive, aggressive, and assertive reactions are illustrated in Exhibit 10.1. Respect for your rights as well as those of others is integral to the philosophy underlying assertion. It is not a "do your own thing" approach in which you express your wishes, regardless of their effects on others, nor does it guarantee that you will achieve your goals. As with any new behavior, learning to be more assertive in specific situations may feel awkward and unnatural at first. And, what will be effective in one social situation may not be effective in another. You may have grown up in a culture in which questioning

EXHIBIT 10.1
COMPARISON OF PASSIVE, ASSERTIVE, AND AGGRESSIVE STYLES AND THEIR EFFECTS

	Passive	Aggressive	Assertive
Behavior patterns	No expression of expectations and feelings	Critical expression of expectation and feelings.	Clear, direct, unapologetic description of expectations and feelings.
	Views stated indirectly or apologetically.	Blaming and judgmental Negative intentions attributed to others.	Descriptive not judgmental criticism.
	Complaints are made to the wrong person.	Problems acted on too quickly.	Persistence.
	Problems not confronted soon enough.	Unwilling to listen. Refuse to negotiate and compromise.	Willing to listen, negotiate, and compromise.
Word choices	Apologetic statements.	Loaded words.	Neutral language.
	Statements about people in general.	"You" statements.	Clear, concise statements.
	General instead of specific descriptions of behavior.	"Always" or "never" statements.	Personalized statements.
	Statements disguised as questions.	Demands instead of requests.	Specific behavioral descriptions.
		Judgments disguised as questions.	Cooperative words.
			Requests instead of demands.
			Absence of statements disguised as questions.

(continued)

EXHIBIT 10.1 (*Continued*)

	Passive	Aggressive	Assertive
Voice characteristics and body language	Pleading or questioning voice tone. Hesitation. Lack of eye contact. Slumping downtrodden posture. Words and nonverbal behavior do not match.	Sarcastic; judgmental, overbearing voice tone. Interruptions. "Looking-through-you" eye contact. Tense, impatient posture.	Even, powerful voice tone. Eye contact. Relaxed. Words and nonverbal messages match.
Results	Rights are violated; taken advantage of. Unlikely to achieve goals. Feel frustrated, angry, hurt, or anxious. Allow others to choose for you.	Violate other people's rights; take advantage of others. Achieve goals at others' expense. Defensive, belligerent; humiliates and depreciates others. Choose for others.	Respect own as well as others' rights. Achieve goals without hurting others. Feel confident. Choose for one's self.

Source: First three sections adapted from *Assertive Supervision: Building Involved Treatment*, by S. S. Drury, 1984, Champaign, IL: Research Press, pp. 294–295. See also E. Gambrill, 2013, *Social Work Practice: A Critical Thinkers' Guide*, New York, NY: Oxford University Press.

authorities was not allowed. Raising questions may feel unnatural and perhaps wrong. But helping clients to make informed decisions obligates us to cultivate and use effective argument skills including raising important questions.

SPEAKING MORE OR LESS

Making informed decisions may require speaking more or less. Skill in resisting interruption and breaking into conversations is helpful. In a fast-moving conversation, you will have to speak up during brief pauses. If you wait for a long pause, the topic might change before you get a chance to share your ideas. This does not mean that you should interrupt people while they are talking. You can resist interruptions by raising your voice if someone tries to interrupt and repeat what you just said. Or, you could ignore the interruption and continue talking. You may remind the other person of the goal of the discussion and the need for commitment to joint sharing. You can start speaking during a pause between the person's sentences when waiting for a natural pause has not been successful. You could let the person know you want to speak by saying, "I'd like to respond to your first point." Turn-taking is integral to deliberative reasoning. Monopolizing a conversation deprives the other party of making their moves (such as criticizing what you say). A key function of group facilitators (paid or unpaid) is to help a group balance talking and listening of each member.

Perhaps you talk too much in some situations. You might mistake a brief pause between statements as an end to a person's speech when it is a transition from one sentence to the next. To prevent this, wait a few seconds after others stop speaking before you talk. You could hand back the conversation after speaking, by asking, "What do you think?" Be sure to offer positive feedback for other people's contributions. Perhaps others are not as talkative as you would like because you show little interest in understanding their views (e.g., ask no questions, offer little eye contact) or have been overly critical of their remarks. You may disagree too often or point out faults in what has been said in ways that offend others (see guidelines for disagreeing). You may fail to acknowledge areas of agreement.

HANDLING CONTROVERSY: RAISING QUESTIONS AND DISAGREEING

Integrating ethical and evidentiary issues often requires questioning what others say as well as welcoming questions others pose. Disagreements (controversies), for example, about the accuracy of a claim, provide opportunities to forward understanding, discover options, and make sound decisions. Popper (1994) argues that "orthodoxy is the death of knowledge, since the growth of knowledge depends entirely on the existence of disagreement" (p. 34). Questioning claims that affect clients' lives in a nonabrasive productive way is vital. Consider the following dialogue:

> *Supervisor to student*: Our state child welfare guidelines require us to use x program with our clients.
> *Student*: I have carefully reviewed the research related to this guideline, and I do not think it applies to Mrs. S. and her children. Mrs. S and her children differ in important ways from people included in research reports related to this program. For example, her children are much younger and have a number of problems (not just one).
> *Supervisor*: We have to use these guidelines.
> *Student*: But do they apply to this family?
> *Supervisor*: I am sure that the state would not require them unless they were best.
> *Student*: But related research shows that this guideline may not apply to Mrs. Sand and her children.
> *Supervisor*: The differences you point out do seem significant. We could refer the family to an agency in which staff consider these differences.

Focusing on shared interests (e.g. avoiding harm) and using diplomatic methods may minimize defensive reactions (see Exhibit 10.2). Let's say a colleague makes a sweeping generalization such as "Cognitive methods help everyone." Rather than saying "That's clearly not true" (not that you would), you could introduce the idea of comparison by asking, "Do you think they work better for some clients than others?" You would use a Columbo style: "Could it be . . . ?" Questions such as Have there been any critical tests of the effectiveness of this intervention?, Are there any data suggesting that this method may harm rather than help clients?, are important to raise in making life-affecting decisions . Cultural differences influence who can question or disagree with whom, about what, when, and what style is most effective. Preferred styles range from indirect to blunt. In some cultures, it is important to avoid conflict. Your own views of asking questions may get in the way:

- Don't ask. It may have been discussed before.
- Don't ask. It may slow down the discussion or group.

EXHIBIT 10.2

CHECKLIST FOR RAISING QUESTIONS AND DISAGREEING

_____ Focus on common goals (helping clients).

_____ Acknowledge other points of view.

_____ View disagreements and questions as learning opportunities.

_____ Make sure you understand other views; acknowledge cogent points, points of agreement, and mutual goals and concerns.

_____ Avoid derogatory comments and negative non-verbal reactions such as rolling your eyes.

_____ Don't interrupt people (unless someone is monopolizing the discussion).

_____ Explain why you disagree or question a view/claim (e.g., refer to relevant research).

_____ Express differences as they arise as appropriate.

_____ Reinforce others for listening.

_____ End or avoid unconstructive exchanges if possible (you could suggest another time for discussion or involve another person).

_____ Consider cultural differences in norms, values, and preferred styles of communication.

- Don't ask. You may be the only one who does not know.
- Don't ask. If it is important, someone else will ask it.
- Don't ask. The other person (or group) may not want to deal with it now.
- Don't ask. Your question may be difficult to describe correctly.
- Don't ask! It may be too big an issue to discuss! (Matthies, 1996)

Raising questions often requires courage; focusing on helping clients will encourage speaking up. Your work and learning environments may not reflect a culture of thoughtfulness in which alternative views are sought and welcomed. Raising questions may be viewed as signs of disloyalty, impertinence, or rudeness. Supervisors or teachers may respond negatively to questions and differences of opinion. They may respond to questions as unwelcome challenges to their authority rather than as efforts to make sound decisions. My students tell me that they are often punished for asking questions about what their professors say or field supervisors promote. This will not help clients.

Effective Disagreement

The answer to the question "What is effective disagreement?" depends on the goals of a discussion, which could include discovering options (see Chapter 7). Be sure you understand a position. You could check your understanding by paraphrasing what is said. People are more likely to consider what you say if they feel understood and are not offended by your style of expression. Recognize points of agreement. This decreases the likelihood of defensive reactions. Raise questions at an appropriate time and acknowledge other views. You might say:

- "That's an interesting view. I like the way you. . . . Another approach might be. . . ."
- "It sounds as if we agree that this program would be helpful, but differ in how to pursue it. . . ." "I think . . . because. . . ."

Take responsibility for points you make by using a personal pronoun such as "I" or "my" and explain the reasons for your views. Questions or disagreements that do not include elaborations may appear abrupt and do not explain reasons for a position. Practice raising questions tactfully and responding constructively to reactions that do not contribute to making informed decisions such as put-downs and question begging. If you start to get upset, focus on service goals, do not take things personally (unless confronted with abusive behavior; see later discussion). Be sure to reinforce tolerant and open-minded reactions by commenting on them. You might say, "It's great to talk to someone willing to consider other views." If you change your point of view after a discussion, tell the other person. You might say: "I did not think of that. Yes, they offered only testimonials to support their claim that their program is effective." Do not let people neutralize you; if you do, clients may lose. Wait until others have finish talking before starting to speak, unless you are not receiving your share of talk time. Raising questions and disagreeing with someone in front of others may be inappropriate in some cultures. This may result in a "loss of face" for the other person. Try not to violate the "pleasantness norm" during initial encounters by introducing a topic or opinion that will lead to conflict. Overlook minor differences.

You may have to be persistent. Your first attempt to question a claim in a case conference may be ignored. You may have to introduce your point more than once and should do so if this would contribute to helping clients and avoiding harm. Let's say you are in a case conference with your supervisor and other staff members.

Supervisor:	Blandy Residential Center was advertised in *Social Work*. I think this setting would be a good one for Jim.
Social Worker 1:	Yes, I've heard about the center. Other agencies also refer to Blandy.
Social Worker 2:	I've visited the center, and the staff seem very dedicated.

Socials Worker 3 (you):	Do you know anything about their success in helping adolescents like Jim?
Supervisor:	Well, they've been around for 50 years. They must be doing something right.
Social Worker 3 (you):	Fifty years is a long time. I wonder if they've collected any data about how effective they have been.
Social Worker 1:	Here's their brochure. It says they offer high-quality services and are sensitive to young people's needs. Sounds good to me.
Social Worker 3 (you):	I think we need information about this center's success rate; perhaps we could offer services at home.
Social Worker 2:	You're new here and don't know the limitations of our resources. I think we should refer him to Blandy.
Social Worker 3 (you):	Yes, I am new to this agency, but perhaps we could find out Blandy's success rate so we can share this with his family.

Avoid put-downs such as "You don't know what you're talking about" and "That's a stupid idea." Put-downs and excessive negative emotion will encourage defensive reactions and increase the likelihood of unproductive conflict. Avoid the build-up of anger by identifying the beginning signs of irritation and using constructive self-statements (e.g., "Take it easy," "What's my goal?"). Unrelenting disagreeing or questioning with the goal of changing someone's mind can be unpleasant and is not likely to be effective. Emphasize shared interests—to help clients. Focus on important points. If you disagree with many small points, your concern about the big points may not be taken seriously. Some people show disagreement by withdrawing their attention (e.g., looking away), leaving the conversation, or avoiding future contact. Silence is not a good option if you can achieve your goals only by expressing your views effectively in a continuing dialogue. If a discussion seems to be escalating into a conflict, you could comment on this and remind participants about shared goals.

SEEKING, RESPONDING TO, AND OFFERING CORRECTIVE FEEDBACK

Seeking and receiving corrective feedback and acting on this, for example, via deliberate practice, are key in enhancing expertise as discussed in Chapter 6. This is key in discovering your ignorance You might ask your supervisor "Could you suggest how I could be more effective in engaging clients?" (See later section on requesting behavior changes.) People may question claims you make and the soundness of your reasoning. Responding effectively to corrective feedback contributes to making sound decisions, continued learning, and maintaining constructive working relationships (see Exhibit 10.3). Learning to offer corrective feedback in ways that encourage positive responses is important such as commenting on specific valuable behaviors first and being specific regarding behaviors of concern and the reasons for this concern.

Negative means of offering feedback may result in (1) withdrawal (avoiding the person, escaping from the situation), (2) attack (name-calling, threats), and (3) defensiveness (counteraccusations, excuses, nonverbal indicators). Signs of defensiveness and closed-mindedness include an unwillingness to listen; raised voices; ridicule, mockery, disgust; crossed arms; shaking the head; and rolling the eyes (e.g., Seech, 1993). Intense reactions concerning feedback (prolonged sadness, anger, or hostility) may reflect unrealistic expectations such as "I must never make mistakes" or "Others have no right to question my behavior." Drury (1984) discusses three kinds of criticism: teasing, blowing off steam, and attempts at problem-solving. The first two may or may not reflect concerns that should be addressed. In criticism as problem-solving efforts, Drury (1984) recommends (1) correcting misperceptions, (2) listening and asking for details to allow others to calm down, (3) identifying problems that should be discussed, (4) acknowledging the other person's feelings and perspectives, and (5) setting limits when people are violent or abusive, or when the time or place is inappropriate.

View feedback as a learning opportunity; your critic may help you to discover flaws in your own thinking or help you to improve a skill. Focus first on understanding

---

EXHIBIT 10.3
CHECKLIST FOR RESPONDING TO CORRECTIVE FEEDBACK

_____ View feedback as a learning opportunity.
_____ Don't take it personally.
_____ Relax and listen (unless the feedback is abusive).
_____ Check your understanding and ask for clarification as needed.
_____ Offer empathic responses (consider the other person's perspective).
_____ Avoid defensive, aggressive, and overly apologetic replies.
_____ Accept responsibility for what you say and do.
_____ Don't let people abuse or neutralize you.
_____ Seek and offer solutions.
_____ Take time to think if you need it.
_____ Arrive at a clear agreement about what will be done and get back on track.
_____ Arrange a time for reviewing results of feedback (e.g., have your skills/ outcomes improved?).

your critic's point of view (e.g., what she wants, feels, or thinks) rather than defending yourself, making suggestions, or giving advice. Relax and listen unless someone verbally abuses you. Avoid counterattacks. Taking time to understand the criticism will help you learn, remain calm, and respond effectively; other people will feel listened to. Check your understanding of what has been said by paraphrasing it and reflecting the feelings expressed. This will indicate that you take the other person's concerns seriously and will allow correction of any misunderstandings. You might say, "You think I've overlooked information that shows that clients are harmed by taking this medication; is that correct?" People may tell you what they do not want but not what they do want. You might say "It sounds as if you want me to. . . . Is this right?" Only if you understand what people want, can you decide whether their requests or objections are reasonable or possible to fulfill. *Your critics have a responsibility to clearly describe their criticisms and the reasons for them.*

Empathic responses can diffuse negative emotions. An example is "I think I'd feel the same way if I thought that." You do not have to agree with criticisms to offer empathic statements such as "I can see how someone may feel this way." Behaviors involved in empathic responses, genuineness, and the therapeutic alliance overlap (Nienhuis et al., 2016). Avoid patronizing comments such as "I know how you feel." Recognize points of agreement. Some people confuse a lack of understanding with a lack of agreement. You may understand what a person wants but not agree that it is a problem. You can demonstrate your understanding by accurately describing his or her position. If the criticism is valid, acknowledge this and work together to seek solutions. But don't let people abuse or neutralize you. You may have to use the "broken record" technique (repeat a statement such as "Let's get back to . . ."). In reply to valid criticism delivered in an offensive way, model an appropriate form. Focus on common goals such as offering effective services (Fisher & Ury, 2011). Reach a clear agreement about what will be done.

REFUSING REQUESTS

You may have to refuse requests from clients, co-workers, supervisors, or other professionals. If so, do so in a way that maximizes positive feelings and minimizes negative ones (see earlier example in this chapter). Let's say your supervisor requests you to use a method you know to be ineffective or harmful. You might say "I know this method has received a great deal of attention in the media, however a recent high-quality Cochrane review found that this method has harmful effects." There is no need to say that you are sorry. Or let's say a client requested you to use a diagnostic method shown to be inaccurate. Here, too, explain your reasons and give the client access to relevant sources so she can examine them. If you offer a sound reason for your refusal and the person rejects it, do not offer new reasons; repeat or elaborate on the one you gave.

Refusing unreasonable demands from supervisors and administrators is important. Staff are often pushed to work longer and harder. Patronizing slogans may be used, such as "work smarter" (as if you were not already working smart). Be informed about your legal rights and stick to your guns; do not be "guilt tripped." For example, a common ploy in response to your refusal may be to say, "But this work must be done" or "Your clients need your help." You could answer, "I agree and I am helping as much as I can. Perhaps you should hire some temporary help." Nicarthy, Gottlieb, and Coffman (1993) provide examples of how to refuse unreasonable work requests in *You Don't Have to Take It!* You as well as your clients can be exploited. Those in the helping professions can be "guilt tripped" into exploitive working conditions because of calls to elevate service to others above self-interest. Limited resources do not mean that your work climate should be punitive (e.g., complaints are punished, and staff are excessively burdened).

REQUESTING BEHAVIOR CHANGES

To protect clients from avoidable harms, you may have to ask people to change their behavior. Examples include staff members who "bad mouth" clients and who promote the use of ineffective or harmful assessment and/or intervention methods. You may request more specific feedback from a supervisor who offers only vague statements. Requesting behavior changes is often regarded as criticism. Considering a situation from the other person's point of view will help you to focus on common interests and reach a mutually acceptable resolution. For example, perhaps your supervisor is overburdened with too many responsibilities (see Exhibit 10.4). Plan how to ask for change in a positive way. Choose the right time and place. Try not to surprise others when they might not be willing or have time to discuss concerns. Avoid criticizing people in front of others and talking about people behind their backs. Start with positive feedback. (This approach might be viewed as manipulative if you offer positive feedback only when you give negative feedback as well.)

Effective feedback is objective rather than judgmental. It focuses on specific behaviors of concern. By being specific, you avoid "characterological blame" (attacks on the whole person; Janoff-Bulman, 1979). Clearly describe what you want and why. You might say, "I value our relationship and look forward to learning more from you. It would help me learn more if you offered me more

EXHIBIT 10.4
CHECKLIST FOR REQUESTING BEHAVIOR CHANGES

____ Ignore minor annoyances.

____ Share concerns as they arise, otherwise select an appropriate time and place to discuss.

____ Give positive comments first, as appropriate.

____ Plan and practice beforehand.

____ Focus on common interests (e.g., to help clients).

____ Be specific; describe what you want and why; give examples.

____ Focus on behaviors desired, not the person. Be brief and to the point; don't overload others with criticisms.

____ Consider the other person's perspective. Find out if there are any handicapping circumstances that get in the way and use the "given that" method.

____ Avoid accusatory "you" statements and name-calling.

____ Use nonverbal behaviors that communicate your seriousness.

____ Offer specific suggestions or solutions.

____ Check the other person's understanding of what you have said and clarify as needed.

____ Use concerns as opportunities to strengthen relationships.

____ Persist when necessary (unless it is a lost cause).

____ Seek the person's commitment to follow through.

____ Reinforce desired behaviors.

detailed feedback about my work. For example, am I overlooking any important areas of assessment in my work with families?" Give specific examples and describe particular situations. Be brief and to the point. Use your feelings as clues as to what you want. Recognize and focus on common interests such as to enhance skills, provide high-quality service, and maintain productive working relationships. Use personal pronouns (I, me) rather than the accusatory "you," which connotes blame. Beginning your comments with a personal pronoun indicates that you take responsibility for your feelings and reactions. You could include the following five steps:

- I feel (describe your feelings, using words that refer to feelings)
- when (describe the behavior of concern)
- because (describe how the behavior affects you)
- I would prefer (describe what you want)
- because (describe how you would feel).

The first step reminds you to use "I" statements and to express what you feel (sad, mad, happy, angry). The error you are most likely to make here is to refer to complaints or beliefs rather than feelings, as in "I feel you should give me more feedback" or "I don't think you like me." Neither statement refers to a specific feeling. If you do not want to start off with "I feel . . ." start with a clear description of the requested behavior change and the reasons for your request. (One disadvantage of starting with a "feeling statement" is that it opens you up to attacks on your feelings, for example, "You women are so sensitive." If this happens, focus on what you want—do not get sidetracked.) The second step calls for a clear description of your concern. Before you bring up a concern, identify what changes you would like. How would you like things to be different? By offering specific suggestions for change, you share responsibility for improving the situation. Here is an example:

- I feel frustrated
- when you ignore the concerns I raised about this intervention program
- because ignoring these concerns may result in harm to Ms. T.
- I would rather we discuss my concerns so that we could determine if they are accurate
- because that may result in a more informed decision regarding what to do.

People are more likely to consider your requests if you use words that communicate mild emotions (e.g., "I feel annoyed" rather than "I feel furious"). Avoid words such as *should, ought, have to,* and *must* that may promote guilt, anger, and defensive statements. You could share any discomfort you feel by saying, "This is difficult for me, but I do want to talk about. . . ." Self-disclosure of this kind communicates that you are vulnerable, too, and do not see yourself in a superior position. *There is no need to apologize or say you are sorry.* Avoid negative comments such as "You're inconsiderate," moralizing (e.g., "you should"), excessive questioning (e.g., "Why did you . . ."), giving orders, and "diagnosing" the other person ("You're doing this because you are bipolar"). Match your style of presentation to your message. When asking for a change in a behavior, be serious and thoughtful. Offer specific suggestions for change. Be willing to compromise and offer positive feedback. You might say, "I'm glad we talked. I appreciate your willingness to talk about this."

People may try to sidetrack you by changing the subject or using positive or negative ad hominems to avoid addressing weaknesses in an argument (see

Chapter 8). You could ignore the sidetrack and repeat or elaborate your request or statement. You might say, "My point is. . . ." Do not react in kind and do not back down when confronted with hostile or defensive reactions unless the other person is becoming very upset or threatening. (Here the best option may be to postpone the discussion.) Agree on changes that will be made. If you are getting "hot under the collar" or ready to "go over the top," you probably have an expectation that the other person "must," "ought to," or "should" change (see books by Albert Ellis). Focusing on common interests increases the likelihood of agreement (Fisher & Ury, 2011). A reluctance to request behavior changes may be related to inaccurate or dysfunctional beliefs about social relationships (e.g., "I have no right to ask others to change") or fear of disapproval. You may incorrectly assume that others know when their action or inactions bother you. Or, you may assume that you are helpless when you are not.

Disliked behaviors often occur because positive alternatives are not reinforced including approximations to them. The most positive and effective way to change disliked behavior is to reinforce positive alternatives. So, ask yourself: Am I reinforcing desired behaviors? Am I reinforcing behaviors I dislike? Supervisors' beliefs such as "She gets paid for this" or "She should know this" may interfere with reinforcing desired behaviors. Suppose you dislike your co-worker dropping by your desk to chat. If he checks with you before he comes over, tell him you appreciate this. If indirect efforts fail (ignoring unwanted behaviors, prompting, and reinforcing positive alternatives), discussing your concerns may be the next step. Always ask: "Does it really matter?" and "Is it likely to happen again?" Here, too, success in resolving concerns will increase your confidence that you can establish and maintain good relationships.

Responding to Put-Downs

Put-downs may be used to deflect attention from a weak argument. In responding, consider your goals. Focusing on put-downs may hinder pursuit of service goals. If so, ignore them and focus on service tasks. You could offer a disarming reaction—acknowledge the truth in the put-down (Burns, 1999). You might say "It is certainly true that I could be wrong, but I wonder if . . ." However, if put-downs are recurrent, you should address them. Those based on race, gender, sexual orientation, ability, age, or ethnicity are a kind of verbal harassment and may be reported to appropriate authorities. (See U.S. Department of Labor, workplace harassment policies/www.dol.gov).Seek support from others who share your concerns and contact governmental agencies to file a complaint as appropriate.

GATHERING AND PROVIDING INFORMATION

Experts compared to novices are more likely to ask questions that provide relevant information regarding how to achieve hoped-for outcomes (see Chapter 6). They are more likely to avoid sources of interview bias including asking questions that suggest certain answers. They are more likely to avoid vague questions and asking multiple questions at one time. Providing information relevant to decisions is a key part of shared decision-making; this helps clients to make rational choices. It is key in empowering clients—helping clients to gain greater influence over their environments (Schwartz & Woloshin, 2011). It is an important component of psychoeducational interventions. Questions often asked by clients in health settings include:

- Is this a problem? What is causing it?
- How does my experience compare with that of other people?
- Is there anything I can do myself to address my concerns and prevent it in the future?
- Should I get a test? Are there alternatives? What is the purpose of the test?
- What are my options?
- What are the risks and benefits of different options?
- What will happen if I do nothing?
- How can I tell if my health care provider is telling me what I need to know to make an informed decision?
- What will it cost?
- Where can I get more information about my concerns and options? (see Jansson, 2011).

Guidelines for offering information are suggested in Exhibit 10.5. Offer information to clients in a form that they find useful. Information can be provided verbally, in written form, via computerized decision aids, websites, videotape, smartphone, or audiotapes. Written handouts or text messages can be used to supplement discussions during interviews. Take advantage of computerized decision aids. Check clients' understanding of material. Clients may need certain skills to make use of relevant information.

EXHIBIT 10.5
GUIDELINES FOR GIVING INFORMATION

- Arrange for an interpreter as needed.
- Check to see how much information the client wants.
- Consider individual and cultural differences (e.g., in how information is presented).
- Use clear, understandable, nontechnical language. Give specific examples. Explain new terms.
- Organize material in a way that contributes to recall.
- Supplement verbal descriptions with audiovisual material and visual graphic aids (diagrams, charts, audiotapes, videotapes, films, brochures).
- Do not over- or undersell.
- Check for understanding. Ask the clients to describe the information given in their own words.
- Do not overload clients with details.
- Tie to personal experience.
- Explore whether the information is compatible with the client's beliefs.
- Encourage clients to raise questions and take notes or write summaries. Repeat important information as needed.
- Describe the rationale for suggested plans (e.g., how they relate to client goals) and the possible consequences of following or not following recommendations.
- Offer an opportunity for clients to share any concerns they may have.
- Give clients written copies of important information (or a tape as relevant).
- Offer an opportunity for clients to be accompanied by a supportive person (e.g., family member).

PROVIDING HIGH LEVELS OF COMMON FACTORS

Common factors refer to "variables found in most therapies regardless of the therapist's theoretical orientation such as empathy, warmth, acceptance, encouragement of risk taking, client and therapist characteristics, confidentiality of the client–therapist relationship, and the therapeutic alliance or process factors" (Lambert & Bartley, 2002, pp. 17–18). There is a spirited debate regarding the relative contribution of "common factors" including the alliance (the helper–client connection), helping skills used, and the person of the helper compared to the specific interventions used (e.g., Wampold & Imel, 2015). Questions and related controversies suggested by Norcross (2011) include (1) do particular characteristics of a helping relationship contribute to positive outcomes and, if so, what are they; (2) what percentage of the variance of outcomes attained is related to relationship variables, the person of the helper, or the particular intervention used; and (3) can important relationship variables be enhanced through training?

In Wampold and Imel's (2015a) contextual model, the client must be actively working toward a goal in a coherent way. In this model, the relationship between helper and client is viewed as key. Critical routes to positive outcomes include: (1) the real relationship, (2) the creation of expectations through explanation of problems and the intervention involved, and (3) the enactment of health promoting actions. They argue that before these pathways can be activated, a therapeutic relationship must be established. Clinicians may offer the same intervention but differ in provision of common factors so attaining different outcomes (Baldwin & Imel, 2013). Attending to important cultural differences contributes to positive outcome (Benish, Quintana, & Wampold, 2011; Huey, Tiller, Jones, & Smith, 2014). Based on a review of the literature, Wampold (2006) argues that there is "not a scintilla of evidence to support empirically supported treatments as more effective than other treatments" (p. 299) in mental health (See also Wampold & Imel, 2015). The person of the helper is intertwined with outcome. So too is choosing interventions clients prefer (Swift & Callahan, 2009). Empathy, warmth, positive regard, and genuineness create a context in which other important elements of helping are offered, such as inspiring hope (Frank, 1991), supporting client assets, clarifying goals, and planning services.

Empathy

Empathy and warmth are important with colleagues as well as with clients. They create the context in which other important elements of effective services are offered, such as clarifying goals and planning services. Types of empathic responses include (1) communicating understanding; (2) affirmations—validating the other's experiences; (3) evocations that try to bring the other's experience alive, such as suggesting an appropriate metaphor; and (4) explorations that attempt to encourage others to discover important information. Empathy is positively associated with outcome (Elliott, Bohart, Watson, & Greenberg, 2011). It may contribute to successful outcomes by increasing client satisfaction, so increasing participation including disclosure. Other benefits include decreasing isolation, feeling respected, and encouraging productive exploration, all of which may contribute to valuable self-change efforts. Empathy facilitates the selection of interventions that are compatible with the client's frame of reference. It requires individualizing responses for particular clients. Research that shows that nonprofessionals may be as effective as professionals in helping clients highlights the importance of empathy and other "nonspecific" relationship factors (e.g., Dawes, 1994).

Lapses in empathy include (1) telling people what they should feel (e.g., "That's not the way to feel when you see her"), (2) an interrogative interview style, (3) overinterpretation, (4) self-disclosure that distracts attention from pursuit of goals, (5) encouragement of dependence by offering excessive help, and (6) negativity (criticizing clients). Examples of physicians' poor attempts at empathy, when they must deliver bad news to patients, are as follows:

> One 72-year-old woman with breast cancer confided to her consultant surgeon that she did not want to lose her breast, only to be told, "At your age, what do you need a breast for?"
>
> A woman of 40 with the same disease asked a different hospital consultant if there was any way she could avoid a mastectomy. He said "There is not much there worth keeping, is there?"
>
> An elderly man with terminal lung cancer was asked by a junior hospital doctor why he was crying and [he] explained that he did not want to die. The house officer's unsympathetic response was: "Well, we all have to die some time." (Collins, 1988, p. A7)

Warmth and Genuineness

Warmth refers to the extent to which you communicate nonevaluative caring and positive regard for clients. Attentive listening, positive feedback, and respect contribute to warmth. Genuineness can be defined as the extent to which helpers are not defensive, are real, and not phony in their exchanges. Being genuine includes not hiding behind a professional role to protect yourself. Other aspects include *self-disclosure, confrontation,* and *immediacy.* The purpose of immediacy is to help clients understand themselves better by discussing some aspect of the immediate exchange. For example, perhaps a client often interrupts you. You could point this out, discuss the effects of such behavior, and suggest alternatives. As with any other skill, effective use is demonstrated both by engaging in it when it would be helpful and avoiding it when it would not.

The Alliance

Wampold (2015) views the alliance as composed of three components: the bond, agreement about the goals of intervention, and agreement about the tasks of helping (p. 272). He argues that the alliance has to be firm to be positively associated with outcome and overlaps with other common factors such as empathy. (See also Street, 2013.)

Respect/Positive Regard

Respect includes involving clients as informed clients in making decisions, considering cultural differences, and not imposing values on clients. Considering client preferences and values is a hallmark of evidence-informed practice. If you show respect for clients, they are more likely to discuss difficult topics, explore how they may contribute to concerns, carry out agreed-on plans, feel better about themselves, and be more hopeful. Positive regard may be especially important when there are differences between clients and helpers or coercive circumstances such as involvement of the criminal justice system.

ATTENTIVE LISTENING

If you are not a good listener, you are unlikely to understand client characteristics and circumstances and cannot offer empathic statements. Good listeners are oriented to other people rather than to themselves. They are good observers of other people. They accurately note what others say and how they say it, as well as nonverbal cues. They listen rather than judge. These features increase the likelihood of understanding clients' experiences and feelings and communicating this to clients. Careful listening is aided by the assumption of ignorance (Kadushin & Kadushin, 1997). Accurate paraphrases and reflections are part of attentive listening. Attentive listening increases the likelihood that clients share useful information and participate in agreed-on plans.

Advice giving is a common error. People often want to be heard, to be understood without being given advice, suggestions, or interpretations, and they want recognition that they have been heard. Poor substitutes for listening include *responding with a cliché*, such as "That's the way the ball bounces," or *parroting* (repeating exactly) what was said (Egan, 2014). Ignoring what has been said is another form of inadequate response. Criteria of value in judging the quality of listening skills include clients sharing relevant material, participating in exploring factors related to concerns, and feeling supported. You could identify your biases about a client that may hinder effective listening by noting what you think a person will say at specific points.

MINIMIZING NEGATIVE BEHAVIOR

Behaviors that hinder working relationships include hostile comments, accusatory "you" comments, assuming rather than checking what others believe or have done, overstructuring of encounters, and empathic failure (ignoring others' experiences; Norcross & Wampold, 2011). Behaviors such as harsh negative evaluations, obvious signs of impatience, and blaming clients decreases the likelihood of engaging clients. Indicators of judgmentalness include blaming or criticizing clients, imposing personal values about what outcomes are good or bad, and ignoring cultural differences in values, norms, or preferred styles of communication. Being nonjudgmental does not imply that you should not identify and respond differently to helpful behaviors that should be supported and dysfunctional ones that should not. Being nonjudgmental is difficult, since we are often unaware of our biases and how we communicate. Biases may be difficult to identify because they are inherent in how problems are defined in a particular society, profession, or practice framework (Gambrill, 2012a). Judgmental views about what is best are imposed on clients in authority-based decision-making. Exploring your reactions to specific individuals, problems, or groups will help you to identify biases that may affect your work.

TEAM MEETINGS AND CASE CONFERENCES

Poor team work and communication contribute to avoidable errors (Williams et al., 2007). Increasing attention has been devoted to enhancing effective communication in teams (e.g., Rosen, DiazGranados, Dietz, Benishek, Thompson, Provonest, & Weaver, 2018). Sensitivity to the feelings and level of knowledge of others and focusing on shared interests (Fisher & Ury, 2011) can avoid unproductive conflicts during team meetings and contribute to resolving conflicts in a constructive manner. In his classic article "Why I Do Not Attend Case Conferences," Meehl (1973) identified characteristics of case conferences and group meetings that decrease the quality of decisions such as rewarding everything, "gold and garbage" alike (no matter what anybody says, it is regarded as profound and informative), and the reluctance to question claims because of not wanting to hurt or embarrass others (Meehl, 1973, p. 235). The latter may result from the false belief that high-quality discussions cannot occur unless harsh criticism is used. Observation of case conferences shows that decisions may be made, not through careful consideration of evidence, but because of influence by pitches or denunciations on the part of influential group members (Dingwall, Eekelaar, & Murray, 1983).

Participants may be reluctant to criticize other views because of the "buddy-buddy syndrome" (not criticizing friends). The power structure in a group may be such that no matter how cogent a point, it will not be persuasive because of the apathy and fear of most participants. Or diplomatic skills that are useful in countering or neutralizing fallacies may be lacking. A history of harsh criticism for speaking up in case conferences or fear of negative evaluation discourage participation. The tendency to be impressed by plausible-sounding but uninformative views is encouraged by failure to raise critical questions such as" "What evidence is there for this view?" or "How does this help us understand and know what to do about this problem?" Participants may believe that raising critical questions is not compatible with caring about clients. They may not have a similar goal, such as discovering the evidentiary status of services provided to clients. Skill in argumentation and attitudes and values integral to critical thinking increase the likelihood that disagreements are fruitful (see Chapters 1 and 6).

Groupthink may occur. This refers to "deterioration of mental efficiency, reality testing, and moral judgments that result from in-group pressures" (Janis, 1982, p. 9). Causes include isolation of a group, cohesiveness, biased leadership, and high stress. Indicators include:

- An illusion of invulnerability that results in over-optimistic and excessive risk-taking.
- Belief in the group's inherent morality.
- Pressure applied to any group member who disagrees with the majority view.
- Collective efforts to rationalize or discount warnings.
- A shared illusion of unanimity.
- Self-appointed "mind guards" who protect the group from information that might challenge the group's complacency.
- Self-censorship of deviations from what seems to be the group's consensus.
- Stereotypical views of adversaries as too evil to make negotiating worthwhile, or too stupid or weak to pose a serious threat (Janis, 1982).

Methods Janis suggests to discourage groupthink include assigning the role of critical evaluation to all group members; every person should be encouraged to air objections and doubts and to look for new sources of information. One member of the group could be assigned the role of devil's advocate.

Enhancing the Effectiveness of Team Meetings and Case Conferences

There are many steps you can take to improve the quality of team meetings and case conferences (see Exhibit 10.6). One is to prepare for meetings, for example, by setting an agenda. If you want to introduce an idea at a case conference, prepare beforehand by rehearsing what you will say and by reviewing your argument and related evidence as well as counterarguments. Anticipate and be prepared to respond to disagreements and counter proposals. Effective skills in entering conversations and expressing opinions are needed. Present your ideas clearly in a way that links your view to a shared goal. Do not take things personally. If you do, your emotional reactions will get in the way of constructive participation. Focus on service goals—helping clients. Be sure to reinforce others for valuable contributions. Valuing truth over winning will help you to contribute to a culture of inquiry. Distinguish between strong opinions and bias so that you do not mistakenly assume that a person with a strong opinion is not open to considering different points of view. Guidelines emphasized by Fisher and Ury (2011) include focusing on the problem not the people, focusing on interests not positions, using objective criteria, and seeking options that benefit all parties.

Knowledge about group process and structure will help you to anticipate and avoid problems. If possible, know whom you are dealing with (be familiar with the goals and preferred interaction styles of participants). Although it may not be possible to totally change styles that compromise the quality of

---

EXHIBIT 10.6

CASE CONFERENCE GUIDELINES THAT CONTRIBUTE TO ETHICAL
DECISIONS

- It is "safe" to disagree.
- It is safe to reveal ignorance and error; participants recognize that knowledge develops through criticism.
- Uncertainty in making decisions is recognized.
- Participants avoid propaganda methods such as inappropriate ad hominems and glittering generalizations such as inflated claims of effectiveness of a method.
- Alternative views are sought.
- Critical appraisal of all views is the norm.
- Blameless: seek information about how to minimize avoidable errors.
- Recognize conflicts between educational needs and clients' rights.
- Focus on maximizing quality of care provided to clients (how best to address client concerns).

decision-making, they can be muted in a number of ways (e.g., by agreeing on group norms, focusing on the problem not the person, and reinforcing positive behaviors). Agreeing on an agenda increases the likelihood that agenda items are discussed. If people get off the track, remind participants of agenda items. Helpful norms include (1) not interrupting other people; (2) not hogging the floor; (3) holding speakers responsible for accompanying assertions with a description of related reasons and evidence; and (4) avoiding personal attacks. Your skill in constructively responding to ploys such as distorting arguments will contribute to productive discussions. Focus on service goals to keep up your courage to raise vital questions. Silence, when confronted with faulty assumptions that may harm clients no matter what the cause, calls for considering the possible consequences for clients (see discussion of the ethics of excuses in Chapter 7). Feeling helpless and saying nothing in a group setting, even though understandable in terms of an unpleasant past history, is an ethical concern if this may result in decisions that harm clients.

OBSTACLES TO EFFECTIVE COMMUNICATION

Both environmental and personal obstacles may interfere with effective communication (see Exhibit 10.7). Environmental factors include lack of opportunities for positive informal exchanges such as a staff lounge and an agreed-on time and place for staff to discuss issues that affect clients such as a support group or journal club. You may work in an agency that does not value a culture of thoughtfulness in which differences of opinion are viewed as learning opportunities. If so, work together with colleagues who share your interests to change your work climate and culture. Not being familiar with the norms, values, and preferred styles of communication of different groups may get in the way. You may be embarrassed or uncomfortable with topics or behaviors of concern to clients and so may not engage them in important discussions. You may have to hone skills in disarming in which you acknowledge the truth in a critic's remarks. Perhaps you have needed skills but do not use them because they have not been reinforced or have been punished. For example, requests for more specific supervisory feedback may have been ignored or punished. Supervisors who have difficulty requesting behavior changes may fail to do so and then threaten an employee with losing her job. This is not fair and in fact, may be grounds for a successful grievance or lawsuit.

Beliefs about how people should act may be an obstacle; you may feel "entitled" to being treated in a certain way with no responsibility for changing a disliked situation. Unrealistic expectations include the belief that you must be successful

EXHIBIT 10.7
FACTORS RELATED TO INEFFECTIVE SOCIAL BEHAVIOR

Problem	Remedy
1. Lack of knowledge about social rules/norms including cultural differences	1. Acquire knowledge.
2. Lack of needed skills	2. Acquire skills.
3. Interfering behaviors (e.g., aggressive reactions)	3. Replace with effective reactions.
4. Inappropriate or inadequate stimulus control (e.g., skills are available but not used)	4. Develop effective self-management skills (see Chapter 12).
5. Interfering emotional reactions such as anxiety and anger	5. Identify related factors (e g., lack of skills or knowledge, taking things personally, fear of negative evaluation, unrealistic expectations), and make needed changes.
6. Fear of negative evaluation	6. Decrease sensitivity to social disapproval.
7. Unrealistic performance standards	7. Identify and decrease unrealistic expectations (e. g, "I must please everyone"), and replace with realistic ones (e.g., "I can't please everyone").
8. Lack of respect for others	8. Increase empathic understanding.
9. A focus on winning	9. Focus on shared goals (e.g., helping clients).
10. Few setting that encourage positive exchanges	10. Increase access to such settings.
11. Agency culture (such as perverse incentives)	11. Rearrange contingencies; involve co-workers.

with all your clients. A belief that everyone must like you or that you must never make mistakes will get in the way of raising questions (and in continuing to learn). Neither belief is likely to be confirmed and thus may result in anger created by nonreward and punishment. Use your feelings as clues to identify your emotional "triggers" such as unrealistic expectations and replace them with helpful self-statements. Dysfunctional beliefs about conflict may get in the way (e.g., it should be avoided at all cost, there is something wrong if you have conflicts, and there must be winners and losers (see Exhibit 10.8); (see descriptions of how the Wright brothers solved problems).

EXHIBIT 10.8

OVERCOMING DIFFICULTIES IN BEING ASSERTIVE

Difficulty	How to Overcome It
Guilt	Identify guilt triggers including irrational beliefs, cognitive distortions, and decide if the guilt is appropriate.
	Develop antidote statements (see Alberti & Emmons, 2008).
Fear of consequences	Ask yourself, "What's likely to happen?" Be alert for irrational beliefs and cognitive distortions.
	Weigh the risks of being assertive against the costs of not being assertive.
Fear of being taken advantage of	Recognize your fear and dispute related assumptions.
Anxiety	Realize that you can act effectively even when you're anxious.
	Practice relaxation techniques including deep breathing or a short meditation prior to confrontations.
Doubt	Do your homework—know what you want to accomplish and the facts of the situation.
	Substitute positive for negative talk.
Anger	Identify and decrease irrational beliefs and cognitive distortions such as anger triggers.
	Empathize—put yourself in the other person's shoes.
Negative self-image	Identify and dispute ways you undermine yourself.
	Recognize your strengths.
	Forgive yourself for your flaws.

Source: Adapted from *Assertive Supervision: Building Involved Teamwork,* by S. S. Drury, 1984, Champaign, IL: Research Press, pp. 304–305.

SUMMARY

Evidence-informed practice requires effective communication skills with a variety of participants in a range of settings including team meetings and case conferences. Examples include offering encouragement, providing critical feedback (e.g., in response to questionable claims), raising questions, disagreeing with others in a nonabrasive manner, supporting positive alternatives to negative behaviors, and engaging clients in a process of shared decision-making. Decision aids are available to communicate information relevant to many decisions. High levels of common factors such as warmth and empathy contribute to positive outcome. You will have many opportunities to protect clients from harm and ineffective service by raising questions about decisions and claims in team meetings and case conferences. Questioning what others take for granted may require courage, especially in environments in which critical appraisal of claims is not viewed as an opportunity to make sound decisions. If criticism is the route to learning and making informed decisions, it is vital not to take it personally but to learn from it—to be aware of and value the ethics of evidence. You may have to develop your assertive skills and encourage related beliefs to speak up when needed as well as take advantage of valuable problem-solving skills such as clearly describing your concerns and what you want; identifying options and considering the consequences, trying the best plan, and evaluating the results.

11

Challenges and Obstacles to Evidence-Informed Decision-Making

AS ALWAYS, CONTEXT is vital to consider. Decisions are influenced by the environments in which they are made, including the preferred approach to framing problems and criteria used to evaluate the accuracy of claims. Implementation challenges include personal, organizational and related social, political, and economic influences. Misinformation abounds in both professional sources and the media (Gambrill, 2012a; Lewandowsky, Ecker, Seifert, Schwarz, & Cook, 2012). Evidence gaps include the relevance gap (of research), the retrievability gap, and the critical appraisal gap (Gray, 1997). Problems differ in their prospects for resolution. The uncertainties associated with making decisions have been emphasized throughout this book as have conflicts of interest that discourage transparency regarding the evidentiary status of practices and policies.

The term *implementation science* refers to efforts to increase the correspondence between the evidentiary status of practices and policies and what is used. Implementation has received increased attention, including identification of facilitators and barriers (e.g., England, Butler, & Gonzales, 2015; Fixen, Blasé, Naoom, Duda, 2015; Fixen, Blasé, Naoom, & Wallace, 2009; Flottorp et al., 2013). Ways in which implementation may go wrong include premature implementation (e.g., promotion of a method based on weak evidence) and low fidelity implementation (e.g., missing important elements and/or components; e.g., Barth et al., 2012). Population-based implementation may be carried out for a program tested with success only locally such as the Troubled Families Program in the United Kingdom (Bonell, McKee, & Fletcher, 2016). Lists of alleged "best practices" may contain programs no better than programs not included (Gandhi, Murphy-Graham, Petrosino, Chrismer, & Weiss, 2007; Gorman & Huber, 2009).

POLITICAL, ECONOMIC, AND SOCIAL INFLUENCES AND RESULTING OBSTACLES

Political, economic, and social influences and related legislation affect practices and policies including transparency regarding what is done to what effect. The professional helping industry, including professional education, is a multibillion dollar one with ties to many other industries such as the pharmaceutical industry. Economic interests may encourage myside bias and related deceptive strategies such as hiding harms of interventions (e.g., Gotzsche, 2013, 2015; Oreskes & Conway, 2010; Young, Ioannidis, & Al-Ubaydli, 2008; see also Bartholomew, 2014). Regulatory agencies such as the Food and Drug Administration and licensing agencies may fail to do their job; they may discourage rather than encourage transparent and accountable practices and policies. A professional license does not guarantee competence. Nor does the filtering process of peer review protect us from misleading claims (retractionwatch.com). The quest for publications has resulted in the creation of hundreds of predatory journals publishing material without review. Prevailing opinion may be an obstacle—influence by standards of practice, opinion leaders, professional education, and public relations advocacy, for example, by pharmaceutical companies and related conflicts of interest.

ORGANIZATIONAL OBSTACLES

Agencies differ in learning opportunities provided to staff and how uncertainties are handled. They differ in the match between resources and goals, which are influenced by their funding sources and legal regulations including accountability requirements (see Exhibit 11.1.) Organizations develop cultures and climates. The latter refers to employees shared perceptions of the psychological impact of their work environment. Culture refers to the social context of the work environment—patterns of social interaction (Glisson, 2007). Components of culture include history, contingencies in effect, patterns of communication, decision-making styles, philosophy, myths, and stories. Certain values are preferred, and certain norms and rules are followed. Contingencies may support going along with dubious

EXHIBIT 11.1

FACTORS THAT INFLUENCE CLINICAL PRACTICE AND OUTCOMES

Uncertainties	About effects of interventions on particular individuals
	Effects of multiple providers
	Knowledge and skill levels of staff
Agency context	Funding sources
	Legal and administrative regulations
	Economic and regulatory context
	Standards of practice
Organizational policies and management practices	Financial resources and constraints
	Organizational structure
	Policy standards and goals
	Safety culture and priorities
	Staffing level and skill mix
	Workload and shift patterns
	Administrative and managerial support including information technologies services
Team characteristics	Verbal and written communication
	Supervisory arrangements
	Team structure (consistency, leadership)
Individual (staff) factors	Competence (knowledge and skills), ethical standards
	Physical health
Task requirements	Task design and clarity of structure
	Availability and use of decision aids
	Availability and accuracy of assessment methods
	Information overload
Client characteristics	Complexity and seriousness of concerns
	Language and communication skills
	Personality and environmental circumstances
	Cultural differences
	Ability to make judgments (health literacy-understanding of options and potential impact on hoped-for outcomes)
	Use of other interventions

Source: Adapted from "The Investigation and Analysis of Clinical Incidents," by C. Vincent and E. Taylor-Adams, 2001, in C. Vincent (Ed.), *Clinical Risk Management: Enhancing Patient Safety* (2nd ed), London, England: BMJ, p. 442, and "How Will Health Care Professionals and Patients Work Together in 2020? A Manifesto for Change, by R. Hertwig, H. Buchan, D. A. Davis, W. Gaissmaier, M. Härter, K. Kolpatzik, . . . H. Wormer, 2011, in G. Gigerenzer & J. A. Muir Gray (Eds.), *Better Doctors, Better Patients, Better Decisions: Envisioning Health Care in 2020*, Cambridge, MA: MIT Press, pp. 317–338.

practices and policies rather than active open-minded thinking so integral to evidence-informed decision-making. Criticism and questions may be taken personally rather than as opportunities to explore the accuracy of claims and to improve services. Harming in the name of helping may be ignored. Little attention may be given to errors, both avoidable and not. The medicalization of social and personal problems may be promoted, as in framing substance abuse and gang violence as mental health problems and ignoring structural influences such as lack of employment that provides a living wage.

Examples of organizational incompetence include lack of any means to check whether key tasks are carried out; not reviewing the quality of communication with clients; lack of feedback concerning the outcomes of decisions made so staff lose opportunities to improve future performance; failure to use interventions most likely to be effective and to harvest and take steps to avoid errors; and continued use of services shown to be ineffective or harmful. Outcomes of referrals may not be tracked. Service systems may be dysfunctional; for example, transfer of records may not be timely. Conflicts of interests that harm clients may be ignored (Cosgrove, Bursztajn, Krimsky, Anaya, & Walker, 2009). Organizations differ in how conflict, uncertainty, and less-than-hoped-for success are handled and in the transparency with which the evidentiary status of services and outcomes attained are clearly and accurately described on their website. They differ in how clearly important dimensions of service quality are described as well as success in meeting these criteria. A review of agency websites in the Bay Area showed that not one clearly described the evidentiary status of services offered and outcomes attained. For example, process measures were often reported (number of clients seen; Gambrill, 2017).

Time pressures and distractions may encourage a mindless approach in which decisions are made with little thought. Staff competencies may not match the tasks they confront and opportunities for coaching and deliberate practice may be absent. Supervisors may have little or no time to carry out their educational role in helping those they supervise to enhance their skills. If line staff work in environments in which supervisors and administrators have little interest in discovering whether clients are helped or harmed (indeed, they may block such efforts), it may be difficult to maintain values and behaviors needed to make evidence-informed decisions. Staff may get "worn down" as their efforts are not reinforced or are punished. The courage to recognize that mistakes will be made and a commitment to learn from them (the "courage to fail"; Fox & Swazey, 1974) may dwindle. Staff may even forget the importance of recognizing information needs, posing related questions, and searching for related research (see discussion of burnout in Chapter 12). Tools such as timely access to up-to-date databases that facilitate a search for needed information may be absent. Technologies that detract from rather than promote quality services may be introduced. The language of managerialism and related activities creep into ever more venues including the increasing press for standardization and efficiency even in areas in which this is not possible without the distortion of reality as with magical uses of statistics (e.g., Stivers, 2001). On the other hand, valuable technologies that could contribute to quality services may be ignored. There may be no clear, supportive whistle-blowing policy.

Administrators may discourage critical appraisal of services (e.g., do they do more good than harm?) and encourage fear-based practice (Whittaker & Havard, 2016). Roberts (2012) draws on Witte, Witte, and Kerwin (1994) to describe kinds and sources of ignorance, both avoidable and not, in organizations. Pressure to conform may result in poor decisions. In the sin of "cordial hypocrisy," we use polite and politically correct language to maintain harmony and minimize friction. There is a "façade of good will and congeniality that hides distrust and cynicism" (Solomon & Flores, 2001, p. 2). Administrators may be complicit in creating and maintaining avoidable ignorance that hinders improvement in services.

> Institutional corruption is manifest when there is a systematic and strategic influence which is legal, or even currently ethical, that undermines the institution's effectiveness by diverting it from its purpose or weakening its ability to achieve its purpose, including, to the extent relevant to this purpose, weakening either the public's trust in that institution or the institution's inherent trustworthiness. (Lessig, 2013)

All these factors influence the overall task environment, which, in turn, influences the quality of decisions.

Knowledge can grow only in an environment in which all involved parties, including clients, are free to raise questions regarding possibilities, evidence, and goals. Criticism provides information that contributes to minimizing avoidable errors. Learning organizations are characterized by ongoing improvements in the quality of decisions as well as the development of new knowledge, including new ways of using and managing knowledge developed by others. User-friendly complaint and compliment systems should be in place and information used to enhance service quality. Gray (2001a) suggests that knowledge in an organization can be increased by transforming tacit into explicit knowledge. He defines an evidence-informed organization as one in which staff at all levels "are able to find, appraise, and use knowledge from research evidence" (p. 249). There is a concern to allocate resources equitably, and in ways in which they can do the most good for the least cost (Ovretveit, 1995, p. 121). (As emphasized in earlier chapters, evidentiary status alone does not imply that a practice or policy should be adopted; there are many other considerations including client characteristics and circumstances including their preferences.)

APPROACH TO ERRORS

Settings differ in how easy it is to make, recognize, and remedy errors. As emphasized in earlier chapters, "reasoning is not only susceptible to error, but constantly prone to it" (Walton, 2015, p. 260). In addition to errors due to a lack of knowledge or skills on the part of individuals, errors may be due to dysfunctional systemic factors (Vincent, 2010). We can consider only so much information at one time. Potential consequences include selective perception, sequential (rather than contextual) processing of information, and faulty memory. In discussing errors, we should consider the extent to which employees control their work. Avoidable errors may reflect avoidable ignorance created by secrecy, taboos, and denials. Organizational cultures range from actively seeking data regarding safety to not wanting to know (Reason, 1997; Vincent, 2010). Are staff encouraged to discover, share, and make informed efforts to decrease errors? Are errors due to lack of important content knowledge and related skills? (see Chapter 6). Forms of denial Singer (1978) proposes include blaming the victim, trivializing error, no response, outright cover-ups, reinterpreting errors as correct, and bureaucratic diffusion of responsibility. Staff may claim that certain errors are unavoidable when they are avoidable or protest that errors have only minor consequences when they have major ones. Ineffective error management strategies suggested by Reason (1997) include:

- They "firefight" the last error rather than anticipating and preventing the next one.
- They focus on active failures rather than latent conditions.
- They focus on personal, rather than situational contributors to error.
- They rely heavily on exhortations and disciplinary sanctions.
- They employ blame-laden, vague terms such as "carelessness," "bad attitude," "irresponsibility."
- They do not distinguish adequately between random and systematic error-causing factors.
- They are generally not informed by current human factors, knowledge regarding error, and accident causation. (p. 126; see also Vincent, 2010)

Organizations have a great deal to gain in the short term by encouraging the view that errors are caused by a particular individual but much to lose in the long run in terms of discovering and altering systemic causes which contribute to avoidable errors that harm clients. Consider, for example, instances in which the death of a child in state care is attributed to a single staff person. This hinders exploration of related agency factors. Singer (1978) suggests that incompetence, callousness, and planned error explain error-related behaviors in organizations. He suggests

> In cases where there is an unwillingness to take action, the second category occurs, errors of callousness. . . . When key people within organizations or institutions are made aware of a problem, persistent or exceptional, and do not take steps to correct it or to rectify injustices, we have errors of callousness. (p. 31)

PERSONAL OBSTACLES

Some barriers to problem-solving are self-imposed such as lack of active open-mindedness (see Chapters 1 and 6). Innumeracy (lack of competence in using numbers) and a reluctance to seek corrective feedback and take action based on this may continue because of lack of intellectual curiosity and fairmindedness. The self-imposed nature of personal obstacles (ourselves) is both an advantage (we may have greater potential to minimize them) as well as a disadvantage (it can be more difficult to spot them). Barriers suggested by Oxman and Flottorp (1998) that remain relevant today include knowledge and attitudes regarding uncertainty, feelings of incompetence regarding new practices, need to act, and information overload.

Motivational Obstacles

Motivational barriers to informed decision-making include a lack of interest in helping clients, a focus on winning over learning and resignation ("What's the use?" Davies & Aitkenhead, 2001). Good decision making involves *sufficient search* for possibilities, evidence, and goals, and *fairness* in the search for evidence and in inference (Baron, 1985). Search is 'sufficient' when it best serves the thinker's personal goals, including the goal of minimizing the cost of thinking (Baron, 2008, p. 63). Deadly sins suggested by Fineberg et al. (2012) include arrogance (I know best no matter what the research says), sloth (being informed takes too much time), greed (the more vague I am, the more money and publications), complacency (acceptance of poor-quality services), denial (refusal to see harms of practices and policies), and fatalism (see but argue that nothing can be done). Other deadly sins include procrastination (I'll do it later), timidity (lack of courage to speak up), and hypocrisy (saying the right thing but taking no related actions). All contribute to avoidable ignorance that may harm clients. Rather than learning from our critics, we may ignore or punish them or misrepresent what they say.

Ethical obligations to clients may be ignored including the obligation to be an honest broker of knowledge and ignorance—to involve clients as informed participants. There may be a reluctance to devote the time needed to acquire valuable knowledge and skills. Critical thinking skills and knowledge may not be valued or have been acquired. There may be a distain for or disinterest for both epistemic and instrumental rationality. Maintaining social bonds with a group may be more important than helping clients and avoiding harm (see discussion of false knowledge in Chapter 3). Conflicts of interest may hinder provision of effective services (Angell, 2009; Cosgrove, Bursztajn, Krimsky, Anaya, & Walker, 2009). Thus, our goals influence the quality of decision-making.

The reasons described in Chapter 2 for creating the process of evidence-based practice highlight ethical lapses such as failing to take advantage of research that can help clients attain valued goals. In his discussion of the moral development of professionals, Rest (1983) uses the term *ethical sensitivity* to refer to four interrelated components: (1) identifying important ethical aspects of a situation, (2) reasoning to find the morally best course of action, (3) being motivated to act in an ethical manner, and (4) acting in an ethical way (moral action; see also Rest & Narvaez, 1994). A lack of ethical sensitivity compromises integration of research and practice; it compromises *evidence-sensitivity*—attention to the evidentiary status of beliefs and actions. Critically appraising beliefs and action is integral to evidence-informed practice. Without what Walton (2013) refers to as a "capacity for criticism," misleading beliefs and assumptions may win the day and hamper learning. Both motivational or learning variables may be related to deficiencies in this area, including misunderstandings about how we learn and preferences for authoritarian decision-making styles (e.g., simply pronouncing what is true or false).

There may be a reluctance to take responsibility for the quality of one's reasoning including accurate description of well-argued alternative views and evidence (or its lack) for favored positions. Moral responsibilities such as fair-mindedness central to critical thinking and so viewed throughout the ages require accurate description of positions, data and their sources, clarity in place of obscurity, and minimizing deceptive use of fallacies and biases.

Failure to perform competently as a professional means two different things. First, there is failure to apply correctly the body of theoretic knowledge on which professional action rests. Failures of this sort are errors in techniques. For surgeons, we have identified two varieties of this type of error—technical and judgmental. Second, there is failure to follow the code of conduct on which professional action rests. Failures of this sort are moral in nature. (Bosk, 1979, p. 168)

Faulty Problem-Solving and Learning Styles

Barriers include inflexible use of problem-solving strategies including lack of active open-minded thinking. Hazardous attitudes include a sense of invulnerability, impulsivity, and resignation (Davis & Aitkenhead, 2001). Focusing on justifying rather than critiquing beliefs encourages confirmation biases in which we seek only data that support our assumptions. There may be a disdain for critical appraisal of claims that impedes arriving at informed decisions. Only if we critically evaluate beliefs and actions including cherished views, can we discover flaws in our reasoning including faulty assumptions and prejudices that may get in the way of helping clients. A preoccupation with finding *the* cause of a problem can be a barrier rather than asking how behaviors or events can be altered to attain desired outcomes (Feinstein, 1967).

Problems may remain unsolved because misleading criteria are relied on to evaluate claims such as tradition or popularity (see Chapter 3). A clinician may believe that good intentions are enough to protect clients from harmful or ineffective services when history shows they are not. Both professionals and clients are vulnerable to propaganda ploys such as appeals to emotion encouraged by use of slogans (e.g., "We care") and inflated claims about the effects of practices and policies (Gambrill, 2012a). Lack of critical thinking values, skills, and knowledge leave us easy prey for marketing pitches for untested methods that may be ineffective or harmful. Lack of or ignoring knowledge regarding how we learn—how expertise can be developed and enhanced (e.g. corrective feedback) will hinder enhancement of knowledge and skills (see Chapter 6).

Lack of Knowledge and Skill

Knowledge about a client's concerns influences success in helping clients as described in Chapter 6. The more knowledge and skills available and needed to solve a problem, the more important it is to have them. Lack of assessment knowledge and skills may hinder collection of valuable information about clients and their characteristics and circumstances, including client strengths and environmental resources. Beliefs about behavior may have little overlap with the science of behavior and related evidence-informed principles (Dishion, Forgatch, Chamberlain, & Pelham, 2016). Let us say you are working with a child labeled "autistic" and know little about autism. Your domain-specific knowledge differs considerably compared to a well-informed professional who specializes in this area. Important contextual circumstances may be overlooked such as coercive aspects of a clients' presence or ambivalence due to cultural differences in problem-solving styles.

Sociocentric biases such as the medicalization of deviance and distress (Conrad, 2007; Speed et Al., 2014; Szasz, 2007) encourage a focus on individual characteristics such as substance abuse, depression, and anxiety, obscuring related environmental factors such as economic inequality (Gigerenzer, 2015). Inequities in life opportunities and related changes in economic and social status contribute to what Case and Deaton (2015) refer to as "death by despair" from alcohol, opioids, and suicide. Skill in prioritizing and discovering interrelationships among concerns may be absent. Lack of skills and knowledge required to locate and critically appraise different kinds of research will impede evidence-informed decisions. Expertise in offering warmth and empathy that contribute to client engagement may be lacking (see Chapter 10). Such factors provide the context in which other important knowledge and skills are used including assessment skills, offering interventions most likely to be of value, and tracking progress using valid indicators of outcome.

Skill in critical thinking and values that encourage their use are needed, including avoidance of myside bias. Innumeracy is high among professionals as well as clients, including statistical innumeracy, resulting in provision of incorrect information (e.g., Gigerenzer, 2002a, 2014). Paulos (1988) defines innumeracy as an inability to deal comfortably with the notions of number and chance. Those who provide faulty information are often confident in their false estimations such as assuring a client that a test for AIDS is always accurate (Gigerenzer, 2002a). Perceptual blocks, such as stereotyping, may hinder accurate understanding of clients and their concerns.

Unrealistic Expectations

Unrealistic expectations may relate to colleagues ("I have to please everyone"), as well as clients ("I have to help everyone"; Ellis & Yeager, 1989). They may be encouraged by promotion of unachievable goals such as "Ensure that no child be harmed in care" on the part of government officials. A belief that you must be successful with all your clients may contribute to burnout. Such beliefs may be due to expectations for success that cannot be realized because individual counseling cannot solve many socially created problems (such as homelessness). Waiting for an ideal alternative may result in unnecessary delays in choosing among available options.

Rationalizations/Excuses Used

Difficult situations breed excuses that help us live with our limitations (Snyder, Higgins, & Stucky, 2005). Excuses can be defined as "explanations or actions that lessen the negative implications of an actor's performance, thereby maintaining a positive image for oneself and others" (p. 45). We may create a disconnect between our actions or inactions and related harm (Bandura, 1999). Excuses serve many functions, including preserving self-esteem, smoothing social exchanges, and helping people to live with their limitations. To the extent that they relieve us from assuming undue responsibility for clients and encourage reasonable risk taking, they are helpful. If they prevent us from recognizing limitations that could be altered, for example, by keeping up with practice-related research, they harm clients. Attributing responsibility for decisions to someone (a supervisor) or to some entity (the legal system, the administration), relieves clinicians from assuming responsibility.

Popular excuses for avoiding responsibility are (1) "I didn't know," (2) "I was just following orders" (from my supervisor, or from an evil administrator), and (3) "I was just doing what others do using the same standards of care" (even though abysmal). We could deny there is a problem (e.g., McDowell, 2000). One or more of the following accounts could be offered: It was not possible to get all the information; this was a difficult case; anyone would have had trouble; I was pressed for time; I didn't have the authority to make a decision. Others include: I was tired; my graduate education didn't prepare me for this kind of client; other people make the same mistakes. Excuses given for less-than-optimal service include lack of resources and high caseloads. These may reflect reality. Caseloads may be high. Many objectives are difficult to attain. Resources are often lacking. Common challenges call for working together with others to address them (see Chapter 11).

Reframing strategies may be used to mute the negative consequences of an action; harm may be underestimated ("He wasn't really harmed"), victims may be derogated ("He did not deserve my help"), or the source of the negative feedback may be attacked ("My supervisor doesn't have experience with such clients"; Bandura, 1999). We may use "cleansing" language that obscures suffering and/or coercion (e.g., use the term *relocated* to refer to a forced eviction). Such reactions are encouraged by our tendency to question the accuracy of negative feedback. Acts of omission may be excused by denying there was need for action. A clinician may protest that others would have acted in the same way. Shortcomings may be attributed to others. A temporary inconsistency in performance may be appealed to decrease responsibility. Variations of the intentionality plea include "I didn't mean to do it" and effort-lowering statements such as "I didn't try" (Semin & Manstead, 1983).

Deceiving yourself that you are doing well with your clients (when you are not) may serve goals of feeling good and saving time and effort. We may convince ourselves that a claim is true despite evidence against it. Biased searches can become a matter of habit so that we do not know that we behave this way. Richard Paul (1993) suggests that "we consistently deceive ourselves about the state of, the degree of, and the nature of our knowledge, our freedom, and our character" (p. viii). This is encouraged by the consumer-oriented culture in which we live, which forwards decisions based on emotion rather than rational thought. As Bernays (1923) suggests, "the average citizen is the world's most efficient censor. His own mind is the greatest barrier between him and the facts" (pp. 109, 122). If the essence of self-deception is not knowing when we are deceiving ourselves, as Baron (2000) suggests, what is possible? The self-deceived can be classified into two categories: (1) those whose values match their self-deception and (2) those whose values do not reflect a match. The latter, unlike the former, can be enlightened by highlighting lack of correspondence between their beliefs and their actions.

White (1971) raises the question: "To what extent, if at all, is self-deception itself 'morally questionable?'" (p. 34). He suggests that the answer depends on what efforts a person has made to minimize self-deception. If we claim that agency services are evidence-informed when research shows that this is not the case, and when confronted with this information, make no effort to look into the situation, this is not being morally responsible. This view is incompatible with professional codes of ethics—the requirement to draw on practice-related research and to be competent. However, competence may be defined as matching standards of practice in a community; such standards may do little to protect clients from ineffective or harmful methods.

Emotional Barriers

Emotional barriers include fear of making mistakes, a low tolerance for uncertainty, and a preference for decision-making based on feelings. Martin Luther King Jr. said, "Many people fear nothing more terribly than to take a position which stands out sharply and clearly from the prevailing opinion. The tendency of most is to adopt a view that is so ambiguous that it will include everything and so popular that it will include everybody." Emotion management skills for handling stress and anxiety may be lacking. Beginning signs of burnout may be ignored.

Memory May Be Faulty

We rely on our memory when processing and organizing data. Memory plays a vital role in deliberative reasoning. With the passage of time, memory may change (Berkowitz, Laney, Morris, Garry, & Loftus, 2008; Bernstein & Loftus, 2009; Loftus, 2005; Steblay & Loftus, 2012). We tend to recall our successes and overlook our failures. False memories can be created through biased interviewing methods (Ceci & Bruck, 1995). Simply being asked a question repeatedly can result in memories of events that did not happen. Memory may be imperfect because events were not accurately noted in the first place. Even if we observe a sequence of events, our memory of these events may not remain accurate. We may make up events to fill in gaps in our memory to create "logical sequences" of actions. We then imagine that we really saw these events. The illusion of having a memory of an event can be created by including inaccurate descriptive data in a question. For example, subjects who watched a car accident and who later received new information about the accident changed their description (Loftus, 1979). High anxiety decreases attention to detail so events may not be noticed. These concerns highlight the importance of using accurate recording systems.

Lack of Assertive Skills

Assertive skills may be required to attain needed resources. These include raising questions about services offered and advocacy skills involved in working with others to seek needed changes (see Chapter 12).

SUMMARY

Ethical obligations to clients require attention to obstacles that compromise quality of services. Personal obstacles include lack of assertive skills for raising questions about practices and a disinterest in basing decisions on well-reasoned arguments, including keeping up-to-date with research that may contribute to helping clients.

Organizations may focus on maintaining funding rather than providing quality services to clients. Policies and legislation reflect economic, political, and social contingencies in effect. We can draw on literature concerning implementation and knowledge transfer in efforts to decrease obstacles to the provision of high quality services. As Gray (1997) suggests, we should start programs found to be effective, stop those found to be ineffective or harmful and place those of unknown effectiveness into well designed research studies. The best care is one in which, "based on the best evidence available, all ineffective interventions have been eliminated; in which the interventions undertaken are of the highest possible effectiveness for those groups most likely to benefit, and in which all services are delivered at the highest possible quality" (p. 13).

12

Being and Becoming an Ethical Professional

THE QUALITY OF becoming characterizes a competent professional. This requires enhancing values, knowledge, and skills that maximize the likelihood of helping clients and avoiding harm, including deliberate practice of important skills. Becoming a skilled professional is like a journey, and, as with all journeys, opportunities are taken and forgone. Maintaining and enhancing effective skills is more likely if you assume responsibility for this yourself by taking advantage of theory and research about how to do so.

PLACE CLIENTS' INTERESTS FRONT AND CENTER

Placing clients' interests front and center will contribute to the courage to act on their behalf including questioning claims that, if acted on, may harm clients. This will encourage you to engage others in a joint quest to "do the right thing" such as blowing the whistle on lack of needed resources and harmful and ineffective practices and policies. It requires paying attention to process (see Chapter 10) as well as outcome. It takes courage as well as empathy to truly see others' miseries, especially in the absence of options to relieve them. Caring, courage, and deliberative thinking are a formidable threesome that contribute to client advocacy as well as informed decisions. This threesome will help you to avoid being bamboozled by yourself or others and, as a result, missing opportunities to help clients and to avoid harm.

ENHANCE SKILLS FOR HANDLING
UNCERTAINTY AND IGNORANCE

The process of evidence-based practice confronts us repeatedly with our ignorance, for example, by identifying information needs related to important decisions and translating these into well-structured questions that contribute to an effective search for related research. Decisions must be made in the face of uncertainty about their likely effects. Use uncertainty as a cue to see if you can decrease it by enhancing your knowledge and skills. Log on to the Database of Uncertainties about the Effects of Treatments (DUETS) occasionally to remind yourself about the uncertainties involved in helping clients. Tracking progress in an ongoing manner offers feedback that contributes to informed decisions.

Cultivate Active Open-Minded Thinking

Active open-minded thinking, including skill in argumentation, will contribute to raising important questions that affect clients' lives such as asking: "Is there any evidence that this parent training program helps clients?" Will it help people like my client? Identifying and decreasing knowledge gaps (ignorance) requires an openness to reviewing your knowledge and skills and continuing to enhance your knowledge and skills including knowledge about important uncertainties. This will be a challenge because of egocentric and sociocentric biases, the allure of authority (experts), and time pressures. Barriers include self-censorship in which important questions are not raised because of fears of "rocking the boat" and offending others (Lowry, 1994).

To offer effective services, new knowledge may have to be discovered and used and old assumptions winnowed out. Effective reasoning "presupposes a questioning attitude, a consideration of arguments and facts, and a willingness to modify one's beliefs when evidence suggests the need for this; it presupposes a commitment to the truth insofar as the truth can be ascertained" (Nickerson, 1986, p. 12). Integral to this commitment is the understanding

> that beliefs should be reexamined from time to time, and that there will be no clear answers for many questions or no way to find out what the answers are. . . . Some issues must be decided on the basis of preferences, tastes, or weakly held opinions regarding what the truth might be. (Nickerson, 1986, pp. 12–13)

We are unlikely to be interested in acquiring new knowledge if we are satisfied with our current knowledge. To paraphrase Perkinson (1993), we must become critical of our own performance (pp. 40–41).

We must learn, in other words, something quite new to us: to identify not with the content of our beliefs but with the integrity of the process by which we arrived at them. We must come to define ourselves, and actually respond in everyday contexts, as people who reason their way into, and can be reasoned out of, beliefs. Only then will we feel unthreatened when others question our beliefs, only then will we welcome their questions as a reminder of the need to be ready to test and retest our beliefs daily at the bar of reason, only then will we learn to think within multiple points of view. (Paul, 1993, p. xii)

Basic to this process is a willingness to critically appraise beliefs and claims no matter who promotes them, to ferret out our blind spots, to view knowledge as tentative, and to view theories as tools rather than dogma to be guarded. Properties of beliefs that influence how difficult it may be to alter them include their strength (confidence in a belief—willingness to act on a belief), longevity (how long it has been held), and value (how important they are to us). Once a belief is formed, we are likely to fall prey to confirmation bias—a selective search for confirming data. Active open-minded thinking will counter this tendency.

Make it a habit to search for disconfirming evidence, such as counter-examples and counter-arguments. Arrange ongoing practice of important skills. Take advantage of sources devoted to detection of bogus claims that may harm clients such as, Plos One-Mind the brain.blog. Personal, work environments, and the media offer opportunities to practice critical thinking skills such as posing questions regarding information needs. Watch how others avoid influence of weak arguments to hone your skills. Respond to mistakes and errors as learning opportunities and value the discovery of ignorance as well as knowledge. Take time-outs for empathic reflection (what if I were in her shoes?), become informed about harmful consequences that result from poor decisions, and weed out dysfunctional personal excuses. (See Chapter 11.)

RECOGNIZE THE LIMITS OF HELP THAT CAN BE PROVIDED

Problems differ in their potential for resolution, even by experts. No one may be able to help clients attain some outcomes such as housing in a particular neighborhood. The expectation to always succeed can only be satisfied by ignoring lack of success. Policies, laws, available research findings, and related resources limit options. Popper (1994) argued that trying to make people happy is not only futile, but results in imposing policies on citizens, even if against their will. He suggests that the pursuit of utopian goals distracts us from working in many small ways to minimize avoidable suffering. You can do no more than give your best. Giving your best includes making informed decisions, helping clients use and expand their own resources, and taking steps to improve services including enhancing your knowledge and skills. Efforts to redress inequities may not benefit today's clients but may help others in the future.

CULTIVATE UNDERSTANDING OF YOUR OWN ENVIRONMENT

An understanding of social, political, and economic factors related to client concerns will protect you from assuming potentials for change that do not exist via services focused on changing individuals (counseling and therapy). Understanding the context of practice, including the agency in which you work, your profession, related policies, legislation and industries, and the environment in which your clients live will help you to avoid blaming clients or yourself for limited options and encourage you to work together with others to advocate for needed changes (see later section on being an activist). It will help you to understand the relationship between the personal and the political (Mills, 1959) including psychological distress due to inequalities many clients confront such as environmental pollution and lack of access to healthcare and employment that provides a living wage (Bakalar, 2011; Braubach, Jacobs, & Ormandy, 2011; Case & Deaton, 2015; Cushon, Vu, Janzen, & Muhajarine, 2011). The medicalization of deviance in our society spurred by related industries such as the pharmaceutical industry encourages a focus on individuals as the cause of their own distress, distracting attention from related environmental contingencies. Understanding the context of behavior encourages empathic rather than judgmental reactions.

Enhance Skills in Propaganda Spotting (Self and Other)

We are surrounded by propaganda—material that encourages beliefs and action with little thought (Ellul, 1965). Related literature highlights the prevalence of misinformation, our vulnerability to it, and the difficulty of correcting it (Gambrill, 2012a; Nyhan & Reifler, 2010). It is impossible to avoid, but we do have a choice whether to just "go with the flow" or try to minimize its effects by educating ourselves about sources, kinds, and causes including deep propaganda that obscures political, economic, and social contingencies that influence our beliefs and behavior and the questionable accuracy of many common assumptions. Keep a copy of Carl Sagan's *Baloney Detection Kit* on your desk and a card listing Rank's (1984) common propaganda cues: *"Hi," "Trust Me," "You Need," "Hurry," "Buy."* Become familiar with informal fallacies, such as glittering generalizations, name calling, plain folks appeal, and card stacking and their use to encourage beliefs and actions with little thought (Gambrill & Gibbs, 2017). Choose a "fallacy-of-the-week" from fallacyfiles.com to practice detecting and avoiding its influence. You can decrease myside bias by making the effects of decisions and criteria on which they are based visible. Thank others for pointing out mistakes in your thinking.

Arrange a Supportive, Learning Environment

In a learning organization, there is a focus on enhancing knowledge and skills that contribute to valued outcomes. What consequences support desired behaviors? What contingencies discourage these? Are undesired behaviors reinforced? What prompts exist for valued behaviors? Are necessary tools available? Even the strongest repertoire can erode in an unsupportive environment. Woo kindred spirits to work together to create conditions that foster evidence-informed decisions. Expertise in contingency analysis—knowledge and skills in identifying and altering the relationships between behaviors of interest and environmental events—will contribute to arranging and maintaining a supportive environment (e.g., Cipani & Schock, 2011; Madden, 2013). Provide prompts and incentives for use of knowledge and skills that encourage sound decisions such as searching for research related to information needs.

If support for valuable competencies is unavailable from colleagues and supervisors in your agency, locate others who share your values and goals and form a support or consultation group, taking advantage of the Internet. You could meet monthly to share successes, seek options for handling setbacks, and discover new ways to help clients. You could start a journal club in which members take turns searching for research findings related to life-affecting questions and sharing what they find (e.g., by preparing CATS; libguides.library.arizona.edu). Select a "fallacy or bias-of-the-week" to practice detecting and avoiding. Thank others for identifying mistakes in your thinking and discovering options that may result in better services (more effective, transparent, and accountable). Take advantage of user-friendly checklists to review the quality of different kinds of research (www.testingtreatments.org).

ENHANCE HELPFUL VIEWS ABOUT KNOWLEDGE AND HOW TO GET IT

Our beliefs about how we learn and how much control we have over what we learn are related to our potential to learn (Hofer, 2001). Lifelong learning requires critically appraising and updating knowledge and skills—it requires active open-minded thinking in which we question initial assumptions and search for alternative views. Learning is an active process in which we question our beliefs, compare perspectives, and seek feedback about our competencies and the outcomes clients attain. We ask: What are arguments against my beliefs? What is the evidence for this possibility? Is there counterevidence? Is this true for all people? Is anything important left out of this argument? What is the main point? How does this relate to other evidence about this topic? Without deep processing, new knowledge may be used to bolster current biases and prejudices, especially when there are strong incentives for maintaining them such as just going along with the prevailing view.

People differ in how open they are to examining their beliefs. Beliefs are often difficult to alter because they are linked to a worldview, a preferred approach to understanding reality. Conceptions of behavior and how it can be changed form a basic part of our beliefs about the nature of human beings and thus have emotional connotations. Information that is not consistent tends to be resisted or "assimilated" (made to fit preferred views). Inconsistencies in beliefs may not be recognized. New beliefs may simply be added without altering old ones. This has been called the *add on* principle (Harmon, 1986).

Perkinson (1993), as well as others, stresses that "students must become critical of their own performances and their own understandings—while remaining confident in their ability to do better- if they are to continue growing" (pp. 40–41). The importance of thinking about why theories do not work has been emphasized by many writers (e.g., Schon, 1983). "Developing theories in use is one of the most important ways critical thinking can be practiced at the workplace. It requires practitioners to reflect on the reasons why espoused theories are not working and to seek alternative forms of practice" (Brookfield, 1987, p. 154). It requires us to distinguish between which theories we think we rely on and which ones we actually use—which may be a surprising revelation. Identifying knowledge gaps requires an openness to reviewing background knowledge and skills and candidly comparing these with what the literature suggests is needed to help clients.

Research showing how difficult it is to alter false beliefs emphasizes the importance of critical thinking values, skills and knowledge (Lewandowsky, Ecker, Seiftert, Schwarz, & Cook, 2012). A willingness to question beliefs requires curiosity and an interest in discovering what is true. A disinterest in examining practice beliefs may be related to a reluctance to accept responsibility for decisions. It is not unusual to hear clinicians say, "I don't make decisions; clients make their own decisions." This stance overlooks the social-influence process inherent in clinical practice (see Chapter 10). A belief on the part of clinicians that they do not make decisions is a key indicator of a sense of powerlessness (or failure to take responsibility) encouraged by inadequate decision making skills and knowledge.

Seek Help When You Need It

The process of evidence-informed practice confronts us repeatedly with our ignorance; information needs related to important decisions are translated into well-structured questions that allow us to see whether there are any research findings that shed light on these questions. A reluctance to recognize that you need help will be a major obstacle, as illustrated by how difficult it is for students to say, "I don't know."

Increase Opportunities for Corrective Feedback

Arranging ongoing feedback regarding both outcome and process (e.g., quality of the alliance) and taking corrective action based on this such as deliberate practice contribute to development of expertise (Miller, Hubble, & Chow, 2017). Evaluating outcome in an ongoing manner allows you and your clients to make timely changes in plans. Data from individual clients can be collected in $N = 1$ designs (see Chapter 4). Take advantage of computer programs to graph data concerning progress. Only via monitoring may harmful effects be detected at an early point (e.g., Vyse, 2005). You could compare your success with the usual trajectories of progress with similar clients (Rousmaniere, Goodyear, Miller, & Wampold, 2017). Monitoring the quality of the alliance with your clients is positively associated with outcome (see Chapter 10). Here, too, you can discover negative trends at an early point. Errors and lack of success are inevitable; they provide valuable learning opportunities. Setbacks offer opportunities to discover what we understand and what we do not, what we can do and what we cannot, and what is effective and what is not. Skill in troubleshooting is one of the cluster of skills that distinguishes novices from experts. Responding to setbacks as learning opportunities focuses attention on problem-solving.

Take Advantage of Helpful Tools and Effective Training Programs

Attention to application obstacles is a hallmark of evidence-informed practice (see Chapter 2). This includes the creation of tools to facilitate the integration of practice and research such as electronic databases and decision aids (https://decisionaid.ohri.ca; van Weert et al., 2016. Apps on smart phones can be used to gather assessment data and monitor progress. Flow charts and checklists are available to review the quality of different kinds of research (www.testingtreatment.org). Use natural frequencies to estimate risk (Gigerenzer, 2002a, 2002b). Brief checklists are available to decrease errors and enhance quality of care (Gawande, 2009). As discussed in Chapter 6, enhancing expertise requires ongoing deliberate practice of important skills informed by feedback.

Seek education programs that use formats that enhance learning and generalization of skills. Problem-based learning is designed to help practitioners to integrate varied sources of information, including external research findings (Straus, Glasziou, Richardson, & Haynes, 2011). Even brief programs may be helpful in counteracting error-producing strategies (Gigerenzer, 2002a; Larrick, 2005). Take advantage of user-friendly resources to help you to review the evidentiary status of widely used interventions such as CriticalThinkRx and www.pharmedout.org. Valuable websites for keeping up with evidentiary concerns include DUETS, EQUATOR, Cochrane and Campbell Databases, and TRIP (see Chapter 4).

INCREASE MOTIVATION TO OFFER HIGH-QUALITY SERVICE

Getting and staying motivated to offer high-quality services is linked to our values including fair-mindedness to possibilities and our skills in "getting motivated." It is linked to a commitment to honor ethical obligations to clients including becoming a lifelong learner. Questions that can help us to honor our ethical obligations include:

1. Will it help clients if I use assessment measures and intervention methods of doubtful validity?
2. Will it help clients if I use outcome measures that are not valid?
3. Will it help clients if I attribute (mis)behaviors to "mental disorders" and ignore related environmental factors?

Apply the goosey–gander test—would you like to be the recipient of services you provide to your clients (Gambrill & Gibbs, 2002)? Become informed about motivational and emotional influences on information processing such as risk aversion (Slovic, 2010). A willingness to question beliefs requires curiosity and moving away from "motivated skepticism" that favors preferred views (Ditto & Lopez, 1992; Taber & Lodge, 2006) to a critical appraisal of the evidentiary status of claims, both favored and not. Cultivating your curiosity will contribute to raising questions and discovering options.

Getting motivated may require uncovering self-deceptions such as overconfidence (Dunning, 2011), misleading world views, and inflated views of success. You may believe you care about the quality of services offered to clients even though you take no steps to discover the evidentiary status of the methods you use. Self-deceptions are not solely of our own making; they are encouraged by special interests reflected in misinformation in the media and professional sources.

Perhaps the best way to "get motivated" is to educate yourself about the sources and kinds of misinformation and its harmful effects. To avoid the influence of misinformation that may contribute to avoidable harm to clients, you must first recognize it including its reflection in your own beliefs. You may discover that because of commonly accepted but false beliefs you engage in "self-censorship" (Loury, 1994): you fail to raise questions about dubious practices and policies because of fear of negative reactions. Learning who is profiting by spreading misinformation that harms clients and hampers your ability to help them can be very motivating.

ENHANCE SELF-MANAGEMENT SKILLS

Self-management involves rearranging the environment or behavior to attain valued goals such as implementing a plan of action for continued learning (Watson & Tharp, 2013). Self-change methods are used to help clients attain a wide range of hoped-for outcomes; you can also take advantage of these methods. Steps include identifying specific goals, planning how to achieve them, acting on plans, monitoring progress, and taking corrective action as needed. For example, if you want to be more consistent and timely in replying to referral requests, you could have e-mail addresses and phone numbers readily available. Use precommitment strategies to avoid future temptations such as momentary mood changes and distractions. For example, make a commitment to spend one hour each week seeking research related to information needs and protect this time from interruptions by planning ahead.

Increase Time-Management Skills

A review of your schedule often reveals room for improvement. You may assume your workdays must have a crisis mentality. A closer examination may reveal opportunities to rearrange your schedule. Feeling disorganized may be a result of not planning the day in terms of priorities; what must be done versus what could be done (discretionary activities). If procrastination is a problem, develop self-management skills to overcome it. If delegating responsibility is difficult, explore the reasons for this.

Enhance Emotion-Management Skills

Anxiety or anger can get in the way of making informed decisions. Anxiety in social situations may be related to a lack of effective assertive skills (see Chapter 10). Use your feelings a clues to discover related contingencies (Skinner, 1974). Enhance your behavioral and cognitive coping skills for regulating arousal. And, keep things in perspective.

> Whenever you are in doubt or when the self becomes too much with you, try the following experiment: Recall the face of the poorest and most helpless man you have ever seen and ask yourself if the step you contemplate is going to be of any use to him. Then you will find your doubts and your self melting away. (Mohandas Ghandi, quoted in Burgess, 1984, p. 38)

Enhance Skills in Keeping Up to Date

Make a plan to keep up to date with information that affects the quality of your decisions. Take advantage of the valuable resources described in this book designed to help you to discover and perhaps decrease important uncertainties regarding decisions. Form a Journal Club in your agency; it could be online. Enhance you skills in locating the highest quality publications that are also clear and client-focused regarding decisions you and your clients make.

EXAMINING RATIONALIZATION, EXCUSES, AND SELF-DECEPTION

Excuses for offering poor quality services may harm clients.(See related discussion in Chapter 11). For example, not evaluating the outcomes of decisions and not keeping up with practice-related research saves time but may result in use of ineffective or harmful methods. So, when you offer an excuse, ask "Does this work for my clients? As Baron (2008) notes, "self-deception can at times be best, at other times it lies behind the most insidious forms of irrationality, as when people convince themselves that some idea or theory is right, despite the evidence against it" (p. 71); biased searches can become such a habit that we are unaware of their biased nature. Professional codes of ethics provide a guide. When confronted with demonstrably poor or unequal services, draw on ethical obligations to encourage needed actions such as bringing harmful or incompetent services to the attention of others.

DEVELOP POSITIVE ALTERNATIVES TO CHALLENGING SITUATIONS

Discrepancies between services needed and resources available may be a key source of discouragement. One dysfunctional response is to assume that what is must be;

there is a fatalism that nothing can be done to alter conditions. I have been struck by the prevalence of reactions such as "There is nothing we can do"; "We have too many cases"; "We have no power"; and "We have to make decisions quickly." There is a feeling of hopelessness and helplessness. Or there is a utopianism—only if all is changed is the effort worthwhile. *Goal displacement* is another kind of dysfunctional reaction: focusing on concerns that are not of key importance to clients. Constructive ways to handle discrepancies between services needed and those available include offering what help you can and taking steps to decrease discrepancies such as bringing them to the attention of supervisors, administrators, and legislators and working together with others to acquire needed resources including valuable training and tools that contribute to informed decisions.

Focusing on helping clients will help you to choose the best course of action in difficult circumstances. And, as Archie Cochrane (1999) noted, outcome "is certainly not the whole story" (p. 95). The manner in which services are provided, including kindliness and the ability to communicate, matter also. He suggests that "we all recognize quality when we see it and particularly when we receive it" (p. 95). Consider the example he gives in *Effectiveness and Efficiency* (Cochrane 1999). As a prisoner of war during World War II, Archie Cochrane took care of other prisoners of war. He was with a dying soldier who was in great pain. Neither spoke a word of the other's language. He had no pain medication. He took the man in his arms and held him until he died.

> In despair, and purely instinctively, I sat on his bed and took him in my arms. The effect was almost magical; he quieted at once and died peacefully a few hours later. I was still with him, half asleep and very stiff. I believe that by personal intervention I improved the quality of care dramatically in this case, and I know it was based on instinct and not on reason. (pp. 94–95)

BE AN ACTIVIST

An understanding of the big picture coupled with a concern for clients will encourage advocacy to decrease avoidable hardships. Become familiar with barriers to informed decision-making and work together with others to address them. A quest for profit at the expense of helping can be seen in treatment centers that harm rather than help (e.g., Alvarez, 2017) and overmedication of children in foster care and the elderly (Gøtzsche, 2013; United States Government Accountability Office,2014). Such harms require action to bring them to light and protest for change. They call for advocacy. Be familiar with whistle-blower laws and regulations and related helpful sources including how to bring fraudulent practices and policies to the attention of authorities (see False Claims Act). Take advantage of Internet resources to advocate for change. The Internet provides a way to link people in pursuit of change. You could form a coalition of interested parties to pursue change using the Internet including social media to inform others and organize meetings and protests. You and your colleagues could document avoidable harms and share these with relevant parties including regulatory agencies, legislators, and attorney generals.

Politics involves efforts to gain or maintain power. Political action is often necessary to achieve desired goals. Some clinicians forgo having a voice in what happens in an organization or in their community because they believe that politics are beneath (or above) them. This decision will be a welcome one to those who wield power. Skill in recognizing various kinds of political tactics such as censorship and distortion is useful in exerting counter control. Political knowledge and skills are important, especially those involved in working with others toward mutually valued aims, such as enhancing the quality of services. Seek changes in dysfunctional practices and policies based on evidentiary grounds. Let's say there is a policy against observing clients and significant others in real-life settings, such as classrooms, playgrounds, and in homes, and research suggest that such observation is valuable in understanding problems and selecting effective plans (e.g., Budd, Poindexter, Feliz, & Naik-Polan, 2001). Not gathering such data when possible and needed may increase the likelihood of the *fundamental attribution error* (attributing behaviors to personality dispositions of clients and overlooking environmental causes). Give copies to your colleagues of the results of studies showing that observation of interaction between clients and significant others can provide important data.

Pursuit of change is more likely to be successful if it involves a small change, is compatible with current beliefs and goals, and focuses on shared interests such as helping clients (Fisher & Ury, 2011). Anticipate objections and prepare counterarguments and seek the support of colleagues and opinion leaders. If many people work together to achieve a change, it is more likely to occur than if one person pursues it alone. Understanding organizations—how they work, how they change, and why change is often difficult—will suggest both opportunities and obstacles.

An historical perspective will remind you that change can occur and that it often takes effort and time. Consider Ignas Semmelweiss who around 1840 discovered that the death rate of mothers from childbed fever could be decreased from 25% to 2% if surgeons washed their hands before delivering babies (Sinclair, 1909). Not until the end of that century did the medical profession act on his recommendations. Women won the vote in the United States only in 1920. Slavery was declared illegal in the United States only in 1865. Only recently did the Equal Employment

Opportunity Commission declare that employers cannot refuse to hire people with disabilities because of concerns about their effect on health insurance costs. We prepare the way, well or poorly, for the next generation of clients and professionals.

PREVENTING BURNOUT AND JOB STRESS

Burnout is common among helping professionals (e.g., Wild et al., 2014). The term *burnout* refers to feelings of stress, boredom, depression, depersonalization, or fatigue related to work, as well as a sense of helplessness and hopelessness (Maslach & Leiter, 2008). There is a loss of concern for clients; services are offered in a routinized uncaring manner. Depersonalization includes a lack of feeling or callous or negative reactions toward clients; clients are treated in a detached, mechanical manner. Stress may result from too much work, personal problems, a job that is boring or too demanding, or low sense of control over work life. Inflexibility and intolerance of ambiguity contribute to stress. Over- or underinvolvement with clients may interfere with informed decision-making. Different stressors may influence problem-solving capability in different ways (e.g., Hammond, 2000). Related organizational factors include unsupportive peer and supervisory relationships, high caseloads, lack of needed resources, unrealistic expectations, lack of positive feedback, and conflicting role demands. You may blame yourself for limited resources overlooking the role of related social, political, and economic contingencies.

Steps to take to prevent burnout, even if working in an agency that encourages it, include forming a support group to pursue valued changes, recognizing the help you do provide, accepting the uncertain nature of decisions, taking advantage of self-management skills for decreasing stress including relaxation skills (e.g., Wild et al., 2014), and increasing use of methods that contribute to success. Burnout is less likely if you pursue and achieve clear, relevant, agreed-on objectives with clients and evaluate progress in an on-going manner. Use stress and dissatisfaction as cues to identify related causes. Perhaps you take your work home with you. Perhaps you have lost sight of the decisions you do make on the job and feel unnecessarily helpless. You may accept unreasonable assignments because of difficulty in refusing requests. You may assume excessive responsibility for your clients.

WHAT ABOUT SELF-EFFICACY AND SELF-ESTEEM?

Performance efficacy refers to the belief that a certain behavior can be performed. *Outcome efficacy* is a judgment of the likely effect of a behavior. Judgments of efficacy influence how long we persist at a task and how much effort we make. Success in real-life situations is the most influential source of accurate efficacy expectations (Baumeister, Campbell, Krueger, & Vohs, 2003). Perceptions of self-efficacy influence our thoughts and emotions as well as the goals we pursue. Some people have a "let me out of here" approach when confronting difficult problems, which, over time, "can result in self-fulfilling prophecies" (Bransford & Stein, 1984, p. 4). Fear of failure interferes with focused attention on problem-solving. Self-efficacy and self-esteem are not necessarily correlated with actual skills levels (for research on flawed self-assessment, see Dunning, 2011). Simply raising self-esteem is unlikely to improve skilled performance, as suggested in the title of Baumeister et al.'s (2003) review: "Does self-esteem cause better performance, interpersonal success, happiness, or healthier lifestyles? Answer: No, no, probably, sporadically" (p. 1). Self-assessment on the part of physicians is not highly correlated with performance (Tousignant & DesMarchais, 2002). Thus, as Baumeister et al. conclude, raising self-esteem should not be an end in itself. Self-efficacy can be enhanced by acquiring additional knowledge and skills.

Low levels of outcome efficacy pose an obstacle to decision-making in several ways. Helpful views may not be presented in a case conference or may be presented in an ineffective manner. Just as the boldness with which comments are made does not necessarily reflect their soundness, so, too, the diffidence with which comments are made does not necessarily reflect a lack of cogency. Low self-efficacy is associated with negative affect, which reduces the quality of problem-solving. Positive emotions encourage flexibility and creativity and enhance helpfulness and generosity, which should add to effectiveness in both interviews and case conferences. Both extremes of self-esteem, excessive and limited, may interfere with making evidence-informed decisions by encouraging a reluctance to examine beliefs.

SUMMARY

Continued learning that enables provision of more effective help to clients is one of the joys of being in the helping professions. Placing clients' interests front and center contributes to the courage to confront challenging situations in a proactive manner including lack of resources (e.g., advocating for better services). Evidentiary and ethical issues are intertwined as emphasized throughout this book. The obligation to place clients' interests front and center provides courage to raise questions about practices and policies that may harm clients—to use active open-minded thinking in making decisions about possibilities, evidence, and goals. The same applies to personal obstacles that compromise services. We are obligated to ferret out our biases and ignorance and seek to decrease them. We can learn how to become better problem solvers by enhancing critical thinking values, knowledge, and skills.

Understanding our environments including the agencies in which we work and related contingencies can help us to identify influences that shape opportunities. We can work with others to arrange supportive environments including pro-vision of ongoing learning opportunities. Responding to mistakes as learning opportunities and recognizing the limits of help that can be provided as well as the uncertainties involved in everyday practice can help us to avoid the negative emotional reactions that contribute to burnout. Understanding how agencies and professional organizations function, as well as social, political, and economic contributors to personal problems will facilitate discovery of options. Other val-uable steps include seeking timely feedback regarding both process and outcome, selecting knowledge and skills based on what has been found to be effective, and focusing on clear outcomes that clients value. Don't let your vision of the potential of practice to be limited by what "is." Offer clients the same quality services you would like to receive.

REFERENCES

Abel, G. A., & Glinert, L. H. (2008). Chemotherapy as language: Sound symbolism in cancer medication names. *Social Science and Medicine, 66,* 1863–1869. doi: 10.1016/j.socscimed.2007.12.016

Adams, J. L. (1986). *Conceptual blockbusting: A guide to better ideas* (3rd ed.). Reading, MA: Addison-Wesley.

Agoritsas, T., Heen, A. F, Brandt, L, Alonso-Coello, P., Kristiansen, A., Akl, E. A., . . . Vandvik, P. O. (2015). Decision aids that really promote shared decision making: The pace quickens. *BMJ, 350,* g7624. doi: 10.1136/bmj.g7624

Akl, E. A., Oxman, A. D., Herrin, J., Vist, G. E., Terrenato, I., Sperati, F., . . . Schunemannn, H. (2011). Using alternative statistical formats for presenting risks and risk reductions. *Cochrane Database of Systematic Reviews, 3,* CD006776. doi: 10.1002/14651858.CD006776.pub2

Alberti, R. E., & Emmons, M. L. (2008). *Your perfect right: Assertiveness and equality in your life and relationships* (9th ed.). Atascadero, CA: Impact.

Alexander, M. (2010). *The new Jim Crow laws: Mass incarceration in the age of colorblindness.* New York, NY: New Press.

Altheide, D. L. (2002). *Creating fear: News and the construction of crises.* New York, NY: de Gruyter.

Alvarez, L. (2017, June 21). Haven for recovery becomes a relapse capital. *New York Times.* Retrieved from http://www.nytimes.com

Angell, M. (2009). Drug companies & doctors: A story of corruption. *New York Review of Books, 56*(1). Retrieved from http://www.nybooks.com/articles/2009/01/15/drug-companies-doctorsa-story-of-corruption/

Apollonio, D., Wolfe, N., & Bero, L. A. (2016). Realist review of policy intervention studies aimed at reducing exposure to environmental hazards in the United States. *BMC Public Health, 16,* 822. doi: 10.1186/s12889-016-3461-7

Arksey, H., & O'Malley, L. (2005). Scoping studies: Towards a methodological framework. *International Journal of Social Research Methodology, 8,* 19–32. doi: 10.1080/1364557032000119616

Armstrong, J. C. (1980). Unintelligible management research and academic prestige. *Interfaces, 10,* 80–86.

Aronson, J. K. (2003). Anecdotes as evidence: We need guidelines for reporting anecdotes of suspected adverse drug reactions. *BMJ, 326,* 1346. doi: 10.1136/bmj.326.7403.1346

Asimov, I. (1989). The relativity of wrong. *Skeptical Inquirer, 14,* 35–44.

Bacon, F. (1985). Idols of the mind. In J. Pitcher (Ed.), *Francis Bacon: The essays* (Index 4). New York, NY: Penguin Books. (Originally published 1620)

Baer, D. M. (1982). Applied behavior analysis. In G. T. Wilson & C. M. Franks (Eds.), *Contemporary behavior therapy: conceptual and empirical foundations* (pp. 277–309). New York: Guilford.

Bakalar, N. (2011, July 5). Researchers link deaths to social ills. *New York Times,* D5.

Baker, M. (2015, April 30). First results from psychology's largest reproducibility test. *Nature.* doi: 10.1038/nature.2015.17433

Bakker, M., & Wicherts, J. M. (2011). The (mis)reporting of statistical results in psychology journals. *Behavior Research Methods, 43,* 666–678. doi: 10.3758/s13428-011-0089-5

Baldwin, S. A., & Imel, Z. E. (2013). Therapist effects: Findings and methods. In M. J. Lambert (Ed.), *Bergin & Garfield's handbook of psychotherapy and behavior change* (6th ed., pp. 258–297). New York, NY: Wiley.

Bandura, A. (1999). Moral disengagement in the perpetration of inhumanities. *Personality and Social Psychology Review, 3,* 193–209. doi: 10.1207/s15327957pspr0303_3

Barlow, D. H., Nock, M. K., & Hersen, M. (2009). *Single-case experimental designs: Strategies for studying behavior change* (3rd ed.). Boston: Pearson/Allyn and Bacon.

Baron, J. (1985). *Rationality and intelligence.* New York, NY: Columbia University Press.

Baron, J. (1996, March 19). Actively open-minded thinking: Talk about teaching. *Almanac, 42*(24). Retrieved from https://almanac.upenn.edu/archive/v42/n24/teach.html

Baron, J. (2000). *Thinking and deciding* (3rd ed.). New York, NY: Cambridge University Press.

Baron, J. (2008). *Thinking and deciding* (4th ed.). New York, NY: Columbia University Press.

Baron, J. (2012, December 24). The point of normative models in judgment and decision making. *Frontiers in Psychology, 3*(577). doi: 10.3389/fpsyg.2012.00577

Baron, J. (2017, August 27). Assessment of actively open-minded thinking. *Brown Bag Talks.* Retrieved from http://www.sas.upenn.edu/~baron/papers/aotwrefs.pdf

Baron, J., Scott, S., Fincher, K., Emlen, & Metz, S. (2013). *Actively open-minded thinking and reflection-impulsivity as alternatives to the sequential two-system theory of the cognitive reflection test and moral judgment.* Working paper, University of Pennsylvania. Retrieved from http://finzi.psych.upenn.edu/~baron/ms/crt/sjdm13.pdf

Baron, J., Scott, S., Fincher, K. M., & Metz, S. E. (2015). Why does the cognitive reflection test (sometimes) predict utilitarian moral judgment (and other things)? *Journal of Applied Research in Memory and Cognition, 4,* 265–284.

Barnum, P. T. (1865). *Humbugs of the world.* New York, NY: Carleton.

Barrett, S., Jarvis, W. T., Kroger, M., & London, W. H. (2002). *Consumer health: A guide to intelligent decision* (7th ed.). New York, NY: McGraw-Hill.

Barth, R. P., Lee, B. R., Lindsey, M. A., Collins, K. S., Strider, F., Chorpita, B. F., . . . Sparks, J. A. (2012). Evidence-based practice at a crossroads. *Research on Social Work Practice, 22,* 108–119. doi: 10.1177/1049731511408440

Barzun, J. (1991). *Begin here: The forgotten conditions of teaching and learning.* Chicago, IL: University of Chicago Press.

Batson, C. D., O'Quin, K., & Pych, V. (1982). An attribution theory analysis of trained helpers' inferences about clients' needs. In T. A. Wills (Ed.), *Basic processes in helping relationships* (pp. 59–80). New York, NY: Academic Press.

Bauer, H. H. (2004). Science in the 21st century: Knowledge monopolies and research cartels. *Journal of Scientific Exploration, 18,* 643–660.

Bauer, H. H. (2015). How medical practice has gone wrong: Causes of the lack-of-reproducibility crisis in medical research. *Journal of Controversies in Biomedical Research, 1,* 28–39. doi: 10.15586/jcbmr.2015.8

Baumeister, R. F., Campbell, J. D., Krueger, J. I., & Vohs, K. D. (2003). Does high self-esteem cause better performance, interpersonal success, happiness, or healthier lifestyles? *Psychological Science in the Public Interest, 4*(1), 1–44. doi: 10.1111/1529-1006.01431

Becker, H. S. (1996). The epistemology of qualitative research. In R. Jessor, A. Colby, & R. A. Shweder (Eds.), *Ethnography and human development: Context and meaning in social inquiry* (pp. 53–71). Chicago, IL: University of Chicago Press.

Bell, T., & Linn, M. C. (2002). Beliefs about science: How does science instruction contribute? In B. K. Hofer & P. R. Pintrich (Eds.), *Personal epistemology: The psychology of beliefs about knowledge and learning* (pp. 321–346). Mahwah, NJ: Erlbaum.

Benish, S. G., Quintana, S., & Wampold, B. E. (2011). Culturally adapted psychotherapy and legitimacy of myth: A direct-comparison meta-analysis. *Journal of Counseling Psychology, 58,* 279–289. doi: 0.1037/a0023626

Berger, Z. D., Brito, J. P., Singh Ospina, N., Kannan, S., Hinson, J. S., Hess, E. P., . . . Newman-Toker, D. E. (2017). Why doctors need to include patients in their diagnoses. *BMJ, 359,* j4218.

Berkowitz, S. R., Laney, C., Morris, E. K., Garry, M., & Loftus, E. F. (2008). Pluto behaving badly: False beliefs and their consequences. *American Journal of Psychology, 121,* 643–660. doi: 10.2307/20445490

Bernays, E. L. (1923). *Crystallizing public opinion.* New York, NY: Boni & Liveright.

Bernstein, D. M. & Loftus, E. F. (2009). How to tell if a particular memory is true or false. *Perspectives on Psychological Science, 4,* 370–374. doi: 10.1111/j.1745-6924.2009.01140.x

Best, J. (2004). *More damned lies and statistics: How numbers confuse public issues.* Berkeley, CA: University of California Press.

Black, N. (1994). Experimental and observational methods of evaluation. *BMJ, 309,* 540. doi: 10.1136/bmj.309.6953.540a

Bless, H. (2001). The consequences of mood on the processing of social information. In A. Tesser & N. Schwartz (Eds.), *Blackwell handbook of social psychology: Individual processes* (pp. 391–421). Oxford, England: Blackwell.

Blenkner, M., Bloom, M., & Nielsen, M. (1971). A research and demonstration project of protective services. *Social Casework, 52,* 483–499.

Bloom, M., & Britner, P. A. (2012). *Client-centered evaluation: New models for helping professionals.* Boston, MA: Allyn-Bacon.

Bonell, C., Mckee, U., & Fletcher, A. (2016). Troubled families: Troubled policy making. *BMJ, 355,* i5879. doi: 10.1136/bmj.i5879

Bonnot, O., Dufresne, M., Herrera, P., Michaud, E., Pivetee, J., Chaslerie, A., . . . Vigneau, C. (2017). Influence of socioeconomic status on antipsychotic prescriptions among youth in France. *BMC Psychiatry*, 17(82). doi: 10.1186/s12888-017-1232-3

Boren, J. H. (1972). *When in doubt, mumble: A bureaucrat's handbook*. New York, NY: Van Nostrand Reinhold.

Bosk, C. L. (1979). *Forgive and remember: Managing medical failure*. Chicago, IL: University of Chicago Press.

Bostrom, N. (2011). Information hazards: A typology of potential harms from knowledge. *Review of Contemporary Philosophy*, 10, 44–79.

Boswell, J. F., Kraus, D. R., Miller, S. D., & Lambert, M. J. (2015). Implementing routine outcome monitoring in clinical practice: Benefits, challenges, and solutions. *Psychotherapy Research*, 25, 6–19. doi: 10.1080/10503307.2013.817696

Bourgois P., Lettiere, M., & Quesada, J. (2003). Social misery and the sanctions of substance abuse: Confronting HIV risk among homeless heroin addicts in San Francisco. In J. D. Orcutt & D. R. Rudy (Eds.), *Drugs, alcohol, and social problems* (pp. 257–278). New York, NY: Oxford University Press.

Boyle, M. (2002). *Schizophrenia: A scientific definition?* (2nd. ed.). London, England: Routledge.

Bransford, J. D., & Stein B. S. (1984). *The IDEAL problem solver: A guide for improving thinking, learning, and creativity*. New York, NY: Freeman.

Braubach, M., Jacobs, D. E., & Ormandy, D. (Eds.). (2011). *Environmental burden of disease associated with inadequate housing*. Copenhagen, Denmark: WHO Regional Office for Europe. Retrieved from http://www.euro.who.int

Brody, H. (2007). *Hooked: Ethics, the medical profession, and the pharmaceutical industry*. New York, NY: Rowman & Littlefield.

Bromley, D. B. (1986). *The case-study method in psychology and related disciplines*. New York, NY: Wiley.

Bromme, R., & Goldman, S. R. (2014). The public's bounded understanding of science. *Educational Psychologist*, 49, 59–69. doi: 10.1080/00461520.2014.921572

Bromme, R., Kienhues, D., & Stahl, E. (2008). Knowledge and epistemological beliefs: An intimate but complicated relationship. In M. S. Khine (Ed.), *Knowing, knowledge, and belief: Epistemological studies across diverse cultures* (pp. 423–441). New York, NY: Springer.

Brookfield, S. D. (1987). *Developing critical thinkers: Challenging adults to explore alternative ways of thinking and acting*. San Francisco, CA: Jossey-Bass.

Brookfield, S. (1995). *Becoming a critically reflective teacher*. San Francisco, CA: Jossey-Bass.

Brouwers, M. C., Kerkvliet, K., Spithoff, K., & AGREE Next Steps Consortium. (2016). The AGREE reporting checklist: a tool to improve reporting of clinical practice guidelines. *BMJ*, 352, i1152. doi: 10.1136/bmj.i1152

Brownlee, S., Chalkidou, K., Doust, J., Elshaug, A. G., Glasziou, P., Heath, I., . . . Korenstein, D.(2017). Evidence for overuse of medical services around the world. *The Lancet, 390*, 156–168. doi: 10.1016/S0140-6736(16)32585-5

Brownlee, S., Wennberg, J. E., Barry, M. J., Fisher, E. S, Goodman, D. C., & Bynum, J. P. W. (2011). *Improving patient decision-making in health care: A 2011 Dartmouth Atlas Report Highlighting Minnesota*. Retrieved from http://www.dartmouthatlas.org/downloads/reports/Decision_making_report_022411.pdf

Bruch, E., & Feinberg, F. (2017). Decision-making processes in social contexts. *Annual Review of Sociology, 43*, 207–227. doi: 10.1146/annurev-soc-060116-053622

Budd, K. S., Poindexter, L. M., Felix, E. D., & Naik-Polan, A. T. (2001). Clinical assessment of children in child protection cases: An empirical analysis. *Law & Human Behavior, 25*, 93–108.

Bunge, M. (1984). What is pseudoscience? *Skeptical Inquirer, 9*, 36–47.

Bunge, M. (2003). The pseudoscience concept, dispensable in professional practice, is required to evaluate research projects: A reply to Richard J. McNally. *Scientific Review of Mental Health Practice, 2*, 111–114.

Burgess, P. H. (1984). *The sayings of Mahatma Gandhi*. Singapore: Graham Brash.

Burnham, J. C. (1987). *How superstition won and science lost: Popularizing science and health in the United States*. New Brunswick, NJ: Rutgers University Press.

Burns, D. D. (1999). *The feeling good handbook*. New York, NY: Plume.

Campanario, J. M. (2009). Rejecting and resisting Nobel class discoveries: Accent on Nobel laureates. *Scientometrics, 81*, 549–565. doi: 10.1007/s11192-008-2141-5

Campanario, J. M., & Acedo, E. (2007). Rejecting highly cited papers: The views of scientists who encounter resistance to their discoveries from other scientists. *Journal of the Association for Information, Science and Technology, 58*, 734–743. doi: 10.1002/asi.20556

Campbell, D. T. (1969). Reforms as experiments. *American Psychologist, 24*, 409–429. doi: 10.1037/h0027982

Campbell, J. A. (1988). Client acceptance of single-system evaluation procedures. *Social Work Research and Abstracts, 24*(2), 21–22. doi: 10.1093/swra/24.2.21

Campbell, D. T. (1996). Can we overcome worldview incommensurability/relativity in trying to understand the others? In R. Jessor, A. Colby, & R. A. Shreder (Ed.), *Ethnography and human development: Context and meaning in social inquiry* (pp. 153–172). Chicago, IL: University of Chicago Press.

Campbell, D. T. & Stanley, J. C. (1963). *Experimental and quasi-experimental designs for research*. Chicago, IL: Rand McNally.

Carey, B. (2017, October 24). How fiction become fact on social media. *New York Times*, D1.

Carroll, L. (1946). *Through the looking glass, and what Alice found there*. New York, NY: Random House. (Originally published 1871)

Cartwright, N., & Hardie, J. (2012). *Evidence-based policy: A practical guide for doing better*. New York, NY: Oxford University Press.

Caruth, D. L., & Handlogten, G. D. (2000). Mistakes to avoid in decision making. *Innovative Leader, 9*(7), 477. Retrieved from www.winstonbrill.com

Case, A., & Deaton, A. (2015). Rising morbidity and mortality in midlife among white non-Hispanic Americans in the 21st century. *PNAS, 112*, 15078–15083. doi: 10.1073/pnas.1518393112

Ceci, S. J., & Bruck, M. (1995). *Jeopardy in the courtroom: A scientific analysis of children's testimony*. Washington, DC: American Psychological Association.

Center for Research and Dissemination. University of York, April, 2004.

Chalmers, I. (1983). Scientific inquiry and authoritarianism in perinatal care and education. *Birth, 10*, 151–166. doi: 10.1111/j.1523-536X.1983.tb01418.x

Chalmers, I. (2003). Trying to do more good than harm in policy and practice: The role of rigorous, transparent, up-to-date evaluations. *ANNALS of the American Academy of Political and Social Science, 589*, 22–40. doi: 10.1177/0002716203254762

Chapman, L. J., & Chapman, J. P. (1969). Illusory correlation as an obstacle to the use of valid psychodiagnostic signs. *Journal of Abnormal Psychology, 74*, 271–280. doi: 10.1037/h0027592

Chorpita, B. F., & Daleiden, E. L. (2009). Mapping evidence-based treatments for children and adolescents: Application of the distillation and matching model to 615 treatments from

322 randomized controlled trials. *Journal of Consulting and Clinical Psychology, 77,* 566–579. doi: 10.1037/a0014565

Cialdini, R. B. (1984). *Influence: The new psychology of modern persuasion.* New York, NY: Quill.

Cialdini, R. B. (2001). *Influence: Science and practice* (4th ed.). Boston, MA: Allyn & Bacon.

Cialdini, R. B. (2008). *Influence: Science and practice* (5th ed.). Boston, MA: Pearson Education.

Cialdini, R. B., & Sagarin, B. J. (2005). Principles of interpersonal influence. In T. C. Brock & M. C. Green (Eds.), *Persuasion: Psychological insights and perspectives* (2nd ed., pp. 143–170). Thousand Oaks, CA: SAGE.

Cipani, E., & Schock, K. M. (2011). *Functional behavioral assessment, diagnosis and treatment* (2nd ed.). New York: Springer.

Cochrane, A. L. (1999). *Effectiveness and efficiency: Random reflections on health services.* Cambridge, England: Nuffield Trust.

Cohen, D. (2013, September 30). ADHD in France and America. *Mad in America.* Retrieved from https://www.madinamerica.com/2013/09/adhd-france-america/

Cohen, J. (1977). *Statistical power analysis for the behavioral sciences.* New York, NY: Academic Press.

Cohen, M. R., & Nagel, E. (1934). *An introduction to logic and scientific method* (2nd ed.). New York, NY: Harcourt, Brace.

Collins, R. (1988). Lessons in compassion for student doctors. *Sunday Times,* Aug. 7, A7.

Colquhoun, D. (2014). An investigation of the false discovery rate and the misinterpretation of *p*-values. *Royal Society Open Science, 1*(3). doi: 10.1098/rsos.140216

Connelly, T., & Beach, L. R. (2000). The theory of image theory: An examination of the central conceptual structure. In T. Connolley, H. R. Arkes, & K. R. Hammond (Eds.), *Judgment and decision making: An interdisciplinary reader* (2nd ed., pp. 755–766). New York, NY: Cambridge University Press.

Conrad, P. (2007). *The medicalization of society: On the transformation of human conditions into treatable disorders.* Baltimore, MD: Johns Hopkins University Press.

Coombs, J. E. & Nimmo, D. D. (1993). *The new propaganda: The dictatorship of palaver in contemporary politics.* New York, NY: Longman.

Cosgrove, L., Bursztajn, H. J., Erlich, D. R., Wheeler, E. E., & Shaughnessy, A. F. (2013). Conflicts of interest and the quality of recommendations in clinical guidelines. *Journal of Evaluation in Clinical Practice, 19,* 674–681. doi: 10.1111/jep.12016

Cosgrove, L., Bursztajn, H. J., Krimsky, S., Anaya, M., & Walker, J. (2009). Conflicts of interest and disclosure in the American Psychiatric Association's clinical practice guidelines. *Psychotherapy and Psychosomatics, 78,* 228–232. doi: 10.1159/000214444

Croskerry, P. (2003). Cognitive forcing strategies in clinical decision making. *Annals of Emergency Medicine, 41,* 110–120. doi: 10.1067/mem.2003.22

Croskerry, P. (2009). Clinical cognition and diagnostic error: Applications of a dual process model of reasoning. *Advances in Health Science Education, 14,* 27–35. doi: 10.1007/s10459-009-9182-2

Croskerry, P., Singhal, G., & Mamede, S. (2013). Cognitive debiasing 1: Origins of bias and theory of debiasing. *BMJ Quality and Safety, 22,* ii58–ii64. doi: 10.1136/bmjqs-2012-001712

Cuccaro-Alamin, S., Foust, R., Vaithianathan, R., & Putnam-Hornstein, E. (2017). Risk assessment and decision making in child protective services: Predictive risk modeling in context. *Children and Youth Services Review, 79,* 291–298. doi: 10.1016/j.childyouth.2017.06.027

Cushon, J. A., Vu, L. T. H., Janzen, B. L., & Muhajarine, N. (2011). Neighborhood poverty impacts children's physical health and well-being over time: Evidence from the Early

Development Instrument. *Early Education & Development, 22,* 183–205. doi: 10.1080/10409280902915861

Damer, T. E. (1995). *Attaching faulty reasoning: A practical guide to fallacy free argument* (3rd. ed.). Belmont, CA: Wadsworth.

Damer, T. E. (2005). *Attacking faulty reasoning: A practical guide to fallacy-free arguments* (3rd ed.). Belmont, CA: Wadsworth.

Davies, P. (2004, February). *Is evidence-based government possible?* Paper presented at the 4th Annual Campbell Collaboration Colloquium, Washington, DC.

Davis, J., & Aitkenhead, A. (2001). Clinical risk management in anesthesia. In C. Vincent (Ed.), *Clinical risk management* (pp. 111–136). London, England: BMJ.

Dawes, R. M. (1988). *Rational choice in an uncertain world.* Orlando, FL: Harcourt, Brace Jovanovich.

Dawes, R. M. (1994). *House of cards: Psychology and psychotherapy built on myth.* New York, NY: Free Press.

Deaton, A. (2015). On tyrannical experts and expert tyrants. *Review of Austrian Economics, 28,* 407–441. doi: 10.1007/s11138-015-0323-y

Deaton, A., & Cartwright, N. (2016). *Understanding and misunderstanding randomized controlled trials.* NBER Working Paper no. 22595.

de Jong, T., & Ferguson-Hessler, M. G. M. (1996). Types and qualities of knowledge. *Educational Psychologist, 31,* 105–113. doi: 10.1207/s15326985ep3102_2

Dijkers, M. (2015, December). What is a scoping review? *KT Update, 4*(1). Retrieved from http://ktdrr.org/products/update/v4n1/

Dingwall, R., Eekelaar, J., & Murray, T. (1983). *The protection of children.* Oxford, England: Basil Blackwell.

DiResta, R. (2017, April 14). This dramatic graph shows how the pro-vaccine movement can win. Retrieved from www.slate.com

Dishion, T. J., Forgatch, M., Chamberlain, P., & Pelham, W. (2016). The Oregon model of behavior family therapy: From intervention design to promoting large-scale system change. *Behavior Therapy, 47,* 812–837. doi: 10.1016/j.beth.2016.02.002

Ditto, P. H., & Lopez, D. F. (1992). Motivated skepticism: Use of differential decision criteria for preferred and nonpreferred conclusions. *Journal of Personality and Social Psychology, 63,* 568–584.

Donner-Banzhoff, N., & Hertwig, R. (2014). Inductive foraging: Improving the diagnostic yield of primary care consultations. *European Journal of General Practice, 20,* 69–73. doi: 10.3109/13814788.2013.805197Dovey, S., Meyers, D., Phillips, R., Green, L., Fryer, G., Galliher, J., Kappus, J., & Grob, P. (2002). A preliminary taxonomy of medical errors in family practice. *BMJ Quality and Safety, 11,* 233–238.

Dragioti, E., Dimoliatis, I., Fountoulakis, K. N., & Evangelou, E. (2015). A systematic appraisal of allegiance effect in randomized controlled trials of psychotherapy. *Annals of General Psychiatry, 14,* 25. doi: 10.1186/s12991-015-0063-1

Dreyfus, H. L., & Dreyfus, S. E. (1986). *Mind over machine: The power of human intuition and expertise in the era of the computer.* New York, NY: Free Press.

Dunning, D. (2011). The Dunning-Kruger effect: On being ignorant of one's own ignorance. *Advances in Experimental Social Psychology, 44,* 247–262. doi: 10.1016/B978-0-12-385522-0.00005-6

Dunning, D., Heath, C., & Suls, J. M. (2004). Flawed self-assessment: Implications for health, education, and the work place. *Psychological Science in the Public Interest, 5,* 69–106. doi: doi: 10.1111/j.1529-1006.2004.00018.x

Drury, S. S. (1984). *Assertive supervision: Building involved teamwork.* Champaign, IL: Research Press.

Eddy, D.M. (1994a). Principles for making difficult decisions in difficult times. *Journal of the American Medical Association, 271,* 1792–1798. doi: 10.1001/jama.1993.03510040124050

Eddy, D.M. (1994b). Rationing resources while improving quality. *Journal of the American Medical Association, 272,* 817–824. doi: 10.1001/jama.1994.03520240079046

Eddy, D. M. (2005). Evidence-based medicine: A unified approach. *Health Affairs, 24,* 9–17. doi: 10.1377/hlthaff.24.1.9

Egan, G. (2014). *The skilled helper: A problem-management and opportunity development approach to helping* (10th ed.). Belmont, CA: Brooks/Cole.

Elder, L., & Paul, R. (2010). *Critical thinking development: A stage theory.* Retrieved from The Foundation for Critical Thinking website: http://www.criticalthinking.org/pages/critical-thinking-development-a-stage-theory/483

Elliott, R., Bohart, A. C., Watson, J. C., & Greenberg, L. S. (2011). Empathy. In J. C. Norcross (Ed.), *Psychotherapy relationships that work: Evidence-based responsiveness* (2nd ed., pp. 132–152). New York: Oxford.

Ellis, A., & Yeager, R. J. (1989). *Why some therapies don't work.* Buffalo, NY: Prometheus Books.

Ellul, J. (1965). *Propaganda: The formation of men's attitudes.* New York: Vintage.

Elstein, A. S. (2009). Thinking about diagnostic thinking: A 30-year perspective. *Advance in Health Science Education, 14,* 7–18. doi: 10.1007/s10459-009-9184-0

Elstein, A. S., Shulman, L. S., Sprafka, S. A., Allal, L., Gordon, M., Hilliard, J., . . . Loupe, M. J. (1978). *Medical problem solving: An analysis of clinical reasoning.* Cambridge, MA: Harvard University Press.

Elwyn, G., Wieringa, S., & Greenhalgh, T. (2016). Clinical encounters in the post-guidelines era. *BMJ, 353,* i3220. doi: 10.1136/bmj.i3200

Elwyn, G., Edwards, A., & Thompson, R. (2016). *Shared decision making in healthcare: Achieving evidence-based patient choice.* New York, NY: Oxford University Press.

Elwyn, G., Barr, P. J., Grande, S. W., Thompson, R., Walsh, T., & Ozanne, E. M. (2013). Developing CollaboRATE: A fast and frugal patient-reported measure of shared decision making in clinical encounters. *Patient Education and Counseling, 93,* 102–107. doi: 10.1016/j.pec.2013.05.009

Elwyn, G., Quinlan, C., Mulley, A., Agoritsas, T., Vandvik, P. O., & Guyatt, G. (2015). Trustworthy guidelines—excellent; customized care tools—even better. *BMC Medicine, 13*(199). doi: 10.1186/s12916-015-0436-y

Ely, J. W., Osheroff, J. A., Ebell, M. H., Chambliss, M. L., Vinson, D. C., Stevermer, J. J., & Pifer, E. A. (2002). Obstacles to answering doctors' questions about patient care with evidence: Qualitative study. *BMJ, 324,* 710–718. doi: 10.1136/bmj.324.7339.710

Engel, S. M. (1982). *With good reason: An introduction to informal fallacies* (2nd Ed.). New York: St. Martin's Press.

Engel, S. M. (1994). *With good reason: An introduction to informal fallacies* (5th Ed.). New York, NY: St. Martin's Press.

England, M., J., Butler, A. S., & Gonzales, M. L. (2015). *Psychological interventions for mental and substance use disorders: A framework for establishing evidence-based standards.* Washington, DC: National Academic Press.

Ennis, R. H. (1987). A taxonomy of critical thinking dispositions and abilities. In J. B. Baron & R. J. Sternberg (Eds.), *Teaching thinking skills, theory, and practice* (pp. 9–26). New York, NY: Freeman.

Entwistle, V. A., Sheldon, T. A., Sowden, A. J., & Watt, I. A. (1998). Evidence-informed patient choice. *International Journal of Technology Assessment in Health* Care, *14*, 212–215. doi: 10.1017/S0266462300012204

Ericsson, K. A., & Pool, R. (2016). *Peak: Secrets from the new science of expertise*. New York, NY: Houghton Mifflin Harcourt.

Evans, J. St. B. T., & Stanovich, K. E. (2013). Dual-process theories of higher cognition: Advancing the debate. *Perspectives on Psychological Science, 8*, 223–241.

Fabrigar, L. R., Smith, S. M., & Brannon, L. A. (1999). Applications of social cognition: Attitudes as cognitive structures. In F. T. Durso (Ed.), *Handbook of applied cognition* (pp. 173–206). New York, NY: Wiley.

False Claims Act. (31 USC 3729).

Farrington, D. P. (2003). Methodological quality standards for evaluation research. *Annals of the American Academy of Political and Social Science, 587*, 49–68. doi: 10.1177/0002716202250789

Fawcett. B. (2011). Post-modernism in social work. In V. E. Cree (Ed.), *Social work: A reader* (pp. 227–235). New York, NY: Routledge.

Feinstein, A. R. (1967). *Judgement*. Baltimore, MD: Williams & Williams.

Feltovich, P. J., Spiro, R. J., & Coulson, R. L. (1993). Learning, teaching, and testing for complex conceptual understanding. In N. Frederickson, R. Mislevy, & I. Bejar (Eds.), *Test theory for a new generation of tests* (pp. 181–218). Hillsdale, NJ: Erlbaum.

Feynman, R. (1974). *Cargo cult science*. California Institute of Technology commencement address. Pasadena, CA.

Fineberg, H. V., Cohen, J., Cuff, P., Erdtmann, P., Kelley, P., Mehler, J., . . . Ziegenhorn, S. (2012). *Deadly sins and living virtue of public health*. Washington, DC: Institute of Medicine of the National Academies.

Fisher, R., & Ury, W. (2011). *Getting to yes: Negotiating agreement without giving in* (2nd ed.). New York, NY: Penguin.

FitzGerald, C., & Hurst, S. (2017). Implicit bias in healthcare professionals: A systematic review. *BMC Medical Ethics, 18*:19 doi: 10.1186/s12910-017-0179-8

Fixen, D., Blasé, A., Naoom, S., & Duda (2015). *Implementation drivers: Accessing best practice*. Retrieved from the FGP Child Development Institute website: http://implementation.fpg.unc.edu/sites/implementation.fpg.unc.edu/files/NIRN-ImplementationDriversAssessingBestPractices.pdf.

Fixen, D. L., Blase, K. A., Naoom, S. F., & Wallace, F. (2009). Core implementation components. *Research on Social Work Practice, 19*, 531–540. doi: 10.1177/1049731509335549

Flexner, A. (1915). Is social work a profession? In *Proceedings of the National Conference of Charities and Corrections* (pp. 577–590). Chicago, IL: Hildmann.

Flottorp, S. A., Oxman, A. D., Krause, J., Musila, N. R. Wensing, M., Godycki-Cwirko, M., . . . Eccles, M. P. (2013). A checklist for identifying determinants of practice: a systematic review and synthesis of frameworks and taxonomies of factors that prevent or enable improvement in healthcare professional practice. *Implementation Science, 8*:35. doi: 10.1186/1748-5908-8-35

Foner, P. S. (Ed.). (1950). *The life and writings of Frederick Douglas. Vol. 2, Pre-Civil War decade, 1850–1860*. New York, NY: International.

Four hours a month can keep a kid off drugs forever: Be a mentor. (2002, December 31). *New York Times*, p. A15.

Fox, R. C. (1957). Training for uncertainty. In R. K. Merton, G. G. Reader, & P. Kendall (Eds.), *The student physician: Introductory studies in the sociology of medical education*. Cambridge, MA: Harvard University.

Fox, R. C., & Swazey, J.P. (1974). *The courage to fail: A social view of organ transplants and dialysis.* Chicago, IL: University of Chicago Press.

Frakt, A. (2013). Half of medical treatments of unknown effectiveness. 1/16/ The Incidental Economist: the health services research blog. https://theincidentaleconomist.com. Originally published in *Clinical Evidence*, BMJ Free Dictionary.

Frank, J. D., & Frank, J. B. (1991). *Persuasion and healing: A comparative study of psychotherapy* (3rd ed.). Baltimore, MD: John Hopkins Press.

Frankfurt, H. G. (1986). On bullshit. *Raritan, 6,* 81–100.

Frankfurt, H. G. (2005). *On bullshit.* Princeton, NJ: Princeton University Press.

Freire, P. (1973). *Education for critical consciousness.* New York, NY: Continuum.

Fugh-Berman, A., & Ahari, S. (2007). Following the script: How drug reps make friends and influence doctors. *PLOS Medicine, 4*:e150. doi: 10.1371/journal.pmed.0040150

Gagnon, M. A. (2010, April). *Veblenian analysis of Big Pharma's intangible assets: Capitalizing medical bias.* Paper presented at Association for Institutional Thought. Reno, NV.

Gambrill, E. D. (1999). Evidence-based practice: An alternative to authority-based practice. *Families in Society, 80,* 341–350. doi: 10.1606/1044-3894.1214

Gambrill, E. (2003). Evidence-based practice: Implications for knowledge development and use in social work. In A. Rosen & E. K. Proctor (Eds.), *Developing practice guidelines for social work intervention: Issues, methods and research agenda* (pp. 37–58). New York, NY: Columbia University Press.

Gambrill, E. (2006). Evidence based practice: Choices ahead. *Research on Social Work Practice, 16,* 338–357. doi: 10.1177/1049731505284205

Gambrill, E. (2010a). Evidence-based practice and the ethics of discretion. *Journal of Social Work, 11,* 26–48. doi: 10.1177/1468017310381306

Gambrill, E. (2010b). Evidence-informed practice: Antidote to propaganda in the helping professions? *Research on Social Work Practice, 20,* 302–320. doi: 10.1177/1049731509347879

Gambrill, E. (2012a). *Propaganda in the helping professions.* New York, NY: Oxford.

Gambrill, E. (2012b). *Critical thinking in clinical practice: Improving the quality of judgment and decision* (3rd ed.). New York, NY: Wiley.

Gambrill, E. (2013). *Social work practice: A critical thinkers' guide.* New York, NY: Oxford University Press.

Gambrill, E. (2015). Avoidable ignorance and the role of the Campbell and Cochrane Collaborations. *Research on Social Work Practice, 25,* 147–163. doi: 10.1177/1049731514533731

Gambrill, E. (2017). *Clarity of information regarding evidentiary status of services on social work agency websites.* Unpublished manuscript.

Gambrill, E., & Gibbs, L. (2002). Making practice decisions: Is what's good for the goose good for the gander? *Ethical Human Sciences & Services, 4*(1), 31–46.

Gambrill, E., & Gibbs, L. E. (2017). *Critical thinking for helping professionals: A skills-based workbook* (4th ed.). New York, NY: Oxford University Press.

Gambrill, E., & Reiman, A. (2011). A propaganda index for reviewing manuscripts and articles: An exploratory study. *PLOS One, 6*(5), e19516. doi: 10.1371/journal.pone.0019516

Gambrill, E., & Shlonsky, A. (2001). The need for comprehensive risk management systems in child welfare. *Children and Youth Services Review, 23,* 79–107. doi: 10.1016/S0190-7409(00)00124-9

Gandhi, A. G., Murphy-Graham, E., Petrosino, A., Chrismer, S. S., & Weiss, C. H. (2007). The devil is in the details: Examining the evidence for "proven" school-based drug abuse prevention programs. *Evaluation Review, 31,* 43–74. doi: 10.1177/0193841X06287188

Gaudet, J. (2013). It takes two to tango: Knowledge mobilization and ignorance mobilization in science research and innovation. *Prometheus, 231,* 169–187.

Gawande. A. (2009). *The checklist manifesto: How it got things right.* New York, NY: Metropolitan Books.

Gawande, A. (2015, May 11). Overkill: An avalanche of unnecessary medical care is harming patients physically and financially. What can we do about it? *The New Yorker.* Retrieved from https://www.newyorker.com

Gellner, E. (1992). *Postmodernism, reason, and religion.* New York, NY: Routledge.

Gibbs, L. (2003). *Evidence-based practice for the helping professions.* Pacific Grove, CA: Brooks/Cole.

Gibbs, L., & Gambrill, E. (2002). Evidence-based practice: Counterarguments to objections. *Research on Social Work Practice, 14,* 452–476. doi: 10.1177/1049731502012003007

Gigerenzer, G. (2002a). *Calculated risks: How to know when numbers deceive you.* New York, NY: Simon & Schuster.

Gigerenzer, G. (2002b). *Reckoning with risk: Learning to live with uncertainty.* New York, NY: Penguin.

Gigerenzer, G. (2005). Fast and frugal heuristics: The tools of bounded rationality. In D. J. Koehler & N. Harvey (Eds.), *The Blackwell handbook of judgment and decision making* (pp. 62–88). Oxford, England: Blackwell.

Gigerenzer, G. (2008). Why heuristics work. *Perspectives on Psychological Science, 3,* 20–29. doi: 10.1111/j.1745-6916.2008.00058.x

Gigerenzer, G. (2014a). *Risk savvy: How to make good decisions.* New York, NY: Viking.

Gigerenzer, G. (2014b). Breast cancer screening pamphlets mislead women. *BMJ, 348,* g2636. doi: 10.1136/bmj.g2636

Gigerenzer, G. (2015). *Simply rational: decision making in the real world.* New York, NY: Oxford University Press.

Gigerenzer, G. (2018). Statistical rituals: The replication delusion and how we got there. *Advances in Methods and Practices in Psychological Science, 1,* 198–218.

Gigerenzer, G., & Brighton, H. (2011). Homo heuristicus: Why biased minds make better inferences. In G. Gigerenzer, R. Hertwig, & T. Pachur (Eds.), *Heuristics: The foundations of adaptive behavior* (pp. 2–27). New York, NY: Oxford University Press.

Gigerenzer, G., & Gaissmaier, W. (2011). Heuristic decision making. *Annual Review of Psychology, 62,* 451–482. doi: 10.1146/annurev-psych-120709-145346

Gigerenzer, G., & Gray, J. A. M. (Eds.). (2011). *Better doctors, better patients, better decisions: Envisioning health care 2030.* Cambridge, MA: MIT Press.

Glasziou, P., & Chalmers, I. (2017, June 5). Can it really be true that 50% of researcher is unpublished? *BMJ Opinion.* Retrieved from http://blogs.bmj.com/bmj/2017/06/05/paul-glasziou-and-iain-chalmers-can-it-really-be-true-that-50-of-research-is-unpublished/

Glasziou, P., Straus, S., Brownlee, S., Trevena, L., Dans, L., Guyatt, G., . . . Saini, V. (2017). Evidence for underuse of effective medical services around the world. *The Lancet, 390,* 169–177. doi: 10.1016/S0140-6736(16)30946-1

Glisson, C. (2007). Assessing and changing organizational culture and climate for effective services. *Research on Social Work Practice, 17,* 736–747. doi: 10.1177/1049731507301659

Gomory, T. (2001). A critique of the effectiveness of assertive community treatment. *Psychiatric Services, 52,* 1394. doi: 10.1176/appi.ps.52.10.1394

Gorman, D. M. (2017). Has the national registry of evidence-based programs and practices (NREPP) lost its way? *International Journal of Drug Policy, 45,* 40–41. doi: 10.1016/j.drugpo.2017.05.010

Gorman, D. M., & Huber, J. C. (2009). The social construction of "evidence-based" drug pre-vention programs: A reanalysis of data from the Drug Abuse Resistance Education (DARE) Program. *Evaluation Review, 33,* 396–414. doi: 10.1177/0193841X09334711

Gotzsche, P. (2008). *Rational diagnosis and treatment: Evidence-based clinical decision making* (4th ed.). New York: NY: Wiley.

Gotzsche, P. C. (2012). *Mammography screening: Truth, lies and controversy.* London, England: Radcliffe.

Gotzsche, P. C. (2013). *Deadly medicines and organized crime: How Big Pharma has corrupted healthcare.* New York, NY: Radcliffe.

Gotzsche, P. C. (2015). *Deadly psychiatry and organised denial.* Copenhagen, Denmark: People's Press.

Graham, R., Mancher, J., Wolman, D. M., Greenfield, S., & Steinberg, E. (Eds.) (2011). *Clinical practice guidelines we can trust.* Institute of Medicine. Washington, D.C.: National Academic Press.

Grandage, K. K., Slawson, D. C., & Shaughnessy, A. F. (2002). When less is more: A practical ap-proach to searching for evidence-based answers. *Journal of the Medical Library Association, 90,* 298–304.

Grant, M. J., & Booth, A. (2009). A topology of reviews: An analysis of 14 review types and as-sociated methodologies. *Health Information and Libraries Journal, 26,* 91–108. doi: 10.1111/j.1471-1842.2009.00848.x

Gray, J. A. M. (1997). *Evidence-based healthcare: How to make health policy and management decisions.* New York, NY: Churchill Livingstone.

Gray, J. A. M. (1998). Where is the chief knowledge officer? *BMJ, 317,* 832.

Gray, J. A. M. (2001a). *Evidence-based healthcare: How to make health policy and management decisions* (2nd ed.). New York, NY: Churchill Livingstone.

Gray, J. A. M. (2001b). Evidence-based medicine for professionals. In A. Edwards& G. Elwyn (Eds.), *Evidence-based patient choice: Inevitable or impossible?* (pp. 19–33). New York, NY: Oxford University Press.

Greenberg, S. A. (2009). How citation distortions create unfounded authority: Analysis of a citation network. *BMJ, 339,* b2680. doi: 10.1136/bmj.b2680

Greenhalgh, T. (2010). *How to read a paper: The basics of evidence-based medicine* (4th ed.). Hoboken, NJ: Wiley-Blackwell.

Greenhalgh, T., & Hurwitz, B. (1998). *Narrative based medicine: Dialogue and discourse in clinical practice.* London, England: BMJ.

Grimes, D. A. (1995). Introducing evidence-based medicine into a Department of Obstetrics and Gynecology. *Obstetrics and Gynecology, 86,* 451–457. doi: 10.1016/0029-7844(95)00184-S

Gross, M., & McGoey, L. (2015). *Routledge international handbook of ignorance studies.* New York, NY: Routledge.

Gross, P. R., & Levitt, N. (1994). *Higher superstition: The academic left and its quarrels with sci-ence.* Baltimore, MD: Johns Hopkins University Press.

Grove, W. M., & Meehl, P. E. (1996). Comparative efficiency of informal (subjective impression-istic) and formal (mechanical algorithmic) prediction procedures: The clinical-statistical controversy. *Psychology, Public Policy & Law, 2,* 293–323. doi: 10.1037%2F1076-8971.2.2.293

Guyatt, G. (1991, March–April). Evidence-based medicine. *ACP Journal Club,* A16. doi: 10.7326/ACPJC-1991-114-2-A16

Guyatt, G., & Rennie, D. (2002). *User's guide to the medical literature: A manual for evidence-based clinical practice.* Chicago, IL: AMA Press.

Guyatt, G., Rennie, D., O'Meade, M., & Cook, D.J. (2008). *Users' guides to the medical literature: A manual for evidence-based clinical practice* (2nd ed.). Chicago: AMA Press.

Guyatt, G., Rennie, D., Meade, M. O., & Cook, D J. (2015). *Users' guide to the medical literature: Essentials of evidence-based clinical practice.* New York: McGraw Hill.

Hafner, K., & Palmer, G. (2017, November 17). Is dermatology doing too much? *New York Times*, p. D1.

Hamm, R. M. (2003). Medical decisions scripts: Combining cognitive scripts and judgment strategies to account fully for medical decision making. In D. Hardman & L. Macchi (Eds.), *Thinking: Psychological perspectives on reasoning, judgment and decision making* (pp. 315–345). New York, NY: Wiley.

Hammond, K. R. (2000). *Judgments under stress.* New York, NY: Oxford University Press.

Han, P. K. J., Klein, W., & Arora, N. K. (2011). Varieties of uncertainty in health care: A conceptual taxonomy. *Medical Decision Making, 31,* 828–838. doi: 10.1177/0272989X11393976

Hanley, B., Truesdale, A., King, A., Elbourne, D., & Chalmers, I. (2001). Involving consumers in designing, conducting, and interpreting randomized controlled trials: Questionnaire survey. *BMJ, 322,* 519–523. doi: 10.1136/bmj.322.7285.519 (

Haran, U., Ritov, I., & Mellers, B. A. (2013). The role of actively open-minded thinking in information acquisition, accuracy, and calibration. *Judgment and Decision Making, 8,* 188–201.

Harmon, G. (1986). *Change in view: Principles of reasoning.* Cambridge, MA: MIT Press.

Hastie, R., & Dawes, R. (2001). *Rational choice in an uncertain world: The psychology of judgment and decision making.* Thousand Oaks, CA: SAGE.

Hatcher, D. L. (2016). *The poverty industry: The exploitation of America's most vulnerable citizens.* New York: New York University Press.

Hathaway, S. R. (1948). Some considerations relative to nondirective counseling. *Journal of Clinical Psychology, 4,* 226–231. doi: 10.1002/1097-4679(194807)4:3<226::AID-JCLP2270040303>3.0.CO;2-V

Hayakawa, S.I. (1978). *Language in thought and action* (4th ed.). New York, NY: Harcourt Brace Jovanovich.

Haynes, S. N. (1992). *Models of causality and psychopathology: Toward dynamic, synthetic and nonlinear models of behavior disorders.* New York, NY: Macmillan.

Haynes, R. B., Devereaux, P. J., & Guyatt, G. H. (2002). Editorial. Clinical expertise in the era of evidence-based medicine and patient choice. *ACP Journal Club,* 136:A11. doi: 10.7326/ACPJC-2002-136-2-A11

Heidari, M., & Ebrahimi, P. (2016). Examining the relationship between critical-thinking skills and decision-making ability of emergency medicine students. *Indian Journal of Critical Care Medicine, 10,* 581–586. doi: 10.4103/0972-5229.192045

Herbst, A. L., Ulfelder, H., & Poskanzer, D. C. (1971). Adenocarcinoa of the vagina: Association of maternal stilbestrol therapy with tumor appearances in young women. *New England Journal of Medicine, 284,* 878–881. doi: 10.1056/NEJM197104222841604

Hertwig, R., Buchan, H., Davis, D. A., Gaissmaier, W., Härter, M., Kolpatzik, K., . . . Wormer, H. (2011). How will health care professionals and patients work together in 2020? A manifesto for change. In G. Gigerenzer & J. A. Muir Gray (Eds.), *Better doctors, better patients, better decisions: Envisioning health care in 2020* (pp. 317–338). Cambridge, MA: MIT Press.

Herzberg, D. (2009). *Happy pills in America: From Miltown to Prozac.* Baltimore, MD: Johns Hopkins University Press.

Hilgartner, S. (2000). *Science on stage: Expert advice as public drama.* Stanford, CA: Stanford University Press.

Hochman, M. E. (2014). *50 studies every doctor should know.* (Rev. ed.). New York: Oxford University Press.

Hofer, B. K. (2001). Personal epistemology research: Implications for learning and teaching. *Journal of Educational Psychology Review, 13,* 353–383.

Hogarth, R. M. (2001). *Educating intuition.* Chicago, IL: University of Chicago Press.

Horton, R. C. (2015). Offline: What is medicine's 5 sigma? *Lancet, 385,* 1380. doi: 10.1016/S0140-6736(15)60696-1

Horton, R. (2017). Offline: Science and the defeat of fear. *Lancet, 389,* 1383. doi: 10.1016/S0140-6736(17)30934-0

Howick, J. (2011). Exposing the vanities—and a qualified defense—of mechanistic reasoning in health care decision making. *Philosophy of Science, 78,* 926–940. doi: 10.1086/662561

Howick, J., Glasziou, P., & Aronson, J. K. (2010). Evidence-based mechanistic reasoning. *Journal of the Royal Society of Medicine, 103,* 433–441. doi: 10.1258/jrsm.2010.100146

Hsu, J., Brozek, J. L., Terracciano, L., Kreis, J., Compalati, E., Stein, A. T., . . . Schünemann, H. J. (2011). Application of GRADE: Making evidence-based recommendations about diagnostic tests in clinical practice guidelines. *Implementation Science,* 6:62. doi: 10.1186/1748-5908-6-62

Huber, R. B. (1963). *Influencing through argument.* New York, NY: McKay.

Huey, S. J., Jr., Tilley, J. L., Jones, E. O., & Smith, C. A. (2014). The contribution of cultural competence to evidence-based care for ethnically diverse populations. *Annual Review of Clinical Psychology, 10,* 305–338. doi: 10.1146/annurev-clinpsy-032813-153729

Huff, D. (1954). *How to lie with statistics.* New York, NY: Norton.

Ioannidis, J. P. A. (2005). Why most published research findings are false. *PLOS Medicine* 2(8):e124. doi: 10.1371/journal.pmed.0020124

Ioannidis, J. P. A. (2012). Why science is not necessarily self-correcting. *Perspectives on Psychological Science, 7,* 645–654. doi: 10.1177/1745691612464056

Ioannidis, J. P. A. (2016). The mass production of redundant, misleading and conflicting systematic reviews and meta-analyses. *Milbank Quarterly, 94,* 485–514. doi: 10.1111/1468-0009.12210

Isaacs, D., & Fitzgerald, D. (1999). Seven alternatives to evidence based medicine. *BMJ, 319,* 1618. doi: 10.1136/bmj.319.7225.1618

Jacobson, J. W., Foxx, & Mulick, J. A. (2005). *Controversial therapies for developmental disabilities.* Mahwah, NJ: Taylor & Francis.

Jadad, A. R., & Enkin, M. W. (2007). *Randomized controlled trials:. Questions, answers and musings* (2nd ed.). Malden, MA: Blackwell.

Janis, I. L. (1982). *Groupthink: Psychological studies of policy decisions and fiascoes* (2nd ed.). Boston, MA: Houghton Mifflin.

Janoff-Bulman, R. (1979). Characterological versus behavioral self-blame: Inquiries into depression and rape. *Journal of Personality and Social Psychology, 37,* 1798–1809.

James, J. (2013). A new, evidence-based estimate of patient harms associated with hospital care. *Journal of Patient Safety, 9,* 122–128. doi: 10.1097/PTS.0b013e3182948a69

James, W. (1975). *Pragmatism.* Cambridge, MA: Harvard University Press.

Jansson, B. S. (2011). *Improving healthcare through advocacy: A guide for the health and helping professions.* New York, NY: Wiley.

Jarvis, W. T. (1990). *Dubious dentistry: A dental continuing education course.* Unpublished manuscript.

Jenicek, M. (2006). Evidence-based medicine: Fifteen years later. Golem the good, the bad, and the ugly in need of a review? *Medical Science Monitor, 12,* RA241–RA251.

Jenicek, M. (2011). *Medical error and harm: Understanding, prevention, and control*. New York, NY: CRC.

Jenicek, M., & Hitchcock, D. L. (2005). *Evidence-based practice: Logic and critical thinking in medicine*. Chicago, IL: AMA.

Jensen, J. M., & Fraser, M. W. (Eds.). (2015). *Social policy for children and families: A risk and resilience perspective* (3rd ed.). Los Angeles: SAGE.

Johnson, D. W. (2015). *Constructive controversy: Theory, research, practice*. Cambridge, England: Cambridge University Press.

Johnson-Laird, P. N. (1985). Logical thinking: Does it occur in daily life? Can it be taught? In S. F. Chipman, J. W. Segal, & R. Glaser (Eds.), *Thinking and learning skills. Vol. 2, Research and open questions* (pp. 293–318). Hillsdale, NJ: Erlbaum.

Kadushin, A., & Kadushin, G. (1997). *The social work interview: A guide for human service professionals* (4th ed.). New York: Columbia University Press.

Kahneman (2011). *Thinking fast and slow*. New York: Farrar, Straus & Giroux.

Kahneman, D., & Klein, G. (2009). Conditions for intuitive expertise: A failure to disagree. *American Psychologist, 64*, 515–526. doi: 10.1037/a0016755

Kassirer, J. P. (1994). Incorporating patient preferences into medical decisions. *New England Journal of Medicine, 330*, 1895–1896. doi: 10.1056/NEJM199406303302611

Katz, J. (2002). *The silent world of doctor and patient*. Baltimore, MD: John Hopkins University Press.

King, L. S. (1981). *Medical thinking: A historical preface*. Princeton, NJ: Princeton University Press.

Klein, G. (1998). *Sources of power: How people make decisions*. Cambridge, MA: MIT Press.

Klein, G. (2009). *Streetlights and shadows: Searching for the keys to adaptive decision making*. Cambridge, England: MIT Press.

Klein, G. (2011). Expert intuition and naturalistic decision making. In M. Sinclair (Ed.), *Handbook of intuition research* (pp. 69–78). Northampton, MA: Edward Elgar.

Kline, N. S. (1962). Factifuging. *The Lancet, 279*, 1396–1399.

Koertge, N. (2009). The moral underpinnings of Popper's philosophy. In Z. Parusniková & R. S. Cohen (Eds.), *Rethinking Popper* (pp. 323–338). Dordrecht, The Netherlands: Springer.

Kolata, G. (2017a, November 3). "Unbelievable": Heart stents fail to ease chest pain in British study. *New York Times International*, p. A8.

Kolata, G. (2017b, June 27). When the lab gets it wrong. *New York Times*, p. D1.

Kuhn, D. (1991). *The skills of argument*. New York, NY: Cambridge University Press.

Kuhn, D. (1992). Thinking as argument. *Harvard Educational Review, 62*, 155–178. doi: 10.17763/haer.62.2.9r424r0113t670l1

Kuhn, D. (1993). Connecting scientific and informal reasoning. *Merrill-Palmer Quarterly, 39*, 74–103.

Kuhn, D., & Udell, W. (2003). The development of argument skills. *Child Development, 74*, 1245–1260.

Kuhn, T. S. (1970). *The structure of scientific revolutions* (2nd ed.). Chicago, IL: University of Chicago Press.

Lambert, M. J., & Bartley, D. E. (2002). Research summary on the therapeutic relationship and psychotherapy outcome. In J. C. Norcross (Ed.), *Psychotherapy relationships that work: Therapists' contributions and responsiveness to patients* (pp. 17–32). New York, NY: Oxford University Press.

Larrick, R. P. (2005). Debiasing. In D. J. Koehler & N. Harvey (Eds.), *Blackwell handbook of judgement and decision making* (pp. 316–337). Malden, MA: Blackwell.

Latour, B. (1988). *Science in action: How to follow scientists and engineers through society.* Cambridge, MA: Harvard University Press.

Layng, T. V. J. (2009). The search for effective clinical behavior analysis: The nonlinear thinking of Israel Goldiamond. *Behavior Analyst, 32,* 163–184.

Leblanc, V. R., McConnell, M. M., & Monteiro, S. D. (2014). Predictable chaos: A review of the effects of emotions on attention, memory, and decision making. *Advances in Health Science Education: Theory and Practice, 20,* 265–282. doi: 10.1007/s10459-014-9516-6

Lenzer, J. (2004). Bush plans to screen whole U.S. population for mental illness. *BMJ, 328,* 1458.

Lenzer, J. (2005). Drug secrets: What the FDA isn't telling. 9/27 Medical Examiner. www.slate.com/articles/health_and_science/medical_examiner.

Lenzer, J. (2013). Why we can't trust clinical guidelines. *BMJ, 346,* f3830. doi: 10.1136/bmj.f3830

Lenzer, J., Hoffman, J., Furberg, C., & Ioannidis, J. (2013). Ensuring the integrity of clinical practice guidelines: A tool for protecting patients. *BMJ, 347,* f5535. doi: 10.1136/bmj.f5535

Lesgold, A., Rubinson, H., Feltovich, P., Glaser, R., Klopfer, D., & Wang, Y. (1988). Expertise in a complex skill: Diagnosing x-ray pictures. In M. T. H. Chi, R. Glaser, & M. Farr (Eds.), *The nature of expertise* (pp. 311–342). Hillsdale, NJ: Erlbaum.

Lessig, L. (2013). *Institutional corruption.* Edmond J. Safra Working Papers no. 1.

Levy, C. J. & Luo, M. (2005, July 18). New York Medicaid fraud may reach into billions. *New York Times.* Retrieved from http://www.nytimes.com

Lewandowsky, S., Ecker, U. K. H., Seifert, C. M., Schwarz, N., & Cook, J. (2012). Misinformation and its correction: Continued influence and successful debiasing. *Psychological Science in the Public Interest, 13,* 106–131. doi: 10.1177/1529100612451018

Lewontin, R. C. (1994). A rejoinder to William Wimsatt. In J. K. Chandler, A. I. Davidson, & H. D. Harootunian (Eds.), *Questions of evidence: Proof, practice, and persuasion across the disciplines* (pp. 504–509). Chicago, IL: University of Chicago Press.

Lexchin, J. (2012). Those who have the gold make the evidence: How the pharmaceutical industry biases the outcomes of clinical trials of medications. *Science and Engineering Ethics, 18,* 257–261.

Lillie, E. O., Patay, B., Diamant, J., Issell, B., Topol, E. J., & Schork, N. J. (2011). The n-of-1 clinical trial: The ultimate strategy for individualizing medicine? *Personalized Medicine, 8,* 161–173. doi: 10.2217/pme.11.7

Lilienfeld, S. O., Lynn, S. J., & Lohr, J. M. (2015). *Science and pseudoscience in clinical psychology* (2nd ed.). New York, NY: Guilford.

Littell, J. H. (2008). Evidence-based or biased? The quality of published reviews of evidence-based practices. *Children and Youth Services Review, 30,* 1299–1317. doi: 10.1016/j.childyouth.2008.04.001

Lo, B., & Field, M. J. (Eds.). (2009). *Conflict of interest in medical research, education and practice.* Institute of Medicine. Washington, DC: National Academy Press.

Loftus, E. F. (1979). *Eyewitness testimony.* Cambridge, MA: Harvard University Press.

Loftus, E. F. (1980). *Memory: Surprising new insights into how we remember and why we forget.* Reading, MA: Addison-Wesley.

Loftus, E. F. (2005). Planting misinformation in the human mind: A 30-year investigation of the mallability of memory. *Learning & Memory, 12,* 361–366. doi: 10.1101/lm.94705

Longino, H. (2002). The social dimensions of scientific knowledge", In E. N. Zalta (Ed.), *The Stanford Encyclopedia of Philosophy* (Spring 2016 ed.). Retrieved from https://plato.stanford.edu/archives/spr2016/entries/scientific-knowledge-social/

Lord, C., Ross, L., & Lepper, M. R. (1979). Biased assimilation and attitude polarization: The effects of prior theories on subsequently considered evidence. *Journal of Personality and Social Psychology, 37*, 2089–2109. doi: 10.1037/0022-3514.37.11.2098

Lowry, G. C. (1994). Self-censorship in public discourse: A theory of "political correctness" and related phenomena. *Rationality and Society, 6*, 428–461. doi: 10.1177/1043463194006004002

Lundh, A., Lexchin, J., Mintzes, B., Schroll, J. B., & Bero, L. (2017). Industry sponsorship and research outcome. *Cochrane Database of Systematic Reviews,* 2:MR00033. doi: 10.1002/14651858.MR000033.pub2

Lynch, E. W., & Hanson, M. J. (2011). *Developing cross-cultural competence: A guide for working with children and their families* (4th ed.). Baltimore, MD: Paul H. Brookes.

MacLean, E. (1981). *Between the lines: How to detect bias and propaganda in the news and everyday life.* Montreal, ON: Black Rose Books.

Madden, G. J. (2013). *APA handbook of behavior analysis.* 2 vols. Washington, DC: American Psychological Association.

Makary, M. A. & Daniel, M. (2016). Medial error—The third leading cause of death in the U.S. *BMJ, 353,* i2139. doi: 10.1136/bmj.i2139.

Marshall, B. J., Warren, J. R. (1984). Unidentified curved bacilli in the stomach of patents with gastritis and peptic ulceration. *Lancet,* 1(8390), 1311–1315.

Maslach, C., & Leiter, M. P. (2008). Early predictors of job burnout and engagement. *Journal of Applied Psychology, 93,* 498–512. doi: 10.1037/0021-9010.93.3.498

Matthies, D. (1996). *Precision questioning.* Stanford, CA: Stanford University Center for Teaching and Learning Mindworks.

McCabe, D. P., & Castel, A. D. (2008). Seeing is believing: The effect of brain images on judgments of scientific reasoning. *Cognition, 107,* 343–352. doi: 10.1016/j.cognition.2007.07.017

McCord, J. (1978). A thirty-year follow-up of treatment effects. *American Psychologist, 33,* 284–289. doi: 10.1037/0003-066X.33.3.284

McCord, J. (2003). Cures that harm: Unanticipated outcomes of crime prevention programs. *Annals of the American Academy of Political and Social Science, 587,* 16–30. doi: 10.1177/0002716202250781

McDowell, B. (2000). *Ethics and excuses: The crisis in professional responsibility.* Westport, CT: Quorum Books.

McGoey, L. (2010). Profitable failure: Antidepressant drugs and the triumph of flawed experiments. *History of the Human Sciences, 23,* 58–78. doi: 10.1177/0952695109352414

McGoey, L. (2012). The logic of strategic ignorance. *British Journal of Sociology, 63,* 533–576. doi: 10.1111/j.1468-4446.2012.01424.x

McNeil, B. J., Pauker, S. G., Sox, H. C., Jr., & Tversky, A. (1982). On the elicitation of preferences for alternative therapies. *New England Journal of Medicine, 306,* 1259–1262. doi: 10.1056/NEJM198205273062103

McPhearson, K., Gon, G., & Scott, M. (2013). *International variations in a selected number of surgical procedures.* OECD Health Working Paper no. 61. doi: 10.1787/18152015

Meehl, P. E. (1973). Why I do not attend case conferences. In *Psychodiagnosis: Selected papers* (pp. 225–302). Minneapolis, MN: University of Minnesota Press.

Michael, M., Boyce, W. T., & Wilcox, A. J. (1984). *Biomedical bestiary: An epidemiologic guide to flaws and fallacies in the medical literature.* Boston, MA: Little, Brown.

Michalos, A. C. (1971). *Improving your reasoning.* Englewood Cliffs, NJ: Prentice Hall.

Mike, V. (1999). Outcomes, research and the quality of health care: The beacon of an ethic or evidence. *Evaluation the Health Professions, 22,* 3–32. doi: 10.1177/01632789922034149

Mill, J. S. (1911). Of the law of universal causation. In *A system of logic* (8th ed., pp. 211–242). New York, NY: Longmans

Miller, D. (1994). *Critical rationalism: A restatement and defense.* Chicago, IL: Open Court.

Miller, S. D., Hubble, M. A., & Chow, D. (2017). Professional development. In T. Rousmaniere, R. K. Goodyear, S. D. Miller, & B. L. Wampold (Eds.), *The cycle of excellence: using deliberate practice to improve supervision and training* (pp. 23–47). Hoboken, NJ: Wiley/Blackwell.

Miller, S. D., Hubble, M. A., Chow, D., & Seidel, J. (2015). Beyond measures and monitoring: Realizing the potential of feedback-informed treatment. *Psychotherapy, 52,* 449–457. doi: 10.1037/pst0000031

Mills, C. W. (1959). *The sociological imagination.* New York, NY: Oxford University Press.

Mirowsky, J., & Ross, C. E. (2003). *Social causes of psychological distress* (2nd ed.). New York, NY: Transaction.

Miser, W. F. (1999). Critical appraisal of the literature. *Journal of the American Board of Family Practice, 12,* 315–333. doi: 10.3122/jabfm.12.4.315

Moncrieff, J. (2016). Misrepresenting harms in antidepressant trials. *BMJ, 352,* i217 doi: 10.1136/bmj.i217

Moncrieff, J., & Cohen, D. (2006). Do antidepressants cure or create abnormal brain states? *PloS Medicine,* July 3, e240.

Monteiro, S. M., & Norman, G. (2013). Diagnostic reasoning: Where we've been, where we're going. *Teaching and Learning in Medicine, 25,* S26–S32. doi: 10.1080/10401334.2013.842911

Montori, V. M. & Guyatt, G. (2007). Corruption of evidence as a threat and an opportunity for evidence-based medicine. *Harvard Health Policy Review, 8,* 145–155.

Mousavi, S., & Gigerenzer, G. (2014). Risk, uncertainty and heuristics. *Journal of Business Research, 67,* 1671–1678. doi: 10.1016/j.jbusres.2014.02.013

Moynihan, R., & Cassels, A. (2005). *Selling sickness: How the world's biggest pharmaceutical companies are turning us all into patients.* New York, NY: Nation Books.

Munz, P. (1985). *Our knowledge of the growth of knowledge: Popper or Wittgenstein?* London, England: Routledge & Kegan Paul.

Munz, P. (1992). What's postmodern anyway? *Philosophy and Literature, 16,* 333–353.

Naftulin, D. H., Ware, J. E., & Donnelly, F. A. (1973). The Dr. Fox lecture: A paradigm of educational seduction. *Journal of Medical Education, 48,* 630–635.

National Patient Safety Foundation Survey. Institute for Health Care Improvement. www.npsf.org.

National Science Foundation. (2006). *Surveys of public understanding of science and technology: 1979–2006.* Retrieved from the Roper Center for Public Opinion Research website: https://ropercenter.cornell.edu/public-understanding-science-technology-nsf/

Nettler, G. (1970). *Explanations.* New York, nY: McGraw-Hill.

New Freedom in Mental Health Commission (2004).

Nicarthy, G., Gottlieb, N., & Coffman, S. (1993). *You don't have to take it!: A woman's guide to confronting emotional abuse at work.* Seattle, WA: Seal.

Nickerson, R. S. (1986). *Reflections on reasoning.* Hillsdale, NJ: Erlbaum.

Nickerson, R. S. (1998). Confirmation bias: A ubiquitous phenomena in many guises. *Review of General Psychology, 2,* 175–220. doi: 10.1037/1089-2680.2.2.175

Nickerson, R. S., Perkins, D. N., & Smith, E. E. (1985). *The teaching of thinking.* Hillsdale, NJ: Erlbaum.

Nienhuis, J. B., Owen, J., Valentine, J. C., Black, S. W., Halford, T. C., Parazak, . . . Hilsenroth, M. (2016). Therapeutic alliance, empathy, and genuineness in individual adult psycho-therapy: A meta-analytic review. *Psychotherapy Research*. doi: 10.1080/10503307.2016.1204023

Nisbett, R., & Ross, L. (1980). *Human inference: Strategies and shortcomings of social judgement.* Englewood Cliffs, NJ: Prentice Hall.

Norcross, J. C. (Ed.). (2011). *Psychotherapy relationships that work: Evidence-based responsiveness* (2nd ed.). New York, NY: Oxford University Press.

Norcross, J. C. & Wampold, B. E. (2011). Evidence-based therapy relationships: Research conclusions and clinical practices. In J. C. Norcross (Ed.), *Psychotherapy relationships that work: Evidence- based responsiveness* (pp. 423–430). New York, NY: Oxford University Press.

Norcross, J. C., Beutler, L. E., & Levant, R. F. (Eds.). (2006). *Evidence-based practices in mental health: Debate and dialogue on the fundamental questions.* Washington, DC: American Psychological Association.

Norman, G. (2009). Dual processing and diagnostic errors. *Advances in Health Science Education, 14,* 37–49. doi: 10.1007/s10459-009-9179-x

Norman, G. R., Monteiro, S. D., Sherbino, J., Illgen, J. S., Schmidt, H. G., & Mamede, S. (2017). The causes of errors in clinical reasoning: Cognitive biases, knowledge deficits, and dual process thinking. *Academic Medicine, 92,* 23–30. doi: 10.1097/ACM.0000000000001421

Notturno, M. A. (2000). *Science and the open society: The future of Karl Popper's philosophy.* New York, NY: Central European University Press.

Nuijten, M. B., Hartgerink, C. H. J., van Assen, M. A. L. M., Epskamp, S., & Wicherts, J. M. (2015). The prevalence of statistical reporting errors in psychology (1985-2013). *Behavior Research Methods, 48,* pp. 1205–1226. doi: 10.3758/s13428-015-0664-2

Nuland, S. B. (2003). *The doctor plague: Germs, childbed fever, and the strange story of Ignaz Semmelweis.* New York: Norton.

Nuzzo, R. (2014, February 13). Scientific method: Statistical errors. *Nature, 506,* 150–152. doi: 10.1038/50650a

Nyhan, B., & Reifler, J. (2010). When corrections fail: The persistence of political misperceptions. *Political Behavior, 32,* 303–330. doi: 10.1007/s11109-010-9112-2

Nyhan, B., & Reifler, J. (2015). Does correcting myths about the flu vaccine work? An experi-mental evaluation of the effects of corrective information. *Vaccine, 33,* 4559–464.

Oakes, M. (1986). *Statistical inference: A commentary for the social and behavioral sciences.* Chichester, England: Wiley.

Oreskes, N., & Conway, E. M. (2010). *Merchants of doubt. How a handful of scientists obscured the truth on issues from tobacco smoke to global warming.* New York, NY: Bloomsbury.

Orwell, G. (1958). Politics and the English language. In S. Orwell & I. Angus (Eds.), *The col-lected essays, journalism and letters of George Orwell.* Vol. 4, *In front of your nose, 1945-1950* (pp. 127–140). London, England: Secker & Warburg.

Øvretveit, J. (1995). *Purchasing for health: A multi-disciplinary introduction to the theory and prac-tice of health purchasing.* Philadelphia, PA: Open University Press.

Oxman, A. D., & Flottorp, S. (1998). An overview of strategies to promote implementation of evidence based health care. In C. Silagy & A. Haines (Eds.), *Evidence based practice in primary care* (pp. 91–109). London, England: BMJ.

Oxman, A. D. & Guyatt, G. H. (1993). The science of reviewing research. In K. S. Warren & F. Mosteller (Eds.), *Doing more good than harm: the evaluation of health care interventions* (pp. 125–133). New York, NY: New York Academy of Sciences.

Paling, J. (2006). *Helping patients understand risks: 7 simple strategies for successful communication*. Gainesville, FL: Risk Communication Institute.

Pashler, H., & Wagenmakers, E. J. (2012). Editor's introduction to the special section on replicability in psychological science: A crisis of confidence? *Perspectives on Psychological Science 7*, 528–530.

Patai, D., & Koertge, N. (2003). *Professing feminism: Education and indoctrination in women's studies* (New ed.). Lanham, MD: Lexington Books.

Pathirana, T., et al. (2017). Too much medicine: What is driving this harmful culture? *BMJ, 358*, 446–448.

Paul, R. W. (1993). *Critical thinking: What every person needs to survive in a rapidly changing world* (3rd ed. rev.). Santa Rosa, CA: Foundation for Critical Thinking.

Paul, R. W., & Elder, L. (2004). *Critical thinking: Tools for taking charge of your professional and social life*. Upper Saddle River: Prentice Hall.

Paul, R. W. & Elder, L. (2014). *Critical thinking: Tools for taking charge of your professional life* (2nd ed.) Upper Saddle River, NJ: Pearson Education.

Paul, R., Binker, A. J. A., & Charbonneau, M. (1986). Critical thinking handbook: K3. Rohnert Park, CA: Center for Critical Thinking and Moral Critique.

Paulos, J. A. (1988). *Innumeracy: Mathematical illiteracy and its consequences*. New York, NY: Hill & Wang.

Pellegrino, E. (1999). The ethical use of evidence in biomedicine. *Evaluation & the Health Professions, 22*, 33–43. doi: 10.1177/01632789922034158

Peng, J., Li, H., Miao, D., Feng, X., & Xiao, W. (2013). Five different types of framing effects in medical situation: A preliminary exploration. *Iranian Red Crescent Medical Journal, 15*, 161–165. doi: 10.5812/ircmj.8469

Penston, J. (2010). *Stats.con—How we've been fooled by statistics-based research in medicine*. London, England: London Press.

Perkinson, H. J. (1993). *Teachers without goals, students without purposes*. New York, NY: McGraw-Hill.

Petrosino, A., Turpin-Petrosino, C., Hollis-Peel, M. E., & Lavenberg, J. G. (2013). "Scared straight" and other juvenile awareness programs for preventing juvenile delinquency. *Cochrane Database of Systematic Reviews, 4*, CD002796. doi: 10.1002/14651858.CD002796.pub2

Petty, R. E. & Cacioppo, J. T. (1986). The elaboration likelihood model of persuasion. In L. Berkowitz (Ed.), *Advances in experimental social psychology* (Vol. 19, pp. 124–206). Orlando, FL: Academic Press.

Petty, R., & Hinsenkamp, L. (2017). Routes to persuasion, central and peripheral. In F. M. Moghaddam (Ed.). *The SAGE Encyclopedia of Political Behavior* (pp. 718–720). Thousand Oaks, CA: SAGE.

Petty, R. E., Cacioppo, J. T., Strathman, A. ., & Priester, J. R. (2005). To think or not to think: Exploring two routes to persuasion. In T. C. Brock & M. C. Green (Eds.), *Persuasion: Psychological insights and perspectives* (2nd ed., pp. 81–116). Thousand Oaks, CA: SAGE.

Pewsner, D., Pattaglia, M., Minder, C., Marx, A., Bucher, H. C., & Egger, M. (2004). Ruling a diagnosis in or out with "SpPln" and "SnNOut": A note of caution. *BMJ, 329*, 209–213. doi: 10.1136/bmj.329.7459.209

Phillips, D. C. (1987). *Philosophy, science and social inquiry: Contemporary methodological controversies in social science and related applied fields of research*. New York, NY: Pergamon.

Phillips, D. C. (1990a). Postpositivistic science: Myths and realities. In E. G. Guba (Ed.), *The paradigm dialog*. Thousand Oakes, CA: SAGE.

Phillips, D. C. (1990b). Subjectivity and objectivity: An objective inquiry. In E. W. Eisner & A. Peshkin (Eds.), *Qualitative inquiry in education: The continuing debate* (pp. 19–37). New York, NY: Columbia University Press.

Phillips, D. C. (1992). *The social scientist's bestiary: A guide to fabled threats to, and defenses of, naturalistic social studies*. New York, NY: Pergamon.

Phillips, J. K., Klein, G., & Sieck, W. R. (2005). Expertise in judgment and decision making: A case for training intuitive decision skills. In D. J. Koehler & N. Harvey (Eds.), *Blackwell handbook of judgment and decision making* (pp. 297–315). Malden, MA: Blackwell.

Plato. (1993). *The last days of Socrates* (H. Tredennick & H. Tarrant, trans.). New York, NY: Penguin.

Popper, K. R. (1970). Normal science and its dangers. In I. Lakatos & A. Musgrave (Eds.), *Criticism and the growth of knowledge*. New York, NY: Cambridge University Press.

Popper, K. R. (1972). *Conjectures and refutations: The growth of scientific knowledge* (4th ed.). London, England: Routledge & Kegan Paul.

Popper, K. R. (1992). *In search of a better world: Lectures and essays from thirty years*. London, England: Routledge & Kegan Paul.

Popper, K. R. (1994). *The myth of the framework: In defense of science and rationality*. (M. A. Notturno, ed.). New York, NY: Routledge.

Popper, K. (1998). *The unknown Xenophanes*. Addendum 2, pp. 62-65

Popper, K. R. (1998). *The world of Parmenides: Essays on the pre-Socratic enlightenment*. New York, NY: Routledge.

Porta, M. (Ed.). (2014). *A dictionary of epidemiology*. New York, NY: Oxford University Press.

Prasad, V., Vandross, A., Toomey, C., Cheung, M., Rho, J., Quinn, S., . . . Cifu, A. (2013). A decade of reversal: An analysis of 146 contradicted medical practices. *Mayo Clinic Proceedings, 88*, 790–798. doi: 10.1016/j.mayocp.2013.05.012

Prasad, V. K., & Cifu, A. S. (2015). *Ending medical reversal: Improving outcomes, saving lives*. Baltimore, MD: John Hopkins University Press.

Prasad, V., & Ioannidis, J. P. A. (2014). Evidence-based de-implementation for contradicted, unproven, and aspiring healthcare practices. *Implementation Science, 9*:1. doi: 10.1186/1748-5908-9-1

Prasad, V., Cifu, A., & Ioannidis, J. P. (2012). Reversals of established medical practices: Evidence to abandon ship. *JAMA, 307*, 37–38. doi: 10.1001/jama.2011.1960

Proctor, R. N. & Schlebinger, L. (Eds.). (2008). *Agnotology: The making and unmaking of ignorance*. Palo Alto, CA: Stanford University Press.

Rampton, S., & Stauber, J. (2001). *Trust us, we're experts: How industry manipulates science and gambles with your future*. New York, NY: Penguin.

Rank, H. (1984). *The peptalk: How to analyze political language*. Park Forest, IL: Counter-Propaganda.

Rapley, M., Moncrieff, J., & Dillon J. (2011). *De-medicalizing misery*. Baringstoke, U.K.: Palgrave Macmillan.

Reason, J. (1997). *Managing the risks of organizational accidents*. Brookfield, VT: Ashgate.

Reason, J. (2001). Understanding adverse events: The human factor. In C. Vincent (Ed.), *Clinical risk management: Enhancing patient safety* (2nd ed., pp. 9–30). London, England: BMJ.

Renner, C. H. (2004). Validity effect. In R. F. Pohl (Ed.), *Cognitive illusions: A handbook on fallacies and biases in thinking, judgement and memory* (pp. 201–213). New York, NY: Psychology Press.

Rest, J. (1983). Morality. In P. Mussen (Series ed.), *Manual of child psychology*, Vol. 3. *Cognitive development* (J. Flavel & E. Markham, vol. eds.; pp. 556–629). New York: Wiley. (

Rest, J. R. & Narvaez (1994). *Moral development in the professions*. Hillsdale, NJ: Erlbaum.

Rittel, H. W. J., & Webber, M. M. (1973). Dilemmas in a general theory of planning. *Policy Sciences, 4,* 155–169.

Roberts, J. (2012). Organizational ignorance: Towards a managerial perspective on the unknown. *Management Learning, 44,* 215–236. doi: 10.1177/1350507612443208

Roberts, J., & Armitage, J. (2008). The ignorance economy. *Prometheus, 26,* 335–354.

Rogowski, S. (2011). Managers, managerialism and social work with children and families: The deformation of a profession? *Practice: Social Work in Action, 23,* 157–167. doi: 10.1080/09503153.2011.569970

Rose, S. C., Bisson, J., Churchill, R., & Wessely, S. (2009). Psychological debriefing for preventing post traumatic stress disorder (PTSD). *Cochrane Library*.

Rosen, M. A., DiazGranados, D., Dietz, A. S., Benishek, L. E., Thompson, D., Pronovost, P. J., & Weaver, S. J. (2018). Teamwork in health care: Key discoveries enabling safer, higher-quality care. *American Psychologist, 73,* 433–450.

Rosenbaum, P. R. (2002). *Observational studies* (2nd ed.). New York, NY: Springer-Verlag.

Rosenthal, R. (1994). On being one's own study: Experimenter effects in behavioral research—30 years later. In W. R. Shadish & S. Fuller (Eds.), *The social psychology of science* (pp. 214–229). New York, NY: Guilford.

Rousmaniere, T. (2017). *Deliberate practice for psychotherapists: A guide to improving clinical effectiveness*. New York, NY: Routledge.

Rousmaniere, T., Goodyear, R. K., Miller, S. D., & Wampold, B. E. (2017). *The cycle of excellence: Using deliberate practice to improve supervision and training*. Hobokan, NJ: Wiley Blackwell.

Ryan, W. (1976). *Blaming the victim* (Rev. ed.). New York: Vintage Books.

Rycroft, C. (1973). *A critical dictionary of psychoanalysis*. Totowa, NJ: Littlefield, Adams.

Sackett, D. L. (1979). Bias in analytic research. *Journal of Chronic Disease, 32,* 51–63.

Sackett, D. L., Richardson, W. S., Rosenberg, W., & Haynes, R. B. (1997). *Evidence-based medicine: How to practice and teach EBM*. New York, NY: Churchill Livingstone.

Sackett, D. L., Straus, S. E., Richardson, W. S., Rosenberg, W., & Haynes, R. B. (2000). *Evidence-based medicine: How to practice and teach EBM* (2nd ed.). New York, NY: Churchill Livingstone.

Salas, E., & Klein, G. (Eds.). (2001). *Linking expertise and naturalistic decision making*. Mahwah, NJ: Erlbaum.

Schilpp, P. A. (Ed.). (1974). *The philosophy of Karl Popper* (2 vols.). LaSalle, IL: Open Court.

Schwartz, L. M. & Woloshin, S. (2011). The drug facts box: Making informed decisions about prescription drugs possible. In G. Gigerenzer & J. A. M. Gray (Eds.), *Better doctors, better patients, better decisions: Envisioning health care 2020* (pp. 233–242). Cambridge, MA: MIT Press.

Schön, D. A. (1983). *The reflective practitioner: How professionals think in action*. New York, NY: Basic Books.

Schraagen, J. M., Militello, L. G., Ormerod, T., & Lipshitz, R. (2008). *Naturalistic decision making and macrocognition*. Burlington, VT: Ashgate.

Scriven, M. (1976). *Reasoning*. New York: McGraw-Hill.

Scriven, M., & Paul, R. (2005). *Critical thinking community: A working definition of critical thinking*. Unpublished manuscript.

Scull, A. (2005). *Madhouse: A tragic tale of megalomania and modern medicine*. New Haven, CT: Yale University Press.

Scull, A. (2015). *Madness in civilization: A cultural history of insanity from the Bible to Freud, from the madhouse to modern medicine*. Princeton, NJ: Princeton University Press.

Secker-Walker, J., & Taylor-Adams, S. (2001). Clinical incident reporting. In C. Vincent (Ed.), *Clinical risk management: Enhancing patient safety* (2nd ed., pp. 419–438). London, England: BMJ.

Seech, Z. (1993). *Open minds and everyday reasoning*. Belmont, CA: Wadsworth.

Seife, C. (2010). *Proofiness: The dark arts of mathematical deception*. New York, NY: Viking.

Semin, G. R., & Manstead, A. S. R. (1983). *The accountability of conduct: A social psychological analysis*. Orlando, FL: Academic Press.

Sharp, V. A. & Faden, A. I. (1998). *Medical harm: Historical, conceptual, and ethical dimensions of iatrogenic illness*. New York, NY: Cambridge University Press.

Shaughnessy, A. F., Vaswani, A., Andrews, B. K., Erlich, D. R., D'Amico, F., Lexchin, J., & Cosgrove, L. (2017). Developing a clinician friendly tool to identify useful clinical practice guidelines: G-TRUST. *Annals of Family Medicine, 15*, 413–418. doi: 10.1370/afm.2119

Sihvonen, R., Paavola, M., Malmivaara, A., Itälä, A., Joukainen, A., Nurmi, H., . . . Finnish Degenerative Meniscal Lesion Study (FIDELITY) Group (2013). Arthroscopic partial meniscectomy versus sham surgery for a degenerative meniscal tear. *New England Journal of Medicine, 369*, 2515–2524. doi: 10.1056/NEJMoa1305189

Silverman, E. (2010). *All that pharma fraud fills the U.S. treasury*. Unpublished manuscript.

Silverman, W. A. (1980). *Retrolental fibroplasia: A modern parable*. New York: Grune & Stratton.

Simon, H. (1982). *Models of bonded bounded rationality*. Cambridge, MA: MIT Press.

Sinclair, W. J. (1909). *Semmelweis, his life and his doctrine: A chapter in the history of medicine*. Manchester, England: University Press.

Singer, B. D. (1978). Assessing social errors. *J. of Social Policy, 9*, 27–34.

Singh, H., Meyer, A. N. D., & Thomas, E. J. (2014). The frequency of diagnostic errors in outpatient care: Estimations from three large observational studies involving US adult populations. *BMJ Quality & Safety*. doi: 10.1136/bmjqs-2013-002627

Skeem, J. L., Douglas, K. S., & Lilienfeld, S. O. (Eds.). (2009). *Psychological science in the courtroom: consensus and controversy*. New York, NY: Guilford.

Skinner, B. F. (1974). *About behaviorism*. New York, NY: Knopf.

Slovic, P. (2010). *The feeling of risk: New perspectives on risk perception*. New York, NY: Earthscan.

Slovic, P., Finucane, M., Peters, E., & MacGregor, D. G. (2002). The affect heuristic. In T. Gilovich & D. Griffin (Eds.), *Heuristics and biases: The psychology of intuitive judgment* (pp. 397–420). New York, NY: Cambridge University Press.

Snyder, C. R., Higgins, R. L., & Stucky, R. J. (2005). *Excuses: Masquerades in search of grace* (2nd ed.). New York, NY: Wiley.

Solomon. R. C., & Flores, F. (2001). *Building trust: In business, politics, relationships and life*. New York, NY: Oxford University Press.

Sperber, I. (1990). *Fashions in science: Opinion leaders and collective behavior in the social sciences*. Minneapolis, MN: University of Minnesota Press.

Staats, A. W. (2012). *The marvelous learning animal: What makes human nature unique*. Amhurst, NY: Prometheus.

Stacey, D., Légaré, F., Lewis, K., Barry, M. J., Bennett, C. L., Eden, K. B., . . . Trevena, L. (2017). Decision aids for teaching people who are facing health treatment or screening decisions.

Cochrane Database of Systematic Reviews, 1:CD001431. doi: 10.1002/14651858.CD001431.pub4

Stanovich, K. E. (2010). *What intelligence tests miss: The psychology of rational thought*. New Haven, CT: Yale University Press.

Stanovich, K. E. (2012). On the distinction between rationality and intelligence: Implications for understanding individual differences in reasoning. In K. J. Holyoak & R. G. Morrison (Eds.), *The Oxford Handbook of Thinking and Reasoning* (pp. 433–455). New York, NY: Oxford University Press.

Stanovich, K. E. (2016). The comprehensive assessment of rational thinking. *Educational Psychologist, 51*, 23–34. doi: 10.1080/00461520.2015.1125787

Stanovich, K. E. & West, R. F. (2002). *Individual differences in reasoning: Implications for the rationality debate?* In T. Gilovich, D. Griffin, & D. Kahneman (Eds.), *Heuristics and biases: The psychology of intuitive judgment* (pp. 421–440). New York, NY: Cambridge University Press.

Stanovich, K. E., & West, R. F. (2008). On the relative independence of thinking biases and mental ability. *Journal of Personality and Social Psychology, 94*, 672–695.

Stanovich, K. E., & West, R. F., & Toplak, M. E. (2013). Myside bias, rational thinking and intelligence. *Current Directions in Psychological Science, 22*, 259–264. doi: 10.1177/0963721413480174

Stanovich, K. E., & West, R. F., & Toplak, M. E. (2016). *The rationality quotient: Toward a test of rational thinking*. Cambridge, MA: MIT Press.

Steblay, N. M., & Loftus, E. F. (2012). Eyewitness memory and the legal system. In E. Shafir (Ed.), *The behavioral foundations of public policy* (pp. 145–12). Princeton, NJ: Princeton University Press.

Sterne, J. A., Eger, M., & Smith, G. D. (2001). Investigating and dealing with publication and other biases. In M. Egger, G. D. Smith, & D. G. Altman (Eds.), *Systematic reviews in healthcare: Metaanalysis in context* (2nd ed., pp. 189–208). London, England: BMJ.

Stivers, R. (2001). *Technology as magic: The triumph of the irrational*. New York, NY: Continuum.

Straus, S. E., & McAlister, D. C. (2000). Evidence-based medicine: A commentary on common criticisms. *Canadian Medical Journal, 163*, 837–841.

Straus, S. E., Richardson, W. S., Glasziou, P, & Haynes, R. B. (2005). *Evidence-based medicine: How to practice and teach EBM* (3rd ed.). New York, NY: Churchill-Livingstone.

Straus, S. E., Glasziou, P., Richardson, W. S., & Haynes, R. B. (2011). *Evidence-based medicine: How to practice and teach it* (4th ed.). New York: Churchill Livingstone.

Straus, S. E., Tetroe, J. M., & Graham, I. D. (2011). Knowledge translation is the use of knowledge in health care decision making. *Journal of Clinical Epidemiology, 64*, 6–10. doi: 10.1016/j.jclinepi.2009.08.016

Street, R. L., Jr. (2013). How clinician–patient communication contributes to health improvement: Modeling pathways from talk to outcome. *Patient Education and Counseling, 92*, 286–291.

Strough, J., Karns, T. E., & Schlosnagle, L. (2011). Decision making heuristics across the lifespan. *Annals of New York Academy of Science, 1235*, 57–74. doi: 10.1111/j.1749-6632.2011.06208.x

Swift, J. K., & Callahan, J. L. (2009). The impact of client treatment preferences on outcome: a meta-analysis. *Journal of Clinical Psychology, 65*, 368–381. doi: 10.1111/j.1749-6632.2011.06208.x

Szasz, T. S. (1961). *The myth of mental illness: Foundations of a theory of personal conduct*. New York, NY: Harper & Row.

Szasz, T. S. (2007). *The medicalization of everyday life*. New York, NY: Syracuse University Press.

Taber, C. S., & Lodge, M. (2006). Motivated skepticism in the evaluation of political beliefs. *American Journal of Political Science, 50,* 755–769. doi: 10.1111/j.1540-5907.2006.00214.x

Tanne, J. H. (2010). AstraZeneca pays $520m fine for off label marketing. *BMJ, 340,* c2380. doi: 10.1136/bmj.c2380

Task Force on Psychological Intervention Guidelines. (1995). *Report of the 2005 Presidential Task Force on Evidence-Based Practice.* Retrieved from the American Psychologicial Association website: https://www.apa.org/practice/resources/evidence/evidence-based-report.pdf

Taussig, M. (1999). *Defacement: Public secrecy and the labor of the negative.* Stanford, CA: Stanford University Press.

Tesh, S. N. (1988). *Hidden arguments of political ideology and disease prevention policy.* New Brunswick, NJ: Rutgers University Press.

Tetlock, P. E. (2003). Correspondence and coherence: Indicators of good judgment in world politics. In D. Hardman & L. Macchi (Eds.), *Thinking: Psychological perspectives on reasoning, judgment and decision making* (pp. 233–250). New York, NY: Wiley.

Tetlock, P. (2005). *Expert political judgment: How good is it? How can we know?* Princeton, NJ: Princeton University Press.

Thompson, J. B. (1987). Language and ideology: A framework for analysis. *Sociological Review, 35,* 517–536. doi: 10.1111/j.1467-954X.1987.tb00554.x

Thomson O'Brien, M. A., Freemantle, N., Oxman, A.D., Wolf, F., Davis, D.A., & Herrin, J. (2001). Continuing education meetings and workshops: Effects on professional practice and health care outcomes (Cochrane Review). In *Cochrane Library, 2.* doi: 10.1002/chp.1340210310

Thouless, R. H. (1974). *Straight and crooked thinking: Thirty-eight dishonest tricks of debate.* London, England: Pan Books.

Thyer, B. A., & Pignotti, M. G. (2015). *Science and pseudoscience in social work.* New York, NY: Springer.

Toulmin, S. E. (2003). *The uses of argument* (Updated ed.). Cambridge, England: Cambridge University Press.

Tousignant, M., & DesMarchais, J. E. (2002). Accuracy of student self-assessment ability compared to their own performance in a problem-based learning medical program: A correlation study. *Advances in Health Sciences Education, 7,* 19–27. doi: 10.1023/A:1014516206120

Toulmin, S. E., Rieke, R., & Janik, A. (1979). *An introduction to reasoning.* New York: Macmillan.

Tracy, T. J. G., Wampold, B. E., Lichtenberg, J. W., & Goodyear, R. K. (2014). Expertise in psychotherapy: An elusive goal? *American Psychologist, 69,* 218–229. doi: 10.1037/a0035099

Tuffs, A. (2004). Only 6% of drug advertising material is supported by evidence. *BMJ, 328,* 485. doi: 10.1136/bmj.328.7438.485-a

Tufte, E. (1983). *Visual display of a quantitative information.* Cheshire, CT: Graphics Press.

Tufte, E. (2006). *Beautiful evidence.* Cheshire, CT: Graphics Press.

Turner, E. H., Matthews, A. M., Linardatos, E., Tell, R. A., & Rosenthal, R. (2008). Selected publication of antidepressants trails and its influence on apparent efficacy. *New England Journal of Medicine, 358,* 252–260. doi: 10.1056/NEJMsa065779

Tversky, A., & Kahneman, D. (1973). Availability: A heuristic for judging frequency and probability. *Cognitive Psychology, 5,* 207–232. doi: 10.1016/0010-0285(73)90033-9

Tweed, R. G., & Lehman, D. R. (2002). Learning considered within a cultural context: Confucian and Socratic approaches. *American Psychologist, 57,* 89–99. doi: 10.1037/0003-066X.57.2.89

Union of Concerned Scientists. (2012). *Heads they win, tails we lose: How corporations corrupt science at the public's expense.* Retrieved from the Union of Concerned Scientists website: https://www.ucsusa.org/sites/default/files/legacy/assets/documents/scientific_integrity/how-corporations-corrupt-science.pdf

US Government Accountability Office. (2014, April). *Foster children. Additional federal guidance could help states better plan for oversight of psychotropic medications administered by managed-care organizations* (GAO-14-362). Retrieved from the US Government Accountability Office website: https://www.gao.gov/products/GAO-14-362

Van Der Weyden, M. B., Armstrong, R. M., & Gregory, A. T. (2005). The 2005 Noel Prize in Physiology or medicine. *Medical Jouranl of Australia, 183*, 612–614.

Venkatesh, A., Savage, D., Sandefur, B., Bernard, K. R., Rothenberg, C., & Schuuer, J. D. (2017). Systematic review of emergency medicine clinical practice guidelines: Implications for research and policy. *PLOS ONE, 12*(6): e0178456. doi: 10.1371/journal.pone.0178456

Vincent, C. (Ed.). (2001). *Clinical risk management: Enhancing patient safety* (2nd ed.). London, England: BMJ.

Vincent, C. (2010). *Patient safety* (2nd ed.). Hobokan, NJ: Wiley-Blackwell.

Vincent, C., & Taylor-Adams, E. (2001). The investigation and analysis of clinical incidents. In C. Vincent (Ed.), *Clinical risk management: Enhancing patient safety* (2nd ed., pp. 439–460). London, England: BMJ.

Volz, K. G. & Hertwig, R. (2016). Emotions and decisions: Beyond conceptual vagueness and the rationality muddle. *Perspectives on Psychological Science, 11*, 101–116. doi: 10.1177/1745691615619608

Vyse, S. (2005). Where do fads come from? In J. W. Jacobson, R. N. Foxx, & J. Mulick (Eds.), *Controversial therapies for developmental disabilities: Fad, fashion, and science in professional practice* (pp. 3–18). Mahwah, NJ: Erlbaum.

Walfish, S., McAlister, B., O'Donnell, P., & Lambert, M. J. (2012). An investigation of self-assessment bias in mental health providers. *Psychological Reports, 110*, 639–644. doi: 10.2466/02.07.17.PR0.110.2.639-644

Walton, D. N. (1995). *A pragmatic theory of fallacy*. Tuscaloosa: University of Academic Press.

Walton, D. N. (1997). *Appeal to expert opinion: Arguments from authority*. University Park, PA: Pennsylvania State University Press.

Walton, D. N. (1999). *One-sided arguments*. Albany, NY: State University of New York Press.

Walton, D. (2005). *Abductive reasoning*. Tuscaloosa, Ala. University of Alabama Press.

Walton, D. N. (2008). *Informal logic: A pragmatic approach* (2nd ed.). New York, NY: Cambridge University Press.

Walton, D. N. (2009). Argument visualization tools for corroborative evidence. In *Proceedings of the 2nd International Conference on Evidence Law and Forensic Science* (pp. 32–49). Beijing, China: Institute of Evidence Law and Forensic Science.

Walton, D. N. (2011). Reasoning about knowledge using defeasible logic. *Argument and Computation, 2*, 131–155. doi: 10.1080/19462166.2011.637641

Walton, D. N. (2013). *Methods of argumentation*. New York, NY: Cambridge University Press.

Walton, D. N. (2015). *Goal-based reasoning for argumentation*. New York, NY: Cambridge University Press.

Walton, D. N., Reed, C., & Macagno, F. (2008). *Argumentation schemes*. New York, NY: Cambridge University Press.

Wampold, B. E. (2006). Not a scintilla of evidence to support empirically supported treatments as more effective than other treatments. In J. C. Norcross, L. E. Beutler, & R. F. Levant (Eds.), *Evidence-based practices in mental health: Debate and dialogue on the fundamental questions* (pp. 299–308). Washington, DC: American Psychological Association.

Wampold, B. E. (2015). How important are the common factors in psychotherapy? An update. *World Psychiatry, 14,* 270–277. doi: 10.1002/wps.20238

Wampold, B. E., & Imel, Z. E. (2015a). *The great psychotherapy debate: The evidence for what makes psychotherapy work* (2nd ed.). New York, NY: Routledge.

Wampold, B. E., & Imel, Z. E. (2015b, March). What do we know about psychotherapy? And what is there left to debate? *Society for the Advancement of Psychotherapy.* Retrieved from http://www.societyforpsychotherapy.org/what-do-we-know-about-psychotherapy-and-what-is-there-left-to-debate

Watson, A. C. & Eack., S. M. (2011). Oppression and stigma and their effects. In N. R. Heller & A. Gitterman (Eds.), *Mental health and social problems: A social work perspective* (pp. 21–43). New York, NY: Routledge.

Watson, D. L., & Tharp, R. G. (2013). *Self-directed behavior: Self-modification for personal adjustment* (10th ed.) Belmont, CA: Wadsworth Cengage Learning.

Webster Third World Dictionary. (1987).

Webster, Y. O. (1997). *Against the multicultural agenda: A critical thinking alternative.* Westport, CT: Praeger.

Welch, H. G., Schwartz, L., & Woloshin, S. (2011). *Overdiagnosed: Making people sick in the pursuit of health.* Boston, MA: Beacon.

Wennberg, J. E. (2002). Unwarranted variations in healthcare delivery: Implications for academic medical centres. *BMJ, 325,* 961–964. doi: 10.1136/bmj.325.7370.961

Wennberg, J. E. & Thomson, P. Y. (2011). Time to tackle unwarranted variations in practice. *BMJ, 342,* d1513. doi: 10.1136/bmj.d1513

West, R. F., Meserve, R. J. & Stanovich, K. E. (2012). Cognitive sophistication does not attenuate the bias blind spot. *Journal of Personality and Social Psychology, 103,* 506–519. doi: 10.1037/a0028857

Weston, A. (1992). *A rule book for arguments* (2nd ed.). Indianapolis, IN: Hackett.

Whitaker, R., & Cosgrove, L. (2015). *Psychiatry under the influence: Institutional corruption, social injury and prescriptions for reform.* New York, NY: Palgrave Macmillan.

White, A. D. (1971). *A history of the warfare of science with theology in Christendom,* Vol. I & II. New York: Prometheus.

Whittaker, A., & Havard, T. (2016). Defensive practice as "fear-based" practice: Social work's open secret? *British Journal of Social Work, 46,* 1158–1174. doi: 10.1093/bjsw/bcv048

Wild, K., Scholz, M., Ropohl, A., Bräuer, L., Paulsen, F., & Burger, P. H. M. (2014). Strategies against burnout and anxiety in medical education—Implementation and evaluation of a new course on relaxation techniques (Relacs) for medical students. *PLOS ONE* 9(12): e114967. doi: 10.1371/journal.pone.0114967

Williams, I. L. (2017). The institutionalized cruelty of biased language: From grand illusion to delusion of normalcy. *Journal of Ethics in Mental Health, 10,* 1–26.

Williams, R. J. (1956). *Biochemical individuality.* Hobokan, NJ: Wiley.

Williams, R. G., Silverman, R., Schwind, C., Fortune, J. B., Sutyak, J., Horvath, K. D., et al. (2007). Surgeon information transfer and communication. Factors affecting quality and efficiency of inpatient care. *Annals of Surgery, 245,* 159–169.

Witte, C. L., Witte, M. H., & Kerwin, A. (1994). Ignorance and the process of learning and discovery in medicine. *Controlled Clinical Trials, 15,* 1–4. doi: 10.1016/0197-2456(94)90020-5

Woloshin, S., Schwartz, L. M., & Welch, H. G. (2008). *Know your chances: Understanding health statistics.* Berkeley, CA: University of California Press.

Woltmann, E. M., Wilkniss, S. M., Teachout, A., McHugo, G. J., & Drake, R. E. (2011). Trial of an electronic decision support system to facilitate shared decision making in community mental health. *Psychiatric Services, 62,* 54–60. doi: 10.1176/ps.62.1.pss6201_0054

Wood, S. F., Podrasky, J., McMonagle, M. A., Raveendran, J., Bysshe, T., Hogenmiller, A., & Fugh-Berman, A. (2017, October 25). Influence of pharmaceutical marketing on Medicare prescriptions in the District of Columbia. *PLOS ONE.* doi: 10.1371/journal.pone.0186060

Woods, D. D., & Cook, R. I. (1999). Perspectives on human error: Hindsight biases and local rationality. In F. T. Durso, R. S. Nickerson, R. W. Schvaneveldt, S. T. Dumais, D. S. Lindsay, & M. T. Chi. (Eds.), *Handbook of Applied cognition* (pp. 141–171). New York, NY: Wiley.

Woods, D. D. & Hollnagel, E. (2006). Prologue. In E. Hollnagel, D. D. Woods, & N. Leveson (Eds.), *Resilience engineering: Concepts & precepts* (pp. 1–8). Boca Raton, FL: Taylor & Francis.

Woolf, S. H., Grol, R., Hutchinson, A., Eccles, M., & Grimshaw, J. (1989). Potential benefits, limitations, and harms of clinical guidelines. *BMJ, 318,* 527–530. doi: 10.1136/bmj.318.7182.527

Young, J. H. (1992). *American health quackery.* Princeton, NJ: Princeton University Press.

Young, N. S., Ioannidis, J. P. A., & Al-Ubaydli, O. (2008). Why current publication practices may distort science. *PLOS Medicine, 5,* e201. doi: 10.1371/journal.pmed.0050201

Zsambok, C. E., & Klein, G. (Eds.). (1997). *Naturalistic decision making.* Mahwah, NJ: Erlbaum.

Zechmeister, E. G. & Johnson, J. E. (1992). *Critical thinking: A functional approach.* Pacific Grove, CA: Brooks/Cole.

INDEX

abductive inferences, 193

acceptability, 204

accountability, 115

accuracy, critical appraisal of, 148–49

active open-minded thinking (AOT)
    cultivating, 285–86
    and decision-making, 5–10, 12, 20–21
    and expertise, 169
    importance of, 72
    lack of, 161

activism, 294–95

actor-observer bias, 178–79

ad hominems, 213, 216–18

ad verecundian fallacy, 201

adverse incident reporting, 184

affective bias, 173

Agency for Health Care Research and Quality
    (AHRQ), 94

aggressive behavior, 244, 245

AGREE, 153–54

AHRQ (Agency for Health Care Research and
    Quality), 94

allegiance effects, 125

alliance, 261–62

AllTrials, 20

American Psychiatric Association, 18

American Psychological Association, 152–53

analogies, inappropriate use
    of, 213, 224–25

analytic thinking, 66

anchoring, 173

"answering question with question," 225

antiscience, 81

AOT. *See* active open-minded thinking

appeals
    to common practice, 218
    to consensus, 220
    emotional, 216
    irrelevant, 216

apriorism, 220

argument-based errors, 178

argument from forced analogy, 225

arguments, 186–210
    from authority, 199–202
    circular, 220–21
    deductive, 193
    defining, 190–94
    enhancing skills in, 202–5
    fouls ways to win in, 215
    illusions of, 189
    individual/cultural differences in, 208–9
    rational, 191

arguments (*cont.*)
  reasoning/evidence/decision making in, 188–89, 205–8
  role of, 186–87
  schemes in, 199
  straw man, 213, 222–23
  unsound, 192–93
  Walton's approach to, 194–99
Armitage, J., 59
assertions, bold, 236
assertive behavior, 244, 245, 268, 282
assessment questions, 90
assumption, defined, 190
asymmetric insight, illusions of, 174
"attacking the example," 219
attentive listening, 262
authority, 199–202, 213, 226–27
authority-based practice, 28–29, 36, 37
autonomy, intellectual, 13
availability, 173
avoidable errors, 14–15, 275
avoiding, collective, 59

Bacon, Francis, 124–25
bad seed fallacy, 217–18
Baer, D. M., 136
Baloney Detection Kit (Sagan), 287–88
Barnum, P. T., 233–34
Barnum Effect, 174, 233–34
Baron, J.
  on argumentation, 186, 208
  on decision-making, 2–4, 10–11
  on evidence, 50–52, 60–61, 76
  on self-deception, 281
Barrett, S., 82–83
barriers, motivational, 276–77
base rate neglect, 173
Bauer, H. H., 55–56
Baumeister, R. F., 296–97
"begging the question," 213, 219–21
behavior
  aggressive, 244, 245
  assertive (*See* assertive behavior)
  negative, 263
  passive, 244, 245
  requesting changes in, 254–57
  social, 267
beliefs, 15, 55–56, 65, 266–67, 289
Bernays, E. L., 281

best evidence, 107
biases
  actor-observer, 178–79
  causing errors, 180
  cognitive, 171–79
  commission, 173
  confirmation, 173, 286
  consistency, 175
  and critical appraisals, 124–28
  defined, 4–5
  detection, 125–27
  egocentric (*See* egocentric bias)
  examples of, 173
  group-serving, 174
  hindsight (*See* hindsight bias)
  information, 173
  in-group, 175
  memory, 175, 282
  observer, 116
  omission, 173
  outcome, 173
  outgroup homogeneity, 175
  performance, 125–27
  projection, 175
  and propaganda, 63–64
  in randomized controlled trials, 126
  reducing, 46
  related to availability, 176
  during research, 111, 116
  selection, 125–27, 130–31
  self-serving (*See* self-serving bias)
  social, 174–75, 178–79
  social desirability, 174
  sociocentric, 61–62, 279
  status quo, 174
  submission, 125
  and validity, 125–28
Biomedical Bestiary (Micheal, Boyce, and Wilcox), 214–15
biomedical literature, false reports in, 17
Black, N., 138
blinding, 136
bold assertions, 236
Bourgois, P., 146–47
Boyle, M., 234
Brighton, H., 69
British Medical Journal, 160–62
Bromme, R., 79
Brookfield (1995), 5

Bruck, M., 179
burden of proof, 204
burnout, 296

Cambridge-Somerville Youth Study, 136–37
Campbell, Donald, 123, 147–48
Campbell Collaboration, 35, 97
CART (Comprehensive Assessment of
　　Rational Thinking), 14, 61–62
Cartwright, N., 127–28, 144–45
Case, A., 279
case conferences, 263–65
case control (case-referent) studies, 140
case example fallacy, 213
case examples, 66
case-referent (case control) studies, 140
case-series studies, 141
CASP (Critical Appraisal Skills Program), 122
causality, 127, 128, 144–45, 207–8
Ceci, S. J., 179
censorship, 63, 230
Center for Evidence-Based Medicine, 94
Centre for Evidence-Based Mental Health, 96
Centre for Evidence-Based Nursing, 96
Centre for Reviews and Dissemination
　　(CRD), 94
Chalmers, I., 121, 122, 123
charity, 204
cherry-picking, 172–76
CINAHL, 94
circular arguments, 220–21
citations, misuses of, 230
claims, 17–19, 51, 66, 134, 190–91
clarity, in arguments, 203–4
clients, 24, 38, 108–11, 284
clinical practices, factors influencing, 272
clustering illusion, 173
Cochrane, Archie, 294
Cochrane Collaboration, 35, 97
Coffman, S., 254
cofounders, 125–27
cognitive biases, 171–79
cognitive conservatism, 181
Cohen, D., 60
Cohen, J., 137
cohort studies, critical appraisals for, 139
CollaboRATE, 114–15
collective avoiding, 59
Combs, J. E., 228

commission bias, 173
communication skills, 242–68
　　for alliance, 261–62
　　with assertive/passive/aggressive
　　　behavior, 244
　　attentive listening, 262
　　and common factors, 259–60
　　and corrective feedback, 251–53
　　for disagreements, 247–51
　　empathy in, 260–61
　　to gather/provide information, 258, 259
　　importance of, 242–44
　　minimizing negative behavior, 263
　　obstacles to, 266
　　with put-downs, 257–58
　　for refusing requests, 253–54
　　for requesting behavior changes, 254–57
　　respect in, 262
　　speaking more/less, 247
　　for team meetings/case
　　　conferences, 263–65
　　warmth in, 261
comparison groups, 130
complex questions, 221
Comprehensive Assessment of Rational
　　Thinking (CART), 14, 61–62
conceptual critique, 143
concurrent validity, 131–32
confidence, 13, 172
confirmation bias, 173, 286
"confusing cause and effect," 213
"confusing correlation and causation," 213
confusion, 226, 234–35
conservatism, cognitive, 181
consistency, 65, 74
consistency bias, 175
CONSORT guidelines, 131
construct validity, 132, 142–43
content knowledge, 10–11, 53
content validity, 131–32
contingency table, 150
contrast effect, 173, 240
control, illusions of, 68, 173, 178
convergent validity, 132
Cook, R. I., 166
corrective feedback, 72, 168, 251–53, 290
correlation, causality vs., 207–8
corruption, 83
cost–benefit questions, 91

courage, intellectual, 13
CRD (Centre for Reviews and
    Dissemination), 94
credibility, 61
criterion validity, 131–32
critical appraisals, of research, 101–3, 120–56
    bias in, 124–28
    discouraging, 274
    issues in, 155
    myths that hinder, 121–24
    practice guidelines in, 152–54
    questions for, 128–52
    skepticism in, 121
Critical Appraisal Skills Program (CASP), 122
critical testing, 65
critical thinking, 7, 10, 13
criticism, 71–73
critique, conceptual, 143
cross-sectional studies, critical appraisals
    for, 140
culture, 208–9, 244, 271–73
curiosity, intellectual, 13
cynics, 12–14

Damer, T. E., 204–5
Daniels, M., 33
databases, examples of, 94
Davies, P., 49
Dawes, R., 60–61
Deaton, A., 279
decision-making, 1–20
    and active open-minded thinking,
        5–10, 14–17
    argumentation in, 186–87
    and Baron's search-inference
        framework, 2–4
    barriers to, 157–59
    context in, 17–19
    drug, 109
    evidence-informed, 270–82
    expertise in (*See* expertise)
    importance of, 1–2
    shared, 108
    skills/knowledge for, 10–12
    uncertainty in, 19–20
    values/attitudes/styles in, 12–14
deductive arguments, 193
deductive inferences, 193
deliberation, 187, 196

democratic knowledge market, 40
description questions, 2, 89, 91
descriptive validity, 127–28, 142–43
detection bias, 125–27
diagnosis, critical appraisal of, 148
diagnostic momentum, 173
Diagnostic Zealot, 33–34
dialogues, 187, 196. *See also* persuasion
        dialogue
disagreements, 249–51
discipline, intellectual, 13
discovery dialogue, 187, 196
distortion, 63, 222
diversion, 63, 223–24, 225
divine fallacy, 214–15
Drake, R. E., 108–11
Dreyfus, H. L., 68–69
Dreyfus, S. E., 68–69
drop-out rates, 132
drugs, 109
Drury, S. S., 252

ecological fallacy, 213, 214–15
ecological validity, 138–39
economics, 32, 271
economy, ignorance, 59
Eddy, D. M., 22
effective disagreement, 249–51
Effectiveness and Efficiency (Cochrane), 294
effectiveness questions, 89, 135
effective reasoning, 285
effect size, 137
egocentric bias, 61–62, 174, 175
Elder, L., 7, 214
Ellul, J., 62
Elwyn, G., 108
Ely, J. W., 92–93, 101
EMB tool kit, 102
emotion, 206–7, 213, 225
emotional appeals, 216
emotional barriers, 281–82
emotional words, 232
emotion-management skills, 292–93
empathy, 13, 173, 253, 260, 261
Ennis, R. H., 164
Entwistle, V. A., 108
Equal Employment Opportunity
        Commission, 295–96
EQUATOR, 94

equivocation, 226
errors
  argument-based, 178
  avoidable, 14–15, 275
  evidence-based, 178
  in evidence-informed
    decision-making, 275–76
  and expertise, 179–83
  fundamental attribution (*See* fundamental
    attribution error)
  human, 179–80
  in integrating information, 111
  knowledge-based, 178
  from lack of AOT, 161
  in language, 228–32
  medical, 179–80
  medication, 178
  memory-based, 178
  in posing questions, 91–92
  sources of, 112
  system, 178
  types of, 178
ethics, 23, 284–98
  and accreditation standards, 32
  of critical rationalism, 76–77
  and evidence, 83–84
  of evidence, 57–58
  on evidence-based practice, 27
  of expertise, 183
  honoring, 36, 37–38
  issues in, 114–15
  and sensitivity, 277–78
euphemisms, 237
"evading the facts," 219
evidence, 48–83
  in argumentation, 188–89
  characteristics of, 58–77
  controversies in, 81–83
  ethics of, 57–58
  gaps in, 270
  genuine, 60, 189
  importance of, 48–54
  politics of, 55–56
  science of, 77–81
  types of, 49
  widely accepted, 60
evidence-based errors, 178
evidence-based medicine, 22
evidence-based practice (EBP), 22–47

appeal of, 35
approaches to, 30
authority-based vs., 28–29, 37
concerns in, 32–34
defining, 22–26
examples of, 26
goals during, 37–40
and internet revolution, 35
key components of, 25
misrepresentations of/objections to, 40–43
obstacles to, 44–46
origins of, 31
philosophies of, 27, 35–37
process of, 85–117
and systemic reviews, 34–35
Evidence-Informed Client Choice Form, 108
evidence-informed decision-making, 270–82
exclusion, reasoning by, 208
excuses, 280–81, 293
expectations, unrealistic, 279–80, 286–87
experience, 67–68, 170
expertise, 157–84
  and cognitive bias, 171–79
  developing, 168
  and errors, 179–83
  ethics of, 183
  novices vs., 163–67
  and problems, 159–62
  strategies for, 169–71
  trusting, 123
  valuable, 165
  See also knowledge
external validity, 127–28, 142–43

fabrication, 63
face validity, 131–32
fair-mindedness, 13
fallacies
  of accident, 213
  ad verecundian, 201
  of alchemist, 231
  and argumentation, 197–99
  avoiding, 212–27
  bad seed, 217–18
  case example, 213
  of composition, 213, 222
  defining, 214–15
  divine, 214–15
  of division, 213, 222

fallacies (*cont.*)
  ecological, 213, 214–15
  examples of, 213
  and expertise, 171–72
  of false cause, 223
  formal, 227
  formal vs. informal, 227
  Gambler's, 173
  of the golden mean, 214–15
  of hasty generalization, 213, 222
  "hush hush," 214–15
  of ignorance, 218
  is/ought, 213
  language-based, 213, 228–37
  of obfuscation, 214–15
  pragmatic, 214–15
  of the single cause, 213
  of stereotyping, 179
  studying, 287–88
  of sweeping generalization, 222
  types of, 216–26
fallacyfiles.org, 214–15
fallibility, 204
false beliefs, 15, 55–56
False Claim Act, 17, 56
false claims, 17–19
false consensus effect, 174, 178–79
false knowledge, 53, 56–57
false memory, 175
Farden, A. I., 38
Farrington, D. P., 127–28, 131, 136, 142–43
feedback, 254–55, 274–75. *See also* corrective
    feedback
feelings, and genuine evidence, 60–61
Feynman, R., 7–8
Fineberg, H. V., 276–77
Fisher, R., 265
Fitzgerald, D., 22
Flexner, A., 68
Follies and Fallacies in Medicine (Skrabanek
    and McComick), 214–15
Food and Drug Administration, 271
forcing extension, 223
Forer Effect, 174, 233–34
Forest Plot, 143–44
formal fallacies, 227
Fox, R. C., 20, 237
framing effects, 173, 177
Frankfurt, H. G., 228
fraud, 83

Freire, P., 209
frequency, critical appraisals for, 146
fundamental attribution error, 174, 176–77, 295

Gambler's fallacy, 173
Gambrill, E., 214–15
Gaudet, J., 59
Gellner, E., 81
genuine evidence, 60, 189
genuineness, 261
Gibbs, L., 91–92, 214–15
Gigerenzer, G., 69, 157–59, 171
Glaszious, P., 86, 105
goals, 3, 293–94
Goldman, S. R., 79
Gottlieb, N., 254
Gøtzsche, P. C., 17, 58
Grading of Recommendations: Assessment,
    Development, and Evaluation
    (GRADE), 153–54
Grandage, K. K., 104
grand cofounder, 214–15
Gray, J. A. M.
  on critical appraisals, 139, 145
  on EBP process, 23, 32, 35, 40, 85, 101
  on effectiveness, 282–83
  on feedback, 274–75
Greenhalgh, T., 148–49
Grice's maxims, 197
group-serving bias, 174
groupthink, 173, 264
G-Trust, 99–100
guidelines
  approach to, 30
  for case conferences, 265
  CONSORT, 131
  critical appraisals of, 152–54
  for offering information, 258, 259
  in research, 97–100
  trust in, 97–98
guilt, 217
Guyatt, G. H., 22, 130, 141

halo effect, 174, 178–79
Haran, U., 7
Hardie, J., 127–28
harm, 33, 38, 91, 141–42
Hastie, R., 60–61
Hawthorne effect, 116, 173
Haynes, R. B., 31, 86, 105

hello–goodbye effect, 116
help, seeking, 290
helping professions, 1–2, 14–15
Herbst, A. L., 140
herd instinct, 174
heuristics, 69, 170–71
hindsight, certainty of, 181
hindsight bias, 116, 173, 175, 177
Hogarth, R. M., 68
homosexuality, 18
honesty, 106
human error, 179–80
Humbugs of the World (Barnum), 233–34
humility, intellectual, 13
hunting tools, 94
"hush hush" fallacy, 214–15

ideology, 209
ignorance, 53, 58–59, 213, 218, 285
ignorance economy, 59
"ignoring the issue," 223–24
illusions
    of argument, 189
    of asymmetric insight, 174
    of control, 68, 173, 178
    of knowing, 64
    of superiority, 175
    of transparency, 174
    of validity, 173
illusory correlations, 173, 178–79, 213
Imel, Z. E., 99
implementation science, 270–71
incident reporting, adverse, 184
incompetence, organizational, 271–74
inductive inferences, 194
inductive reasoning, 193
inert knowledge, 53
inferences, 192–94
    abductive, 193
    deductive, 193
    defined, 3
    inductive, 194
    plausible, 194
informal fallacies, 227
information
    need for, 86–89
    seeking, 187, 196, 258, 259
    vivid, 172
information bias, 173
informed experience, 170

in-group bias, 175
inquiry, 187, 195–96
instinct, herd, 174
integrity, intellectual, 13
intellectual autonomy, 13
intellectual courage, 13
intellectual curiosity, 13
intellectual discipline, 13
intellectual empathy, 13
intellectual humility, 13
intellectual integrity, 13
intellectual perseverance, 13
intent, 194–95
internal validity, 125–27, 142–43
internet, 35, 62, 93
interpersonal skills, 242–43
interventions, uncertainty in, 19–20
intuition, 66, 68–69, 123, 169, 170–71
Ioannidis, J. P. A., 17, 33–34
irrelevant ad hominems, 216–18
irrelevant appeals, 216
irrelevant conclusion, 223–24
Isaacs, D., 22
is/ought fallacy, 213

James, William, 209
Janis, I. L., 264
jargon, 70, 231–32, 240–41
Jenicek, M., 163, 179–80
job stress, 296
just world phenomenon, 175

Kahneman, D., 171
Kerwin, A., 274
"Killer Bs," 39, 105
King, L. S., 68
King, Martin Luther, Jr., 281–82
Klein, G., 166–67
knowledge
    building, 288–89
    content, 10–11, 53
    and criticism, 71–73
    defining, 52–54
    and expertise, 168
    false, 56–57
    illusions of, 64
    inert, 53
    lack of, 278–79
    objective, 61
    personal, 61

knowledge (*cont.*)
  procedural, 53, 210–11
  self, 53
  types of, 53
  See also expertise
knowledge-based errors, 178
knowledge dissemination, 33–34, 36–37, 40
Koertge, N., 77
Kuhn, D., 60, 189
Kuhn, T. S., 77–78, 188

labeling, 232–37
Lake Wobegon effect, 175
language
  effective use of, 238
  errors in, 228–32, 240–41
  fallacies through, 213, 232–37
  importance of, 228
  missing, 230
learning, problem-based, 291
Lettiere, M., 146–47
lifelong learning questions, 91
likelihood ration (LR), 150
liking, principle of, 239
listening, attentive, 262
logic, 65–66
logical positivism, 79
LR of negative test result (LR-), 150
LR of positive test result (LR+), 150

Makary, M. A., 33
marketing, 18–19
McAlister, D. C., 44
McCord, John, 136–37
McHugo, G. J., 108–11
medical errors, 179–80
medication errors, 178
medicine, evidence-based, 22
Meehl, P. E., 263–64
meetings, team, 263–65
Mellers, B. A., 7
memory-based errors, 178
memory biases, 175, 282
mental illness, 18
meta-analyses, critical appraisals
  of, 142–44
meta-cognitive skills, 11–12, 168–69
metaphors, 232
Meta-Research Innovation Center
  (METRICS), 20, 34

mindset, 166
Miser, W. F., 152
misinformation, 15, 55–56, 287–88
missing language, 230
mistakes, 75. *See also* errors
Moncrieff, J., 60
Monteiro, S. M., 169–70
motivation, increasing, 291–92
motivational barriers, 276–77
Munz, P., 56–57, 73, 81–82

naming, 232–37
National Council for Excellence in Critical
  Thinking, 7
negative behavior, 263
negative predictive value (NPV), 150
negotiation, 187, 196
Nettler, G., 208
New Freedom Commission on Mental Health
  (2003), 150–51
newsspeak, 236–37
Nicarthy, G., 254
Nickerson, R. S., 54, 217
Nimmo, D. D., 228
Nisbett, R., 171
N of 1 (single-case) studies, 115, 141
Norcross, J. C., 259–60
normal science, 77–78
Norman, G. R., 169–71, 180–81
normative question, 2
novices, experts vs., 163–67
NPV (negative predictive value), 150
numerator monster, 214–15

objective knowledge, 61
objectivity, scientific, 75
observational studies, critical appraisals
  for, 137–41
observer bias, 116
odds, 149
omission bias, 173
order effects, 236
organizational incompetence, 271–74
Orwell, G., 236
outcome bias, 173
outcome resistance, 108–11
outgroup homogeneity bias, 175
overconfidence, 173, 181
oversimplifications, 177, 230
Oxman, A. D., 130

parroting problem, 163
parsimony, 74
passive behavior, 244, 245
Patient-Oriented Evidence That Matters
   (POEMS), 96
Paul, Richard
  on arguments, 208
  on decision-making, 4–5, 7, 8, 12, 281
  on fallacies, 214
Paulos, J. A., 279
peer-review sources, 17
Pellegrino, E., 57
performance bias, 125–27
Perkinson, H. J., 286, 289
perseverance, intellectual, 13
personal knowledge, 61
persuasion dialogue, 187, 197, 198, 228–41
pharmaceutical companies, 18–19, 240
Phillips, D. C., 61, 79
physical attractiveness stereotype, 175
PICO questions, 89
Pitch, The (Rank), 55
plausible inferences, 194
pleading, special, 218
POEMS (Patient-Oriented Evidence That
   Matters), 96
politics, 55–56, 271, 295
Popper, Karl
  on critical appraisals, 209
  on decision-making, 12–14, 15–16
  on disagreements, 247–48
  on evidence, 54, 58–59, 61
  on expectations, 286–87
  facts defined by, 65
  and falsifiability, 73
  on knowledge, 71–72
  on mistakes, 77
  moral philosophy of, 76–77
  on normal science, 78
  on scientific objectivity, 75
  view of science, 72
positive predictive value (PPV), 150
positivism, logical, 79
Poskanzer, D. C., 140
possibilities, defined, 3
post hoc ergo propter hoc, 213
postmodernism, 81
posttest odds, 149
posttest probability, 149
PPV (positive predictive value), 150

pragmatic fallacy, 214–15
Prasad, V., 32
prediction questions, 90
predictive validity, 131–32
premature closure, 173
pre–post studies, 140–41
prescriptive question, 2
presentation, manner of, 237
presumptions, 194
pretest odds, 149
pretest probability, 149
prevention questions, 89, 90
probability, 149
problem-based learning, 291
problem framing, 162–63
problem-solving
  barriers to, 45, 276, 278
  and expertise, 159–62
  steps of, 161, 167–68
  training for, 293–94
procedural factors, 182–83
procedural knowledge, 53, 210–11
process resistance, 108–11
Proctor, R. N., 59
prognosis, critical appraisals for, 151–52
projection bias, 175
proof, burden of, 204
propaganda, 22, 30, 55–56, 62–63, 287–88
pseudoauthority, 239
pseudoevidence, 60, 189
pseudoexplanations, 233
pseudoscience, 80, 226–27
put-downs, communication skills with, 257–58

quackery, 82
qualitative research, critical appraisals for, 146–51
quality filters, 95
quality of care, 39
quarrel, 187, 196
Quesada, J., 146–47
questions
  for disagreements, 249
  for EBP, 86–93
  obstacles to well-structured, 92–93
  well-structured, 87

RAIT (Restoring Invisible and Abandoned
   Trials), 20
randomized controlled trials (RCTs), 43–44,
   126, 135–37

Rank, H., 55, 287–88
rational argument, 191
rationality, 61–62, 195, 280, 293
RCTs. *See* randomized controlled trials
Reason, J., 180, 275
reasoning, 61–62
    from analogy, 205–6
    and argumentation, 188–89
    by cause, 207
    effective, 285
    from emotion, 206–7
    by exclusion, 208
    inductive, 193
    and logic, 65–66
    from samples, 206
    from signs/symptoms, 206
    and truth, 64
    types of, 205–8
rebuttals, 204
reciprocity rule, 239
red herring, 213, 223–24, 226
reflection, 5
reflective thinking, 169
reflex, Semmelweis, 174
refusing requests, 253–54
reification, 234, 240–41
relativism, 81
relevance, in arguments, 204
reliability, of measures, 131–32
Rennie, D., 141
repetition, 235
representativeness, 173
representative thinking, 172
requests, refusing, 253–54
research, 93–105
    applying, 104
    common errors in, 100, 102
    critical appraisal of, 101–3 (*See also* critical
        appraisalsof research)
    databases/hunting tools for, 94
    decision-making from, 103
    importance of, 104–5
    lack of relevant, 107
    obstacles/remedies for, 100–1, 103
    practice guidelines in, 97–100
    purpose of, 120–21
    searching for, 93–97
resolutions, 205
respect, 262

responsibility, avoiding, 280
Rest, J., 277
retractions, 189
Retractionwatch.com, 34
Richardson, W. S., 31, 86
risk, critical appraisals for, 151–52
Ritov, I., 7
Roberts, J., 59, 274
Rogowski, S., 237
Rosenbaum, P. R., 138–39
Rosenberg, W., 31
Rosenthal, R., 33–34
Rosenthal effect, 116
Ross, L., 171
rule-based errors, 178

Sackett, D. L., 31, 39, 121
safety-specific factors, 182–83
Sagan, Carl, 287–88
Saket, D. L., 23
sample sizes, 130–31
San Francisco General Hospital, 28–29
scarcity principle, 240
Schliebinger, L., 59
SCIE (Social Care Institute for Excellence), 95
science
    characteristics of, 76
    defining, 71
    implementation, 270–71
    importance of understanding, 70
    misunderstandings of, 78–79
    normal, 77–78
    as testable, 73
scientific criteria, 70
scientific objectivity, 75
Scientific Rating Scale, 153
scientism, 70
screenings, critical appraisal of, 148, 150–51
Scriven, M., 7
search-inference framework (Baron), 2–4,
        50–52, 157
selection bias, 125–27, 130
self-deception, 281, 293
self-efficacy, 296–97
self-esteem, 296–97
self-evaluation questions, 118
self-fulfilling prophecy, 175
self knowledge, 53
self-management skills, 292

self-serving bias, 175, 178–79
semantic linkages, 235
Semmelweis reflex, 174
Semmelweiss, Ignas, 295–96
sensitivity, 138–39, 149, 277–78
shared decision making, 108
Sharp, V. A., 38
Shaughnessy, A. F., 99, 104
Sheldon, T. A., 108
Significance Turkey, 33–34
Simon, H., 167–68
Singer, B. D., 275, 276
single-case (N of 1) studies, 115, 141
situation awareness, 166–67
skepticism, 12–14, 121, 291
Skeptics Dictionary, The, 214–15
skill-based errors, 178
skills
    for argumentation, 202–5
    for decision making, 6, 10–11
    developing, 288, 293
    interpersonal, 242–43
    lack of, 278–79
    meta-cognitive, 11–12, 168–69
    self-management, 292
    time-management, 292
Slawson, D. C., 104
slippery slope, 213
SMS, 136
social behavior, ineffective, 267
social biases, 174–75, 178–79
Social Care Institute for Excellence (SCIE), 95
social desirability bias, 174
social desirability effect, 116
social influences, 271
social proof, principle of, 240
social-psychological persuasion
    strategies, 238–40
*Social Scientist's Bestiary: A Guide to Fabled
    Threats to and Defenses of Naturalistic
    Social Science, The* (Phillips), 79
sociocentric bias, 61–62, 279
Socrates, 50, 167
Socratic questioning, 8, 9.
Sowden, A. J., 108
special pleading, 218
specificity, 149
sponsorship, 134
Stanovich, K. E., 14, 171

statistical conclusion validity, 142–43
statistical significance, 133
statistics, 133
status quo bias, 174
stereotypes, 175
stereotyping, 174
Straus, S. E., 31, 44, 86, 105
straw man arguments, 213, 222–23
stress, job, 296
subjective validation effect. *See* Barnum
    Effect
submission bias, 125
suggestibility, 175
sunk costs, 174
superiority, illusions of, 175
surveys, critical appraisal for, 145
suspension of judgment, 205
system error, 178
systemic review, 34–35, 142–44
Szasz, T. S., 232

Teachout, A., 108–11
team meetings, 263–65
technical factors, 182–83
Tesh, S. N., 205
testimonials, 66, 213
Tetlock, P. E., 178–79
theory-driven standards, 181
thinking
    active open-minded, 5–10
    critical (*See* critical thinking)
    defined, 2–3, 4
    intuitive (*See* intuition)
    reflective, 169
    representative, 172
    wishful (*See* wishful thinking)
"Thinking as Argument" (Kuhn), 189
Thompson, J. B., 209
Thouless, R. H., 5, 235
time-management skills, 292
time pressures, 273–74
Toplak, M. E., 14
Toulmin, S. E., 190, 191
training, 290–91
transparency, 34–35, 36, 38–39, 174
trick questions, 221
TRIP database, 95
trust, in guidelines, 97–98
truth, 61, 204

Tufte, E., 172–76
Tversky, A., 171

Ulfelder, H., 140
uncertainty, 41
  in critical practice, 19–20
  in evidence, 58–59
  skills for handling, 285
unrealistic expectations, 279–80, 286–87
unsound arguments, 192–93
untested methods, 106–7
Ury, W., 265

vague language, 231–32, 233–34
validity
  concepts reviewing, 149–50
  concurrent, 131–32
  construct, 132
  content, 131–32
  convergent, 132
  criterion, 131–32
  descriptive, 127–28, 142–43
  ecological, 138–39
  external, 127–28, 142–43
  face, 131–32
  illusions of, 173
  internal, 125–27, 142–43
  of measures, 131–32
  predictive, 131–32
  statistical conclusion, 142–43
variation, 31

verbal speculation, 235
vivid information, 172

Walton, D. N., 58–59
  on argumentation, 194–202
  on correlation vs. causation, 207–8
  on criticism, 277
  on fallacies, 214
Wampold, B. E., 99, 260, 261–62
warmth, 261
Watt, I. A., 108
Wennberg International Collaborative, 31
West, R. F., 14
whistle-blowing, 17
White, A. D., 281
"Why I Do Not Attend Case Conferences"
    (Meehl), 263–64
widely accepted evidence, 60
Wilkniss, S. M., 108–11
Williams, I. L., 233
wishful thinking, 174, 178, 220
Witte, C. L., 274
Witte, M. H., 274
Woltman, E. M., 108–11
Woods, D. D., 166
"Woozle Effect," 65
words, assumptions with, 233

You Don't Have to Take It! (Nicarthy, Gottlieb,
    and Coffman), 254

CPSIA information can be obtained
at www.ICGtesting.com
Printed in the USA
BVHW041342300821
615476BV00002B/3